THE WORLD ENCYCLOPEDIA OF
MILITARY VEHICLES

THE WORLD ENCYCLOPEDIA OF
MILITARY VEHICLES

- A COMPLETE REFERENCE GUIDE TO OVER **100** YEARS OF MILITARY VEHICLES, FROM THEIR FIRST USE IN WORLD WAR I TO THE SPECIALIZED VEHICLES DEPLOYED TODAY

- FEATURING OVER **185** VEHICLES WITH **540** HISTORICAL AND MODERN PHOTOGRAPHS

PAT WARE

LORENZ BOOKS

Contents

This edition is published by
Lorenz Books, an imprint of
Anness Publishing Ltd, Blaby Road,
Wigston, Leicestershire LE18 4SE;
info@anness.com

www.lorenzbooks.com;
www.annesspublishing.com

Anness Publishing has a new picture
agency outlet for images for publishing,
promotions or advertising. Please visit our
website www.practicalpictures.com for
more information.

Publisher: Joanna Lorenz
Senior Editor: Felicity Forster
Editor: Jasper Spencer-Smith
Designer: Nigel Pell
Editorial Assistant: Lizzie Ware
Copy Assistant: Maree Brazill
Scanning: Reaction Ltd,
    Poole BH12 1DJ
Produced by JSS Publishing Limited,
    PO Box 6031, Bournemouth BH1 9AT
Proofreading Manager: Lindsay Zamponi
Production Controller: Wendy Lawson

© Anness Publishing Ltd 2012

PUBLISHER'S NOTES
Although the advice and information in this book
are believed to be accurate and true at the time
of going to press, neither the authors nor the
publisher can accept any legal responsibility or
liability for any errors or omissions that may be
made.
    The nationality of each vehicle is identified
in the relevant specification box by the national
flag that was in use at the time of service.

PAGE 1: **Canadian 30cwt Chevrolet 1533X2.**
PAGE 2: **The 2¹/₂-ton 6x6 GMC CCKW.**
PAGE 3: **The Willys MA.**

Introduction

In 1879, Karl Benz had been granted a patent for his first internal combustion engine, and by 1885, Benz had designed and constructed the first recognizable motorized vehicle. He was awarded a patent for its invention in January 1886. Around 25 Benz vehicles were sold between 1888 and 1893, when his first four-wheeler was introduced. During the last years of the 19th century, Benz ran the largest motor company in the world, producing 572 units in 1899.

A handful of forward-thinking military officers in Europe and North America soon began to realize that the motor vehicle offered distinct advantages over the traditional horse or mule for carrying supplies, as well as being more adaptable in the prime mover role than teams of horses or steam traction engines. Within a decade, definite military roles had started to evolve for trucks, tractors, motor cars and motorcycles and, by the beginning of World War I, Germany, Britain, France, Belgium, Canada and the USA had all started the process of mechanization of their armies.

At the end of World War I, thousands of surplus military vehicles found their way into civilian hands. There was little appetite for military spending during the 1920s and, in most countries, there was little serious development in the military truck. Germany began a process of illegal rearmament in the 1930s which included some attempts at producing a range of standardized military trucks. Britain was ill-prepared for another war and, having lost literally thousands of military vehicles during the retreat from northern France, the British motor industry spent much of the next two to three years catching up and the War Office was forced to appeal to the USA and Canada for assistance.

US truck production during World War II reached a total of more than three million vehicles, and US trucks were supplied to all of the Allies under the Lend-Lease arrangements. Even Canada managed to build close to one million trucks, and the standardized Canadian Military Pattern (CMP) vehicles also became a familiar sight in all of the theatres of the war. By contrast, Germany and Japan struggled to provide sufficient logistics vehicles to their armies and were frequently forced to use captured and impressed civilian vehicles.

By 1945, German industry was close to collapse and truck production had slowed to a trickle. Most of the trucks in the hands of the *Wehrmacht* were destroyed after VE Day, while Allied surplus vehicles were disposed of in their hundreds of thousands. The armies of the newly liberated European nations were equipped with surplus British, Canadian and American vehicles, many of which remained in service into the 1970s and '80s. In Britain and the USA new vehicles were designed and produced which reflected the harsh lessons learnt in the six-year conflict. The Soviet Union also embarked on a rearmament

BELOW: **GMC 6x6 trucks leaving the D-Day beachhead. A number of amphibious DUKWS are on the beach, having ferried supplies from ship to shore.**

LEFT: **As in World War I, mud was often the greatest enemy, and without all-wheel drive it was all too easy for vehicles to be brought to a slithering halt. This column of *Wehrmacht* vehicles includes a standardized Auto-Union Horch Kfz 21 heavy personnel carrier (extreme left), a Ford V3000S or V3000A 3-ton truck (centre left), and a Zündapp KS750 heavy motorcycle combination (foreground, centre).**

programme, modelling the first generation of post-war military vehicles on the Lend-Lease trucks that had been supplied to them since 1941.

In the West, logistical military vehicles became ever more capable and sophisticated, while the Soviet Union opted for a more basic approach that relied heavily on quantity. All-wheel drive became commonplace, as did the use of diesel engines and multi-fuel units, and the availability of more powerful engines made it possible to design heavy equipment transporters which could carry tanks weighing up to 70 or 75 tons. The crossing of water obstacles remained an obsession on both sides, and the DUKW of World War II had shown that it was possible to design reliable amphibious vehicles, while many logistical vehicles were designed to be able to wade

through deep water with the minimum of preparation. Floating bridge and ferry equipment and sophisticated vehicle-launched bridges were developed that could be carried on regular trucks by both Western and Soviet forces.

By the end of the century, military vehicles had come a long way. Today's sophisticated trucks would be scarcely recognizable to the drivers and mechanics of the primitive machines known to the opposing sides between 1914 and 1918. But, curiously, many of the roles have remained unchanged.

This book explores the diversity of cargo trucks, artillery tractors, ambulances, ammunition carriers, gun trucks, and signals and reconnaissance vehicles which have always been vital to support the fighting men in every conflict across the world since the first such vehicle appeared.

LEFT: **The Bedford MK was introduced in 1970–71 as a replacement for the RL of 1951. In 1981, the MK was replaced by the near-identical, but turbocharged MJ. This example is one of those vehicles constructed by AWD after Bedford went into administration. The trailer mounts the Rapier 2000 with an Alenia Marconi "Dagger" 3D pulse doppler-radar search system.**

The History of Military Vehicles

The 100-year story of the military vehicle can be divided into two periods. During the first four decades, military vehicles differed little from civilian types. The first trucks used on the Western Front in 1914 were basic commercial vehicles. In reality many were simply civilian vehicles commandeered by the military. Few were equipped with four-wheel drive or even pneumatic tyres. These primitive early trucks were unreliable and easily stopped by the cratered ground of the battlefield.

The advent of World War II changed everything and the design of trucks for the military and civilian markets began to diverge. Few civilian companies had any need for all-wheel drive, or for vehicles that could float or be driven in deep water. Specialized vehicles began to emerge, including powerful artillery tractors, missile transporter-erector-launchers, tank transporters, bridging vehicles and amphibious vehicles.

In the six decades since the end of World War II this divergence has continued. Most military planners recognize that standard commercial vehicles are fit only for non-battlefront duties. The modern purpose-designed military vehicle is a powerful and manoeuvrable machine, which has little similarity to the design of vehicles available for use by commercial companies.

LEFT: **A parade in Madrid, May 12, 1939, by a mechanized FlaK unit of the *Legion Kondor* (Condor Legion) in Krupp light trucks. The salute is being taken by General Franco.**

The importance of horsepower

One of the problems facing any army is the logistics of supply. The successful delivery of men and materials to the right place at the right time has frequently been crucial to the success of a military campaign. In 218BC, the Carthaginian general Hannibal used horses and elephants to move supplies from Spain to northern Italy for his 40,000-strong army. It is also said that he oversaw the construction of special barges to cross the River Rhône. Nearer our own time, Cromwell clearly understood the importance of logistics, and appointed officers to oversee transport and supplies. The Duke of Marlborough even contracted civilians to transport men and equipment for his armies and to ensure that sufficient food was always available.

Until the end of the 19th century, transport was generally carried out using pack animals and wagons. Horses, mules and oxen could be put into harness to pull a wagon, or loaded with

ABOVE: **Austro-Hungarian Army horse-drawn artillery column photographed at Galizien/Bukowina on the Eastern Front in 1915. Horse-drawn artillery was commonplace throughout the conflict.**

supplies in panniers. It was not long before the general-service type of wagon was joined by purpose-designed vehicles; for example, special wagons or carriers began to appear which could carry 24 men together with their personal equipment and weapons, and purpose-built gun carriages allowed teams of horses to pull heavy field guns. Outside of Europe and North America, camels and elephants were also used by the military.

BELOW: **Bulgarian artillery unit photographed during the Mittelmächte Offensive in October–November 1915. Each unit is drawn by four horses pulling an ammunition limber and a gun. The gun crew ride on the limber.**

This is how military transport continued until the late 19th century when a different kind of horsepower began to be developed. The Frenchman Joseph Cugnot had designed a three-wheeled steam-powered artillery tractor as far back as 1769, but it was not adopted. It was to be another 100 years before steam power began to have any significant impact on military transportation.

Towards the middle of the 19th century, the steam traction engine had started to make an impact on agricultural practice across Europe. Clearly these new machines were capable of hauling considerable loads, albeit slowly, and it was equally clear that the machines might thus have some military application. In Britain, steam tractors were used experimentally to haul heavy guns, but weight and the lack of manoeuvrability was generally a hindrance to general usage. Lighter tractors, such as the "Steam Sapper" produced by Aveling & Porter, saw service in the Boer War. The French company Lotz produced a steam-powered artillery tractor in 1867 and a number of British-built Fowler steam engines were supplied to the German Imperial Army in 1905.

By the end of the 19th century it had become obvious that mechanized transport was no passing trend and that there were real advantages to be gained from the use of motorized ambulances, wagons and staff cars. The British War Office established a Mechanical Transport Committee to investigate and report on the relative merits of steam and internal-combustion engines and to recommend suitable vehicles for military use. At first, there were doubts about the safety of petrol and the reliability of supplies, but the British Army had

purchased its first petrol-engined military vehicle in 1902, and had established a Motor Transport Company at Woolwich in 1903. By 1910 the end was in sight for steam power with the petrol engine being universally adopted as the way of the future.

In 1911, the British Secretary of War announced that he was considering the large-scale replacement of horses by motor vehicles. A so-called "subsidy scheme" encouraged civilians to purchase suitable 30cwt and 3-ton trucks at a reduced price on the understanding that they could be taken into military service should the need arise. Elsewhere, in France, Germany and in the Austro-Hungarian empire, similar schemes were established.

It was as much the availability of these trucks, as well as the appearance of the tank, which led to World War I being described as "the mechanized war".

ABOVE: Horse-drawn and motor transport were not the only options. Photographed in 1915 on the Eastern Front, This pedal-operated German vehicle uses railway tracks. BELOW: British steam-powered ammunition and supplies train. The legend on the wagons reads "HM War Office steam road transport, Aldershot".

Motor transport before World War I

In 1899, the German Imperial Army purchased its first internal-combustion engine vehicle in the form of a Daimler six-seater car. Within three years, the British Army had taken delivery of a Wolseley four-seater light car which was trialled for possible use as a staff car. In 1904, Austria had also started to buy motor cars for military use. In the USA, the US Army Signal Corps started to buy Winton cars in 1904 and, as a stand-by measure, also took delivery of some White steamers in 1910. Motorized ambulances were in use with the armies of Britain, France and the USA by 1905, often based on civilian motor car chassis.

As regards the transportation of cargo and other supplies, although the horse continued to reign supreme, the German Imperial Army had started to use Daimler Canstatt light trucks from 1900, with a medium-weight variant around 1910. Daimler had already been supplying heavy motor trucks to the Russian Imperial Army since 1903 and later to the German Imperial Army in 1907. In Britain, Leyland and Milnes-Daimler 3- to 5-ton trucks were taken into service from 1907. In the USA, trucks started to enter military service from around 1904/05, although some Woods Electric battery-powered delivery vans and cars had been purchased by the Signal Corps as early as 1899.

These early vehicles were frequently under-powered and often unreliable, but the technology was constantly improving and the military authorities in Britain and elsewhere began to organize automotive trials, which allowed the motor-vehicle manufacturers to demonstrate advances in performance. The trials often tested the products of one manufacturer against another and also allowed units of the military services to see, at first hand, how the vehicles performed.

ABOVE: **Generally only heavy steam tractors had sufficient power to move the heaviest guns. This Holt caterpillar tractor is towing a 6in howitzer.**
RIGHT: **Pre-war vehicles were frequently requisitioned by the British Army. This motor lorry, previously owned by the Anglo American Oil Company is being unloaded at Rouen, France, in 1914.**

the "subsidy" type or impressed civilian vehicles, forming a well-established, functioning logistics organization. In France, large numbers of vehicles were requisitioned, while Belgium started to purchase vehicles from France, Italy, Britain and the USA. On the other side, Austria had been mechanizing its army since 1898 and was an early user of all-wheel drive designs, particularly as field artillery tractors. In Germany, something like three-quarters of the 64,000 motor vehicles available in the country in 1914 were passed into the control of the military authorities.

While it might be an exaggeration to say that there were huge advances in motor-vehicle technology during World War I, it would certainly be true to note that there were significant improvements in reliability. The motor truck of 1918 was a very different vehicle from its pre-war predecessor.

At the same time, the motor vehicle was providing the basis for a number of specialized applications which would not previously have been a practical proposition. For example, the US Army had started to experiment with motorized scout cars before the end of the 19th century and had started to mount guns on to motor car chassis in the first decade of the new century. In France, CGT Charron had developed an armoured car as early as 1902. The same thinking led to the use of a Panhard 24CV chassis as the basis for a machine-gun car in 1906. An anti-aircraft gun had been mounted on the chassis of a De Dion Bouton 35CV car in 1910, with a similar chassis converted to carry the ammunition. Self-propelled searchlight vehicles began to appear in 1905, generally using a dynamo driven by the vehicle's engine.

By 1914, when World War I broke out, the motor truck was a well-established component of the armies of Europe's leading nations. This enabled a serious reduction in the amount of horse transport used.

The British Expeditionary Force (BEF) went to France in 1914 with large numbers of motor lorries, either of

RIGHT: **The Halford was typical of early British Army trucks used in World War I. This 1914 model was powered by a 5,300cc four-cylinder petrol engine and had a four-speed gearbox with chain drive to the rear wheels.**

Military vehicles during World War I

Although World War I was by no means the end of the use of the horse in military service, it was certainly a time when the motorized military vehicle started to develop. In fact mechanization advanced at a faster rate during this period than many would have believed possible.

The vast majority of those motor vehicles which entered service during World War I were equipped as "General Service" or cargo vehicles, and were used to deliver men and supplies to the front line, or as close to the front line as the cratered ground and primitive suspension systems would allow. However, it was not long before strategists and logistics specialist began to realize that these motor vehicles could be adapted for other, more specialized roles, including some which required the fitting of guns and crude armour. By the end of the war, there really was a surprising variety of roles for which motor trucks had been adapted, including fuel and water tankers, gun tractor, machinery workshop, artillery and ordnance repair. Other adaptions included photographic processing, gas supply, machine-gun, gun carriage, gun portee, troop carrier, searchlight carrier, signals, balloon winch, timber carrier, field kitchen, and road building vehicles.

Personnel carriers were in general not developed or required, but then World War I was not a mobile war. Nevertheless, the British Army famously used AEC Type B buses as personnel carriers in 1914–15, and France constructed personnel carriers on a De Dion Bouton and Schneider bus chassis.

As regards the technology, it must be remembered that these were early days in the development of the motor vehicle and, although a design consensus had yet to emerge, it was a period of steady development rather than of great leaps of innovation. Throughout the war, the typical engine was a big, slow-revving four-cylinder unit, generally with the cylinders cast in pairs. The valves were fitted alongside the cylinders in the block. Nevertheless, there were also examples of six-cylinder engines, and some manufacturers had already started to use overhead valves. Daimler, at least, continued to use sleeve valves.

TOP: **A US Army field radio station during World War I, circa 1917.** ABOVE: **German** *Kraftfahrttruppen* **mechanics working on a Praga truck. Note the chains fitted on the rear wheels designed to improve traction.** BELOW: **British-built Napier 3-ton War Office-pattern lorries awaiting delivery.**

LEFT: **A Halley 3-ton motor lorry displayed in France after being declared the winning vehicle in a reliability trial. This was based on the length of time on active service and the number of repairs required during that period.**

Most trucks had a three- or four-speed crash gearbox with final drive to the wheels by either an open roller chain or a propeller shaft. With the exception of the Austrian-built Austro-Daimler artillery tractors, two French manufacturers and the US-built Jeffery and FWD trucks, rear-wheel drive was standard. In Italy, Fiat adopted an unusual axle arrangement which employed two large T-shaped pressings for the rear axle, the rearmost pressing providing a housing for the crown wheel and pinion (differential gears). The forward pressing, which acted as a torque tube and contained the propeller shaft, was hinged to a chassis cross-member. Although pneumatic tyres had been introduced in 1887, the technology was still in its infancy, particularly for heavy vehicles; the tyres tended to be easily damaged. For this reason, trucks either retained solid tyres or had solid tyres at the rear and pneumatic tyres at the front. Brakes were almost exclusively fitted on the rear wheels or the transmission and, of course, were mechanically operated. Vehicle suspension remained primitive. Almost universally, trucks were fitted with axles mounted on semi-elliptical multi-leaf springs. Notable exceptions include the German company Büssing which fitted shock-damping auxiliary coil springs at each end of the semi-elliptical front springs.

The German companies Benz-Bräuer, Daimler and Nacke-Aquilon all produced experimental half-track vehicles during the war years. The Benz-Bräuer allowed the caterpillar tracks to be lifted and the vehicle to revert to wheeled operation.

Trailers were widely used by the German and Austrian armies. In the USA and Britain, the Knox and Lacre companies, respectively, produced tractor/semi-trailer units although, of course, they were yet to be described as such.

BELOW: **A Russian motor convoy using French Berliet trucks during World War I.**

LEFT: **Photographed on the Franco-Belgian front in 1914, these British soldiers and supplies are travelling up to the battlefront in impressed civilian vehicles.**

The World War I motor lorry

In the years leading up to World War I, the governments of Britain, France, Germany, Austria and France had all recognized the growing importance of motor trucks to the military, and had devised subsidy schemes which encouraged civilian truck users to purchase standardized, or at least unified, designs at a discounted price. In exchange for this financial assistance, the purchaser had to agree that the vehicles could be taken into military service should the need arise. Obviously such a need did arise and, from the outset of World War I, all five of these nations were in a position to supply their armies with large numbers of cargo-carrying vehicles all produced to something approaching a standard design.

In Britain, the subsidy scheme had described two classes of vehicle and, by 1913, around 1,000 of these were in civilian use. Neither class included all-wheel drive. The "Subsidy A" vehicle was rated at 3 tons, and manufacturers of such machines included Karrier, Thornycroft, Leyland, Maudslay, Rover, Dennis and Wolseley. The lighter "Subsidy B" truck was rated at 30cwt, and manufacturers of this type included Napier, Albion and Wolseley. Non-subsidy trucks were supplied in large numbers by AEC, Austin, Lacre, British Berna, Commer and Halley; the most numerous was probably the 3-ton AEC Y-Type. At the end of the war, Britain had a total of 66,352 motor trucks in service as well as 1,293 steam wagons. Thousands were put up for sale as surplus, creating a considerable problem for the domestic motor industry.

The French scheme appears to have been rather loosely defined, but purchasers of approved trucks received a subsidy of 8,200 francs in return for making the trucks available to the government for a period of four years.

LEFT: **British Army transport at La Ferte-Sous-Jouarre, using a commandeered "Robertson's Golden Shred" delivery van.**

ABOVE: **World War I was the first conflict where women had become involved in the day-to-day business of warfare, either as nursing volunteers or munitions workers.**

The German subsidy scheme, which was introduced in 1908, covered a 4-ton truck which was designed to be used with a 2-ton four-wheeled trailer. By 1914, around 500 of these vehicles were available. The manufacturers included Benz, Büssing, Daimler, Durkopp and Mannesmann-Mulag. A further 12,000 German subsidy-type trucks were produced during the war. By 1918, the German Army had 25,000 trucks in service, most of which had to be destroyed at the end of the war.

Austrian subsidy trucks were generally rated at 3 tons, and were often also used in conjunction with a four-wheeled 2-ton trailer. Manufacturers of such vehicles included Austro-Fiat, Fross-Büssing, Berna-Perl, Saurer and Graf und Stift. Although the standard Austrian subsidy truck was equipped only with rear-wheel drive, out of all the European combatant countries, France and Austria appear to have understood the importance of all-wheel drive. From around 1905, various types of heavy locomotive, suitable either for use as part of a land train or as an artillery tractor, were produced by Latil and Renault in France, and Austro-Daimler in Austria, with drive to all four wheels. Ferdinand Porsche was involved in the design of a number of these vehicles. Italian lorries of the period were built almost exclusively by Fiat, with a small number from Lancia and Itala.

The USA did not enter World War I until 1917 and was thus in a position to supply vehicles to Britain and France. By 1918, the US motor industry had produced 275,000 vehicles for the military, with thousands being put up for disposal in France at the end of the war. It is also interesting to note that the US Army was not only keen on the use of all-wheel drive vehicles, using chassis coming from FWD and Jeffery, but also tried to develop, with some degree of success, a range of standardized military vehicles including the 4x4 Militor.

At the same time all of the armies found themselves desperately short of transport vehicles, and many civilian trucks, often of less suitable design, were also purchased or pressed into service, particularly during the early years of the conflict.

BELOW: **The Irish Brigade returning to camp in 3-ton Wolseley CR6 trucks after taking Guillemont, on the Somme, September 1916.**

The US Army-standardized "Liberty" designs

Alone of all of the combatants of World War I, the US Army, through the Ordnance Department, attempted to develop a range of standardized military vehicles. The programme started in 1912 with the intention of simply providing a guide for the purchase of commercial vehicles for military use. It was also considered desirable that parts should be interchangeable across vehicles produced by a range of manufacturers. Soon the Ordnance Department was trying to develop specifications for commercial 1¹/₂- and 3-ton trucks with both 4x2 and 4x4 drive.

In 1916, the Truck Standards division of the Society of Automotive Engineers began to draw-up standard specifications for military Class A (1¹/₂- to 3-ton) and Class B (3- to 5-ton) trucks, with the lighter weight Class AA (1¹/₂-ton) added subsequently. The specifications were issued in 1917 but before the scheme could be put into proper effect, the USA declared war on Germany. In the scramble to procure sufficient vehicles that followed the declaration of war each arm of the US military service started to purchase its own trucks. In an attempt to prevent the complete collapse of the scheme, the Ordnance Department stated that only sufficient commercial trucks should be purchased to satisfy the immediate need. Nevertheless, it is said that the US Army had a total of 294 different makes of truck in service during World War I.

ABOVE: **Not all of the trucks used by the US Army during World War I were of the Standard B "Liberty" design. Other types included Packard, Riker, White, Mack and Moreland.** RIGHT: **The 3- to 5-ton US Standard B "Liberty" trucks were produced by 15 manufacturers but were simply identified by the letters "USA" cast into the radiator header tank. The steel-spoked wheels identify this as a late model.**

Work continued on the design of what were now being described as the Standard AA, Standard A and Standard B "Liberty" trucks. Standard AA trucks were prototyped by Willys-Overland, Maxwell, Federal and Reo, powered by a 4,113cc Northway four-cylinder engine. All were replaced by the GMC Model 16, but the vehicle never entered production. The Standard A was powered by a four-cylinder 5,113cc engine and was prototyped by Autocar, Denby and White but, again, never entered series production.

Of the three designs, only the Standard B – not to be confused with the FWD Model B – entered series production. The first trucks were assembled and ready for service within 10 weeks of the standardized design being approved! There were 15 manufacturers, including Bethlehem, Brockway, Diamond T, Garford, Gramm-Bernstein, Indiana, Kelly-Springfield, Packard, Pierce-Arrow, Republic, Selden, Service, Sterling, US Motor Truck and Velie. A total of 9,452 were completed, with 7,000 being shipped overseas. The largest number came from Gramm-Bernstein and Kelly, who built 1,000 each, while Packard built just five. All of the parts were interchangeable and none of the trucks carried any manufacturer identification, the radiator header tank simply carrying the legend "USA".

The Standard B was powered by a 6,965cc four-cylinder engine driving the rear wheels through a four-speed gearbox to a worm-gear rear axle. The engines were manufactured by Continental, Hinkley, Waukesha and Wisconsin. Suspension was by semi-elliptical multi-leaf springs. Solid tyres were fitted at the front and rear.

It was a strong, durable truck, indestructible, some might say, with many remaining in military service until the 1920s.

ABOVE: **The forward-control 3-ton FWD 4x4 was widely used by the US Army during World War I. In 1916, the British company Peerless built 500 for the British Army.**

Later field modifications included the use of pneumatic tyres and the addition of front mudguards (fenders), which were not fitted during assembly.

Although the design lacked four-wheel drive, there is no doubt that the Liberty truck project was an incredible effort bearing in mind the timescale and the technology available. The project was abandoned in 1918 and the US Army effectively de-activated, but the US Ordnance Corps did not give up on the concept of standardization, returning to the idea in 1928.

ABOVE: **The Peerless TC-3 was a 3-ton truck built for both the British and US armies. The cargo body was produced by coachbuilder J. G. Brill.**

ABOVE: **Peugeot ambulance of the French Red Cross. Like many French ambulances of the period, this example appears to be built on a heavy motor car chassis. The photograph is dated 1916.** LEFT: **A British Red Cross heavy ambulance. The ambulance body is the standard British type of the period and was mounted on Rover or Sunbeam chassis.**

Motorized ambulances

The total number of men wounded during the five years that World War I raged across Europe was estimated at 22 million. Although the medical evacuation procedures of the period were surprisingly sophisticated, nevertheless the sheer numbers of casualties must have kept those concerned with their treatment at full stretch.

The first step in the evacuation procedure was often nothing more than a simple stretcher carried by two men across ground that no-one could expect a wheeled vehicle of the time to negotiate. If the casualty could not be satisfactorily treated at a field dressing station, then he would be passed up the medical chain. At the next stage in this process, it may well have been that a motorcycle was involved since many of the wounded were moved on a sidecar outfit but, eventually,

most casualties would have been moved in a motorized ambulance. This type of vehicle had started to enter military service before the outbreak of World War I and offered the benefit of speedy evacuation of the wounded. Most of the combatant nations were quick to adopt a variety of such vehicles. Many were converted from heavy motor cars or taxi cabs, while others were fitted on light truck chassis. In some cases, the casualty was carried on a stretcher which was simply slung across a tubular framework which replaced the rear body. If any weather protection was available, this was likely to be little more than a tarpaulin. One particularly primitive type was the French-built Bedelia cyclecar, where the patient was carried ahead of the driver, on a stretcher which was strapped to the bathtub-shaped body.

RIGHT: **"The Prince George", an ambulance for the Belgian Field Hospital outside Buckingham Palace, January 1916. The vehicle was presented by readers and friends of The Children's Story of the War.**

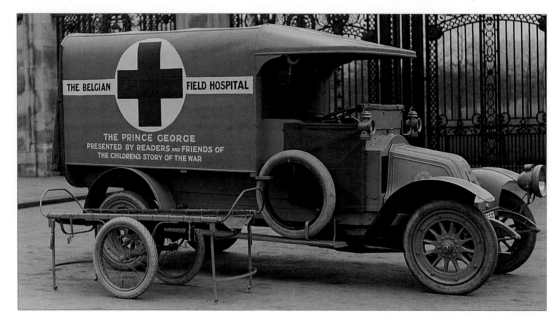

RIGHT: **Renault chassis were commonly used as a basis for ambulance conversions. Easily identified by the scuttle-mounted radiator and distinctive bonnet, the vehicle also saw service in many cities as a taxi cab.**

Some casualties were more fortunate and were carried in a vehicle which was fitted with a fully enclosed, sometimes heated, body which included space for an attendant. By the latter years of the war, the British Army, at least, had devised a standard specification for a heavy ambulance which incorporated an insulated body, heating system, and a central passage between the stretchers. Sunbeam and Rover chassis were used, and both incorporated twin rear wheels in an effort to provide a smooth ride. This question of comfort was an important issue, regardless of the type of vehicle involved. For a badly injured casualty, the often primitive suspension of the period meant that the journey must have been agony. One Fiat-based ambulance offered the combination of cast-steel wheels and solid tyres! In an effort to alleviate this discomfort, the stretcher mountings were sometimes sprung to reduce the jolting and shaking to which the unfortunate casualty would otherwise have been subjected. The British Straker-Squire and Wolseley-Siddeley ambulances of around 1906–08 actually incorporated an air suspension system for the body.

The German Imperial Army operated a fleet of ambulance road trains made up of a car towing three softly sprung two-wheeled trailers. The canvas-covered bodies each had provision for two or three stretcher cases.

In the US Army, the most common chassis for the heavy ambulance was a GMC or King, of which more than 5,500 were produced. In both cases, there was provision inside an enclosed body for eight seated casualties or four stretchers. For the light ambulance, a long-wheelbase version of the Ford

Model T was widely used. More than 10,000 were ordered during the conflict, some 50 per cent of which had been delivered by 1918. The Model T was also used by the British Army and others.

Of course, ambulances were not the only medical-service vehicles used during this period. Medical supply vehicles, mobile dental surgeries and mobile first-aid posts were also developed and mounted on suitable chassis.

LEFT: **The German Imperial Army used large numbers of these light two-wheeled trailers. Often several were coupled together to form an ambulance train for transporting the wounded. The trailer was well sprung and could accommodate two or three stretchers. Photographed on the Eastern Front in 1915.**

Improvised armour

Alongside the rapid growth in the use of motor vehicles for roles such as transporting the wounded and carrying cargo and ammunition, the opposing armies of World War I started to invent new ways in which these vehicles might be used to gain military advantage. A decade or more before the appearance of the first tanks, most of the major combatants had already begun to experiment with the use of armoured steel – often little more than heavy boiler plate – to provide some protection for crews against machine-gun fire.

In 1899, Frederick R. Simms, in conjunction with Vickers Sons & Maxim Limited, had mounted a Maxim machine-gun behind an armoured shield on a quadricycle, dubbing it the "motor scout". Simms had effectively created the first armoured car and, in doing so, had also established the three elements which remain the basics of armoured-vehicle design – firepower, mobility and protection. The French-built Charron armoured car followed in 1902, and Austro-Daimler produced a turreted four- or five-seat armoured car a year later. In Germany, Opel built its first armoured car in 1906. By 1914, wheeled armoured vehicles were being produced by most of the major combatants.

In Britain, AEC, Austin, Lanchester, Sheffield-Simplex, Rolls-Royce and Wolseley all built turreted vehicles during World War I, typically armed with a 0.303in Vickers machine-gun in a rotating turret. Peugeot, Renault and Laffly, the latter using US-built White chassis, were producing similar vehicles in France. Büssing, Daimler and Erhardt were assembling such machines in Germany. The Royal Canadian Army took delivery of 20 Autocar-based machine-gun cars in 1918. Even in Belgium, a number of improvised armoured cars were produced by adapting Minerva touring motor cars.

These early vehicles were literally "armoured" cars, little more than a front-engined heavy motor car or light truck chassis on to which had been mounted a turreted box-shaped armoured body. Engines, suspension and running gear were generally unchanged from the standard vehicle, which often

ABOVE: **An early British armoured vehicle, almost certainly improvised using a motor car chassis. There is no turret (the vehicle is clearly open-topped) but attempts have been made to protect the vulnerable radiator and the rear wheels.**

meant that the vehicle was underpowered and unstable. The increased weight also meant that the steering was heavy and the suspension prone to collapse. Most lacked all-wheel drive which meant that off-road use was also extremely limited. Whenever roads became impassable, the armoured cars could no longer be used.

The armour of these early machines was thin and generally offered protection only from small arms and rifle fire. The art of manufacturing thin armour plates was still in its infancy, resulting in wide variations in quality. Furthermore, the method of manufacture, which invariably involved bolting or riveting the plates together to form the box-like hull,

LEFT: **French Fusiliers in an improvised armoured car, crossing the Yser Canal on a locally built raft; note the hinged ramps at the rear.** BELOW: **A German car with improvised armour captured by the Belgian Army at Antwerp. In this instance, the bodywork has been left intact but has been protected by appliqué armour.**

LEFT: **French Renault armoured trucks which have been fitted with a machine-gun to be used as a basic armoured car. The armoured screen, to protect the driver, would in reality give very little defence against even rifle fire.**

offered little protection against large-calibre weapons. Indeed, rivets or bolts would frequently fly out under the effect of direct hits, ricocheting around the interior and causing considerable risk to the crew. This could result in the effective loss of an armoured vehicle even though the vehicle itself remained driveable.

Armour-piercing ammunition was soon developed for rifles and machine-guns, and it was not long before this was followed by small-bore (up to 0.5in) anti-tank rifles. Even where bullets failed to penetrate the armour, the crew were still subject to the hazards of "bullet splash", where molten lead, which resulted from the impact of a projectile on the armour plate, found its way through gaps, burning exposed skin and damaging eyes.

However, by the end of the war, it was clear that there was a continuing and valuable role for the armoured car in providing fire support for infantry and cavalry, also for conducting long-range reconnaissance missions. The early improvised designs had already given way to purpose-built vehicles that addressed the early shortcomings and vulnerabilities. Although many of these were still recognizably derived from the motor car, the design path of the armoured vehicle had already begun to diverge from standard soft-skin military vehicle design.

LEFT: **Not an armoured car but an early (1914) example of a gun portee. The weapon is a Krupps anti-aircraft gun mounted on a Daimler chassis. The elaborate curved chocks for the gun's wheeled carriage suggest that it could have been fired from this vehicle after being raised to a suitable elevation.**

The inter-war period

At the end of World War I, it was obvious that the motorized military vehicle was here to stay. Nevertheless, the demobilization of the Allied armies meant that thousands of surplus military vehicles were put up for sale to civilians. This offered many returning soldiers the opportunity to establish a transport business using a fleet of war-surplus trucks. Surplus trucks also created serious problems for the vehicle industry, which had worked hard to expand production capacity and was now faced with an unprecedented drop in demand. On the other hand, the Treaty of Versailles forced the German and Austro-Hungarian armies to hand vehicles over to the Allies for destruction. For many years, the Treaty prevented these nations from rearming.

However, even following destruction and disposal, so many thousands of vehicles remained available after 1918 that military procurement during the 1920s was at a very low level. In France, for example, some World War I vehicles remained in service right up to the outbreak of World War II. The US Quartermaster Corps had purchased fewer than 800 new vehicles by June 1929, and most of these were motor cars. Although there was little interest in rearmament in Britain, in 1923 the government had introduced a new subsidy scheme

TOP: **New vehicles outside the Marmon-Herrington factory in Indianapolis circa 1933. These 2¹/₂-ton TL29-6 6x6 trucks were designed for use as artillery prime movers.** ABOVE: **A 5-ton diesel-engined Armstrong-Saurer tested by the British Mechanisation Experimental Establishment in 1935. Saurer was a Swiss company and the truck was assembled under licence by Armstrong-Whitworth.**

for 30cwt and 3-ton vehicles, with vehicles coming from AEC, Guy, Leyland, Crossley, Morris-Commercial and Thornycroft. By 1926, some 1,000 had been acquired and registered with the authorities, but the scheme became discredited and had been abandoned by the mid-1930s.

By this time, the military organizations of most nations had virtually agreed on the categorization of cargo trucks into three classes – light, medium and heavy – even if they were unable to agree on the exact weight range for each class. But this was also a period of development and innovation, with the use of four-wheel drive becoming more commonplace. Experiments were also made with features such as four-wheel steering, lockable differentials and independent front suspension. In Britain, the War Department favoured the 6x4 format for cross-country trucks and a standardized articulated rear bogie was developed and patented by Herbert Niblett. Any manufacturer was free to use the patented design on vehicles designed to the requirements of the War Office.

Steam power was little used by any army after the end of World War I, and petrol remained the favoured fuel for the next

LEFT: **A Marmon-Herrington TH310-A6 of 1933, assigned to the US Army 19th Ordnance Company, fitted with an unusual van body.**

LEFT: **Not a manufacturer usually associated with the military, Trojan built this 6x4 truck which was trialled by the British War Office. Like most Trojans of the period it was powered by a four-cylinder two-stroke engine that the manufacturer boasted had just seven moving parts. Note the chains carried on the side step which could be fitted around the tyres of the rear bogie.**

30 to 40 years. However, the diesel engine had supporters, particularly in Germany, where Daimler-Benz, Büssing and MAN started producing military diesels from the mid-1930s.

Heavy recovery vehicles and tank transporters had yet to make any real impact. The artillery tractor was to provide the automotive designer with the greatest scope for ingenuity. French tractors from Laffly, Hotchkiss and Latil included un-ditching rollers at the front and incorporated multi-wheel steering and complex independent suspension. In Italy, the Pavesi P4-100 tractor steered on all four wheels via a centre articulated coupling.

There were also experiments with half-tracks. The first really successful half-tracked vehicles were produced in France by Citroën, using the endless rubber tracks devised by Adolphe Kégresse. The British Army tested similar vehicles from

manufacturers such as Burford, Guy and Crossley using both Kégresse and Roadless track systems, but the army never made any serious commitment to the design. In the USA, the Kégresse system was adopted and modified by the US Army for the White and International half-tracks of World War II. Only Germany deployed any significant numbers of soft-skin half-tracked vehicles. These started to appear in the mid-1930s and used a more complex steel track system, with overlapping wheels and torsion bar suspension.

It was not until the mid-1930s, when Germany and Italy embarked on major rearmament programmes, that military mechanization once again started in earnest. But, by the time World War II broke out in 1939, it would be fair to say that Britain and the USA were still a long way behind in vehicle development and production.

LEFT: **First built in 1915, but remaining in production until 1920, the Fiat 20B *Autocarro-Trattore Pesante* heavy artillery motor tractor. Rather like the Trojan (above), tracks for the solid-tyred rear wheels were carried in racks on the body sides. Note the larger diameter rear wheels which were driven by chains.**

ABOVE: **Dating from around 1936–37, Horch, BMW, Hanomag and Stoewer produced standardized chassis for both light and medium motor cars.**
LEFT: **The US Army's 3- to 5-ton Class B "Liberty" truck of World War I was a standardized design produced by 15 manufacturers.**

The emergence of standardized designs

During World War I little attention was paid to the question of the standardization of makes, models or types of vehicle procured for military service. Nowhere was this more apparent than in the US Army, where there were reputed to be some 200 different makes of vehicle in service. The result was a logistics nightmare as supply officers and quartermasters struggled to purchase and store the parts required to maintain their mixed fleets in battle-ready condition. It is not difficult to understand why standardization might have seemed something unachievable, but during the 1920s, Italy, Germany and the USA all made some progress in this direction. For some other nations, including Britain, it was a step too far and any standardization that did take place merely allocated disparate vehicles to standard weight classes.

Despite being on the losing side during the conflict, Italy had been fortunate in one respect by virtue of having only a small number of domestic vehicle manufacturers. This had made it possible to standardize on a small number of vehicle

designs following a common layout and, in the mid-1930s, the Italian Army drew up specifications for standardized vehicles in the medium and heavy weight classes. Described as *Autocarro Unificato Medio* and *Autocarro Unificato Pesante*, the trucks were designed to carry a payload of $2^{1}/_{2}$–3 tons and 6 tons, respectively. Examples were manufactured by Alfa Romeo, Bianchi, Breda, Isotta Fraschini and Lancia.

Germany was a different matter, with many competing manufacturers. In 1926, the German *Reichswehr* attempted to specify a series of standardized military vehicles, which included light (*leichte*), medium (*mittlere*) and heavy (*schwere*) personnel carriers, and a chassis for a light ($1^{1}/_{2}$-ton) load carrier. Within 10 years, there were so many other makes and models in service that a rationalization plan had to be drawn up. This resulted in new specifications for light, medium and heavy cars/personnel carriers and also light, medium and heavy trucks. Unfortunately, there was little real standardization achieved because manufacturers were free to interpret the requirements, including

RIGHT: **As part of the inter-war standardization programme, the 5-ton Class C truck was assembled at the US Quartermasters Depot at Fort Holabird, Maryland, for the US Marine Corps. The date is 1924.**

LEFT: **As part of the** *Autocarro Unificato* **programme, the Italian Army standardized trucks in medium (***medio***) and heavy (***pesante***) classes. Produced between 1940 and 1944, the 6-ton Alfa Romeo 800RE fell into the heavy class.**

the fitting of their own engines. The only truly standardized military truck produced as a result of this programme was the 2¹/₂-ton 6x6 cross-country load carrier described as the *leichter geländegängig Einheits Lastkraftwagen*. Production of the vehicle started in 1937 and continued until 1940, with examples built by Borgward, Büssing-NAG, Daimler-Benz, FAUN, Henschel, Magirus and MAN.

The US Army had enjoyed some success at standardization with the "Liberty" Standard B trucks that had been deployed during World War I but, with the war over, the design was not developed further. In the late 1920s, engineers at Fort Holabird, in Maryland, started to design prototypes of purpose-made military vehicles in a number of weight categories from 1¹/₄ to 12 tons, with 4x2, 4x4, 6x4 and 6x6 drive. The vehicles were categorized into groups from I to V according to payload and were described as the QMC Standard Fleet. Approximately 60 trucks were completed at Fort Holabird in the early 1930s,

with the cost said to be considerably lower than that of a comparable commercially produced vehicle. It should be no surprise that political lobbying by the US truck manufacturers soon brought the programme to an end.

In the event, it seems that the dream of a truly unified range of military vehicles, sharing common parts, and equally suitable to being produced by more than one manufacturer, was one that could not be realized within technology of the 1930s. While few would have argued with the objective, it appears that the political and financial will to achieve the objective was lacking.

It would take the impetus of the coming war to bring the question of standardization back to the forefront. But it was to be Canada, rather than one of the more highly industrialized nations such as Britain, Germany and the USA, who would show the way forward with the Canadian Military Pattern (CMP) vehicles built between 1940 and 1945.

LEFT: **With almost identical vehicles produced in several load classes by both Chevrolet and Ford, the Canadian Military Pattern (CMP) trucks were probably the most successful attempt at military standardization during World War II. The smallest vehicles in the series were the 8cwt C8 and F8 trucks, which used a slightly narrower version of the standard CMP cab.**

German rearmament and the standardized military vehicle

ABOVE: **Despite making several serious attempts to standardize military vehicle designs, the *Wehrmacht* continued to use a multiplicity of both domestic and commercial trucks.**

The Treaty of Versailles, signed in June 1919, ended the state of war between Germany and the Allied powers. The Treaty required that Germany and its allies accept responsibility for having caused the war, make substantial territorial concessions, and pay reparations to certain of the Allied countries. At the same time, Germany was specifically banned from producing, manufacturing, importing, or exporting weapons, including poison gas, tanks, military aircraft and artillery. However, the Treaty was soon being undermined in small ways and, by the mid-1930s, was being openly ignored by the Nazi regime.

Rearmament in Germany started under a cloak of secrecy in the 1920s and for this reason, trucks purchased for military service were of a lightly modified civilian pattern. However, there were problems inherent in using civilian vehicles and, by 1926, the Army (*Reichswehr*) encouraged the German motor industry to produce a series of standardized vehicles for military service. Specifications were drawn up for light (*leichte*), medium (*mittlere*) and heavy (*schwere*) personnel carriers, and a 1¹/₂-ton 6x4 chassis which would be suitable for use as a light load carrier.

MIDDLE: **Produced between 1934 and 1936, the BMW 315 was typical of German light motor cars, which used a basic civilian chassis on to which was fitted a military-type body. The chassis was also fitted with the standardized Kfz 2 body.** RIGHT: **Replacing hybrid military/civilian vehicles such as the BMW 315, the Stoewer R200 *Spezial* was a standardized light military motor car which remained in production from 1936 to 1943. Early examples had selectable four-wheel steering.**

ABOVE: **Although it never entered series production, the Trippel SG6/38 was an early attempt by the** *Wehrmacht* **to produce a practical military amphibian. The first prototypes date from 1935.** RIGHT: **For most of World War II, the** *Wehrmacht* **lacked sufficient supplies of logistics trucks and always suffered from having too many differing types in service.**

The latter went into production in 1929, firstly with Mercedes-Benz, and subsequently with Büssing-NAG, and Magirus. By 1938, some 6,000 examples had been produced. But this design was not suitable for all military uses and by 1929, it was being acknowledged that it would be necessary to design special types of motor vehicle for transporting anti-aircraft guns and field artillery. This policy led to the development of the family of standardized tactical half-track vehicles, which remained in service throughout World War II.

In 1936, the German government announced the implementation of an economic Four Year Plan which was designed to promote the development of key heavy industries, and to encourage increased domestic production of strategic materials such as steel, rubber and petroleum. By this time, there were 36 domestic motor manufacturers producing military vehicles, or vehicles which could be used by the military should the need arise. Once again, this led to a multiplicity of types being available to the *Reichswehr*. In an attempt to rationalize the situation, plans were drawn up for a series of standardized (*Einheitsfahrgestell*) vehicle chassis.

The scheme described light, medium and heavy cars/personnel carriers, and light, medium and heavy trucks. Most were fitted with an open cargo body, but different types of standardized body were also available for specific roles. All of these vehicles were to be fitted with all-wheel drive and two, three or four independently sprung driven axles according to weight classification. However, the specifications did not include any detailed aspects of design and the manufacturers were free to interpret the requirements in their own way including the use of their own engines.

In truth, the level of standardization actually achieved was minimal and the only truly standardized military truck produced as a result of this programme was a 2.5-tonne 6x6 cross-country load carrier. Described as the *leichter geländegängig Einheits Lastkraftwagen* (abbreviated to leglELkw – standardized cross-country light truck), the vehicle was effectively a product of the Ordnance Department.

Production of what was often referred to as the *Einheitsdiesel* began in 1937 and continued until 1940. Seven manufacturers, Borgward, Büssing-NAG, Daimler-Benz, FAUN, Henschel, Magirus (as Klockner-Humboldt-Deutz after 1937), and MAN were involved in production. Medium and heavy standardized vehicles were also planned along similar lines, but there never was any series production.

Unsurprisingly, the problems of a multiplicity of chassis types persisted. In 1938, as part of the Four Year Plan, General Major Adolph von Schell, Director of Automotive Affairs, once again, attempted to rationalize the number of military vehicle types in service with the intention of speeding production, reducing cost and simplifying parts inventories. Schell's office continued to oversee automobile production with regard to military requirements until it was absorbed into Albert Speer's Ministry for Armaments and War Production.

Even so, the problem was never really solved, and the *Wehrmacht* continued to struggle throughout World War II with an inventory that included too many types of logistical support vehicles.

ABOVE: **The Deutz-powered 40-ton Faun ZR was one of the few wheeled heavy tractors available to the** *Wehrmacht.*

The US QMC "Standard Fleet"

In 1918, responsibility for the design of military vehicles for the US Army had been centralized in the Motor Vehicle Board. The Board standardized three types of motor car, three motorcycles and a number of different truck chassis. By 1920, this responsibility had been passed to the US Quartermaster Corps (US QMC), but significant numbers of World War I vintage vehicles remained on strength, and purchases of new vehicles were at a minimum. Nevertheless, the QMC remained interested in standardization. In the early 1920s, the US QMC Depot at Fort Holabird, Maryland started to assemble experimental military vehicles using parts from existing types, together with production proprietary components.

By the end of the decade, the engineers involved had discovered that they were able to produce vehicles which would meet the requirements of the Army, but which would cost considerably less than the equivalent commercial product, should such a product actually be available. For the fiscal year 1930–31, the US Congress finally allocated a total of $406,800 for the purchase of new military trucks, specifiying how much could be spent on each. It proved impossible to buy vehicles

of the specified performance for the stated price so the Quartermaster General proposed that the USQ MC purchase components and assemble the trucks.

A team of Army engineers led by Colonel Arthur W. Herrington who later founded the Marmon-Herrington company with Walter C. Marmon in 1931, started to build prototypes for what was being referred to as the QMC "Standard Fleet" or as USA/QMC trucks. The vehicles were classified into five groups by payload: Group I covered the weight classes 1½ to 2½ tons; Group II was for 3- to 4-ton vehicles; Group III covered the 5- to 7-ton class; vehicles in

RIGHT: **Designated TTSW (truck, tractor, six wheeled), this Hinckley-engineered 1½-ton QMC "Standard Fleet" Group I truck is fitted with twin wheels all round.**
BELOW: **Largest of the QMC "Standard Fleet" was this 10- to 12-ton Group V Sterling-engined 6x6 at Fort Holabird, Maryland in 1932.**

LEFT: **Dating from 1932, the 5-ton 4x2 Group III truck of the US QMC "Standard Fleet" was powered by a 8,210cc Hercules RXB six-cylinder engine. Compared to most vehicles in the "fleet", this appears to have been on a long-wheelbase chassis.**

Group IV had the weight range 7½ to 9 tons; and Group V vehicles were designed for a payload of 10 to 12 tons. In total, the scheme designated 129 different vehicles.

These were purpose-built trucks, assembled from carefully selected proprietary components that offered adequate power, speed and performance for the anticipated usage. Engines were supplied by Franklin, Continental, Hercules and Sterling. The smallest being a Franklin 4,490cc air-cooled four-cylinder and the largest being 12,765cc Sterling LT6 six-cylinder. Four-, six- and even eight-speed transmission was used, sometimes in combination with a two- or three-speed transfer box. Suppliers included Brown-Lipe, Wisconsin and Spicer. Axles were supplied by Wisconsin, Timken, Rockwell and Hendrickson, and the smaller trucks were generally of 4x2, 4x4 or 6x4 configuration, but in Groups III, IV and V there were also 6x6 vehicles. Suspension was by semi-elliptical multi-leaf springs.

Some 60 prototypes were built during 1931–32, and put through extensive trials both at Aberdeen Proving Ground and at Holabird, where, by all accounts, the vehicles performed well. So well, in fact, that the US motor industry felt sufficiently threatened to lobby Congress to bring the programme to a premature end. There was no series production of any of the "Standard Fleet" but the US truck industry was at least forced into producing all-wheel drive trucks that were suitable for the military. When Marmon-Herrington started producing military trucks in the 3½- to 7-ton class, the vehicles bore a remarkable similarity to some of the prototypes that Arthur Herrington had overseen for the US QMC.

BELOW: **The QMC "Standard Fleet" Group III also included 4x4 and 6x4 chassis all rated for a 5-ton payload. This is the six-wheel drive variant, photographed at US QMC Depot, Fort Holabird, Maryland in 1932.**

RIGHT: **The 15cwt 4x2 truck was one of the types most widely used by the British Army during World War II, with vehicles being produced by most of the leading manufacturers. This convoy is led by a Bedford MW, followed by a Morris-Commercial (second row, right) and a Guy (second row, left).**

British military vehicles between the wars

In 1918, after the Armistice was signed, the British Army held a stock of 165,128 military vehicles, made up of 48,175 motorcycles, 43,187 motor cars and ambulances, 66,352 trucks, 1,293 steam wagons, and a further 6,121 miscellaneous vehicles. Thousands were left in Europe, but hundreds more were parked in vehicle dumps in Great Britian, and the Government started to dispose of these surplus vehicles through a series of auctions starting in the spring of 1919.

The Army kept sufficient for immediate requirements, but so many trucks remained in service that there was little need to purchase any new vehicles for most of the 1920s and thus equally little need for development. One exception was the series of abortive experiments with full- and half-tracked trucks that had been carried out under the aegis of the Department of Tank Design and Experiment at Woolwich. By 1923, these trials had been abandoned as impractical and expensive. There were later experiments with half-tracked vehicles using the Citroën-Kégresse and Roadless systems, but the British Army did not procure any significant numbers.

However, there remained a shortage of medium-weight vehicles and in 1922 a new subsidy scheme was introduced which covered 30cwt and 3-ton vehicles. There was little interest from the motor industry until the following year when some aspects of the specifications were simplified.

ABOVE: **The 15cwt Commer "Beetle" of 1939 was never produced in significant numbers.** LEFT: **Although the design was patented, the WD standardized rear bogie was used by several manufacturers producing 6x4 trucks for the British Army. Thornycroft elected to use their own double-sprung bogie.**

Albion, Karrier, Clement-Talbot and Crossley all built prototypes. In 1925, Guy, Halley, Thornycroft and Vulcan also built prototype vehicles. A plan to extend the scheme to cover 15cwt vehicles was abandoned.

In 1924, Louis Renault had produced a 6x4 heavy motor car which he believed could offer similar performance to the rival Citroën-Kégresse in cross-country performance. One of these was acquired by the Royal Army Service Corps (RASC) Training College. The rear wheels of the Renault were mounted on two axles in a self-contained bogie which was articulated to the frame in a way that allowed maximum ground contact regardless of the terrain. Realizing the advantages of this, but believing that the design could be improved, Colonel Herbert Niblett and his team designed and patented an improved version which was known as the "War Department Pattern articulated rear bogie". The bogie was suitable for both 30cwt and 3-ton vehicles and could be used freely by any manufacturer designing vehicles to meet the requirements of the British Army. By 1927, most of the big manufacturers in the British truck industry were producing subsidy vehicles, but the specification was not updated again and the design soon became obsolete.

It was also at this time that responsibility for the research, experimental work and design of British military vehicles was transferred from the Department of the Quartermaster General to the Master General of Ordnance. The RASC resisted the change, arguing that valuable experience would be lost, but it was to no avail and the Mechanical Warfare Experimental Establishment (MWEE) was created to oversee the function.

The MWEE established a series of annual vehicle trials in which manufacturers could demonstrate their trucks against those of competitors in the hope of being rewarded with valuable military contracts. These trials were held from the mid-1930s on the mountain roads in north Wales and were intended to encourage technological development. All types of experimental vehicles were tested, including a number from overseas

ABOVE: **The 3-ton 6x4 Leyland Retriever was typical of British heavy military trucks in service during the late 1930s.**

manufacturers. It was all a curiously gentlemanly business and the British truck industry appeared as reluctant to try new ideas as the Army was to buy them.

By the time the Government realized that another war with Germany was inevitable, it was suggested that the answer to the shortage of general transport vehicles lay in being able to impress or hire suitable civilian trucks. By 1938, the RASC had compiled a register of 10,000 vehicles which could be readily mobilized should it become necessary. It would be true to say that few, if any, of these were really suitable, but did at least allow the existing military 6x4s to be replaced in the general service role and converted for more specialized tasks.

So, when the British Expeditionary Force left for France it was equipped with a miscellany of some 85,000–100,000 often ageing and unsuitable vehicles. Most were abandoned in May 1940, and many foolishly believed that this presented the perfect opportunity for future British military vehicles to be manufactured to a standardized design.

LEFT: **Soldiers of the 1st Battalion of the King's Own Scottish Borderers prepare their Morris-Commercial 6x4 vehicles in Nazareth, November 17, 1936.**

Artillery tractors, tank transporters and recovery vehicles

During World War I the largest vehicles used by the opposing sides were those deployed for moving heavy artillery. Often steam powered, and almost universally heavy and slow, these vehicles continued to develop through the post-war years. But, as artillery pieces became more sophisticated, the weight and size for a given calibre were reduced, allowing the tractors to become more manageable in size. The typical artillery heavy tractor of the 1930s was a steel-bodied truck, which provided accommodation for the gun crew together with supplies, equipment and ammunition. The artillery piece was mounted on a wheeled carriage. A powered winch was almost always provided to assist with emplacing and recovering the gun.

Tanks were another matter altogether and the trend over the years was for tanks to become ever larger and heavier. At one end of the scale, the French Renault light tank of World War I weighed little more than 7 tons. Although no trucks of the period were capable of carrying such a load, by 1921, Charles Dewald of Paris had demonstrated a 7½-ton truck that could carry the tank on the flat bed, loaded by means of a capstan winch. The vehicle was copied by other nations who found that the smaller tanks of the period could be accommodated relatively easily as trucks became more powerful. The US Army used a development of the Mack Bulldog with a special flat-bed body for this purpose. There was even a tank carrier of this type in the US QMC "Standard Fleet". In the mid-1930s, the French

ABOVE: **The Scammell Pioneer 6x4 chassis was developed in 1929. It was ultimately used as a tank transporter, heavy artillery tractor and recovery vehicle by the British Army.**

Army developed a flat-bed tank carrier which used an overhead hoist for loading. Both Britain and Germany continued to use flat-bed tank carriers into the early years of World War II, but the heavy tanks presented a different problem.

During World War I, the typical British heavy tank weighed some 28 tons. This was way beyond the capacity of the trucks of the period and tanks were either moved under their own power or were loaded on to flat-bed railcars. In 1919, the London-based company H. C. Bauly modified an AEC K Type truck by mounting a fifth-wheel coupling across the rear axle. This allowed a semi-trailer, designed to carry a large crawler tractor or a medium tank, to be towed. The vehicle was close to being a tank transporter in the modern sense and would appear to have shown the way forward, but it was to be a further 10 years before the first specialized tank transporter appeared.

In 1929, Oliver North designed the Scammell Pioneer. A huge machine for the time and intended as a heavy tractor for pipeline work, Scammell realized that it also had military potential. In 1932, the British War Office purchased a single petrol-powered Pioneer, together with a low-loading trailer capable of carrying 18 tons. The trailer featured a removable rear bogie which allowed a tank to be easily loaded. It appears that, at first, the Army failed to see how such a vehicle might be useful and the vehicle was quickly assigned for training duties. It was not until 1937 that further purchases were made when the original was replaced by an updated version, this time with a 20-ton low-loading trailer.

The rear-mounted loading ramps, which these days provide the normal means of loading tanks on to trailers, did not appear until 1939. As a tractor-trailer configuration with a heavy-duty loading winch and hinged ramps, the Scammell Pioneer effectively became the modern tank transporter.

But it was not just the transportation of tanks that was creating problems – recovery was also an issue. Disabled tanks were frequently recovered using a heavy breakdown vehicle and a suitable drawbar trailer. The increasing weight of many trucks also demanded heavier recovery vehicles. The British Army had purchased a number of FWD R6T 6x6 tractors equipped for the heavy breakdown role in 1929, and this tractor was often used with a tank-transporter trailer. When the R6T was found to be unable to move the increasing weight of tanks and other vehicles, it was superseded by a recovery version of the same

ABOVE: **In the artillery tractor role, the Pioneer was designated R100. The spacious steel body had room for the gun crew plus supplies and ammunition. The gun is a British 60pdr on a pre-World War II solid-tyred carriage.** BELOW: **Dating from 1929, the FWD R6T was used both as a recovery vehicle (shown) and as an artillery tractor. AEC took over production in 1932.**

powerful Pioneer 6x4 chassis. It was a similar story in the USA, where the M1 6x6 heavy wrecker was originally developed as a tank transporter in the late 1930s.

Inevitably, the outbreak of World War II served simply to further increase the weight of tanks, bringing a fresh set of technical challenges.

LEFT: **Although first designed in 1928, the US Army's TCSW (tank carrier, six wheeled) eventually formed part of the US QMC "Standard Fleet". Rated at 7¹/₂ tons, and assigned to Group IV, the steel body incorporated folding ramps at the rear. The vehicle is the second prototype, dating from 1930; later vehicles were fitted with pneumatic tyres.**

Other specialized roles

The inter-war years saw the motor lorry gain universal acceptance as the primary military logistics vehicle. Although the vast majority of such vehicles were bodied for the cargo role, the inevitable advances in technology allowed adaption to other more specialized roles.

Aircraft refuelling

During World War I aircraft had generally been refuelled manually, simply by pouring fuel into the tanks from containers. But the use of ever-larger fuel tanks made it imperative to find a better way of dispensing fuel. Hand pumps on trolleys soon gave way to trucks that were fitted with a large cylindrical fuel tank. A motor-driven pump and hose apparatus were fitted to deliver the fuel to the aircraft tanks. By the outbreak of World War II, the RAF had developed three types of such vehicle using chassis built by Albion, Morris-Commercial and Karrier.

Bridging vehicles

The crossing of water obstacles has always played a part in warfare. The destruction of bridges can delay an advancing army just as surely as a shortage of men or ammunition; and

TOP: **Commer Q2 complete with the 3-ton "Queen Mary" trailer used for transporting aircraft.** ABOVE: **Sharing many components with the Model 0853 Matador artillery tractor, the AEC Model 0854 chassis was used as an 11,350 litre/2,500 gallon aircraft refuelling tanker. Pumping equipment was fitted in a compartment at the rear of the tank.**

all armies have sought the means to overcome such delays. The Romans used the fascine, a bundle of sticks or brushwood, to facilitate ditch crossing. The technique continued through World War I and persists today, although the brushwood has given way to plastic piping.

RIGHT: **In Britain, as in the USA and Germany, new vehicles were generally reserved for the military services. Although closely related to the military designs, the Bedford OWS tractor, complete with Scammell tanker semi-trailer, was allocated to the Petroleum Board for essential deliveries.**

LEFT: **Albion BY5 bridging trucks used by the Royal Engineers. The chassis was built to carry pontoons for building a floating bridge. A collapsible boat could also be carried.**

The first regular bridging train in the British Army was formed in 1812, using floating pontoons to form a crude ferry. While development of this technology continued, the tanks of World War I suggested that there were other ways to cross, at least, smaller water obstacles and a small portable bridge was designed by William Tritton of William Foster & Company. A Foster tractor was modified to carry Tritton's bridge, which could be positioned across a 2.5m/8ft gap in around three minutes. Other designs which emerged at the time included the sledge bridge, designed to be towed into position by a tank and the canal lock bridge which was lowered across the gap.

While these early designs required the weight and power of the tank for reliable deployment, smaller types of bridge which could be carried by a specially adapted truck began to appear in the 1930s. The British Army, for example, used several types of bridge during this period, including the prefabricated floating pontoon bridge, trestle bridge, small box girder bridge and the sliding bay bridge. All could be carried on a fleet of typical 3-ton 6x4 military trucks.

Signals and communications

Primitive mobile wireless equipment had been used during World War I and had even been truck-mounted to allow mobility. Dogs had been used as cable layers, the lightweight signals cable simply being free to unroll from a reel carried on the dog's back. During the 1920s and 1930s advances in wireless technology allowed smaller, more powerful, equipment to be vehicle-mounted. It became possible for reliable speech and Morse transmission to be made on the move. Tanks and fighting vehicles were fitted with wireless equipment that allowed the commanders to communicate, and keep in contact with mobile command posts. Cables could be laid by means of special equipment mounted on trucks or trailers. Telephone switchgear could also be vehicle-mounted.

Workshop facilities

The development of small mobile generators and relatively lightweight lathes, power drills and heat-treatment facilities allowed quite sophisticated workshops to be mounted on the chassis of a typical medium truck. This was a practice that had actually started during World War I, but the general workshops of that period soon gave way to more specialized workshops devoted, for example, to ordnance or motor vehicle repair.

ABOVE: **A Bedford MWC chassis on which has been fitted a YMCA canteen body.**

LEFT: **Canadian Military Pattern (CMP) vehicles were used by Canada, Britain and the Commonwealth countries. The standardized vehicles were produced in a range of load classes, and fitted with a wide range of bodies.**

Military vehicles during World War II

When Britain declared war on Germany in September 1939, British forces were ill-prepared and ill-equipped. The invasion of France which followed the six-month "phoney war" was ill-advised and was unlikely to succeed. Germany had been mobilizing for war since the mid-1930s, while Britain had spent little on rearmament during that period, hoping that a major conflict could be avoided. The events of May 1940 were a serious setback and, at the time, it appeared that there was little prospect of help from the USA who believed that this time Europe should sort out its own problems.

Few would have dared to predict the long struggle that lay ahead. World War II became a truly global conflict and there is little doubt that the pressures and exigencies of the moment created an incredible technological hothouse effect which, among other things, had an enormous influence on the design of military vehicles. Certainly for Britain and the USA there was little comparison between the vehicles that were in service at the beginning of the conflict and those being produced in 1945.

ABOVE: **The GAZ-67 was the Soviet equivalent of the US Army's Jeep.**

It was not a contest of equals and each of the participating nations brought its own particular strengths and weaknesses to the battlefront. The British Army had been forced to abandon thousands of military vehicles in France in 1940. Faced, then, with terrible shortages of all kinds of equipment Britain took whatever was available from the domestic motor industry, with little standardization between the products of different manufacturers. The result was that many vehicles were far from satisfactory and the Army faced an ongoing logistical nightmare in producing and distributing parts to keep this fleet of vehicles running.

The situation in the USA was an altogether different matter. When the USA finally realized that the war in Europe really was a global affair, that nation's massive industrial production capacity rightly earned it the title of the "Arsenal of Democracy". The USA was more successful in standardizing on a small number of specialized military vehicles, concentrating on turning these out in large numbers for all of the Allies. The standardized Jeep, GMC, Chevrolet, and Dodge vehicles played a valuable part in the conflict, but there were also trucks from many lesser known companies, including Available, Hug, Biederman, Thew, Hendrickson, Walter, Sterling and Corbitt.

Canada understood the significance of standardization, but perhaps with just three domestic manufacturers this should be no surprise. The standardized Canadian Military Pattern (CMP) vehicles combined technical competence with ease of production and might be considered to have established a pattern for the design of military vehicles in the post-war years.

Curiously, Germany was behind in innovation, producing military vehicles which were technically superior, but were complex and difficult to produce in sufficient numbers. It is a paradox that the nation that invented the concept of Blitzkrieg entered the war at least partially dependent on horse-drawn transport, mounted troops and a multiplicity of civilian vehicles.

LEFT: **Fiat's TM40 4x4 medium artillery tractor. Also available with solid tyres, it was powered by a 9,365cc six-cylinder engine. It was also built as a truck (T40) with an** *Einheits* **cab.** BELOW: **The British-built Ford WOA1 was based on the company's pre-war Model 62 and produced from 1941 to 1947. The example shown is a staff car, but there was also a heavy utility vehicle (WOA2) built on the same chassis.**

Rearmament had started in earnest with Hitler's rise to power in 1933, and military spending rose accordingly. Truck manufacturers were encouraged to produce any vehicle thought to be worthy. By the middle of the decade, there was such a multiplicity of vehicle types in service that several attempts were made to reduce the number of designs, to little avail.

Germany entered the war with far too many different types of vehicle and with an obsession with technical quality that slowed production. There was also a heavy reliance on civilian and captured vehicles that exacerbated the problem. As the war progressed, Allied bombing began seriously to affect the ability of the German motor industry to produce sufficient transport vehicles. Many vehicle types were simplified, while others were abandoned in an attempt to maintain production – but it was probably too late to affect the outcome of the war.

In the end it was down to volume – standardization did not win the war, but standardization and simplification allowed production to be maintained at the highest levels.

LEFT: **Produced from 1941, in two wheelbase lengths and with both open and closed cabs, the GMC CCKW 2^1/$_2$-ton 6x6 truck was used by all of the Allies in every theatre of the war. A total of more than half a million were built. The truck was to become the logistics "backbone" of many countries around the world after the end of the war.**

Changing technology and the importance of all-wheel drive

Although Germany had embarked on a programme of rearmament during the mid-1930s, little attention was paid to the question of logistics. Like most of the major combatants of World War II, Germany entered the war with vehicle designs that dated from the first half of the 1930s. Clearly the design of motor vehicles had rapidly progressed since the first faltering military applications during World War I. Outside of Germany, there had been little progress in the design of purpose-built military vehicles; the majority of the vehicles in use during the 1930s were recognizably derived from civilian designs.

However, there were two major areas of diversion between military and civilian vehicle technology – the first was in the provision of all-wheel drive, the other was in the use of all-wheel steering.

All-wheel drive

During World War I, driven front axles had employed simple Hardy-Spicer universal joints and, although these were fine for use at limited speed, it was not until the invention of the constant-velocity (or homo-kinetic) joint that the modern all-wheel drive vehicle became a possibility. The constant-velocity joint allows a smooth transfer of power to the wheels regardless of the angle to which the joint is bent. The first such joint was patented by Pierre Fenaille in 1926 under the name Tracta and was promoted by the French designer Jean-Albert Grégoire in his front-wheel drive motor cars.

ABOVE: **Most nations tested four-wheel steering during the late 1930s but eventually rejected the idea as dangerous. This is a Mercedes-Benz G4.**

ABOVE: **The Marmon-Herrington company was one of the pioneers of four-wheel drive in the USA, supplying conversion kits to other manufacturers as well as building trucks to their own designs.**

A year later, Alfred H. Rzeppa produced the joint vehicles which bore his name – it was a better product but was expensive to manufacture and maintain. This was followed by the more cost-effective Bendix-Weiss joint.

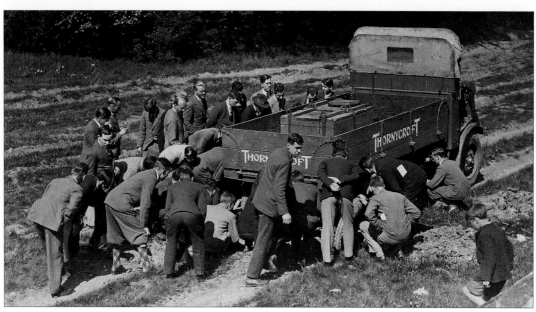

RIGHT: **In the 1930s, the British War Office appeared reluctant to accept that all-wheel drive had any real benefits. It was believed that 6x4 trucks fitted with a WD-pattern standardized rear bogie could provide almost the same level of performance. Here a Thornycroft 6x6 is undergoing trials.**

Despite the ready availability of these joints, the use of all-wheel drive for military vehicles was by no means universal in 1939. While Germany had developed a range of all-wheel drive light car and truck chassis, in Britain, for example, the War Office had placed greater emphasis on the use of the 3-ton 6x4 chassis. Britain had produced all-wheel drive artillery tractors, but the only 4x4 trucks were prototypes produced in very small numbers by Guy and Karrier for trials in 1938.

The advantages of all-wheel drive soon became obvious, and, as the war progressed, Britain, the USA and Canada began to produce more all-wheel drive vehicles. By 1945, there is little doubt that, for military trucks, such vehicles had become the norm.

Four-wheel steering

While all-wheel drive became more commonplace as the war continued, the early experiments in the provision of all-wheel steering were quickly abandoned.

The German standardized light car chassis (*leichter Personnenkraftwagen* or l Pkw) of 1936 was produced with both four-wheel drive and selectable four-wheel steering. It must be presumed that the use of four-wheel steering was intended to enhance manoeuvrability. The Willys Jeep, which followed in 1940, was also prototyped with steering on both the front and rear axles.

The complexity of the linkages involved and the general unpredictability of handling when all-wheel steer was selected soon led to the abandonment of the technology.

Diesel engines

There was one other major area of development where it could be argued that military vehicles lagged behind contemporary commercial practice and that was in the application of diesel power. The world's first compression-ignition engine was developed by Dr Rudolph Diesel in Augsburg, Germany, between 1893 and 1897. It was not until 1923 that compact diesel engines that were suitable for use in commercial trucks were produced by Daimler-Benz and MAN in Germany. The use of such engines became more widespread in the early 1930s in commercial vehicles, but two schools of thought seem to have emerged over the use of these more efficient power units in military trucks.

Germany and Japan were both forced to synthesize fuels, and since diesel oil was easier to produce, it is not surprising that both nations were enthusiastic users of the diesel engine. However, in Britain, Canada and the USA, despite the use of powerful diesel engines in tanks, the diesel-powered military vehicle remained in a minority. Notable exceptions include the Scammell Pioneer and the Diamond T Model 980/981.

ABOVE: **A Jeep fitted with experimental wheel extensions to provide traction through deep snow (known as "Spuds" when used on tanks).**

RIGHT: **A steel-cabbed Ford V3000S bogged down in the mud of the Russian Front as a VW *Kübelwagen* struggles past. Small numbers of the V3000S were also produced with all-wheel drive.**

German military vehicles

Despite explicit prohibitive conditions laid down in the Treaty of Versailles, during the 1930s Germany had embarked on an ambitious illegal programme of rearmament, spending millions of *Reichmarks* on tanks, armoured vehicles, U boats, artillery and aircraft and other military equipment. The number of men serving in the German Army increased ten-fold and the army was re-equipped and trained in the lightning Blitzkrieg tactics. However, it appears that little attention was paid to the design and procurement of the logistics vehicles that were required to support this formidable war machine.

Perfunctory attempts had been made at standardizing trucks during the mid-1930s, but the numbers of different types of

motor vehicle in use were still spiralling out of control. Over a period of years, two separate attempts were made to rationalize the types of vehicle and, for much of the war, the military struggled to maintain hundreds of different vehicle types.

In 1938, Major General Adolph von Schell, Director of Automotive Affairs, attempted to reduce the number of military vehicle types in service with the intention of speeding production, reducing cost and simplifying parts inventories. According to records of the *Fahrzeugministerium* (Motor Vehicle Ministry), the number of truck types, which had previously totalled 131, was reduced to 23. The number of car types was reduced from 55 to 29. Manufacturers in the occupied countries were also enlisted

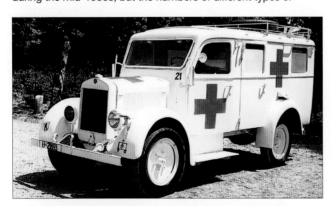

ABOVE: **A Mercedes-Benz ambulance Type L1500S which served with the 12th SS Panzer Division *Hitlerjugend*.** RIGHT: **Early examples of the Stoewer R200 *Spezial* light car were fitted with a four-wheel steering system. The chassis was also produced by BMW and Hanomag. Most were fitted with a four-seat passenger car body, but other variants included a signals car, maintenance/repair vehicle and light survey car.**

into producing trucks to German designs, but the Army was not averse to using impressed civilian vehicles – French-built Citroën and Renault trucks were widely used – or to purchasing the products of the Czechoslovak companies Tatra and Škoda. None of this helped with vehicle standardization.

Three years later, the number of cars was reduced further, with only the Volkswagen *Kübelwagen* remaining in production. At the same time, production of the previous, often complex, *Einheits*-pattern vehicles was terminated and all future German military trucks were standardized in four weight classes – 1$\frac{1}{2}$, 3, 4$\frac{1}{2}$ and 6$\frac{1}{2}$ tons, each of which included both S *Typ* (4x2, standard) and A *Typ* (4x4, *Allradantrieb* – all-wheel drive) variants. At the same time, von Schell rationalized the 164 types of dynamo, 269 light bulbs, 113 starter motors and 112 hydraulic cylinders that the army was forced to stock in order to keep the trucks serviceable.

Although existing vehicles remained in service, including many pre-1935 *Reichswehr* types, which were frequently of civilian pattern, no more were built. The trucks of the von Schell programme were of simplified design and were easier to manufacture. In some cases, more than one manufacturer was contracted to produce the same type of vehicle. But the problems continued and, in October 1943, more vehicle types fell victim to the standardization programme and, by the end of the year, there were just nine different types of truck being produced. Light trucks were produced only by Steyr and Phänomen; medium trucks came from Opel, Daimler-Benz (who were producing the Opel design under licence), Ford and Borgward. Heavy trucks came from Daimler-Benz, Büssing-NAG, and Tatra, the latter, a decidedly non-standard 6x6 design with a V12 air-cooled diesel engine. Continued shortages of materials also led to the adoption of the *Wehrmacht Einheitsfahrerhaus* cab of compressed

ABOVE: **Although it lacked all-wheel drive, the VW *Typ* 82 *Kübelwagen* was the *Wehrmacht*'s closest equivalent to the Jeep. Some 52,000 were produced.**

cardboard and timber that could be fitted to any of the standardized vehicles of the von Schell programme.

After this date, there was also a marked preference for diesel engines, since the fuel was easier to produce. By mid-1944, Magirus diesel engines were being used in trucks produced by other manufacturers.

Even if the problems of standardization had been solved, there were also continual difficulties with procurement and Allied bombing. This combined with a lack of production capacity, meant that there was a continual shortage of vehicles. During the period 1939–45, the USA manufactured more than three million soft-skin motor vehicles, Britain produced 680,000 and Canada delivered more than 810,000. By contrast, the German motor industry believed that world domination was possible with less than 500,000 transport vehicles.

LEFT: **The *Wehrmacht* was always an enthusiastic user of *Halbkettenfahrzeug* (half-tracked vehicles). Dating from 1934–35, the Krauss-Maffei-m-8 medium artillery tractor was also built by Daimler-Benz and Büssing-NAG. Early examples had shorter tracks with four road wheels. The vehicle is towing a 15cm sFH 18 howitzer.**

British military vehicles

Britain had failed to recognize the threat posed by the rapid rearmament of Germany, initiated in 1936, and had not spent sufficient time or resources in re-equipping its own armed forces. Many prototypes had been designed and tested during the closing years of the decade, but few had

TOP: **Dating from the immediate pre-war years, the 15cwt Bedford MW remained in production until 1945, with some 66,000 completed.**

ABOVE: **The light utility vehicles – known as "Tillies" – were produced by Hillman (shown), Austin, Morris and Standard.**

been cleared for production. When Britain declared war on Germany in September 1939, the British Army was equipped with a miscellany of motor vehicles, many of which were obsolete. Almost all of the British vehicles in service in 1939 lacked front-wheel drive and the most numerous types were the 4x2 15cwt, as typified by the Bedford MW and the Morris-Commercial CS8. The 30cwt and 3-ton 4x2 and 6x4 trucks were typically produced by Morris-Commercial, Leyland and Thornycroft dating from the early 1930s.

Just 5,000 of the vehicles shipped to France with the British Expeditionary Force (BEF) in 1939 were returned following the rescue from Dunkirk. Faced with a devastating shortage of vehicles, and the threat of imminent German invasion, the Government had little choice. All civilian motor vehicle production was halted and the motor industry was put on to a war footing. There was little time available to develop new designs, which meant that many pre-war types were continued in production. Many of the vehicles which remained in production for the duration of the conflict were far from satisfactory, but possessed the sole virtue of being available. At the same time, Britain turned to the USA and Canada for assistance, resulting in an enormous variety of vehicle types in service.

There was little co-operation between manufacturers and no standardization of even the most basic design elements. Consider the "Tilly", a British light utility vehicle which, during the early days of the war, served in many of the roles for which the Jeep was so well suited. Little more than a pick-up truck based on a 10hp or 12hp motor car, the "Tilly" was produced by Austin, Morris, Hillman and Standard. Each vehicle was produced to its own design and lacked all-wheel drive. No attempt was made to encourage the four manufacturers to standardize design.

At the other end of the scale, the Scammell Pioneer chassis was used as a heavy tractor for tank transport, a heavy recovery vehicle and artillery tractor. It was slow, but possessed a sturdy reliability which endeared the vehicle to its crews but, for the entire duration of the war, was in short supply. In the tank-transporter role, the Pioneer was supplemented by the superb US-built Diamond T, and by the somewhat less-than successful Albion CX24S, which possessed brakes so inadequate that drivers were obliged to use the engine and transmission to reduce speed, leading to many crankshaft breakages. However, the shortage of heavy artillery tractors meant that the British Army was obliged to operate the diesel-engined Scammell alongside the similarly equipped Albion CX22S and the petrol-engined US-built Mack NO series.

British all-wheel drive trucks started to be produced in 1940, but were never available in sufficient numbers to replace the 4x2 and 6x4 types. Dating from February 1941,

LEFT: **Morris-Commercial C8 field artillery tractor. A typical load for these tractors was the British 17 or 25pdr field gun on a two-wheeled carriage, together with a two-wheeled ammunition limber.**

Bedford's forward-control 3-ton QL was probably the most successful. Other 3-ton trucks were produced by Albion, Austin, Thornycroft, Karrier, Fordson, Guy and Crossley, with no attempts made to standardize design or components.

By VE Day, the British Army possessed 1¼ million logistics vehicles, but resources were wasted through abortive attempts to produce British versions of standard US-designed vehicles. Austin and Standard, for example, were asked to investigate the production of a British Jeep. Austin prototyped a substitute for the ¾-ton Dodge WC series. Thornycroft designed an eight-wheel skid-steer amphibian which could have replaced the DUKW, but the production vehicles, assembled by Morris-Commercial, did not perform to specification, mainly due to inadequate development at prototype stage. Like Germany, Britain struggled through World War II trying to produce and support too many makes and types of vehicle.

ABOVE: **The 3-ton WOT6 was Ford's largest World War II military vehicle, with more than 30,000 produced from 1942–45. Most were fitted with the standard cargo body, but there were also breakdown, container and machinery variants. The truck was fitted with a V8 side-valve petrol engine.**

ABOVE: **The Scammell Pioneer R100 was the British Army's largest artillery tractor. Although lacking front-wheel drive, the slogging power of the Gardner 6LW diesel engine gave the vehicle superb haulage capacity. Approximately 780 examples were built between 1939 and 1945.**

US military vehicles and Lend-Lease

In September 1939, the British Army had in service 85,000 motor vehicles, slightly less than one-third of which were impressed civilian types. At the end of May 1940, the British Expeditionary Force (BEF) was forced to abandon thousands of military vehicles in France following the retreat from Dunkirk. Most were destroyed, but many were painted grey by the Germans and given a new lease of life. Faced with a desperate shortage of all types of vehicle, Britain turned to the domestic motor industry for assistance and, at the same time, appealed to the USA and Canada. US-built vehicles, which had been destined for France, and may have been paid for by France, were diverted to Britain. At the same time, the British Government started placing orders with truck manufacturers in the USA to help bolster the inadequate supplies coming from the British factories.

ABOVE: **GMC CCKW (left) and Diamond T Model 969 medium wrecker (right), both fitted with the canvas-topped military cab adopted to reduce steel consumption and to provide a reduced shipping height.**

When Britain declared war on Germany in 1939, the US Government had changed its neutrality law to allow the nations that were at war in Europe to buy military vehicles and supplies from the US. During most of 1940, Britain was obliged to pay for those vehicles which came from the US, including tanks. It soon became obvious that Britain, standing alone against the might of Hitler's Germany, was facing a serious financial crisis.

British Treasury officials convinced President Roosevelt and Treasury Secretary Henry Morgenthau that, if Britain were to continue to hold back the German war machine, then some form of credit or loan would be required. In the face of US public opposition, Roosevelt was anxious that the USA should not be drawn into another European conflict. At the same time it must

ABOVE: **A 10-ton Brockway dump truck as supplied to the Ministry of Supply during early World War II.** LEFT: **Dodge 1¹/₂-ton WC62 weapons carrier.**

ABOVE: **The Diamond T Model 980/981 was produced in both open and closed cab form and was initially intended for the British. It was adopted by the US Army as the M19 tank transporter initially classified as "substitute standard", later downgraded to "limited standard" when the M26 "Dragon Wagon" entered service.**

ABOVE: **Rated at a nominal 7¹/₂ tons, the Mack NO was a heavy prime mover intended for towing the US Army's 8-inch howitzer or the 155mm field gun.**

have been obvious that the survival of Britain was in the best interests of the USA. By December 1940, Roosevelt thought of a way of providing aid to Britain that did not involve the use of the words "loan", "credit" or "subsidy". On March 11, 1941, US Congress passed the "Lend-Lease Act" into law, enabling the mighty industrial base of the USA to produce and supply hundreds of thousands of tons of military equipment to America's wartime allies without leaving a residue of war debts when the conflict was over.

Lend-Lease continued until the end of the war and the USA supplied somewhere around $42 billion in food, military goods, oil and fuel, industrial production and technical services. More than $2 billion, some 4.9 per cent of the total aid, was in the form of motor vehicles and parts, with a further $3.5 billion (8.4 per cent) in the form of tanks and armoured fighting vehicles. Britain and the Commonwealth were the major beneficiaries of the scheme.

Lend-Lease goods were also delivered to China and the Soviet Union. Lend-Lease ensured that American tanks, Jeeps and trucks became a familiar sight wherever the Allies were fighting.

Well-versed in mass-production techniques and safe from German bombing raids, for six years the US automotive industry turned out millions of rugged, reliable trucks and the parts to keep them running. In 1945, these vehicles would go on to provide the backbone of the armies of the newly liberated European nations, as well as providing the pattern for military vehicles produced the world over during the next two decades.

There is little doubt that by agreeing to become the "Arsenal of Democracy" the USA ensured that Germany could not win World War II. Aided by the English Channel and Hitler's ill-advised invasion of the Soviet Union, Britain had managed to hold out against Nazi Germany. There is no doubt that Britain or the Soviet Union would not have been able to defeat Germany without the industrial and military might of the USA.

LEFT: **Using the same cab as the more numerous GMC CCKW and powered by the same six-cylinder engine, Chevrolet's 4100/7100 series was produced in a range of variants, including this earth auger (drill) intended for erecting telephone poles. Production began in 1940 and continued to the end of the war.**

RIGHT: **January 1, 1941, two US soldiers in a ¹/₄-ton 4x4 Willys MA Jeep prior to the entry of the United States into World War II.**

The Jeep

In June 1940, William F. Beasley, Chief Engineer of the US Ordnance Department, produced a small sketch for an open-sided four-wheeled all-wheel drive utility vehicle that was intended to replace the motorcycle and the horse and rider in the military reconnaissance role. Some preliminary work had been carried out in conjunction with American Bantam that had helped to refine the specification of what was wanted, but, in mid-July, 135 motor manufacturers in the USA were approached to bid for the detailed development and eventual production of the vehicles. Just two companies responded – American Bantam, who believed that they were already ahead, and Willys-Overland.

Having appointed Karl Probst to head the design team, American Bantam had their bid papers approved within the allotted 10-day period and had a prototype running by late September. Given the opportunity to examine the Bantam prototype, the Willys-Overland vehicle was delivered some eight weeks later, on November 13. Political pressure was put on the Ford Motor Company and their prototype was submitted 10 days later. All three of the companies involved had experienced difficulties in achieving the Ordnance Department's target weight, but the Jeep was still light enough to be man-handled when necessary. Inside the simple open bodywork there was room for four men, and there was a mounting for a machine-gun or anti-tank rifle. This vehicle was also equipped to tow a

field gun. For the first time, the US Army had a light four-wheel drive vehicle that could go almost anywhere that a tracked vehicle – or a motorcycle – could go.

ABOVE: **Early Willys MBs had a slatted radiator grille. Note the "A" frame which allowed two Jeeps in tandem to tow a light field gun.**

Following a period of trials, the Ordnance Department was undecided as to the relative merits of the different vehicles. The three companies each received a contract to build 1,500 examples of their vehicles based on Beasley's design – the Bantam was described as the 40BRC, Willys designated their vehicle MA and the Ford was known as the GP.

Once the manufacturing work was underway, elements of the Willys and Ford vehicles were combined to produce a standardized design which was described as the Willys MB, and the Ford GPW – the "W" indicating that the Ford included elements of the Willys design. Bantam received no further contracts, but Willys and Ford went on to build some 640,000 examples of the standardized Jeep between 1941 and 1945.

The MB/GPW was light enough to be able to go almost anywhere and yet powerful enough to be able to carry out tasks that the designer had almost certainly not envisaged. Although it dated from the early 1930s, Willys' Go-Devil four-cylinder engine, which was also used in the Ford GPW, was superbly reliable. When coupled to a three-speed gearbox and two-speed transfer box, it allowed a maximum road speed of 106kph/65mph, combined with the ability to tackle the worst possible terrain.

The availability of large numbers of Jeeps brought to an end the widespread use of the military motorcycle. For example, US Army standing orders had initially decreed that motorcycles be attached to each armoured division, but this practice came to an end in March 1942 when the vehicle type was removed from the "Tables of Organization and Equipment" (TOE), having been replaced by the Jeep.

ABOVE: **The Willys MA was the improved version of the company's Quad prototype, the immediate predecessor to the standardized MB/GPW. A total of 1,500 examples were produced during 1941, most of which were supplied to the Soviet Union. The model differed from the standardized Jeep. Note the radiator and grille and the depth of the body cut-outs. A column gear-change was fitted.**

The Jeep demonstrated that it was possible to provide effective four-wheel drive for a light military truck. Vehicle types such as the British light utilities became obsolete. It was no longer necessary to compromise on transport for officers in the field, the Jeep was equally useful on or off the road. During the course of World War II, senior figures such as Churchill, De Gaulle, Patton and Montgomery – even European royalty – were all photographed riding in Jeeps.

LEFT: **Designed by the US company American Bantam and the US Ordnance Department, the Jeep was the first vehicle of the type that effectively replaced the motorcycle in military service. In the standard form some 640,000 Jeeps were produced by Ford and Willys-Overland.**

Canadian Military Pattern

In 1937, Syd Swallow, an engineer with the Ford Motor Company of Canada, designed what was effectively a Canadian version of the 15cwt British War Office-pattern truck using a strengthened chassis from a Ford 1-ton commercial vehicle. The Ford prototype was followed by a similar vehicle from General Motors, Oshawa. A year later, the Canadian Army asked Ford and GM to produce a light version of the 6x4 Scammell Pioneer, which the British Army was using as a heavy artillery tractor. The resulting prototypes were displayed at Petawawa alongside a 6x6 Marmon-Herrington. From inauspicious beginnings these vehicles became a range of standardized Canadian military vehicles. At first described as "Department of National Defence Pattern" (DNDP) they were subsequently to be better known as the "Canadian Military Pattern" (CMP). The vehicles followed British War Office patterns, but were designed for mass production in Canada.

In truth, neither Ford nor General Motors believed that the essentially British design of the vehicles was suited to Canadian production methods and produced alternative specifications. But the Department of National Defence in Canada insisted that the trucks be produced according to the British pattern.

In late 1939, it was proposed that the vehicles be fully standardized and that Ford produce the cab, engine and transmission, with GM contributing chassis, axles and body. This idea was eventually dismissed and both companies went on to build their own versions. Although there was a

ABOVE: **Chevrolet C8A; with variations, the type 1C house-type body was used for various roles, including ambulance (1C5), heavy utility (1C7), radio (1C2), machinery (1C10) and staff car (1C11).**

high degree of commonality, the Ford-built vehicles were powered by a 3,917cc V8 side-valve petrol engine driving through a four-speed gearbox; if the vehicle had all-wheel drive then a two-speed transfer box was fitted. However, General Motors vehicles used a 3,548cc six-cylinder overhead-valve petrol engine, with the same drive-line assembly. Ford fitted "split" axles, while GM fitted "banjo-type" axles.

The earliest vehicles to be supplied were of the 4x2 pattern, but 4x4, 6x4 and 6x6 vehicles were subsequently produced. The smallest CMP vehicle in the family was an 8cwt,

RIGHT: **Chevrolet CGT field artillery tractor; a similar vehicle was also produced by Ford, designated FGT. The body was based on then-current British War Office practice. The vehicle was generally used as a tractor for the 25pdr field gun and its ammunition limber.**

ABOVE: The 30cwt CMP truck was designated C30 or F30 according to manufacturer and most were of the 4x4 configuration.

ABOVE: Chevrolet C15A bodied by the British company Edbro as a mount for a 20mm anti-aircraft gun.

designated either C8 (Chevrolet) or F8 (Ford), according to manufacturer. If the chassis was fitted with all-wheel drive the designations became C8A and F8A. Next was the 15cwt chassis (C15, C15A, F8, F8A), followed by a 30cwt (C30, C30A, F30, F30A) design. Largest of the series was the 3-ton chassis, which was produced in 4x2 and 4x4 long-wheelbase (C60L, CC60L, F60L, FC60L), and in 4x4 short-wheelbase form (C60S, FC60S). There were also 3-ton 6x4 (F60H) and 6x6 (C60X) chassis, and Ford also produced a 2-ton 4x2 in both long- and short-wheelbase. The 6x4, which was only built by Ford, was unusual in that the front axle and the forward of the rear axles were driven.

Standard variants included cargo, artillery tractor, workshop, breakdown, heavy utility, machinery, ambulance, recovery, wireless, anti-aircraft, van, office, water tanker, fuel tanker, anti-tank portee and stores. There were also armoured variants. Regardless of manufacturer, the vehicles shared a common cab design, only the details of how the cab was mounted to the chassis varied. The first type of cab – described as the Number 11 – was copied from the British cabs of the period and received considerable criticism, being cramped and hot. It was soon replaced by the Number 12 cab; this was a little better, and featured an alligator-type bonnet to improve engine access. The most numerous of the designs was the Number 13 cab which was fitted from late 1941. The cab featured the distinctive reverse-slope windscreen.

The majority of the vehicles were shipped to Britain first in completely knocked down (CKD) form, and subsequently in semi-knocked down (SKD) form for local assembly. In Britain, large numbers were assembled at the Citroën works in Slough, and at Pearsons in Liverpool. There were many instances where Ford-built cabs were fitted on to GM chassis and vice-versa, because shipping losses caused an imbalance in the availability of components. In Australia,

the vehicles were assembled by Holden and were often fitted with locally produced bodies.

Less than 15,000 vehicles were produced in 1939, the first year of production, but by 1941, Canada was the largest producer of motor vehicles in the British Empire. By September 1, 1945, Canada had produced almost 410,000 CMP vehicles, of which the largest number were of the 3-ton 4x4 type. The CMP vehicle was probably the most successful example of standardization during World War II and was used by all of the Allies. Thousands remained in service in Europe after the end of the war.

ABOVE: Chevrolet C15A 15cwt general service cargo truck. Both 4x2 and 4x4 chassis were produced. The cab is a 1941 Number 12 design with an "alligator" bonnet.

RIGHT: **The GAZ-61 was produced between 1941 and 1948. It was effectively a 4x4 version of the GAZ-11-73. Powered by a 3,480cc six-cylinder petrol engine, it was widely used as a staff car for junior and middle-rank officers.**

Soviet military vehicles

Dating from 1924, the first Soviet-built truck was the 1½-ton AMO-F-15. The Moscow-based AMO plant was renamed ZIS in honour of Joseph I. Stalin (Zavod Imeny Stalin) in 1933. AMO and GAZ became the two most significant truck plants in the Soviet Union. The GAZ factory in Nizhni Novgorod had been constructed during 1931–32 with American assistance and was equipped with tooling for the Ford Model A shipped from the Ford plant in Germany. By 1932, GAZ was producing what were essentially Ford Model A trucks and cars under the designation GAZ-A and GAZ-AA, with a GAZ-AAA 6x4 truck variant entering the

range in 1935. During the second Five Year Plan, Soviet factories produced some 200,000 vehicles. Although the output of trucks grew at an impressive rate during the period 1933–38, the vehicles were essentially civilian in design and little attention was paid to the needs of the military.

When the Soviet Union was invaded by Germany on June 22, 1941, the Red Army was equipped with standard GAZ and ZIS trucks, the design of which dated from the beginning of the 1930s. Faced with the might of the *Wehrmacht*, it was clear that the nation's factories were not in a position to produce the modern military vehicles that would be required to mobilize

LEFT: **ZIS-5 searchlight trucks. Powered by a 5,550cc six-cylinder engine, the ZIS-5 was rated at 3 tons and produced from 1933 to 1944. The vehicle was often nicknamed the "Stalin Truck". Variants included cargo, gas producer, compressed gas carrier and dump truck.**

ABOVE: **Produced for a decade or more from 1943, and powered by a licence-built Ford engine, the GAZ-67 and 67B was the Soviet version of a Jeep-type vehicle.**

ABOVE: **The Jeep was not the only vehicle supplied to the Soviet Union under the Lend-Lease Program. Trucks were supplied from the USA, Britain and Canada. For example, Studebaker supplied more than 100,000 US6 trucks. Introduced in 1941, the US6 was produced as a 6x6 and 6x4, the latter designated US6X4. Other vehicles supplied to the Soviets included GMC CCKW trucks, Dodge T214s, GPA amphibians, Chevrolet and Dodge trucks as well as Mack tractors.**

the Red Army. But, help was soon available. In November 1941, the Soviet Union was included in the US Lend-Lease arrangements and, between 1941 and 1945, US aid to the Soviets amounted to 16.6 million tons of material at an overall cost of almost $10 billion. This included more than 400,000 trucks and tank transporters as well as artillery prime movers, guns and armoured fighting vehicles.

Alongside the US-built trucks, which included Chevrolet, Studebaker and GMC, Jeeps, Dodge and Mack vehicles were also delivered. Vehicles were also supplied by Canada and Britain. At one time, almost half of Soviet military supplies were being carried in Lend-Lease trucks. The Soviets also used large numbers of captured vehicles.

The 1½-ton GAZ-AA was replaced by the modernized GAZ-MM in 1938, although the improvement was confined to the use of a more powerful engine. Both this, and the GAZ-AAA remained in production throughout the war years but, in 1942–43, GAZ started to produce a second generation of military vehicles, based on the Lend-Lease

types which had been coming from the USA. First of these was the GAZ-64 (later GAZ-67) a small 4x4 field car similar to the Jeep. Heavier trucks were produced in small numbers by the JAG (YAG) and JAS factories. Also a number of half-tracks were produced using the ZIS-5 chassis, under the designation ZIS-33 and ZIS-42.

The German invasion forced the relocation of the ZIS plant from Moscow to the Urals where it was known as either Ural or Ural-ZIS, and later UAZ. Production was restarted in the new factory in 1943.

Many of the Lend-Lease vehicles remained in service during the immediate post-war years. It was not until almost the late 1950s that the Soviet Union began to produce modern military vehicles. The GAZ, ZIS (now renamed ZiL) and UAZ plants continued to be the major suppliers.

LEFT: **Russian anti-aircraft troops on parade in unidentified trucks with planes flying overhead in Kiev, 1935.**

RIGHT: **Japanese forces enter Peking, China, July 31, 1937. The light tank is at the head of a column of Isuzu Type 94 trucks.**

Japanese military vehicles

The world force that is today's Japanese motor industry is a comparatively recent phenomenon. At the end of the 1920s, the Japanese home market was dominated by the products of the United States "big three", General Motors, Ford and Chrysler. The domestic manufacturers had assembled less than 500 vehicles a year. In 1931, the Japanese Government purchased some 6x4 trucks from Britain and Czechoslovakia and set about developing designs using the vehicles as patterns. The Government also set up a Motor Industry Establishment Committee to produce a specification for a standardized medium truck that could be used by both civilians and the military.

The military vehicle divisions of DAT and Ishikawajima were merged to form a new company to manufacture what was effectively a subsidy-type truck. The company was named Jidosha Kogyo and the products were designated Isuzu. The first product of the new company was the Isuzu TX, a 4x2 civilian truck rated at 2 tons and powered by a 4,390cc six-cylinder engine. The larger TU10 was a 6x4 design rated for 3 tons which was also produced as a military vehicle, the Type 94 – the number being derived from the Japanese date 2594 (1934). Three years later, a 4x2 version was produced, designated Type 97.

In 1936, the Japanese Imperial Army had decreed that all Japanese vehicle manufacturers should agree to produce

RIGHT: **The Isuzu TU10, or Type 94A, was first supplied to civilians under a subsidy scheme, and rated at 3 tons. The chassis was assembled in several factories. The vehicle was one of the Japanese Imperial Army's standard tactical trucks.**

LEFT: The 1½-ton Isuzu Type 94 appeared in 1934 and was the Japanese Imperial Army's standard cross-country truck. Based on typical European practice of the early 1930s, it featured a 6x4 drive-line and was produced in a variety of configurations. The Type 94A was powered by a petrol engine; the 94B used a diesel power unit.

products under military licence and that 50 per cent of the capital, shareholders and company officials should be Japanese. By 1939, all production of American cars and trucks in Japan had ceased and the factories had been taken over by local companies. From 1941, military trucks were being produced by Nissan (formerly DAT), Isuzu and Toyota. During 1941–42, the three companies produced 45,500 trucks and buses, approximately half of which were intended for military use.

Following the Japanese attack on Pearl Harbor in December 1941, the motor industry was placed under direct government control and civilian output was severely restricted. Truck production was reduced by American air raids. Shortages of raw materials, and the pressures of manufacturing aircraft engines saw production continue to decline during the years that followed. Just 6,726 vehicles were produced in 1945. Continual shortages of petrol forced the Japanese to develop a family of standardized diesel engines which were intended for use in trucks, tanks and submarines.

Standard military trucks deployed by the Imperial Army during World War II included the Nissan 80 and 180, a semi-forward control 1½-ton vehicle powered by a 3,670cc six-cylinder engine; a 1½-ton Toyota, equipped with a four- or six-cylinder engine, and designated G1, GA, GB, AK, KB or KC according to date and specification; and the 1½-ton 6x4 Isuzu Type 94 and the 4x2 Type 97. Isuzu also produced 2-ton trucks in both 4x4 (designated YOK1) and 6x6 (ROK1) form, as well as a 3-ton 6x4, the TU23 of 1941, built in both petrol- and diesel-engined form. The heaviest Japanese trucks of the period were the 7-ton Isuzu Type 2, a 4x2 cargo truck powered by an 8,550cc engine, and the 20-ton Isuzu TH10 dump truck that was produced for the Japanese Imperial Navy.

Isuzu and Ikegai produced half-tracked vehicles with multiple crew seats in an open body, very much in the German style. Both were designated Type 98, indicating that the date of introduction was 2598 (1938), and were powered by a six-cylinder standardized diesel engine. The vehicles were intended for use either as artillery tractors or as mounts for anti-aircraft guns. The Army also used large numbers of captured American and British vehicles.

BELOW: The Nissan 180 was produced from 1940 until 1944. After the war, the vehicle continued in production for the civilian market and was rated at 2½ tons. This captured example was photographed at Aberdeen Proving Ground, Maryland, USA.

Half-tracked vehicles

During World War I, continuous heavy shelling of the front line, combined with the inevitable flooding of the shattered ground, frequently rendered huge areas all but impassable to wheeled vehicles. With their endless track systems, the early tanks and heavy artillery tractors were less easily defeated by ground conditions. However, their unreliability and the lack of suspension made for a slow and uncomfortable ride, and even a tank of the period was easily defeated by a water obstacle.

Searching for improved mobility, in 1915 the French Delahaye company had produced a tracked bogie which could be used to replace the rear wheels of a conventional vehicle. During World War I, the German Daimler company had also started experimenting with trucks on which the rear wheels were replaced by a tracked bogie and, in the USA, both Holt and Lombard had also produced primitive half-tracked machines.

The first successful vehicle of this type to be developed was almost certainly the Citroën-Kégresse half-track of the early 1920s. Adolphe Kégresse had developed his endless rubber track system to enable the Russian tsar to drive with equal facility over metalled roads, deep mud and snow in what was effectively little more than a modified car or light truck. His system demonstrated how the mobility of wheeled vehicles could be improved without necessarily involving the expense and complexity of a fully tracked machine. Forced to leave Russia after the 1917 Revolution, Kégresse brought the system back to his native France,

ABOVE: **Although there was no series production, there were experiments conducted in the USA with a view to producing a half-track Jeep.**

where he managed to convince André Citroën that there was merit in developing half-tracked vehicles for use in the French territories overseas, where metalled roads were poor or non-existent.

The French Army started to buy half-tracks and there were demonstrations of the system in Britain and the USA. Despite experiments with half-tracked vehicles from Albion, Burford, Guy and Crossley, the British Army remained unconvinced. In the USA, Kégresse tracks were fitted to a Model T Ford, but it was experiments by GMC, Cunningham and Marmon-Herrington with the US Ordnance Department which led to the appearance of the well-known armoured US half-tracks of World War II, using a heavily modified form of the Kégresse bogie and suspension system.

RIGHT: **Load-carrying 3-ton truck constructed using the chassis of the Sd Kfz 11 medium half-track; these vehicles were built by Hansa-Lloyd-Goliath, Borgward, Adler, Horch and Wanderer (both of them part of the Auto-Union conglomerate), Hanomag, and Škoda. The cab is typical of the utility *Einheits*-type fitted to German trucks from late 1943, while the bonnet and radiator grille do not conform to the standard pattern.**

ABOVE: **Japanese Ikegai KO-HI Type 98 semi-track prime mover. Produced from 1937 as a tractor and self-propelled mount for anti-aircraft guns.**

ABOVE: **Italian-built Fiat 727SC** *trattore semi-cingolato* **(half-tracked tractor). It was fitted with a Fiat 5,750cc six-cylinder petrol engine and a five-speed gearbox with reduction gear, giving ten forward speeds.**

There were also US experiments with a half-tracked Jeep, using at least two different track systems, and an experimental 2½-ton half-tracked truck was built by Autocar for possible use in the Soviet Union.

Half-tracked cars and trucks were also produced in the Soviet Union by both ZIS and GAZ. The vehicles were generally based on a conventional wheeled chassis, but the lack of front-wheel drive and use of low-powered engines restricted their performance.

In Germany, a series of standardized half-track vehicles was developed in six weight classes from the mid-1930s. Eschewing the endless rubber Kégresse bogie, the sophisticated German half-tracks employed pin-jointed all-steel tracks suspended on torsion bars or semi-elliptical leaf springs. The vehicles were originally intended for use as prime movers for artillery, but, late in the war, their weight, expense and complexity saw them

replaced by the *Maultier* – a standard military truck on which the rear wheels had been replaced by a far simpler track system. In Britain, the bogie system of a captured German 8-ton Sd Kfz 7 half-track was used by Bedford to produce a prototype artillery tractor dubbed the Traclat, but there was no series production and the idea was abandoned once the war was over.

After 1945, the improvements in all-wheel drive trucks saw the half-tracked vehicle fall from favour.

BELOW: **Chassis for the** *schwere Wehrmachtsschlepper* **(sWs) heavy half-track tractor. Designed by Büssing-NAG, the first prototype appeared in the spring of 1943. The vehicle's appearance was that of a heavy truck to which had been fitted a standard rear track and bogie assembly.**

RIGHT: **By the end of World War II, the US Army was experimenting with ever larger and more powerful trucks. Designated T20, this chain-driven 8-ton 8x8 cargo vehicle was produced by Cook Brothers in late 1944. The engine was a 9,865cc Continental six-cylinder producing 240bhp. The vehicle was also prototyped as a tractor-truck, but there was no series production of either type.**

The end of World War II

As World War II progressed, it was not only the military strengths and weaknesses of the opposing sides that became more apparent. Faced with relentless Allied bombing, Germany's industrial capacity was being slowly eroded, forcing the High Command to decide on military priorities. Choosing tanks and guns over transport vehicles, the German truck industry practically stopped and such development as did take place was directed towards saving scarce raw materials.

ABOVE: **The British-built Leyland Hippo Mk II was a 10-ton cargo vehicle intended for long-distance road use in Europe following the D-Day landings.**

Continued shortages of materials also led to the adoption of the *Einheitsfahrerhaus* cab in October 1943. It was fabricated from compressed cardboard on a timber frame, to save vital supplies of steel, and could be fitted on any standardized truck chassis that remained in production.

In Britain, the motor industry continued to mass-produce trucks, but these were to the same designs that had been in production since the early years of the war. Precious little time was available to think about developing new designs or even of making modifications which might improve some of the existing vehicles. One notable exception was the Leyland Hippo Mk II, a 10-ton 6x4 truck that was specifically designed in 1943 to meet the needs of the military. Various experimental vehicles were produced, including the Bedford Traclat, a half-tracked light artillery tractor that borrowed heavily from German practice. Prototypes were built for Albion and AEC of low-silhouette heavy artillery tractors. Albion designed the curious double-ended 8x8 tank transporter. None entered series production.

Similarly, in the USA, the motor industry continued to produce the trucks which had helped the Allies, while the US Ordnance Department was also working on new designs. In 1941–42, there were experiments with low-profile versions of existing ³/₄-ton 4x4 trucks, as well as designs for low-profile 2¹/₂-ton 6x6 trucks and 3-ton 4x4s. Prototypes of these vehicles were produced by, among others, Dodge, GMC, Corbitt, Reo, International and Ford. None were put into production, but the work did lead to the development of the 1¹/₂-ton 4x4 Ford GTB.

The Ordnance Department was also investigating the development of larger trucks which could provide greater mobility combined with increased load-carrying capability.

LEFT: The British had not tended to use half-track logistics vehicles during World War II. The Bedford-built Traclat (Tracked Artillery Tractor) was prototyped towards the end of the war. The track system is an obvious copy taken from a German heavy half-track.

In 1942, Cook Brothers produced a strange rear-engined chain-driven 8x8 vehicle which was used for desert mobility trials in California. This went no further, but some of the drive components were re-used in prototypes for an 8-ton 8x8 cargo truck and tractor, designated T20. This was also produced by Cook Brothers in 1943–44 using a Continental six-cylinder engine in combination with a five-speed gearbox and two-speed transfer box. A similar machine was produced by Corbitt, featuring turntable steering and a swan-necked

chassis frame designed to reduce the overall height. Sterling used the same approach for the 12-ton T26 8x8 cargo truck, which was powered by a LaFrance V12 engine. The company also produced a tractor variant. Corbitt designed an 8-ton 8x8, designated T33, with a Continental engine.

The end of the war saw most existing military vehicle contracts cancelled, leaving many uncompleted. At the same time, all urgency for further development was lost. Although more than one of these huge trucks survived into the 1950s before being scrapped or otherwise disposed of, none of the designs were put into production.

ABOVE: German truck production and development had virtually come to an end by early 1945, but from October 1943 most trucks were fitted with the *Einheits* utility cab. RIGHT: Singularly unsuccessful, the double-ended Albion CX33 heavy tank transporter was an interesting development. There were two engines, originally driving all eight axles, but later modified to 8x6. The rear cab housed the winch controls.

The immediate post-war years

During World War II, the USA, Britain and Canada produced approximately five million military transport vehicles. In May 1945, following VE Day, hundreds of vehicle production contracts were cancelled. In Europe there was an abundance of surplus military vehicles for which there was no longer any demand. There is a persistent story that few trucks were returned to the USA, manufacturers there being anxious to avoid a repeat of the market collapse which had followed the repatriation of surplus vehicles after Armistice Day in 1918. "War Claims Settlement" agreements were made between Britain, the USA and Canada which provided for the disposal of unclaimed vehicles and other assets remaining in Britain. Huge dumps were established across Europe where vehicles were examined – the worst vehicles were scrapped, cannibalized or simply dumped in the sea. The best were allotted for further

ABOVE: **At the end of the war, hundreds of outstanding contracts were cancelled, and surplus military vehicles were collected in large open areas to be disposed of by auction.**

military use, but the remainder were auctioned or sold to civilians as surplus. There were also thousands of tons of vehicle spares stored in depots across the world.

Thousands of surplus military vehicles were gifted or sold to the newly liberated European nations. France, Belgium, Denmark, Norway and the Netherlands all mobilized their post-war armies with a miscellany of pre-war vehicles and Allied vehicles of US, British and Canadian origin. Only France standardized on US-supplied equipment and, for a period, even new French military vehicle designs tended to follow the same basic specifications.

ABOVE: **Although thousands remained in service, surplus Jeeps were also sold to civilians and many were modified to match the owners' preferences.**
LEFT: **Much modified, the powerful Pacific M26 made an excellent heavy-haulage tractor for Wynns Heavy Haulage.**

In Britain, all military vehicle contracts came to an end. Sufficient vehicles were retained for the Army's immediate need, and the numbers and variety of types of truck in service were rationalized. Most of the vehicles retained were of British manufacture, but the bigger, more specialized US-built vehicles, such as the Diamond T and Mack tractors, were retained, as were thousands of Jeeps. Plans were put in hand for a new generation of wheeled military vehicles, but a lack of money and foresight meant that these plans were slow to come to fruition. Many of the World War II vehicles were to remain in service for a further 25 years.

During the war, Canada had produced what might be considered hybrid vehicles that embraced US automotive technology and design practice, but tended to attempt to follow British War Office specifications. Although many of these CMP vehicles remained in service in Canada, and for that matter in Australia, after the end of the war obsolescence was imminent. Not long after 1945, this policy was abandoned when the Canadian Government elected to supply their armed forces with US equipment.

In Germany, many military vehicles were destroyed while others were overhauled for civilian use. New German-built trucks were frequently supplied to the Allied occupying powers. It was not until 1956 that the newly formed *Bundeswehr* was allowed to start purchasing military vehicles.

The US Army continued to use vehicles of World War II origin during the immediate post-war years – vehicles such as the Jeep, the GMC CCKW and the Dodge WC series remained a common sight, serving in Korea, Berlin, Japan and anywhere that US troops were deployed. New designs began to appear in the early 1950s and the opportunity was taken to rationalize

ABOVE: **Many trucks were left in scrapyards across Europe. This is a rare US-built Federal 605 or 606 tractor, originally equipped as a wrecker.**

the weight classes and types of vehicle produced. The 1¹/₂-ton 4x4 class was abandoned and new 5-ton 6x6 trucks replaced the mixture of 4-, 6- and 7¹/₂-ton vehicles that remained from the war years. A similar 10-ton 6x6 chassis was also subsequently produced. These post-war US trucks were produced by more than one manufacturer to the same design and were widely exported. Many remained in service to the end of the century.

BELOW: **All across Europe, companies offered surplus military vehicles that had been converted to better suit a civilian usage. This Canadian-built Dodge T110 has been converted to a timber tractor by Sworder Motors in Britain.**

The US Military Assistance Program (MAP)

In 1947, during one of the coldest winters of the century, US General George C. Marshall returned from a fact-finding mission. He was shocked by conditions in the shattered and starving countries of Europe. Marshall told President Truman that all of Europe could fall to Communism unless steps were taken to stimulate the ailing economies. Despite a counter-proposal from Treasury Secretary Henry Morgenthau who suggested that Germany should be made to pay massive reparations, Truman agreed with Marshall. On July 12, 1947, the Marshall Aid Plan was unveiled to a meeting of the 16 participating European nations. Congress voted for $13 billion in aid, the major beneficiaries of which were Britain and France. Although invited, Stalin saw the plan as a plot to undermine the Soviet Union, and he vetoed participation by any of the Soviet satellite countries.

The enabling legislation was passed on April 3, 1948, and the first ships, containing 19,000 tons of wheat, set sail from Texas to France. The Plan also saw Europe receive supplies of fuel, raw materials, goods and food. There were also loans of money and expertise to rebuild shattered factories. For four years (1948–52) US aid flowed into Europe, stimulating rapid economic growth and halting the spread of Communism.

As part of this same strategy of containing Communism, the USA had already pledged an initial $650 million in foreign aid as part of a plan to promote economic development, create political stability and build military strength among US allies. The aid was generally extended to countries bordering the Soviet Bloc as well as to those located in strategic areas such as South Asia and

ABOVE LEFT: **Convoy of Marshall Aid Plan trucks bringing Ford agricultural tractors to the Netherlands.** ABOVE: **The US post-war M Series 6x6 trucks were widely used during the Vietnam War. Many were supplied to the Army of the Republic of Vietnam, seen here withdrawing from Cambodia in 1989.**

the Middle East. Key beneficiaries included South Korea, the Philippines and Iran, but aid also went to Latin America to support pro-United States regimes.

In October 1949, Truman went further and a "Military Assistance Program" was created as a key part of the "Mutual Defense Assistance Act". The Act promised assistance to any US ally that might be threatened by the Soviet Union or one of its allies. Aid and assistance would be suspended to nations that traded in strategic materials and technologies with the Soviet Union. The initial budget was $1.3 billion but, during the first three years, military aid was supplied to the nations of Western Europe, including military vehicles to the value of $8 billion.

By 1951, the "Mutual Security Act" had replaced the Marshall Aid Plan, and economic and military aid was being offered to Europe and across the developing world. During the first year alone, European nations received military aid amounting to $1.02 billion. A year later Taiwan and Indochina received $202 million in military support. Between 1949 and 1952, less than one third of the $28 billion in aid parcelled out by the Marshall Plan had been for military use. In the following eight years, military aid grew to 50 per cent of the $43 billion in total. Aid was used to promote a free market that was seen as being beneficial to the US.

LEFT: **The Philippines was among the recipients of US aid. Here, combat-ready Philippine troops head to the front in a US-built M Series 6x6 truck. The wire mesh grille is typical of late production but the "MAP" versions of these trucks lacked various features of the US Army versions.**

With regard to military vehicles, the recipients of US "MAP" aid were given access to budget or austerity versions of standard vehicles of the period, including a restricted range of armoured fighting vehicles. This not only brought the money back into the US defence industry but also helped to spread US military influence around the world. For example, there were militarized versions of the Jeep CJ3B, designated M606; a simplified version of the M38A1 under the designation CJ5M (M606A1 etc), a simplified MAP version of the M715 designated AM715; and low-cost versions of the 2 $\frac{1}{2}$-ton and 5-ton 6x6 trucks. All of these were supplied to Vietnam, the Philippines and other friendly nations. In some cases, the vehicles were assembled under licence in the country concerned.

Critics levelled the accusation that US military assistance promoted corrupt government, funded the imperial ventures of France and the Netherlands in South-east Asia and established the basis for modern multi-national corporations. While these accusations may or may not have been true, the plans did do little to hurt American interests around the globe.

LEFT: **Built between 1964 and 1968, the M606 was a militarized version of the standard Kaiser-Jeep CJ3B model and was intended for recipients of "MAP" aid. A licence-built version was also produced by Mitsubishi in Japan.**

The British post-war military vehicle programme

For the British Army, the multiplicity of vehicle types used during World War II had been a salutary reminder of the dangers of poor planning. A War Office Policy Committee document produced in September 1944 stated that there were close to 600 different makes and types of soft-skin transport (described as Category B) vehicles in service. Many of these were based on commercial types not suited to the needs of a modern mechanized army. A large number had been assembled by companies with no British production facility, so servicing and maintaining this diverse fleet was a huge problem.

Anxious to avoid future repetition, even before the war was over, the War Office and the Ministry of Supply had approached the Society of Motor Manufacturers & Traders (SMMT) for assistance in planning new standardized vehicles. However, a rigidly held view in War Office departments was that military-vehicle design had become widely divergent from mainstream commercial vehicles. Thus there was a curious reluctance to ask the motor industry to simply get on with the job. This view led to the notion that all Category B vehicles should be originated by the Government's design and research body – at the time, the Fighting Vehicle Design Department (FVDD). By June 1947, this principle had been agreed upon and protected by a General Staff Policy Statement, but it soon became clear that the country could not afford such luxury. By 1950, it was

ABOVE: **With some 11,500 examples built, the FV1801 Austin "Champ" was the most numerous of the British post-war "combat" vehicles. It was intended as a replacement for the Jeep and was fitted with a torsion-bar independent suspension and a five-speed gearbox which provided all gears in both directions.**

being suggested that British military vehicles should be divided into three categories – Combat (abbreviated to CT), General Service (GS) and Commercial (CL).

The combat vehicles were described as being "specialized military vehicles with multi-wheel drive, manufactured from components not used for commercial purposes and required to give the best possible cross-country performance". Five weight classes were defined – $\frac{1}{4}$, 1, 3, 10 and 30 tons, together with a 60-ton tank transporter. Much of the design

RIGHT: **The Humber FV1600 series 1-ton truck was produced in cargo and communications variants. The vehicle was the basis for the "Pig" armoured trucks and personnel carrier.** BELOW: **Rated at 3 tons, the Vauxhall FV1300, a 6x4 tractor that never entered production.**

LEFT AND BELOW: **The FV1100 series 10-ton Leyland Martian was powered by the eight-cylinder version of the Rolls-Royce B Series engine and was the largest of the "combat" trucks. Drive to the front wheels was by revolving kingpins the same as on the wartime Mack. The rear bogie was a walking-beam design as used on the Scammell. Standard variants included a cargo truck, recovery vehicle (left) and heavy artillery tractor (below). Like the Austin and the Humber, it was also offered to the civilian market with a different engine, but the price and mechanical complexity restricted sales.**

work for these machines would be carried out at what eventually became the Fighting Vehicles Research & Development Establishment (FVRDE). The smaller vehicles were fitted with independent suspension and unconventional transmission arrangements and, aside from the two larger weight categories, the vehicles were to be powered by a Rolls-Royce B Series engine. This engine was produced in four-, six- and eight-cylinder versions, with a high percentage of component commonality. Experience gained during the D-Day landings also required the vehicles to deep-wade with a minimum of preparation.

General-service vehicles were described as being "modified versions of standard civilian vehicles, for example down-rated commercial trucks with the addition of all-wheel drive, heavy-duty wheels and tyres and standardized electrical equipment". The commercial vehicles, in the third category, were simply standard-production trucks.

All of the vehicles were described by "FV" numbers: four-figure numbers were used for vehicles in the Combat category, five-figure numbers for General Service vehicles and six-figure numbers for Commercial Vehicles. The numbers were assigned in series to each vehicle type, with a different final digit used for each variant produced. For example, the FV1600 series covered the Humber 1-ton CT family; FV16000 was used to describe the Austin K9WD, which was the equivalent 1-ton GS vehicle. FV160000 would have been assigned to the 1-ton CL range had there been one.

Endless lists of vehicles and classes were produced as the War Office and the Army wrestled with the logistics of the scheme. Weight categories were changed and dropped and, at one time, it was suggested that the CT vehicles be abandoned altogether as being too costly and complex.

By 1955, the Army had spent £150 million, with just three types of vehicle produced in quantity. First of these was the FV1800 Austin Champ, a 1/4-ton 4x4, which had been intended to replace the Jeep, but which was superseded by the cheaper and more reliable FV18000 Land Rover. The FV1600 Humber 1-ton 4x4 was a superb vehicle, but was generally surplus to requirements. Finally, there was the FV1100 Leyland 10-ton 6x6 chassis, which was eventually produced as a cargo vehicle, artillery tractor and recovery vehicle.

While all of this had been happening, there had been a growing awareness that the GS vehicles had been far more successful than had originally been envisaged. In 1956, those CT vehicles which had been produced were downgraded to GS and the War Office proposed that future British military vehicles might be better designed by the motor industry and that FVRDE's role should be one of trial and assessment.

And broadly, that was the end. Future British military vehicles shared electrical equipment and minor components, but little else. The dream of a unified range of specialized types was lost.

The US post-war programme

At the end of World War II the US Government cancelled almost all of the outstanding contracts for military vehicles, and for the next five years or so the Army continued to use those that had been produced during the war years. However, this did not stop the development of new designs and, around 1950, the first of these new, so-called "M Series", vehicles started to enter service.

Occasionally described as the "Korean War vehicles" to differentiate them from the vehicles used during World War II, these were effectively improved versions of the best of the wartime trucks. Major improvements included the use of radio-screened 24V electrical equipment and built-in basic waterproofing. More importantly, having learned the lessons of standardization during World War II, these prototype trucks were produced under development contracts that provided for the design parent company to work in conjunction with the newly formed Ordnance Tank-Automotive Center (OTAC). As a result, the trucks could not be considered to be standard commercial products and the development and manufacturing processes were contracted separately, with the intention of making it easy for more than one manufacturer to assemble any given vehicle type.

At the same time, the number of types of vehicle in service was reduced by around half, with the future fleet standardized in five weight classes – $^1/_4$- and $^3/_4$-ton trucks using a 4x4 drive line, and $2^1/_2$-, 5- and 10-ton trucks with 6x6 configuration drive.

First to enter service was the $^3/_4$-ton 4x4 M37 which was produced by Dodge as a replacement for that company's WC series, and the $2^1/_2$-ton M35 6x6, which was an improved

ABOVE: **The post-war M Series 6x6 trucks were produced in $2^1/_2$-, 5- and 10-ton versions, to a very similar design. The $2^1/_2$- and 5-ton versions are difficult to distinguish between. An M51 5-ton dumper truck variant leaves a landing craft.**

version of the iconic "Jimmy" of the war years. The M35 was not the only $2^1/_2$-ton truck produced at this time and it was eventually superseded by the Reo-designed M44 series. As well as being manufactured by Reo, and often described as such regardless

RIGHT: **New $2^1/_2$-ton M Series 6x6 trucks being prepared for shipment. Note how the US Army continued to use open cabs into the post-war years.**

LEFT: **The Ford-designed M151 MUTT (Military Utility Tactical Truck) was the first attempt by the US Army to improve on the Jeep of World War II. Unfortunately, despite two attempts (M151A1 and M151A2) at redesigning the suspension, the combination of a high centre of gravity and swing axles led to instability when cornering. Nevertheless, thousands were produced. The directional indicators show that the first and third vehicles in the line are the M151A1 variant.**

of origin, it was also produced by Studebaker, Kaiser-Jeep, Curtiss-Wright, White and AM-General. It was a very successful design and was produced in a very large number of variants, including a tractor truck. Early versions were petrol-powered, but subsequent upgrades saw the truck fitted with diesel and multi-fuel engines.

From 1950 on, the World War II-type Jeep was replaced by the broadly similar M38 – also known as the Willys MC – and, in 1952, by the more powerful M38A1 (Willys MD). However, in 1951, the Ford Motor Company was awarded a contract to develop an entirely new Jeep-type vehicle. Although the resulting M151 "Military Utility Tactical Truck" (MUTT) was eventually built in very large numbers from 1960 by Ford, Willys, Kaiser-Jeep and AM-General, handling problems meant that it was never entirely successful.

Introduced in 1950, the 5-ton M39 6x6 trucks were very similar in design and appearance to the 2½-ton model, and were intended to replace the 4-, 6- and 7½-ton 6x6 trucks of the war years. Production was undertaken by Kaiser-Jeep, Diamond T, AM-General and International Harvester, and the trucks were powered by either a petrol, diesel or multi-fuel engine according to the date of production.

The 10-ton M123 series was introduced in 1953, and was produced by Mack and Consolidated Diesel Electric (Condec), the latter using Mack axles and transmissions. All of the 10-ton trucks used a LeRoi multi-fuel or diesel engine.

Many of this first generation of US post-war military vehicles remained in service with the US Army until the end of the century. These vehicles were also being supplied to other nations across the world, often as part of the Military Assistance Program (MAP).

LEFT: **The GMC CCKW was the US Army's standard logistics truck during World War II, with more than half a million produced. The CCKW remained in service into the 1950s and many were used during the Korean War. This photograph, taken in July 1950, shows British infantry being transported from Taegu up to the battlefront.**

Soviet technology

Until the 1930s, the Soviet Union had no domestic automotive industry, and even during the Great Patriotic War – as the Soviets termed World War II – it had little spare production capacity for transport vehicles. Domestic truck production during the war years amounted to fewer than 350,000 vehicles, but large numbers of military vehicles were supplied to the Soviets from both the USA and Britain, almost half a million coming from the USA alone.

During the period 1944–45, the Soviet authorities started work on the first generation of post-war military vehicles, but designs tended to follow the pattern of existing American vehicles. For example, the 1¹/₂-ton GAZ-63A 4x4, and the 2¹/₂-ton ZiL-157 6x6, both became the mainstay of the Red Army during the immediate post-war years. These clearly leaned heavily on the design of the Studebaker US6 trucks, some 100,000 of which had been supplied

under the Lend-Lease program during the war years. Similarly, the ZiL-485 amphibian closely resembled the GMC DUKW and the GAZ-46 was little more than an enlarged Ford GPW amphibian. Even the GAZ/UAZ-69 field car was similar to the American Jeep.

During the late 1950s, these vehicles started to be replaced by a second generation of trucks, with many of the older vehicles being passed on to the Warsaw Pact nations which formed the Soviet Union's first line of defence. The Soviet automotive industry grew rapidly in the years following World War II with major truck-manufacturing plants established, under State control, in Bryansk (BAZ), Gorkiy (GAZ), Kremenchug (KrAZ), Minsk (MAZ), Ul'yanovsk (UAZ) and Likhachev (ZiL). By 1967, the Soviet Union was one of the largest producers of trucks in the world.

RIGHT: **Developed from the 6x6 trucks supplied to the Soviet Union under the Lend-Lease Program during World War II, the ZiL-157 entered production in 1958 to replace the earlier ZiL-151. This is a licence-built version, built in China. The vehicle is here in service with the Cambodian Army in 1983.**

ABOVE: **Rated at 4¹/₂ tons, the Ural 375 series was introduced in 1961. This vehicle has been equipped as a "Stalin's Organ" multiple rocket launcher.**

By this time, a third generation of military vehicles had been introduced, many of which were also produced in civilian form. While these may still have some traces of American influence, they would certainly not have been considered sophisticated by the standards of the West, but like many Soviet products of the time they were sturdy, straightforward and reliable. Most importantly, the vehicles were available in large numbers and were capable of being operated reliably in the freezing depths of the Russian winter. The most numerous of this new generation

was probably the ZiL-131, a 3¹/₂-ton 6x6 truck which was powered by a 6,000cc six-cylinder engine. Produced in large numbers and adapted for a wide variety of roles, the ZiL-131 was supplied to all the armies of the Warsaw Pact.

The Soviets also produced a number of large 8x8 chassis which were designed to be used as "Transporter-Erector-Launcher" (TEL) vehicles for the growing range of surface-launched missiles. These were either trailer-mounted or carried on launch rails attached directly to the chassis of the truck. One of these, the ZiL-135L4 was powered by two large capacity V8 petrol engines, each arranged to drive the wheels on one side of the vehicle through hydro-mechanical transmission. Again, the emphasis was on the use of simple or well-proven technology which could be relied upon to produce uncomplicated vehicles in large numbers. While the Soviets might not have been able to win the technology race, if a war did occur it is probable that they could have overwhelmed the Western forces by sheer numbers.

In recent years, the break-up of the former Soviet Union has either resulted in the collapse of the former State-owned enterprises or, as in the case of Minsk Tractor (the former MAZ plant), has encouraged companies to look for overseas markets. Soviet technology remains uncomplicated to Western eyes, but it is becoming increasingly common to see Soviet trucks that have been improved by the use of an American or German diesel engine and transmission.

LEFT: **Dating from 1978, the 4-ton Ural-4320 was a diesel-engined development of the Ural-375D.** BELOW: **The GAZ-66 4x4 truck dates from 1963 and was widely used by the Soviet Army. A version was available for the civilian market.**

The Jeep effect

The Jeep of World War II was an extraordinary vehicle. Although nothing like it had really existed before, its designers worked against the clock, lacking sufficient time to reason through the inevitable design problems and the lack of any extended development period. It could be argued that it was actually rather too small but, at the same time, it quickly proved to be both reliable and durable. More than 635,000 were produced. Jeeps were used by all of the Allies and the vehicle was adapted to a wide range of roles, both in support and

ABOVE: **The Soviet Union received large numbers of US-built Jeeps during World War II and produced their own version, the GAZ-67, during the war. In 1956, this was replaced by the GAZ/UAZ-69 (above) which was constructed both as a light truck and as a five-seater field car.**

combat. Thousands of Jeeps remained in service after the end of the war and large numbers were allocated to the newly liberated European nations.

In the US, the original MB/GPW was replaced by the very similar M38 and then by the heavier and more powerful M38A1. The US Marine Corps purchased the lightweight "Mighty Mite" which was designed by members of the same

ABOVE: **In 1948, the prototype for the Land Rover was actually built on the chassis of a military surplus Jeep.** RIGHT: **Built by Willys-Overland from 1954, the M606A2 and A3 Jeeps were militarized versions of the CJ5 intended for the "MAP" programme. This M606 has been restored and painted in Israeli Defense Force finish.**

LEFT: **In the mid-1950s, Auto-Union DKW produced the MUNGA field car for the *Bundeswehr* (West German Army). It was an unusual design featuring a three-cylinder two-stroke engine and independent suspension using transverse leaf springs. The components of the front and rear axles were interchangeable. Production continued until 1968. The vehicle was also supplied to the Dutch Army.**

team that had been responsible for the original Bantam BRC40 in 1940. During the early 1950s, Ford started the design work on the M151 which, despite being produced in large numbers, suffered from handling problems. After 25 years of service, the M151 was replaced by the High-Mobility Multi-purpose Wheeled Vehicle that is generally described by the acronym "HMMWV".

The "HMMWV" effectively ended the career of the Jeep in US military service, but it appears that every country who received supplies of Jeeps believed that they could produce a better version. Many tried but failed!

The War Office intended that the FV1800 Austin Champ would be the replacement for the Jeep in British service but with its independent suspension, 5F5R transmission and Rolls-Royce engine, the design was complex and expensive. The vehicle was so unreliable that within 10 years of its introduction it had been replaced by the cheaper and simpler Land Rover. Although not originally intended as a military vehicle, it is well known that the Land Rover design had been inspired by the Jeep. The prototype used a war-surplus Jeep chassis.

Like the British, the French military authorities believed that they could design and produce a Jeep-type vehicle as a replacement for the original. The Delahaye VLR-D that was introduced in 1950 suffered transmission, handling and reliability problems so severe that it was superseded by a licence-built Hotchkiss version of the original Jeep. The French-built Hotchkiss M201 remained in service with the French Army until the end of the 20th century.

In 1955, the newly liberated West German *Bundeswehr* chose the curious Auto-Union MUNGA, independently sprung three-cylinder engined vehicle, over similar types produced by Porsche and Goliath. Following an abortive Franco-German-Italian amphibious field car designed by Hotchkiss, Büssing-NAG and Lancia, the MUNGA was replaced by the VW Iltis,

ABOVE: **In Japan, Mitsubishi produced a version of the CJ3B Jeep. Designated CJ3B-J4, production began in 1953, with large numbers supplied to the Japanese Self Defence Force, South Korea and South Vietnam. A number were also supplied to the US forces in Japan and to the domestic market. An ambulance variant was also available.**

a vehicle which perhaps owed more to the original VW *Typ* 82 *Kübelwagen* of 1939 than the Jeep.

Both Alfa-Romeo and Fiat built small Jeep-like vehicles at the beginning of the 1950s, the 1900M *Matta* (Crazy) and the AR59 Campagnola respectively. Both featured independent front suspension. Similarities with the original Jeep were there and both would have been very familiar to the men who had designed it 10 years earlier. In the Soviet Union, GAZ and later UAZ, produced small four-wheel-drive field cars which owed more than a modest debt to the original Jeep. Similar vehicles appeared in other countries as far apart as Czechoslovakia, India, Turkey and Japan.

In the near-70 years which have elapsed since American Bantam produced the first Jeep prototype, the type has become both a legend and an icon. The Jeep is probably the most recognizable vehicle in the world. An unnamed American advertising copywriter probably got it exactly right when he wrote "The sun never sets on the Willys Jeep" in 1942.

RIGHT: **The US Army's "M Series" 6x6 was produced by Diamond T, International, Mack, Kaiser-Jeep and AM-General for more than 30 years. The original power unit was a Continental petrol engine, but this was later superseded by a multi-fuel diesel.**

NATO and US influence

Formed in 1949, the North Atlantic Treaty Organization (NATO, or OTAN in French) is an alliance of 26 countries from Europe and North America dedicated to upholding the principles of the North Atlantic Treaty, specifically with regard to uniting their efforts "for collective defence and for the preservation of peace and security". The Treaty was signed in Washington, DC on April 4, 1949, and the signatories included the five Treaty of Brussels states (Belgium, France, Luxembourg, the Netherlands and the United Kingdom), as

ABOVE: **Rated at 10 tons, the British-built AEC Militant was used with the Leyland Hippo as part of the UK's force in NATO.**

well as the United States, Canada, Portugal, Italy, Norway, Denmark and Iceland. Three years later, on February 18, 1952, Greece and Turkey also joined. In 1954, the Soviet Union suggested that it should join NATO to preserve peace in Europe. The proposal was rejected by the NATO countries, who suspected the Soviet Union's motives.

When West Germany was incorporated into the organization on May 9, 1955, the Soviet Union responded by creating the Warsaw Pact, thereby defining the two opposing sides of the "Cold War". The Warsaw Pact was signed on May 14, 1955, by the Soviet Union, Hungary, Czechoslovakia, Poland, Bulgaria, Romania, Albania and East Germany. In 1966, France withdrew from the military membership of NATO.

For the first few years, NATO was not much more than a political association and even during the height of the "Cold War", NATO did not participate in any actual military engagement as an organization. However, the Treaty provided for mutual defence in the face of an armed attack on any member, and it became apparent that a military role for NATO was unavoidable. During the Korean War member states agreed to the development of an integrated military structure, which was built-up under the direction of two US Supreme Commanders. This has brought about considerable standardization of military terminology, procedures and technology among the NATO countries, although in practice it has meant that the European countries have largely adopted US military practice. Standardization is controlled by the publication of so-called Standardization Agreements – known

LEFT: **Post-war DAF military vehicles were part-financed by US aid and for this reason were fitted with Hercules engines. This is the 3-ton YA314 dating from 1955.**

as STANAGs – by the NATO Standardization Agency in Brussels. They are written in English and French, the two official languages of NATO. Something like 1,300 STANAGs have been published covering an enormous variety of military land, sea and air related topics. Vehicle-related standardization has covered road signs, sizes and capacities of vehicle batteries, inter-vehicle starting sockets, towing hitches, vehicle marking, bridge classifications, trailer connectors, load markings and many other topics.

In 1955–56, NATO laid down standardization requirements for vehicles in load classes of $1/4$, 1, 3, 6 and 10 tons. Despite a number of US-German and Franco-German initiatives,

efforts aimed at producing a series of standard military vehicles in each class, for use by all member countries, have failed. In the main, however, member nations have produced vehicles which fall into the standard weight classes and which have been designed under the relevant STANAG agreements – with the notable exception of the USA. For some unaccountable reason they have decided to retain $1/4$-, 1-, $2^1/2$-, 5- and 10-ton class vehicles.

It is unlikely that NATO would ever be able to agree on a standard vehicle range, but these standards have at least ensured a high level of commonality and interchangeability.

LEFT: **The British Humber FV1600 was a 1-ton 4x4 truck produced in cargo and radio variants. It was a sophisticated vehicle, powered by a Rolls-Royce petrol engine. This vehicle is fitted with torsion-bar independent suspension on all four wheels.**

Warsaw Pact military vehicles

The Soviet-sponsored "Treaty of Friendship, Co-operation and Mutual Assistance" – more generally known as the Warsaw Pact – was signed on May 14, 1955, at the Presidential Palace in Warsaw, Poland. In the West it was seen as a direct response to West Germany joining the North Atlantic Treaty Organization (NATO) in 1955. It was, effectively, the Communist Bloc's counterpart to NATO and was a military-treaty organization of Communist states in central and eastern Europe. The founding members were Albania, Bulgaria, Czechoslovakia, Hungary, Poland, Romania and the Soviet Union. The Soviet Union cited the Warsaw Pact when crushing the Hungarian Revolution in 1956, while Albania withdrew from the Treaty in September 1968 in protest against the Soviet invasion of Czechoslovakia. This was never recognized by the Soviet Union.

ABOVE LEFT: **Dating from 1962, the East German-built (GDR) P3 was a seven-seat field car, powered by a 2,407cc six-cylinder engine. Independent torsion-bar suspension and differential locks at front and rear.** ABOVE: **Also produced in East Germany, the IFA W50LA/A was introduced in 1969 and was equipped for a variety of roles. This is a public-address van intended for internal security service.**

The Warsaw Pact was divided into two branches – the Political Consultative Committee, which co-ordinated non-military activities, and the Unified Command of Pact Armed Forces, which had authority over the troops assigned to it by member states. The latter was headed by a Supreme Commander, who was also the First Deputy Minister of Defence of the USSR.

Since 1945, the Soviet Union had been acting as the arsenal of Eastern Europe, and the Warsaw Pact simply ensured that

RIGHT: **The Soviet ZiL-157 was widely used by all of the Soviet Bloc nations and was also produced under licence in China. Standard variants included the cargo/ personnel truck (shown), tractor, shop van, multiple rocket launcher, tanker, snow plough and bridging vehicle. Like many Red Army vehicles, it was fitted with a Central Tyre Inflation System (CTIS).**

this situation would continue. The signatory nations were "encouraged" to buy Soviet military equipment, including uniforms and all kinds of vehicles, or were allowed to build vehicles and other equipment under licence. For example, the Polish Lublin-51 was effectively the GAZ-51 while the UMMM M-461 produced in Romania was similar to the Soviet GAZ/UAZ-69. This not only helped the Soviet economy, but also resulted in the standardization of military equipment across the Pact states. However, some of the vehicles supplied were effectively obsolete types superseded by the introduction of new designs in the Soviet Union.

Beginning in the late 1960s, the Soviet Union conducted a dramatic increase in the mechanization of their ground combat forces, but the technology remained resolutely outdated. Soviet military vehicles, for example, were robust and easy to operate. When new vehicles were introduced they were fitted wherever possible, with equipment and proven sub-assemblies and components already in use.

The Soviet Union was never able to achieve total standardization among the member states of the Warsaw Pact. The nationalized and state-run motor industries of Poland, Czechoslovakia, Hungary, East Germany and Romania produced military trucks, motorcycles and armoured vehicles for use by their own forces. There was also considerable trading among the member states. For example, trucks produced by Robur in East Germany and Tatra in Czechoslovakia were exported to Romania and Poland.

In 1973, the Warsaw Pact nations were able to call upon a regular army of more than three million men, plus a further three million reservists; these were equipped with more than 78,900 tanks. More than 10,000 surface-to-air missiles were ranged along what most considered to be the European border. Papers released since the demise of the Warsaw Pact have revealed that, until the 1980s, military plans in the case of war

ABOVE: **A late model of the East German-built Robur LO-1800A truck. The Robur factory was based in Zittau until 1961 and continued production of the Phänomen Granit. Production then turned to the LO-1800A.**

with the West were for a swift land offensive, the objective of which would be to secure Western Europe quickly. There was no ban on the use of nuclear weapons and Poland alone was home to 178 nuclear missiles, increasinging to 250 in the late 1980s. Warsaw Pact commanders made very few plans for the possibility of fighting a defensive war on Soviet territory.

The end came with the fall of the Berlin Wall in 1989 and the subsequent political collapse of the Soviet Union. On March 12, 1999, the former Warsaw Pact members and successor states Hungary, Poland and the Czech Republic joined NATO. Bulgaria, Estonia, Latvia, Lithuania, Romania and Slovakia joined in March 2004.

LEFT: **A ZiL-151 mounted *Katyusha* rocket launcher being used to attack an apartment building, photographed in Lebanon in 1975. The vehicle is one of thousands supplied to Syria by the Soviet Government. The 6x6 ZiL-151 was produced from 1947 until 1958 when it was replaced by the ZiL-157.**

RIGHT: **To fit a Jeep into a glider, in this case an Airspeed AS.51 Horsa, it was necessary to cut back the ends of the front bumpers, remove the steps behind the front mudguards, and provide some means of easily and quickly removing the steering wheel. Only then could the vehicle be turned at the top of the ramp and fitted under the main wing spar which ran across the inside of the fuselage.**

Air-portable vehicles

The concept of air portability for vehicles dates back to World War II when motorcycles, light trucks and, eventually, light tanks were delivered by glider. The size of the transport aircraft of the period meant that, at first, it was necessary to adapt existing vehicles for this purpose. For example, in 1943, Nuffield Mechanizations shortened and otherwise heavily modified a Willys Jeep for possible delivery by air. In the USA, Willys, as well as Crossly Chevrolet and Kaiser, also produced lightweight versions of the Jeep.

Improvements in the load-carrying capabilities of transport aircraft and gliders finally rendered these experiments unnecessary. During the Normandy and Arnhem operations, modified Jeeps were carried in Waco Hadrian and Airspeed Horsa gliders. Experiments were also conducted on dropping a Jeep on an airborne platform or "crate" slung underneath, for

example, a Handley Page Halifax. The British Ministry of Supply ordered 2,000 such platforms for airborne operations in 1944.

Throughout World War II one of the major constraints affecting delivery by air of all types of load, not only vehicles, was the size and shape of the aircraft cargo door and the volume of the fuselage. By the late 1950s, aircraft such as the Blackburn Beverley, with a huge rear loading door, removed this constraint and paved the way for the development of new equipment.

In Britain, heavy dropping equipment (the delivery of vehicles by parachute) included the AATDC (Army Air Transport and Development Centre) platform, which had capacity for a Jeep and trailer or 3,636kg/8,000lb of stores, the 8,181kg/18,000lb Medium Stressed Platform (MSP), and the Heavy Stressed Platform (HSP) which was suitable for air-dropping a bulldozer for example. Similarly, a vehicle

RIGHT: **Air-portable (APD) variant of the Bedford QLD GS truck, shown here with the upper part of the cab and doors removed to reduce the overall height. The top of the cab is stowed in the rear body. Once the truck had been stripped, the chassis was mounted on castors and was carried in one Dakota, while the body parts and the wheels were carried in a second aircraft.**

ABOVE: **Austin "Champ" loaded on to the Medium Stressed Platform (MSP) ready for air-dropping. LEFT: US "HMMWV" slung beneath a Chinook heavy-lift helicopter in Afghanistan. Although perfectly practical, and often the only feasible method of moving vehicles across hostile territory, this is an expensive solution.**

could be slung under a helicopter; the Royal Marines deployed Citroën 2CV pick-ups in this way.

Similar equipment was developed in other countries. The US Army, for example, used a system of modular platforms to rig vehicles for air-dropping. Adjustable diagonal braces were used to secure the load to the platform and thick honeycomb packing was employed as a shock absorber.

Over the years, the increasing size and capability of transport aircraft began to make the weight of individual vehicles in drops less relevant. However, this did not prevent many armies from developing vehicles specifically designed to

maximize the dimensions and capabilities of transport aircraft. In Britain, one of these was the Land Rover "Air Portable General Purpose" (APGP), an amphibious vehicle dating from the early 1960s designed to be stacked two-high inside an aircraft fuselage or dropped on the medium stressed platform. In 1964, a specification was issued for a lightweight version of the Land Rover that could be stripped to the minimum for air-portability, while remaining fully operational. It was intended that this vehicle would be carried by the Beverley, Argosy and Belfast aircraft which made up the RAF heavy airlift fleet at the time. The vehicle could also be under-slung beneath a Belvedere or Wessex helicopter.

Other specialized vehicles began to appear which were sufficiently small and versatile to allow easy delivery by air. Examples include the Belgian FN AS24, which weighed just 220kg/485lb and yet could carry four lightly equipped troops. In France, the LOHR FL500 was developed for use by airborne troops, with six vehicles carried in a C-130 Hercules or C-160 Transall aircraft. The M274 "Mechanical Mule" was a similar vehicle produced for the US Army. The German Kraka 640 folding lightweight vehicle was even more versatile, and 16 folded or 10 unfolded vehicles could be carried in a C-160. Similarly, the EINSA MM-1 multi-purpose all-terrain vehicle from Spain is sufficiently small to allow ten to be carried in a C-130.

Common standards and procedures have been developed by NATO to simplify the air delivery of all kinds of supplies. In Britain, for example, the co-ordinating body is the Joint Air Delivery Test & Evaluation Unit (JADTEU). The US-built Lockheed Martin C-130 remains the standard military transport aircraft in the West and can carry a range of loads, including utility helicopters and six-wheeled armoured vehicles. In an air-delivery role, loads up to 19,090kg/42,000lb can be dropped.

ABOVE: **An air-portable and amphibious 8x8 vehicle of the Chinese Peoples' Liberation Army.**

Reconnaissance and special operations vehicles

ABOVE: **The long-wheelbase Land Rover provides the perfect platform for the modern special operations and reconnaissance vehicle.** BELOW: **The Jeep was soon found to be the ideal vehicle for long-range covert operations by the British Special Air Service Regiment in World War II.**

The development of the Jeep effectively created a new class of military vehicle. With a powerful four-cylinder engine and excellent four-wheel drive, the Jeep could go almost anywhere. The Special Air Services Regiment (SAS) in Britain soon adapted the vehicle for special behind-the-lines operations. The vehicles were stripped to the bare essentials, loaded with food rations, water, personal kit and jerrycans of fuel. SAS Jeeps were able to carry everything, including machine-guns, the crews needed to conduct interdiction raids on enemy airfields, and fuel and ammunition dumps.

In the early 1950s, with the Jeeps beginning to wear out, the SAS adapted the short-wheelbase Series I Land Rover for the same role. In Belgium, the Para-Commandos similarly converted the Minerva TT to this role, carrying out a series of similar

modifications. The SAS Series I remained in service until the late-1960s when it was replaced by the long-wheelbase Series IIA which provided more stowage space and allowed the operating range to be increased.

The military requirements for what was officially known as "Truck, GS, SAS, $^3/_4$-ton, 4x4, Rover 11" – but which everyone refers to as the "Pink Panther" – were drawn up by the SAS Regiment in 1964 and derived from experience gained on operations. Some improvised prototypes were produced in conjunction with the Royal Electrical & Mechanical Engineers (REME) workshop, but it was clear that the standard Series II chassis was not suitable. Final development of the vehicle was passed to the Fighting Vehicles Research & Development Establishment (FVRDE) who produced a development vehicle based on a long-wheelbase Series II equipped with heavy-duty springs and over-sized wheels fitting 9.00–15 sand tyres.

LEFT: **A beautifully restored Land Rover Series I as used by the British Special Air Service.**

ABOVE: **Built by Marshalls of Cambridge, and dating from the late-1980s, the SAS special patrol vehicle finally replaced the iconic "Pink Panther".**

RIGHT: **Constructed by Marshalls of Cambridge, the iconic Series IIA-based "Pink Panther" is typical of long-range patrol vehicles, carrying weapons, stores, spare parts, fuel and whatever is needed to allow the crew to survive behind enemy lines for days at a time.**

Other changes included the use of two long-range fuel tanks, which increased the average operating range to 2,500km/ 1,500 miles, and the inclusion of various weapons mounts.

By May 1967, a final specification had been prepared and Marshalls of Cambridge was contracted to develop the vehicle, and build 72 examples. The first, by now using the Series IIA chassis, was ready in August 1968. Following some inevitable detail changes, the SAS received the first vehicle on October 2, 1968.

Following stalwart service, the "Pink Panthers" started to be replaced in the late 1980s by a heavily modified Defender 110 "Desert Patrol Vehicle" (DPV). Superficially resembling the "Pink Panther", the DPV lacked doors, windscreen, top and frame. At the rear, the body was of the civilian high-capacity pick-up truck. An external roll-over bar was fitted behind the front seats. Also there were additional fuel tanks, as well as generous stowage capacity for additional petrol and water jerrycans, ammo and personal kit. A pair of machine-guns was mounted in the rear, with a third pedestal-mounted on the scuttle.

In 1992, Land Rover introduced the "Special Operations Vehicle" (SOV), based on the long-wheelbase four-door Defender 110, featuring a combined roll bar and weapons mount. The SOV was originally designed to provide the US Army Rangers with a rapid-reaction, air-portable, all-terrain weapons platform. Believing that the ubiquitous High-Mobility Multi-purpose Wheeled Vehicle (HMMWV) was too large, the Rangers had been impressed by the performance of the British Army's Defenders during the first Iraq War, seeing it as a better replacement for the M151A2 gun Jeep. The Rangers took delivery of 60 examples in 1993, and the SOV was also offered to other defence customers.

A year later, Land Rover showed the "Multi-Role Combat Vehicle" (MRCV) at the British Army Equipment Exhibition (BAEE). Developed partly in conjunction with Longline, who had produced the "desert buggies" favoured by the SAS, the MRCV was also derived from the Defender and was originally

demonstrated on the short-wheelbase Defender 90, but users could also choose the Defender 110 or 130 platform. The MRCV was subsequently renamed the "Rapid Deployment Vehicle" (RDV).

The RDV was intended to provide maximum versatility, acting either as a weapons platform or reconnaissance vehicle. The modular construction enabled the vehicle to be converted for seven distinct roles. These included pedestal mount, MILAN anti-tank platform, multi-purpose ring mount, and personnel or cargo carrier. Conversion from one role to another required only hand tools, and no modifications were required which would have compromised the vehicle's ability to be used for general service duties. The RDV could also accept the "Weapons Mount Installation Kit" (WMIK), which was developed for use with the British Army's Wolf Defender XD 110 models.

Like the original SAS Jeeps, these special operations vehicles are designed to get special forces in and out of an area fast and have given rise to a whole new sub-category of military vehicle – the soft-skin combat vehicle. It is a category in which the Land Rover has a unique position.

ABOVE: **The distinctive brush guard identifies this special operations vehicle developed for the US Rangers following "Operation Desert Storm", the first Gulf War.**

RIGHT: **Leyland-Scammell "Medium Mobility Load Carrier" (MMLC) DROPS vehicle. Note how the load-carrying area can be used to transport a light armoured fighting vehicle such as the Scorpion.**

Cargo vehicles and DROPS

The cargo vehicle, or simple load carrier, forms the basis of military logistics and provided the first steps towards the mechanization of most armies. Almost all of the early motorized military vehicles were assigned to the cargo-carrying role, and by the end of World War I most mechanized armies had divided load carriers into three categories – light, medium and heavy – covering payloads of up to 1 ton, 1¹/₂–4 tons, and over 5 tons respectively. By the mid-1930s, trucks were also being categorized as those that were suitable only for road use, and those equipped with all-wheel drive to enhance off-road performance.

While the development of trucks continued rapidly after the end of World War I, there were no particular advances in those designed for a logistical role. The cargo carriers of the 1920s and 1930s were generally rigid chassis four- or six-wheeled trucks, often with fixed sides that meant loading had to be done from the rear. Tractor and trailer units were not much

ABOVE: **Although these are standard cargo trucks, the US Army's Oshkosh 8x8 "Heavy Expanded Mobility Tactical Truck" (HEMTT) was also fitted with the "Palletized Loading System" (PLS). The trucks are being unloaded prior to deployment in "Operation Desert Storm", the first Gulf War.**

favoured, even during World War II, although, at least by the end of the war, the upper limit for the heavy class vehicles had risen to 10 tons. The story was no different during the post-war years. Trucks became larger, more powerful and more reliable, but remained little different in concept from vehicles of 50 years earlier. From the late 1960s it started to become common practice to fit larger trucks with hydraulic cranes for loading and unloading – these were described by the British Army as "Crane Appliance, Lorry Mounted" (CALM).

The biggest, and really the only technological improvement in load carrying, came in the 1980s with the use of self-loading "Demountable Rack Off-loading and Pick-up System" (DROPS) vehicles designed to handle flat-racks.

Work on DROPS had begun in the 1970s when it became obvious that the British Government would not be prepared to fund the numbers of logistical vehicles required to keep battle supplies flowing to the combat units in the event of war. Clearly a more radical approach was required to the problems of supply. Commercial transport companies had been using demountable bodies for some time and, at the end of the 1970s, the Royal Corps of Transport (now the Royal Logistics Corps) undertook feasibility studies into the adaptation of this system for military use. In July 1982, the Ministry of Defence requested submissions from vehicle and load-handling system manufacturers for trials. A year later, Foden Lorries and the Scammell Trucks Division of Leyland were asked to produce "Medium Mobility Load Carriers" (MMLC) and "Improved Medium Mobility Load Carriers" (IMMLC) incorporating DROPS equipment for evaluation.

The DROPS system is made up of a removable vehicle container body and flat-rack pallets, manufactured to the ISO (International Standards Organization) standard dimensions. These flat-racks, which carry 10 NATO pallets to a total weight of 15 tons, are designed to be carried by vehicles equipped with special mechanical load-handling systems. The equipment allows the container or flat-rack to be picked up from the ground

ABOVE: **The Foden "Improved Medium Mobility Load Carrier" (IMMLC) DROPS vehicle incorporated the same equipment as the Scammell. The Foden proved to have better cross-country performance.**

ABOVE: **Foden 10-ton 6x6 cargo truck fitted with a hydraulic lifting arm to facilitate the loading and unloading of cargo – the British Army describe this as a "Crane Appliance, Lorry Mounted" (CALM).**

ABOVE: **Although it was subsequently re-rated at 4-tons, the 3-ton Bedford RL 4x4 is a typical type of military cargo vehicle since the early days of World War II. Most such vehicles can also be used as troop carriers.**

and loaded over the rear axles on to the chassis of the transporter vehicle without any need for manual handling or breaking down of the load. This means that the load can be moved from stores to end user, across a variety of vehicles if necessary, without ever needing to be unpacked. Indeed, the flat-racks and containers can be easily transferred from road to rail and back again with no need for conventional mechanical-handling equipment. The system can be operated by one man, and the speed of loading means that the DROPS system provides increased efficiency.

The military version of this bulk transportation system, which is described by the US Army as the "Palletized Loading System" (PLS), includes features which are not required by civilian users, including below-ground pick-up, high tolerance to mis-alignment of the LHS and flat-rack, and the ability to travel across country without compromising the security of the load.

Since the initial deliveries and deployment of the British Army's DROPS system began in early 1990, the range of body options has been expanded to include, for example, vehicle-handling pallets, communications shelters, tankers, hospital modules, workshops and radar installations.

Similar load-handling systems are also in use with most armies in the West, using standard ISO-dimensioned flat-racks and container bodies. In the USA, for example, Oshkosh fits an OTC/Multilift LHS on the 10-ton M1120 8x8 "Heavy Expanded Mobility Tactical Truck" (HEMTT) chassis. In Germany, Multilift load-handling equipment has been installed on MAN chassis. In France, the Renault TRM 10,000 6x6 is equipped with the Bennes-Marrel load-handling system. Users include Astra, Volvo, Scania, Sisu, Steyr and others.

LEFT: **Although most commonly specified as a basic cargo vehicle, the French-built ACMAT is a versatile vehicle which can be readily adapted for a variety of roles including gun tractor, personnel carrier, mortar carrier, shelter carrier and water tanker. The vehicle shown is in service with the French Foreign Legion during UN operations.**

RIGHT: **This 1-ton forward-control Land Rover was fitted with a four-stretcher Marshalls body for use as an ambulance for forward areas. The red cross markings are applied to hinged flaps which can be closed to show just the camouflaged green finish. A similar type of ambulance was produced for the Luxembourg Army.**

Ambulances and medical vehicles

Motorized ambulances were among the first types of military vehicle to be developed, with all of the major combatants of World War I using small van-type ambulances, and motorcycle combinations also used as stretcher carriers. Most offered very little in the way of comfort for the casualty and many injured soldiers must have perished as a result of the jolting ride across country, never actually reaching sanctuary. The development of bodies for military ambulances continued during the inter-war period, with Germany and Britain both producing standard designs that could be fitted to a number of chassis.

ABOVE: **The current British Army forward area ambulance is based on a Land Rover Wolf Defender XD long-wheelbase chassis.**

During World War II, if there was nothing else available, the Allied armies favoured the use of the Jeep for front-line evacuation. There were three standard designs employed, one of which placed the stretchers above the driver, the other two placing the wounded men in a lower, less precarious position, either behind the driver or across the bonnet.

The British Army's standard heavy ambulance of World War II was based on the Austin K2Y chassis and provided accommodation for four stretchers or ten seated casualties in an enclosed and heated body. The US equivalent was the Dodge WC54, which could also accommodate four stretchers or eight seated in a somewhat smaller body, but with the benefit of four-wheel drive. Both types were supplied to other Allied armies. Germany and the USA also used standard bus bodies in the ambulance medical role behind the lines. The standard *Wehrmacht* front-line ambulance (*Krankenwagen*) body of World War II was designated Kfz 31, and could be fitted to a number of light 4x2, 4x4 and 6x4 chassis.

By the time the war was over, armoured ambulances had begun to be used, the best of these being a vehicle based on the Canadian-built C15TA armoured truck. Others were based on the White M3A1 scout car or the International half-track. The *Wehrmacht* also used the half-tracked Hanomag SdKfz 251/8 as a front-line armoured ambulance.

The requirements of the medical evacuation role have changed little since World War II, and front-line military ambulances have continued to be produced on 4x4 type chassis. The standards of care available to casualties during evacuation to a clearing station or hospital have been much improved.

ABOVE: **A field ambulance based on the Renault R2087 4x4 chassis which was used in service by the French Army during the 1950s.**

ABOVE: **With go-anywhere performance, the Jeep was adapted to serve as a front-line ambulance, although it must have been far from comfortable.**

In the USA, there have been field ambulances built on the M38A1 and M151 chassis, and the current US front-line ambulance is based on the ubiquitous AM-General "High-Mobility Multi-purpose Wheeled Vehicle" (HMMWV). The British Land Rover Series I and the Austin "Champ" were both fitted with stretcher kits in the early 1950s, rather in the style of the wartime Jeep. Later, the long-wheelbase Land Rover was adopted for the standard British field ambulance, and mountain crash rescue vehicle in the mid-1950s. The current British vehicle of this type uses the 3,327mm/ 130in variant of the Land Rover Defender chassis.

Medium and heavy ambulances have tended to be built on a suitable truck chassis, often with softer suspension to minimize discomfort. For example, in Britain there have been larger ambulances based on the Ford Thames E3, Austin K9 and Bedford RL chassis. There were also armoured ambulance variants of the Alvis Saracen, FV430 series and Humber "Pig". In France, Peugeot and Renault medium truck chassis have been used, while in the USA, the ³/₄-ton Dodge and 1-ton Kaiser-Jeep chassis have both been fitted with ambulance bodies.

Other military medical vehicles produced over the years include mountain search and rescue vehicles, mobile operating theatres, dental surgeries, medical laboratories, X-ray units and medical supply vehicles. These included various refrigerated vehicles for the delivery of blood and plasma.

LEFT: **A** *Bundeswehr* **armoured battlefield ambulance built on a Bucher/MOWAG 6x6 DURO chassis. The vehicle has more space for stowage of medical equipment and supplies and also additional personnel accommodation. The larger, boxy body enables the medical teams to provide more than basic first-aid treatment to battlefield casualties.**

RIGHT: **A Jeep, equipped for signals equipment cable laying, in Normandy, 1944, with a GMC truck in the background.**

Communications vehicles

Marconi made his history-making cross-Channel radio transmission in 1898. It was obvious that wireless would have military applications, and a British Royal Engineer Committee, headed by Captain J. C. Kennedy, was set up the following year to keep a watching brief on his progress. By 1901, Marconi had proposed a mobile wireless station for military use, the heavy equipment being mounted on a Thornycroft steam-powered wagon. Within five years, the Royal Engineer Signal Service had accepted wireless as a standard means of communication, and mobile equipment was mounted in Daimler and Rolls-Royce motor vehicles, as well as in horse-drawn wagons.

Alongside more traditional messaging systems, which included the use of pigeons and motorcycle despatch riders, both sides used telegraph and telephone transmissions for messages during World War I, as well as establishing wireless stations in the trenches and behind the lines. Mobile wireless equipment was also carried in motor vehicles, fitted with a telescopic mast-type or folding aerial made of steel tubing which could be quickly raised or lowered.

In 1920, the British Army established the Royal Corps of Signals and during the 1920s and 1930s there was considerable development in both cable and wireless

communication. Gradually, Morse code began to be replaced, or at least supplemented, by voice communication. Command tanks were among vehicles to be fitted with wireless equipment.

By the time World War II broke out, radio sets – although the British persisted in calling them "wireless" – had been reduced in size sufficiently to allow installation in vehicles as small as a Jeep or staff car. It became common practice with both the Allies and the Axis armies to equip most, though not all, armoured cars and tanks with a radio set that would allow communication both with headquarters and between individual vehicles. The *Wehrmacht* pioneered the use of unit construction, with interconnection between radio sets made by plug and socket. Multi-channel "Frequency Modulation" (FM) sets began to be developed which provided front-line troops with reliable, static-free communications. These were followed by "Very-High Frequency" (VHF) and "Ultra-High Frequency" (UHF) sets which increased range and reliability, particularly where line-of-sight transmission was not possible. Specialized communications vehicles, often with a self-contained generating capability, were used by both sides during the war.

Equipment became smaller, more powerful and considerably more sophisticated during the 1950s and 1960s. The development of printed-circuit technology

and transistors allowed a degree of miniaturization that was further exploited when the integrated circuit appeared. Another breakthrough came in December 1958 when the US Signal Corps launched its first communications satellite, "Project Score", demonstrating the feasibility of world-wide communications by means of relatively simple active-satellite relays. During the Vietnam War, the US Army utilized "troposcatter" technology, whereby a radio signal is beamed up into the atmosphere and bounced back down to earth, by-passing challenging terrain which might interfere with more conventional communications.

In 1988, the US Signal Corps embarked on the production and deployment of the "Mobile-Subscriber Equipment" system (MSE) which effectively created a dedicated mobile telephone network serving the battlefield. This allowed a commander or communications centre to connect mobile telephones and fax machines in vehicles with each other, sending and receiving secure information. It even allowed connection to the public telephone network. The MSE was mounted in "High-Mobility Multi-purpose Wheeled Vehicles" (HMMWVs), rather than the larger, less-mobile 2¹/₂-ton 6x6 trucks.

By the 1990s, new military communications technology allowed signals to be transmitted across many frequencies, hopping from one to another at high speed. This allowed many channels of talk to share an already crowded frequency spectrum. Later generations of these radios combined encryption devices with the receiver/transmitter, making it possible to send and receive digital traffic with great fidelity.

Alongside the advances in voice and signals communications, there have been similar technological improvements in electronics devoted to target acquisition, surveillance and intelligence gathering, fire-control and digital data processing. While the specialized vehicles that were used for voice communications may be a thing of the past, the modern army continues to deploy formidable electronic resources, much of it mobile and vehicle-mounted.

ABOVE: **The Land Rover Vampire, a signals-equipped variant built on the forward-control 101 chassis. It is also thought to have been used as a re-broadcast or relay vehicle.**

ABOVE: **Bedford QL fitted with mobile teleprinter equipment.** BELOW: **The Bedford QLR was equipped with a house-type body for signals, command and similar roles. The electrical system was interference suppressed, and equipment included a 600W auxiliary generator.**

Heavy equipment transporters

As World War II progressed, the size and weight of tanks deployed by the opposing armies increased inexorably. The massive German *Königstiger* (King Tiger), which appeared in 1944, weighed some 70 tons, and the Germans had even larger tanks on the drawing board. After the end of the war, there was no relief and the trend increased. Post-war tanks such as the British Conqueror and the Soviet *Iosif Stalin* (Joseph Stalin) still weighed more than 60 tons. Most current "Main Battle Tanks" (MBTs) tend to weigh around 65–70 tons. The challenge has been to produce tank transporters – or "Heavy Equipment Transporters" (HETs) – to move these enormous vehicles.

During the war years, the Allies had three tank transporters available – the Diamond T Model 980/981 ballasted tractor, which was used with a 40–45-ton multi-wheeled draw-bar

ABOVE: **The British-built Scammell Commander replaced the Thornycroft Antar in 1982. In 2001, the Commander was replaced by the Oshkosh M1070F.**

trailer; the Pacific TR-1 – better known as the M26 "Dragon Wagon" – which was available in both soft-skin and armoured form, and designed to be coupled to a Fruehauf 40-ton semi-trailer; and the Scammell Pioneer, which was used only by Britain, and which was also designed for use with a semi-trailer. In Germany and the Soviet Union, it was common practice to move tanks on their tracks or on railway wagons. The heavy purpose-designed transporters favoured by Britain and the US Army did not exist.

Having never been rated as "standard", the Diamond T was quickly phased out by the US Army, who continued to use the

RIGHT: **In the early 1970s, Germany and the USA agreed to co-operate in the development of a new main battle tank, the MBT-70. It was also agreed that there would be a jointly developed heavy equipment transporter, the HET-70, to carry the new tank. The HET-70 project was eventually abandoned but each country continued with the development of the HET. The US-designed vehicle was the Chrysler XM745.**

LEFT: Dating from 1997, the Scania T144GB6 x 4NZ350 has been purchased by both the Belgian and Swedish Armies. The engine is a Scania V8 diesel producing 530bhp, driving the rear bogie through a nine-speed gearbox. The standard semi-trailer used by the Belgian Army is a six-axle LOHR design. The tractor is rated for a gross train weight of 150 tons.

"Dragon Wagon". However, both the Pacific and the Diamond T remained in service in Britain and Europe into the early post-war years. Britain even chose to re-engine the aging, but very capable, Diamond T, keeping some examples in reserve service into the 1970s.

The US Army experimented with a number of tractor and trailer combinations during the 1950s and 1960s, including a double-ended twin-tractor outfit designed at Detroit Arsenal towards the end of the 1950s. In the 1960s, there were further experiments with a 10x4 heavy tractor coupled to a semi-trailer. Although the development of the joint US-German MBT-70 main battle tank was cancelled, the associated transporter evolved into the Chrysler XM745 8x8 tractor and the German Faun SLT-50 *Elefant*. In US service, the Chrysler was replaced by the 50-ton Oshkosh M911 6x6 in 1976 and then, when the M1A1 Abrams MBT started to enter service in 1992, by the Oshkosh M1070 tank with a 70-ton semi-trailer.

In Britain, attempts were made to produce specialized 30- and 60-ton tractors, but when these were abandoned, the Diamond Ts were supplemented by the Thornycroft Antar. Initially rated at 50 tons and designed for use with a draw-bar trailer, it was subsequently upgraded to 60 tons and produced both as a ballasted tractor and for use with a semi-trailer. Although the Rotinoff Super Atlantic was trialled in the late 1950s, the Ministry of Defence (MoD) retained the Antar until 1982 when it was replaced by the 65-ton Scammell Commander. By the time the Commander was due for replacement, in the 1990s, the European Union had imposed a 12-ton axle loading limit which forced a rethink. In 2001, the MoD announced that it had chosen a European version of the US-built Oshkosh M1070, with a seven-axle 72-ton King trailer, in preference to the Alvis-Unipower MH 8875.

By the late 1950s, the heavy equipment transporter had standardized its present design configuration; essentially a powerful diesel-engined tractor, not necessarily with all-wheel drive, coupled to a multi-axle semi-trailer. A winch is usually fitted behind the cab to aid the loading of disabled tanks. As well as those described, similar tractors have been produced in France by Renault, Willème, Berliet and Saviem, in Germany by Magirus, Mercedes-Benz and Faun, in Spain by Fiat. Other types have been produced in Sweden, China, South Africa, Belarus and elsewhere.

The Soviet Army still prefers to move tanks on their tracks, but the 8x8 MAZ-537 tractor has been used as a heavy equipment transporter in conjunction with a low-loader semi-trailer.

ABOVE: The Thornycroft Antar was originally designed as a private venture for oil-field use but was adopted by the British Army as a replacement for the Diamond T Model 980/981. This is the Antar Mk 3, fitted with a ballast body.

Missile transporters

Although dating back several centuries, the military rocket began to find new favour in the mid-1930s. Its reappearance coincided with the development of solventless cordite which could be shaped into a solid propellant. The use of liquid propellants allowed the Germans to develop long-range rockets as a substitute for artillery, a method also used by the Soviet Union. During World War II, the *Wehrmacht* and Soviet armies both employed mobile rocket launchers, mounting electrically operated multiple tube launchers on to trucks and half-tracks. The modern form of this weapon is the US-built "Multiple Launch Rocket System" (MLRS) carried on a tracked chassis.

The German V2 was the first modern ground-launched missile, but, lacking a guidance system, it was really only useful as a terror weapon. Although the V2 gave rise to similar rockets in both the USA and the Soviet Union, it was not considered to be transportable.

The US Army's "Honest John" missile of the early 1950s was probably the first transportable surface-launched artillery missile, although it still lacked a guidance system. It was widely deployed by NATO armies and saw service in the USA, Canada, Britain, Japan and West Germany during the 1950s and 1960s. Designed to deliver either a conventional or nuclear warhead, the missile was carried on a special "Transporter-Erector-Launcher" (TEL) which was mounted on the chassis of a standard US Army 5-ton 6x6 truck. Reload missiles were carried in open-backed trucks and on special trailers.

The "Honest John" had actually been preceded by the Firestone "Corporal" guided-weapon system, which was derived from the German V2 rocket, but the system was large and complex and required specially designed launch and transport vehicles, as well as erector vehicles, servicing platforms, fuel dispensers, and firing systems. A similar surface-to-surface missile system was produced in Britain under the designation "Blue Water". Although it never entered service (the project being

TOP: **Soviet ZiL-131 tractors towing semi-trailers for transporting surface-to-air missiles during a May Day parade.** ABOVE: **The US Army's "Honest John" missile was also deployed by Britain, West Germany, Canada and Japan.**

ABOVE: **US Army "Tube-launched, Optically guided, Wire-tracked" (TOW) battlefield anti-tank missile launched from a "HMMWV" vehicle.**

cancelled in August 1962) "Blue Water" was sufficiently compact to allow transport and launch from a 3-ton Bedford RL.

The "Corporal", "Honest John" and its replacement, "Sergeant", were eventually superseded by the "Lance" missile which was carried on a tracked chassis derived from the US Army's M113 armoured personnel carrier.

LEFT: **A "Javelin" anti-tank missile being fired from a Pinzgauer vehicle of 42 Commando, Royal Marines, during a live fire demonstration.**

During the two or three decades following the end of World War II, the Soviet Union developed a range of huge "Transporter-Erector-Launcher (TEL) vehicles to handle the nuclear and conventional ballistic missiles deployed by the Red Army. The first of these were the V2-based mobile missiles, mounted on a railway launcher, which were developed during the late-1940s. Truck-mounted launchers began to be used by the mid to late-1950s. The most notable of Soviet rocket was probably the MAZ-543 truck-mounted SCUD which saw service with Iraqi forces during the Gulf War of 1992. The Soviet Union continued to develop transportable ground-launched ballistic missiles long after the concept had fallen from favour in the West, where the military tended to favour submarine launch or aircraft delivery. The longest-range Soviet ballistic missile of this type was the Temp-S, SS-12 (NATO codename: "Scaleboard"), which had a range of 900km/550 miles. It was in service between 1965 and 1979 and was carried on a MAZ-543 truck.

The equivalent US missile systems include the M48 "Chaparral", which is carried on a tracked chassis, and the "Patriot", which is mounted on a wheeled "Transporter-Erector-Launcher" (TEL) vehicle and requires support vehicles carrying radar and data-processing equipment.

For battlefield use, there has been a trend towards the miniaturization of both anti-tank and anti-aircraft guided weapons and associated equipment. British surface-to-air anti-aircraft missiles like the "Thunderbird" of the 1960s could be carried on a small trailer and towed by a Bedford 3-ton truck, or even a Land Rover. Surface-to-air anti-aircraft missile systems such as the "Rapier" can be trailer-mounted and towed behind a Land Rover or mounted in the back of a tracked launcher vehicle. As regards anti-tank missiles, even first-generation weapons such as the "Malkara", "Vigilant" and "Swingfire" were sufficiently compact that the launch system and guidance equipment could be carried in a small armoured vehicle such as a "Ferret" or "Saladin". Current practice is to mount modern anti-tank weapons, such as the wire-guided Franco-German MILAN system or the US-built TOW and "Dragon" missiles, on to small soft-skin vehicles such as the "HMMWV", Land Rover or Jeep.

LEFT: **Soviet MAZ-543 9P120 "Transporter-Erector-Launcher" (TEL) loaded with a Temp SS-12b missile (NATO name: "Scaleboard"). The missile is contained inside a protective cylinder which, until ready for launch, allows the fuel for the solid-fuel rocket motors to remain at a controlled temperature.**

Bridging vehicles

ABOVE: **The US Army "Mobile Assault Bridge" (MAB) dates from 1959. Each 4x4 transporter vehicle carries either an end bay or an interior bay.**

Despite the development of heavy-lift helicopters, surface crossing of water obstacles continues to play a vital role in the capability of the modern army. As early as 1812, the British Army had used floating pontoons to provide a simple ferry. Tank bridges began to be developed during World War I. Smaller types of portable bridge, which were carried by specially adapted trucks, began to appear in the 1930s. During this period, the British Army, for example, used several types of bridge, including the prefabricated floating pontoon, trestle, small box-girder bridge and sliding bay bridge; all were designed to be carried on a 3-ton 6x4 truck.

In 1941, the British-developed "Bailey" bridge system was adopted by the Allied armies as the standard military bridging system, providing a versatile means of quickly building a range of bridges from prefabricated standardized girder components. Part of the design criteria was that the individual components could be carried by a six-man party, and the parts had to be transportable in a 3-ton truck. The system was used extensively throughout the European campaign and was also produced in the USA, with a total of

490,000 tons of bridge components manufactured, sufficient to build a 40km/25-mile long bridge. One example, the "Springbok" bridge, which was constructed over the River Po at Pontelagasco in Italy, used 1,900 tons of equipment. In 1942, the "Bailey" suspension bridge was introduced, designed for clear spans of up to 122m/400ft. In modified form, the "Bailey" bridge remains in use to this day.

During World War II, the US Army also used the H10 and H20 box-girder bridges, a steel pontoon bridge and two types of floating pontoon bridge. Once again, all of these were carried on specially adapted trucks. The *Wehrmacht* used pneumatic boats to assemble light bridges. Some of their engineer units were equipped with box-girder bridges, while permanent river crossings were built using the *Typ B* (pontoon trestle), *Typ K* (box-girder), *Typ J* (tank bridge) or *Typ LZ* (through-girder bridge).

Floating pontoon and girder bridges are the mainstay of military bridging equipment, as are the mechanized "Armoured Vehicle Launched Bridges" (AVLBs) mounted on what are essentially modified tank chassis. More recently, floating

RIGHT: **The Gillois-EWK bridge and ferry system was a joint Franco-German project, at first using rubber floats. Subsequently these were replaced by fabricated aluminium buoyancy units. The system of a separate ramp and bridging units can be used to assemble either a floating bridge or a motorized ferry.**

ABOVE: **Folding float unit carried on a US Army Oshkosh (HEMTT) truck.**
LEFT: **Royal Engineers assembling elements of the British Army's "Bridging in the 90s" (BR90) system (see caption below).**

bridge and ferry systems have been developed which allow speedy crossing of water obstacles.

NATO strategy of the 1950s and 1960s had decreed that repelling a Soviet invasion across the plains of East German would require considerable amphibious capability. While this might have been all very well for small numbers of tactical vehicles, it was impractical for the larger numbers of supply vehicles that are required to keep an army fighting. The question of providing mechanized bridges occupied much military thinking, and various kinds of floating and folding bridges were developed by both NATO and the Warsaw Pact.

Floating bridges were not a new idea, the US Army having already deployed such devices during World War II. What was new was the idea of using vehicles equipped for transporting and erecting the bridge, remaining a part of it while it was being used. One of the earliest of these was a unique amphibious bridging and ferrying system designed in the early 1950s by a French General, Jean Gillois. The first example in this development programme was the Gillois-EWK bridge and ferry system, "an amphibious vehicle, which can be used as a water-crossing ferry or can be assembled with other such vehicles to form a pontoon bridge... (it includes) a hull section hinged to two ramp sections". Essentially, the system is made up of separate ramp and bridge vehicles that were used to build either a Class 60 floating bridge or a navigable ferry. Both types of vehicle were equipped with huge inflatable rubber pontoons, supported on curved frames and carried on rigid arms hinged on the sides of the hull. Some 264 of these vehicles were produced before the design was superseded by the improved M2, on which the easily damaged rubber floats were replaced by rigid aluminium buoyancy units which folded up and on to the hull for transport.

At the same time, the US Army also developed a similar bridging vehicle which was described as the "Mobile Assault Bridge" (MAB).

LEFT: **The BR90 system is a beam-launched bridge which can be assembled on one side of a river crossing and levered across. This photograph was taken during trials.**

Amphibious vehicles

During the 1950s and 1960s, NATO placed considerable emphasis on the development of amphibious vehicles. It was believed that a Soviet invasion would cross the East German plains and that the Soviets would have destroyed as many river crossings as possible. Serious experiments were conducted with a view to making vehicles of all sizes capable of floating or deep-water wading, and various amphibious vehicles were produced as a result. Most armies were able to field small armoured vehicles which were amphibious or capable of being made amphibious. Russia remains an enthusiastic user of the amphibious combat vehicle.

Wartime amphibious vehicles included the US-built DUKW, which was based on the GMC 6x6 truck, the Jeep-based Ford GPW, and the Porsche-designed VW *Schwimmwagen*. The DUKW can almost certainly be considered the most successful amphibious military vehicle of all time and, unsurprisingly, provided the model for many of the vehicles which followed. Other less successful vehicles were produced by Britain and Japan.

In the USA, GMC produced prototypes for the so-called "Super Duck" around 1953, with a $2^1/_2$- to 4-ton cargo capacity. In 1956, this was followed by the 8x8 "Drake" with an increased payload of 8–10 tons. Both were amphibious trucks which were equally suited (or equally unsuitable) on roads or relatively calm water. The LARC (Lighter, Amphibious, Resupply, Cargo) and BARC (Barge, Amphibious, Resupply, Cargo) were more like boats that were also fitted with wheels, enabling them to traverse beaches or loading ramps. There is no question that these vehicles could have been used in road-going supply convoys. Other US trucks which were required to provide some degree of amphibious operation included the M561 "Gama Goat" and the Caterpillar "Goer" family. Also the 5-ton 8x8 cargo vehicle prototyped in 1959–60 by Ford and others, such as the "Mover". It would be better to consider these as trucks which could float, should it be necessary, rather than fully amphibious vehicles.

The DUKW remained in service with the British Army for many years after the war, but it was eventually superseded by the Alvis Stalwart, a 5-ton 6x6 high-mobility load carrier

ABOVE: **The 5-ton Alvis Stalwart used Dowty Hydrojet units driven from the main engine for both propulsion and directional control in the water.** RIGHT: **Prototyped in 1962–63, the US Army's Ford XM656 amphibious 8x8 truck was fitted with inflatable seals on the cab and body doors.**

that was fully amphibious. Unlike the US-built DUKW, and the "Super Duck" and "Drake" experiments, the Stalwart was both steered and powered in the water by a Dowty Hydrojet system that provided improved performance. Notwithstanding drive-line problems caused by having just one differential, the Stalwart remained in service for 25–30 years. For the last 10 years in service the truck lacked any amphibious capability since the Hydrojet system was removed. There were also experiments with amphibious Land Rovers, both in Britain and Australia.

Berliet almost negotiated a licence to manufacture the Stalwart under the name Aurochs, but declined at the last minute. Marmon-Bocquet produced a similar 4-ton 4x4 amphibious truck which used Dowty Hydrojets for propulsion in the water. France, Germany and Italy also co-operated on the early development stages of an amphibious Jeep-type vehicle that would have been manufactured by Hotchkiss, Büssing and Lancia, but the project never passed the prototype stage.

The Soviet Union had used large numbers of Ford GPW amphibians during World War II and built a virtual copy, the GAZ-46 in the post-war years. Similarly, a DUKW copy was built from 1952 as the ZiL-485. Dating from the end of the 1950s, the LuAZ-967M was a small amphibious vehicle intended for ferrying supplies to the front line across difficult terrain, or for evacuating casualties carried on stretchers either side of the central driving position.

The truth is that the performance requirements for the two modes of operation of an amphibious vehicle are in conflict and most such vehicles are neither good trucks nor good boats. By the end of the century it was widely accepted that heavy-lift helicopters could be used to fulfil the role previously allocated to amphibious trucks, and such vehicles that remained in service were consigned to ferrying supplies from ship to shore.

ABOVE: **Britain's attempt at building a domestic rival to the DUKW was the eight-wheeled skid-steered Morris-Commercial Terrapin of which 500 examples were built. Designed by Thornycroft, the vehicle was powered by two Ford V8 petrol engines, each driving the four wheels along one side of the vehicle. The lack of suspension made it difficult to drive on the road.**

Directory of Military Vehicles

The production of motor vehicles was confined to the industrial nations in the USA and Europe, and military vehicles produced by those nations were deployed along the Franco-Belgian border in 1914. Today, military vehicles are produced across the globe. Many companies have been attracted into the defence industry by what appears to be an endless supply of government money. Many have failed by not understanding the nature of the industry, falling victim to technical failure or defence spending cuts. Others have survived by merger or acquisition, or purely by the excellence of the product.

In Britain and France, once-great companies such as Leyland, AEC, Thornycroft, Latil, Laffly and Hotchkiss have closed, yet Renault has managed to survive. Of the German truck manufacturers of World War II, Mercedes-Benz and MAN have prospered, while Henschel, Magirus, Phänomen and Büssing-NAG are barely remembered. Many of the familiar US company names from World War II have closed or left the defence market. Diamond T, Pacific, Dodge, FWD and International have been replaced by newcomers such as Stewart & Stevenson, AM-General and Oshkosh. In Russia, the former state-owned companies such as GAZ and ZiL once manufactured hundreds of thousands of military vehicles for service with the Red Army and the nations of the former Soviet Bloc.

However, this constant maelstrom of technology and development, commercial success and failure has left a rich and varied legacy that cannot fail to fascinate the military vehicle enthusiast.

LEFT: **A line-up of restored GMCs. Note the .50in Browning heavy machine-gun on the third truck in line, typical of air-defence vehicles used on the supply routes.**

Chevrolet C15A, Ford F15A

During World War II, the Canadian motor industry produced almost a million vehicles for service with the British Army and Commonwealth forces. It is well known that many were supplied to Australia, but what is less well known is that large numbers of these Canadian-produced Chevrolet and Ford chassis were also imported into Australia in "Completely Knocked-Down" (CKD) form for assembly by GM-Holden and the Ford Motor Company Australia. Often described as Canadian War Office (CWO) or CMP Australian trucks, they were effectively standard Canadian Military Pattern (CMP) vehicles. The cab (either the number 12 or 13) and the body were produced in Australia. Early vehicles were fitted with a canvas-topped open cab, but this was subsequently replaced by a steel-roofed design. Although superficially similar in appearance, there were many differences between the Australian and Canadian products.

Rated for a ³/₄-ton payload, the Chevrolet C15A and Ford F15A were typical of these Australian-built trucks. The C15A was powered by a 3,548cc GM 216 six-cylinder engine, while the F15A used Ford's V8 petrol engine. In both cases, the engine was connected to all four wheels through a four-speed gearbox and single-speed transfer box. Live axles were fitted at front and rear, suspended on semi-elliptical leaf springs.

Standard variants included a wooden-bodied general-service (GS) truck, office, fire-tender, field artillery tractor, anti-aircraft tractor, and signals/communications vehicle.

ABOVE: Produced by both Ford and Chevrolet, the 15cwt 4x4 C15A and F15A were among the smallest of the Canadian Military Pattern (CMP) trucks. Large numbers of these Canadian-built chassis were imported into Australia in CKD form for local assembly by GM-Holden and Ford Australia. Described as Canadian War Office (CWO) or CMP Australian trucks, the result was effectively a standard CMP vehicle with an Australian-built cab and bodywork.

The chassis were also used to build Australian-designed armoured cars and reconnaissance vehicles.

RIGHT: **Assembling the cab of a Canadian Military Pattern (CMP) truck at the General Motors plant in Oshawa, Canada.**

Chevrolet C15A, Ford F15A

Type: Truck, cargo, (Aust) No 1, ³/₄-ton, 4x4
Manufacturer: Ford Motor Company of Canada; Windsor, Ontario. General Motors Products of Canada; Oshawa, Ontario. Final assembly and bodywork by Ford Motor Company Australia, and General Motors Holden, both based in Melbourne
Production: 1941 to 1945
Powerplant: Ford variants – Ford 239; eight cylinders in V configuration; petrol; water-cooled; 3,917cc; side valves; power output, 95bhp at 3,600rpm. GM-Chevrolet variants – GM 216; six cylinders in-line; petrol; water-cooled; 3,548cc; overhead valves; power output, 85bhp at 3,400rpm
Transmission: 4F1R; part-time 4x4
Suspension: Live axles on semi-elliptical multi-leaf springs
Brakes: Hydraulic
Electrical system: 6V
Dimensions: Length – 4,343mm/171in
Width – 2,235mm/88in
Height – tilt in place, 2,439mm/96in
Wheelbase – 2,565mm/101in
Weight: Unladen – 3,402kg/7,500lb
Payload – 1,134kg/2,500lb
Performance: Maximum speed – 80kph/50mph

GMC "Maple Leaf" series 1600

Type: Truck, breakdown, (Aust) LP3, 3-ton, 4x2
Manufacturer: General Motors Products of Canada;
    Oshawa, Ontario. Final assembly and bodywork
    by General Motors Holden; Melbourne
Production: 1937 to 1942
Powerplant: GM 216; six cylinders in-line; petrol;
    water-cooled; 3,548cc; overhead valves;
    power output, 85bhp at 3,400rpm
Transmission: 4F1R; 4x2
Suspension: Live axles on semi-elliptical
    multi-leaf springs
Brakes: Vacuum-assisted hydraulic
Electrical system: 12V
Dimensions: Length – 6,350mm/250in
    Width – 2,230mm/88in
    Height – 2,540mm/100in
    Wheelbase – 4,013mm/158in
Weight: Not available
Performance: Maximum speed – 56kph/35mph

GMC "Maple Leaf" series 1600

Introduced in 1937, the Canadian Chevrolet "Maple Leaf" series 1600 was a 3-ton 4x2 truck based on the similar US-built GM 9600H heavy-duty chassis, but using a more powerful six-cylinder engine. Many of these vehicles were exported to Australia in CKD form during the immediate pre-war years and into World War II. They were assembled by GM-Holden at Woodville, South Australia, with GM-Holden-built cabs and bodies. The cabs were similar to those fitted

to the Canadian vehicles, but differed in many minor details.

The chassis was powered by a 3,548cc six-cylinder overhead-valve petrol engine driving the rear wheels through a four-speed gearbox. Live axles were suspended on semi-elliptical multi-leaf springs. The chassis were produced in both left- and right-hand drive. There were long and short-wheelbase options, including 3,352mm/132in, 4,013mm/158in and 4,445mm/175in, identified as

model 1660, 1670 and 1680, respectively. Although essentially a civilian truck, the "Maple Leaf" 1600 chassis was also pressed into military service with the Royal Australian Army and with the Royal Australian Air Force, where it was adapted for use as a cargo vehicle, breakdown vehicle, gantry vehicle, and aircraft refueller. Militarization was frequently confined to little more than a coat of matt finish paint and the use of over-sized tyres for the twin rears.

ABOVE: **The Canadian-built Chevrolet "Maple Leaf" series 1600 was a 3-ton 4x2 truck based on the US-built GM 9600H, but with a more powerful six-cylinder engine. Many of these vehicles were exported to Australia in knocked-down form and were assembled by GM-Holden at Woodville in South Australia, with Holden-built cabs and bodies. Although essentially a civilian truck, the "Maple Leaf" 1600 was also taken into military service with the Australian Army and Royal Australian Air Force. This example is equipped as a wrecker in the British style.** RIGHT: **Other body types on the 1600 chassis included cargo vehicles and stake-bodied trucks.**

International Aust No 1, Mks 1–4

International Aust No 1, Mks 1–4

Type: Truck, 2¹/₂-ton, cargo, 4x4
Manufacturer: International Harvester Company of Australia; Melbourne
Production: 1959 to 1971
Powerplant: International AGD-282; six cylinders in-line; petrol; water-cooled; 4,621cc; overhead valves; power output, 148bhp at 3,800rpm
Transmission: 5F1Rx2; part-time 4x4
Suspension: Live axles on semi-elliptical multi-leaf springs; double-acting hydraulic shock absorbers
Brakes: Air-assisted hydraulic
Dimensions: Length – 6,375mm/244in
 Width – 2,438mm/96in
 Height – tilt in place, 2,896mm/114in
 Wheelbase – 3,683mm/145in
Weight: Unladen – 5,525kg/12,181lb
 Payload – 2,490kg/5,489lb
Performance: Maximum speed – 80kph/50mph

Launched in 1959, and remaining in production until 1971. A design project aimed at producing a tactical truck with a high national content of parts was initiated by the Army Design Establishment in 1953. International Harvester was the only company to show any interest, and prototypes were tested during 1955–59. The first 100 production vehicles were delivered in April 1959.

ABOVE: **The International 2¹/₂-ton truck was the Royal Australian Army's standard vehicle during the 1960s and 1970s.**

A further 600 were ordered in 1962 and by 1966 more than 1,500 examples were in service. More than 90 per cent of the components originated from Australia.

Aside from the use of glass-fibre mudguards on the steel cab, the design was thoroughly conventional, with a 4,621cc six-cylinder water-cooled petrol engine driving both axles through a five-speed gearbox and two-speed transfer box. The live axles were suspended on semi-elliptical springs.

Standard variants include cargo/personnel, fire-tender, machinery, office/stores, tipper, road-layer and water tanker.

International Aust No 1, Mk 5

With the 2¹/₂-ton variant of the Australian designed and produced military truck entering service in April 1959, work had begun in 1958 on a 6x6 variant. Launched in 1966, and rated at 5 tons, the larger vehicle shared many components with the earlier Mks 1–4 (4x4). Alongside the standard cargo body, there were dumper, tractor, pole-borer, and garbage-compactor variants. The two trucks formed the basis of the Army's logistics fleet and both were used widely during the Australian involvement in Vietnam.

Like the smaller truck, the Mk 5 was powered by the same 4,621cc International six-cylinder petrol engine, driving both axles through a five-speed gearbox and two-speed transfer box. The live axles were suspended on semi-elliptical springs. Prototypes had twin rear wheels, while the production trucks used singles of larger section.

LEFT: **Both versions of the Aust No 1 were assembled at the International Harvester plant at Dandenong, Victoria, alongside the company's civilian truck range.**

International Aust No 1, Mk 5

Type: Truck, 5-ton, cargo, 6x6
Manufacturer: International Harvester Company of Australia; Melbourne
Production: 1966 to 1971
Powerplant: International AGD-282; six cylinders in-line; petrol; water-cooled; 4,621cc; overhead valves; power output, 148bhp at 3,800rpm
Transmission: 5F1Rx2; part-time 4x4
Suspension: Live axles on semi-elliptical multi-leaf springs; double-acting hydraulic shock absorbers
Brakes: Air-assisted hydraulic
Electrical system: 12V
Dimensions: Length – 6,528mm/257in
 Width – 2,438mm/96in
 Height – tilt in place, 3,302mm/130in; minimum, 2,515mm/99in
 Wheelbase – 3,783mm/149in
 Bogie centres – 1,120mm/44in
Weight: Unladen – 6,624kg/14,604lb
 Payload – road, 6,804kg/15,000lb; cross-country, 4,990kg/11,000lb
Performance: Maximum speed – 80kph/50mph

Land Rover MC2 Perentie

Land Rover MC2 Perentie

Type: Truck, 1-ton, cargo, 4x4
Manufacturer: Jaguar-Rover (Australia); Sydney
Production: 1987 to 1990
Powerplant: Isuzu 4BD1; four cylinders in-line; direct-injection diesel; water-cooled; 3,856cc; overhead valves; power output, 84bhp at 3,200rpm
Transmission: 4F1Rx2; full-time 4x4
Suspension: Live axles on dual-rate coil springs; hydraulic double-acting telescopic shock absorbers
Brakes: Servo-assisted hydraulic
Electrical system: 12V
Dimensions: Length – 4,877mm/192in
    Width – 1,778mm/70in
    Height – tilt in place, 2,057mm/81in
    Wheelbase – 2,794mm/110in
Weight: Unladen – 2,250kg/4,960lb
    Payload – 950kg/2,094lb
Performance: Maximum speed – 115kph/72mph

From the early 1960s, the Royal Australian Army had used Series IIA and Series III Land Rovers produced by Leyland Australia (later Jaguar-Rover Australia (JRA)). During 1981, JRA started development work on a heavy-duty 3-ton 6x6 truck using components of the Land Rover 110, based on a

BELOW: **The MC2 Perentie was based on the Land Rover 110, but was powered by an Isuzu 4BD1 diesel engine.**

development vehicle produced by SMC Engineering. At the same time, the Army announced its intention to procure 25,000 1-ton and 400 2-ton vehicles under "Project Perentie". Seven companies submitted tenders, and three, including JRA and Jeep, were asked to provide vehicles for trials. At the conclusion of the trials, JRA received contracts for both types of vehicle, with deliveries taking place between 1987 and 1990.

The 1-ton vehicle was designated the MC2 4x4 Perentie. Based on standard Land Rover 110, the chassis was galvanized, and lengthened at the rear to allow the spare wheel to be carried under the body. The vehicle was powered by an Isuzu four-cylinder diesel engine driving through the four-speed transmission of the early Range Rover.

Standard variants included a soft-top cargo vehicle, hardtop and soft-top communications vehicles.

Land Rover MC2HD Perentie

Land Rover MC2HD Perentie

Type: Truck, 2-ton, cargo, 6x6
Manufacturer: Jaguar-Rover (Australia); Sydney
Production: 1989 to 1998
Powerplant: Isuzu 4BD1; four cylinders in-line; turbocharged direct-injection diesel; water-cooled; 3,856cc; overhead valves; power output, 115bhp at 3,200rpm
Transmission: 4F1Rx2; full-time 4x4, selectable 6x6
Suspension: Live axles; dual-rate coil springs at front; dual-rate semi-elliptical multi-leaf springs and cranked rocker beam at rear; hydraulic double-acting telescopic shock absorbers
Brakes: Servo-assisted hydraulic
Electrical system: 12V, 24V
Dimensions: Length – 6,147mm/242in
    Width – 2,057mm/81in
    Height – tilt in place, 2,083mm/82in
    Wheelbase – 3,048mm/120in
    Bogie centres – 1,500mm/35in
Weight: Unladen – 3,660kg/8,069lb
    Payload – 2,000kg/4,409lb
Performance: Maximum speed – 100kph/62mph

In the early 1980s, Jaguar-Rover Australia (JRA) announced a heavy-duty 3-ton 6x6 civilian truck, based on developments from SMC Engineering, Bristol in the UK. When the Royal Australian Army announced it was planning to procure 400 2-ton vehicles under "Project Perentie", JRA submitted an upgraded version of this 6x6 vehicle for consideration. Following trials, the vehicle was accepted for production.

Known as the MC2HD 6x6 Perentie, the vehicle was built on a purpose-designed heavy-duty galvanized-steel chassis, with a fabricated rear section of rectangular tube to support the rear bogie. Power came from an Isuzu 4BD1 four-cylinder diesel engine, driving through Range Rover transmission. Drive to the rearmost axle was by a separate propeller shaft from the transfer box power take-off. The front and rear axles were fitted with lower ratio gears and were wider than standard to accommodate the increased weight.

Production variants included a pick-up truck, personnel carrier,

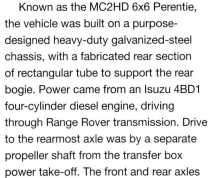

LEFT: **Work on the MC2HD began in March 1989. The vehicle was also offered worldwide, with an option to fit the 3,500cc Range Rover V8 petrol engine.**

water tanker, air-defence vehicle, gun tractor, four-stretcher ambulance, box body and shelter carrier. A long-range patrol vehicle was also produced for Australian special forces.

MACK RM600 Series MC3

Mack Trucks (Australia) is a wholly owned subsidiary of the US company, and has been supplying heavy-duty military vehicles to the Australian Defence Force (ADF) since 1981. The company also refurbishes all Australian military vehicles regardless of origin.

The RM600 Series is a bonneted truck with the front axle set well back, and with a centre cab. It is powered by an 11,000cc Mack six-cylinder turbocharged diesel engine driving all three axles through a Maxitorque five-speed gearbox and two-speed transfer box. The first three prototype vehicles were supplied for a two-year evaluation in 1979. Following successful performance in a range of conditions, from the tropical climate found in the north-west of the continent, to the dry, searing heat of the central desert. The first order, for 906 vehicles, was placed in 1981 with deliveries scheduled for the following year.

The standard 8-ton cargo vehicle is fitted with a drop-side body manufactured by Walsh Engineering. Some vehicles were fitted with an Abbey hydraulic loading crane mounted between the cab and the body. Other standard variants include a heavy recovery vehicle, artillery tractor, fuel tanker, water distributor, dump truck, concrete mixer, bitumen layer and bridge laying/recovery vehicle. In the typical style of Australian road trains, the vehicle is often required to tow two 12.2m/40ft container trailers. More than 1,000 of the vehicles have now been supplied to the ADF. In 2003, Mack were contracted to convert 158 trucks to the heavy-recovery and fuel-tanker roles.

Some RM600s were fitted with a front-mounted 10-ton Ateco winch. Mack Trucks was taken over by Volvo in 2001.

ABOVE: **An Australian Army Mack RM600 fitted with a heavy recovery body.** LEFT: **The standard 8-ton cargo vehicle is fitted with a drop-side body manufactured by Walsh Engineering. This example has had the drop-down sides removed to carry a container.**

MACK RM600 Series

Type: Truck, 8-ton, cargo, 6x6
Manufacturer: Mack Trucks Australia; Wacol, Queensland
Production: 1981 to date
Powerplant: Mack EM6-285 Maxidyne; six cylinders in-line; water-cooled; turbocharged diesel; 11,000cc; overhead valves; power output, 285bhp at 1,800rpm
Transmission: 5F1Rx2; full-time 6x6 (6x4 for bitumen layer and fuel tanker variants)
Suspension: Live axles on semi-elliptical multi-leaf springs; some trucks retro-fitted with rear air-bag suspension
Brakes: Air-pressure
Electrical system: 24V
Dimensions: Length – 9,601mm/378in
    Width – 2,490mm/98in
    Height – 3,150mm/124in
    Wheelbase – 5,461mm/215in
    Bogie centres – 1,397mm/55in
Weight: Unladen – 13,413kg/29,570lb
    Payload – 8,000kg/17,637lb
Performance: Maximum speed – 90kph/56mph

Austro-Daimler ADGR

In 1899, the German manufacturer Daimler Motoren Gesellschaft, made an agreement with Bierenz-Fischer to build 100 Daimler cars in Austria. Meanwhile, Österreichische Automobil Gesellschaft, which had been founded during 1906 in Wien, had commissioned Daimler to build Maja cars. When Österreichische Automobil Gesellschaft went into receivership, the design was adopted by Daimler. In 1911, all contact with the German company was severed and the enterprise adopted the name Austro-Daimler.

During World War I, Austro-Daimler supplied cars, 1½- and 3-ton 4x2 trucks, and all-wheel-drive artillery tractors to the Austro-Hungarian Army. In 1928, the company merged with Puch-Werke and started to produce both cars and trucks using Puch designs, some of which were used in military service. First of these was the 2-ton 6x4 ADG – the initials stood for Austro-Daimler *Geländewagen* (command car) – based on a heavy car chassis dating from 1931. Less than 200 were supplied to the Austrian Army during 1935–36, built as trucks, ambulances, tankers, and command vehicles. The ADG was developed into the more numerous 2½-ton 6x4 ADGR of which 361 examples were built for the Romanian Army between 1936 and 1940. Both also saw service with the *Wehrmacht* during World War II.

The truck was unusual for the period in featuring independent rear suspension by means of swing axles and leaf springs. The engine was a 3,915cc six-cylinder unit driving through a seven-speed gearbox which included two reverse gears. Although the drive-line was a conventional 6x4, there were front rollers as well as free-running spare wheels mounted either side, to help prevent the chassis from grounding when driven cross-country. Standard variants included a cargo/personnel, ambulance, tanker and command car.

In 1934, Austro-Daimler-Puch merged with Steyr-Werke and the company became known as Steyr-Daimler-Puch. New products introduced after this date were generally badged "Steyr".

LEFT: **The twin spare wheels were mounted in such a way as to permit them to revolve freely, which helped to prevent the truck grounding. The two front rollers were an aid for crossing ditches.**

Austro-Daimler ADGR

Type: Truck, 2½-ton, cargo, 6x4
Manufacturer: Steyr-Daimler-Puch; Wien
Production: 1936 to 1940
Powerplant: Austro-Daimler M640; six cylinders in-line; petrol; water-cooled; 3,915cc; overhead valves; power output, 72bhp at 3,800rpm
Transmission: 7F2R; 6x4
Suspension: Live axle on semi-elliptical multi-leaf springs at front; independent suspension by swing axles on semi-elliptical multi-leaf springs at rear
Brakes: Mechanical at front; hydraulic at rear
Electrical system: 6V
Dimensions: Length – 6,500mm/256in
    Width – 2,135mm/84in
    Height – tilt in place, 2,230mm/88in
    Wheelbase – 3,720mm/146in
    Bogie centres – 1,200mm/47in
Weight: Unladen – 4,420kg/9,744lb
    Payload – 3,000kg/6,614lb
Performance: Maximum speed – 68kph/42mph

LEFT: **Manufactured by Steyr-Daimler-Puch from 1937 to 1941, the Steyr 640 was not dissimilar in appearance to the Austro-Daimler ADGR although it was actually a replacement for the Steyr Model 440. The front axle was suspended on semi-elliptical leaf springs, at the rear were swinging half-axles which helped to maintain ground contact; twin spare wheels were provided to help prevent bellying on rough ground.**

Steyr 640

Originally established in 1864 as an arms manufacturer, Österreichische Waffenfabriks Gesellschaft started producing trucks under the name Steyr in a former weapons factory in a town of the same name near Wien in 1922. Four years later, the company name was changed to Steyr-Werke. In 1934, Steyr merged with Austro-Daimler-Puch to form Steyr-Daimler-Puch. The company produced a range of light trucks including many which were intended for military use.

The 1¹/₂-ton 6x4 Model 640 was introduced in 1937 as a replacement for the earlier, and very similar, Model 440. It was powered by a 2,260cc Steyr six-cylinder engine, driving the rear wheels through a four-speed main gearbox and two-speed auxiliary

box. At the front, there was a live axle suspended on semi-elliptical leaf springs. At the rear, there were swinging half-axles, again using semi-elliptical leaf springs. Free-running spare wheels were fitted alongside the cab, to prevent grounding on rough terrain.

Standard variants included a cargo/ personnel carrier, an open four-door heavy command car, with a coach-built body and an all-steel four-stretcher ambulance (Kfz 31 *Krankenkraftwagen*).

The 640 remained in production until 1941, with most of the total of 3,780 being built during 1940–41. Almost all of the vehicles produced were supplied to the *Wehrmacht*, although the command car was also used by the Austrian Army.

Steyr 640

Type: Truck, cargo, 1¹/₂-ton, 6x4
Manufacturer: Steyr-Daimler-Puch; Wien
Production: 1937 to 1941
Powerplant: Steyr M640; six cylinders in-line; petrol; water-cooled; 2,260cc; overhead valves; power output, 55bhp at 3,800rpm
Transmission: 4F1Rx2; 6x4
Suspension: Live axle on semi-elliptical multi-leaf springs at front; swinging half-axles on semi-elliptical multi-leaf springs at rear
Brakes: Hydraulic
Electrical system: 12V
Dimensions: Length – 5,330mm/210in
  Width – 1,730mm/68in
  Height – tilt in place, 2,330mm/92in
  Wheelbase – 3,030mm/119in
  Bogie centres – 1,060mm/42in
Weight: Unladen – 2,400kg/5,291lb
  Payload – 1,500kg/3,307lb
Performance: Maximum speed – 70kph/44mph

ABOVE AND RIGHT: **Some 3,780 examples of the Steyr 640 were produced, with many supplied to the *Wehrmacht*. Most were bodied as standard cargo carriers.**

Steyr 270 1500A

Designed by Ferdinand Porsche, the Steyr 270 4x4 was in production between 1941 and 1944 for the *Wehrmacht*. The vehicle was co-produced by Steyr in Austria, who made 12,450 and by Auto-Union in Germany. The chassis was designated 1500A/01 and 1500/A2, and the most numerous of the three variants produced was an eight-seater utility-bodied personnel carrier (Kfz 70), which largely replaced the *Wehrmacht*'s

ABOVE: **Auto-Union and Steyr produced almost 12,500 examples of the 1500A heavy cross-country car chassis for the *Wehrmacht* between 1941 and 1945.**

earlier assortment of heavy cross-country cars. There was also a convertible staff/command car (Kfz 21) and a light cargo truck.

The engine was a 3,517cc V8 air-cooled unit, coupled to both axles via a four-speed gearbox and two-speed transfer box. A differential

lock was fitted in the rear axle. Suspension was independent with torsion bars at the front. At the rear there was a live axle suspended on semi-elliptical multi-leaf springs.

Steyr 270 1500A	
Type: Car, heavy, personnel, 4x4	
Manufacturer: Steyr-Daimler-Puch; Wien. Auto-Union; Siegmar	
Production: 1941 to 1944	
Powerplant: Steyr 1500A; eight cylinders in V configuration; petrol; air-cooled; 3,517cc; overhead valves; power output, 85bhp at 3,000rpm	
Transmission: 4F1Rx2; part-time 4x4	
Suspension: Independent at the front using wishbones and torsion bars; live axle at the rear on semi-elliptical multi-leaf springs	
Brakes: Hydraulic	
Electrical system: 12V	
Dimensions: Length – 5,080mm/200in Width – 2,030mm/80in Height – tilt in place, 2.320mm/91in; minimum, 2,032mm/80in Wheelbase – 3,250mm/139in	
Weight: Unladen – 2,485kg/5,478lb Payload – 1,675kg/3,693lb	
Performance: Maximum speed – 90kph/56mph	

Steyr-Puch 700AP Haflinger

Launched in 1959, the Steyr-Puch Haflinger was designed by Erich Ledwinka, son of the famous Tatra designer Hans Ledwinka. The vehicle incorporated the designer's trademark tubular backbone chassis on to which were attached the coil-sprung independent swing-arm axles. Despite being small, the Haflinger offered an extremely high level of off-road performance. The basic vehicle was little more than a flat platform to which was attached a front panel and windscreen. Both two- and four-door canvas hoods were available. A glass-fibre cab was also offered. Variants included rocket-launcher, communications vehicle and mount for a recoilless anti-tank gun. A longer wheelbase variant was introduced in 1962.

Power was provided by a rear-mounted 643cc horizontally opposed

two-cylinder air-cooled engine driving through a five-speed gearbox. Manual differential locks were fitted in both axles and final drive was through step-down spur gears in the hubs.

The Haflinger saw service with the armies of Austria, Indonesia, Italy, the Netherlands, Nigeria, South Africa, Sweden and Switzerland.

Steyr-Puch 700AP Haflinger	
Type: Truck, light, cargo, 4x4	
Manufacturer: Steyr-Daimler-Puch; Graz	
Production: 1959 to 1973	
Powerplant: Puch 700AP; horizontally opposed two cylinders; petrol; air-cooled; 643cc; overhead valves; power output, 24bhp (27bhp from 1967) at 4,800rpm	
Transmission: 4F1R (5F1R from 1966); part-time 4x4; differential locks in both axles	
Suspension: Independent suspension by swing arm half-axles with coil springs	
Brakes: Hydraulic	
Electrical system: 12V	
Dimensions: Length – 2,845mm/112in Width – 1,350mm/53in Height – 1,740mm/69in Wheelbase – 1,500mm/59in, 1,800mm/71in	
Weight: Unladen – 635kg/1,400lb Payload – 515kg/1,135lb	
Performance: Maximum speed – 75kph/47mph	

LEFT: **Despite its small size, the Ledwinka-designed Haflinger was an agile performer off the road.**

Steyr-Daimler-Puch Pinzgauer 710M, 712M

LEFT: This armoured variant of the 712M was originally intended for New Zealand, but has subsequently been trialled by a number of other nations.

During the UK trials in 1993, the company Automotive Technik was established, in Aldershot, Surrey, to provide trials support and to handle deliveries into the UK. However, when commercial production in Austria ceased in June 2000, Automotive Technik acquired the rights to the design and the production line was moved to the company's new premises in Guildford.

Alongside the basic cargo/personnel vehicles, the Pinzgauer has been produced for the command, cargo and shelter carrier, weapons carrier, special forces, radio, workshop, fire-tender and ambulance roles. Automotive Technik have also produced armoured and so-called "extreme mobility" variants with electronic traction control.

In 1965, Steyr-Daimler-Puch showed a prototype of the Model 710 Pinzgauer 4x4, intended to replace the Haflinger. This was soon followed by the 6x6 Model 712. By 1971 both models were in production. Both were initially offered with either a fully enclosed steel body or a military-type cargo body with a folding windscreen. The cargo area has removable top hoops, and bench seats fitted down both sides of the body for either eight men (Model 710) or 12 men (Model 712).

The vehicle is assembled around a torsion-resistant tubular backbone chassis on which are mounted independent swing axles with coil springs (rocking beam leaf springs at the rear of 6x6 variants). Early examples used a 2,460cc Steyr four-cylinder petrol engine but, from 1983, the petrol-engined versions were joined by 2,499cc six-cylinder turbocharged diesel engine. Subsequently, a Volkswagen five-cylinder turbocharged diesel engine has also been specified. The engine is coupled to a five-speed ZF gearbox and two-speed transfer box, with lockable differentials, front and rear. A four-speed ZF automatic gearbox is also available.

More than 20,000 Pinzgauer vehicles are in use by the armed forces of more than 15 countries including Austria, Ghana, Nigeria, Oman, Sudan, Switzerland, Tunisia, the former Yugoslavia and the UK. Also other nations in the Middle East and South America.

LEFT: Although the design is now more than 40 years old, the Pinzgauer remains in production and is in service with 15 countries. The combination of a tubular backbone chassis combined with swinging half axles gives the vehicle a formidable off-road performance, further enhanced by traction control.

Steyr-Daimler-Puch Pinzgauer 710M, 712M

Type: Truck, 1-ton, cargo/personnel, 4x4; or 1½-ton, cargo/personnel, 6x6

Manufacturer: Steyr-Daimler-Puch; Graz. Automotive Technik; Guildford

Production: 1965 to date

Powerplant: Steyr; four cylinders in-line; petrol; water-cooled; 2,460cc; overhead valves; power output, 92bhp at 4,000rpm. Five- and six-cylinder turbocharged 2,499cc diesel engines also offered.

Transmission: 5F1Rx2, or 4F1Rx2 automatic; part-time 4x4

Suspension: Independent suspension at all wheels using swing axles and coil springs; rocking beam at rear of 6x6 variants with semi-elliptical multi-leaf springs; dual-action hydraulic shock absorbers

Brakes: Hydraulic with vacuum servo-assistance; late models have ABS and electronic brake distribution

Electrical system: 24V

Dimensions: Length – (4x4 variants) 4,528mm/178in; (6x6 variants) 5,308mm/209in
Width – 1,800mm/71in
Height – tilt in place, 2,045mm/80in
Wheelbase – 2,400mm/95in
Bogie centres – (6x6 variants) 980mm/39in

Weight: Unladen – (4x4 variants) 2,450kg/5,401lb; (6x6 variants) 2,600kg/5,732lb

Performance: Maximum speed – 120kph/75mph

MZKT 74135 *Volat*

First seen in the early 1990s, the Minsk Wheel Tractor Plant (MZKT) *Volat* (Hero) 74135 is a massive 8x8 tractor designed for use with a 70-ton semi-trailer or a 60-ton drawbar trailer. MZKT's vehicle heritage includes such monsters as the MAZ-535, 537 and 547 which

were used as missile "Transporter-Erector-Launcher" (TEL) rigs by the army of the former Soviet Union.

Weighing more than 26 tons, the *Volat* is powered by a 21,600cc Deutz-MWM V12 turbocharged inter-cooled diesel engine producing 788bhp. Alternatively, a 21,930cc Daimler-Chrysler 780bhp engine may be specified. The transmission is a joint US-Belarus project, a fully automatic Allison six-speed hydro-mechanical gearbox coupled to a two-speed Minsk transfer box which incorporates a lockable inter-axle differential. Each of the axles includes automatic and manual differential locks. There is also an automatic "Central Tyre-Inflation System" (CTIS) that operates on both the tractor and the three-axle MWTP-99941 semi-trailer.

The spacious four-door seven-man cab incorporates a full-width bonnet and a reverse-raked, divided windscreen. A 25-ton German-manufactured ITAG winch is mounted on the chassis behind the cab.

RIGHT: **The huge bonnet conceals either a Deutz-MWM V12 turbocharged diesel engine producing 788bhp, or a 780bhp Daimler-Chrysler OM 444LA. Transmission is by a fully automatic Allison six-speed hydro-mechanical gearbox and a two-speed Minsk transfer box.**

ABOVE: **Produced by the Minsk Wheel Tractor Plant, the *Volat* 74135 is a massive 8x8 tractor which can be coupled to either a 70-ton semi-trailer or a 60-ton drawbar trailer and is rated for a gross train weight of more than 200 tons.**

There is also a crane for handling the spare wheels.

The standard MWTP-99941 semi-trailer is rated at 70 tons and has a load-bed length of 13.9m/45.5ft. Loading is carried out via hydraulic ramps which are raised and lowered by an auxiliary power unit carried on the trailer. The trailer is large enough to accept a main battle tank or two armoured personnel carriers or infantry fighting vehicles. Other Soviet and East European semi-trailers may also be used and the tractor has been demonstrated coupled to both a semi-trailer and a drawbar trailer, with a gross train weight in excess of 200 tons.

MZKT describe this monster vehicle in their dual-language sales literature as being a "heavy-duty autotrain – suitable for the transportation of heavy caterpillar rigs".

MZKT *Volat* 74135

Type: Truck, 60- to 70-ton, tractor, 8x8
Manufacturer: Minsk Wheel Tractor Plant (MZKT); Minsk
Production: 1998 to date
Powerplant: Deutz-MWM TBD-234; 12 cylinders in V configuration; turbocharged diesel; water-cooled; 21,600cc; overhead valves; power output, 788bhp at 2,000rpm. Daimler-Chrysler OM 444LA; 12 cylinders in V configuration; turbocharged diesel; water-cooled; 21,930cc; overhead valves; power output, 780bhp at 1,800rpm.
Transmission: 6F2Rx2, automatic; full-time 8x8 with central and axle differential locks
Suspension: Independent suspension, front and rear, using torsion bars
Brakes: Air-pressure
Electrical system: 24V
Dimensions: Length – 9,700mm/382in
 Width – 3,070mm/121in
 Height – 3,670mm/145in
 Wheelbase – 6,650mm.262in
 Bogie centres – 2,200mm/87in + 1,700mm/67in
Weight: Unladen – 26,000kg/57,319lb
 Gross train weight – 205,400kg/452,822lb
Performance: Maximum speed – 90kmph/55mph

LEFT: The FN 4RM/62C, manufactured between 1952 and 1954, was also co-produced by the Belgian companies Brossel Frères and Auto-Miesse. The standard variant was a steel-bodied canvas-covered cargo truck. There was also a quadruple anti-aircraft gun mount and a tipper. BELOW: The vehicle was powered by an FN 4,275cc six-cylinder unit with either overhead or side valves.

FN 4RM/62C

Based in the city of Herstal, near Liége, the Belgian armaments company FN (originally established as Fabrique Nationale des Armes de Guerre) started producing bicycles in 1895, progressed to trucks in 1900, with motorcycles following a year or so later. Trucks, artillery tractors and motorcycles

FN 4RM/62C

Type: Truck, cargo, 4$\frac{1}{2}$-ton, 4x4

Manufacturer: Fabrique Nationale Herstal; Herstal. Auto-Miesse; Brussels. Etablissements Brossel Frères Bovy et Pipe; Brussels

Production: 1952 to 1954

Powerplant: FN62C; six cylinders in-line; petrol; water-cooled; 4,275cc; side valves (overhead valves available as an option); power output, 92–134bhp at 2,400rpm

Transmission: 4F1Rx2; part-time 4x4

Suspension: Live axles on semi-elliptical multi-leaf springs

Brakes: Hydraulic

Electrical system: 12V

Dimensions: Length – 5,670mm/239in
Width – 2,300mm/90in
Height – tilt in place, 2,950mm/116in; minimum, 2,150mm/85in
Wheelbase – 2,870mm/113in

Weight: Unladen – 3,185kg/7,022lb
Payload – 4,500kg/9,921lb

Performance: Maximum speed – 73kph/45mph

were supplied to the Belgian Army during World War I and after the outbreak of World War II. The company resumed the production of military vehicles after 1945 and produced a number of excellent tactical truck designs that were used in large numbers by the Belgian Army.

The 4RM/62C was typical of these post-war types, many of which served in the British-occupied zones of Germany where the Belgian 1st Army Corps assisted the occupation. Designed and manufactured between 1952 and 1954, and also co-produced by Brossel Frères and Auto-Miesse, the 4RM/62C was a 4$\frac{1}{2}$-ton 4x4 truck powered by a

4,275cc six-cylinder petrol engine, with either side valves or overhead valves: the latter offered a near 50 per cent increase in power output. Power was transmitted to both axles via a four-speed gearbox and two-speed transfer box; the rear wheels were twinned. Suspension was by live axles on semi-elliptical multi-leaf springs.

Standard variants included a steel-bodied cargo/personnel carrier, quadruple anti-aircraft gun mount and a tipper. A winch was fitted under the chassis. The total number produced was between 3,700 and 4,050. The company remains involved in defence work, but truck manufacture ceased in 1970.

LEFT: **A superbly restored Minerva TT being displayed by its enthusiastic owner at a military vehicle show in Beltring, Kent.**

Minerva TT

The Belgian Minerva car company was established in 1899 by Sylvain de Jong, a Dutchman living in Antwerp. During World War I the company's large touring car chassis was used as the basis for a primitive armoured car. By the outbreak of World War II the company was producing commercial vehicles. Following a period when the works were used for aircraft repairs under German occupation, Minerva resumed commercial-vehicle production after the war.

At the end of the 1940s, the Belgian Army was seeking a replacement for the ageing US-supplied Jeeps. In 1951 they agreed to buy an initial 2,500 Land Rovers from a consortium established between Minerva and the British Rover Company.

Manufacture started on September 12, 1951. Rover supplied kits of parts

to Belgium which were made up of the complete rolling chassis together with the vital bulkhead. The bodies were built locally. Lighting equipment, fuel tanks and upholstery were also sourced from Belgian manufacturers, with Minerva claiming that there was 60 per cent national content. At first, the vehicles used the 2,032mm/80in chassis but, in 1954, production changed to the 2,184mm/86in chassis. Some sources suggest that the chassis of late production vehicles were built in Belgium.

The body differed from that produced in the UK by mainly being manufactured from steel. It was fitted with non-standard flat-fronted mudguards which were easier to produce. There was also a fixed panel at the rear in place of the usual Land Rover-style tailgate.

Alongside the standard vehicle, there was a 24V "Fitted For Radio" (FFR) variant with a screened electrical system, and a two-stretcher field ambulance. A special forces model was

LEFT: **Even as late as 1985, some 2,500 Minervas remained in service, and many were sold from war reserve stock with very low mileage showing.**

built with strengthened suspension, increased stowage and gun mounts. In 1980, 13 vehicles were converted to carry the MILAN anti-tank missile.

From October 1953, the type was also offered to civilians. Total military production was 5,921 vehicles, with a further 4,000 sold on the civilian market. Minerva went into liquidation in 1958.

Minerva TT

Type: Truck, ¼-ton, utility, 4x4
Manufacturer: Sté Nlle Minerva, Bruxelles
Production: 1951 to 1956
Powerplant: Rover; four cylinders in-line; 1,997cc; petrol; water-cooled; overhead inlet valves, side exhaust; power output, 52bhp at 4,000rpm
Transmission: 4F1Rx2; part-time 4x4
Suspension: Live axles on semi-elliptical multi-leaf springs; hydraulic double-acting shock absorbers
Brakes: Hydraulic
Electrical system: 12V, 24V
Dimensions: Length – 3,600mm/141in
  Width – 1,550mm/61in
  Height – tilt in place, 1,900mm/74in; minimum, 1,400mm/55in
  Wheelbase – 2,032mm/80in, 2,184mm/86in
Weight: Unladen – 1,227kg/2,705lb
  Payload – 600kg/1,323lb
Performance: Maximum speed – 89kph/55mph

Chevrolet C8, C8A

Dating from 1940, the 4x2 Chevrolet C8, and the very similar all-wheel drive C8A variant, was an 8cwt truck. It was designed to the same parameters as the equivalent British military types of the time, such as those produced by Humber, Morris-Commercial and Ford. Although not strictly forming a part of the Canadian Military Pattern (CMP) programme, the vehicle was fitted with the standard CMP-type Number 11 cab.

The vehicle had a right-hand drive open-topped cab, and the standard body was a small welded-steel well-type design intended for general service use. A "wireless" body was also fitted, which could be dismounted and supported on internal folding legs to provide either an office or radio station in the field. The wireless vehicle was generally fitted with a "Chorehorse" generator mounted between the cab and the body.

BELOW: **Ford of Canada also built versions of both vehicles, designated F8 and F8A.**

Chevrolet C8, C8A	

Type: Truck, 8cwt, cargo, 4x2
Manufacturer: GM Canada; Oshawa
Production: 1940 to 1941
Powerplant: Chevrolet; six cylinders in-line; petrol; water-cooled; 3,548cc; overhead valves; power output, 85bhp at 3,400rpm
Transmission: 4F1R; 4x2
Suspension: Live axles on semi-elliptical multi-leaf springs
Brakes: Hydraulic
Electrical system: 6V
Dimensions: Length – 4,216mm/166in
  Width – 2,108mm/83in
  Height – 2,286mm/90in
  Wheelbase – 2,565mm/101in
Weight: Unladen – 1,932kg/4,260lb
  Payload – 635kg/1,400lb
Performance: Maximum speed – 80kph/50mph

The vehicle was powered by a 3,548cc Chevrolet six-cylinder petrol engine driving the rear wheels through a four-speed gearbox. Suspension was by semi-elliptical multi-leaf springs.

Dodge T212-D8A

The Canadian-built Dodge T212-D8A could be regarded as something of an Anglo-American hybrid. Although fitted with right-hand drive, the chassis was similar to the US Army's ½-ton T207-engined series of 1941, albeit the Canadian variant used a smaller engine. The open-topped rear body was typical of British War Office style of the period. Standard variants included cargo, personnel and wireless bodies.

The engine was a 3,572cc six-cylinder side-valve unit, driving all four wheels through a four-speed gearbox and single-speed transfer box. The live axles were mounted on semi-elliptical leaf springs.

Although there is some controversy concerning the number of vehicles actually produced, the WD registration numbers indicate that the production total was 3,002.

BELOW: **The T212 was used extensively by Allied forces during the campaign in North Africa.**

Dodge T212–D8A	

Type: Truck, cargo, 8cwt, 4x4
Manufacturer: Chrysler Corporation of Canada, Dodge Division; Windsor, Ontario
Production: 1941
Powerplant: Dodge T212; six cylinders in-line; petrol; water-cooled; 3,572cc; side valves; power output, 89bhp at 3,000rpm
Transmission: 4F1R; part-time 4x4
Suspension: Live axles on semi-elliptical multi-leaf springs
Brakes: Hydraulic
Electrical system: 6V
Dimensions: Length – 4,369mm/172in
  Width – 1,930mm/76in
  Height – tilt in place, 2,108mm/83in; minimum, 1,880mm/74in
  Wheelbase – 2,946mm/116in
Weight: Unladen – 2,337kg/5,152lb
  Payload – 702kg/1,548lb
Performance: Maximum speed – 88kph/55mph

Chevrolet and Ford CMP series

During World War II, the Canadian motor industry manufactured what was probably the most successful standardized truck designs. Almost identical vehicles were produced in a range of capacities and drive configurations by Ford and GM-Chevrolet throughout the war. Described as Canadian Military Pattern (CMP) vehicles, the design, co-developed by the two companies from 1936, managed to combine British War Office specifications with US automotive manufacture.

The major difference was in the power unit. The Ford-produced vehicles were powered by that company's ubiquitous V8 side-valve petrol engine. The Chevrolet trucks used a General Motors (GM) straight-six engine, but in other respects the trucks were virtually identical, with standard cab and body designs. The smallest of the series was

the 8cwt chassis, designated C8 when produced by Chevrolet, and F8 for Ford. The "A" suffix indicated all-wheel drive. Next was the 3/4-ton C15/F15 and C15A/F15A. Both companies also produced a 1 1/2-ton 4x4 truck, designated C30 and F30. Also a 3-ton 4x2 designated CC60 or FF60. There was also a 4x4 variant of the 3-ton chassis, on either long or short wheelbase, designated C60S/F60S and C60L/F60L. These were specialized versions for gun tractor and portee applications. Ford also produced a 3-ton 6x4, designated F60H and Chevrolet produced a 3-ton 6x6 identified as C60X.

Standard types included a heavy utility, general-service cargo truck, dump, van, water and fuel tanker, signals and communications vehicles, artillery tractor, ambulance, stores, machinery workshop and office. There were also armoured variants.

In total, more than 390,000 Canadian Military Pattern trucks were produced between 1940 and 1945, of which the majority were of the 3-ton 4x4 configuration. CMP vehicles were used by all of the Allies.

ABOVE: **The majority of the CMP trucks produced were the 3-ton 4x4 type, with a total of around 209,000. This Ford F60L, with a Number 13 cab, dating from 1942–43, has been fitted with Gar Wood twin-boom recovery gear.** LEFT: **The 1 1/2-ton chassis was designated C30 or F30, according to manufacturer. This Chevrolet C30 truck has the earlier Number 11 cab and carries a British-built timber cargo body.**

Chevrolet C60S, Ford F60S CMP

Type: Truck, 3-ton, cargo, 4x4
Manufacturer: Ford Motor Company of Canada; Windsor, Ontario. General Motors Products of Canada; Oshawa, Ontario
Production: 1940 to 1945
Powerplant: Ford variants – Ford 239; eight cylinders in V configuration; petrol; water-cooled; 3,917cc; side valves; power output, 95bhp at 3,600rpm GM-Chevrolet variants – GM 216; six cylinders in-line; petrol; water-cooled; 3,548cc; overhead valves; power output, 85bhp at 3,400rpm.
Transmission: 4F1Rx2; part-time 4x4
Suspension: Live axles on semi-elliptical multi-leaf springs
Brakes: Hydraulic with vacuum servo-assistance
Electrical system: 6V
Dimensions: Length – 5,182mm/204in
  Width – 2,134mm/84in
  Height – tilt in place – 2,946mm/116in; minimum, 1,905mm/75in
  Wheelbase – 3,404mm/134in
Weight: Unladen – 3,558kg/7,845lb
  Payload – 2,994kg/6,600lb
Performance: Maximum speed – 80kph/50mph

Beijing Jeep BJ212

Beijing Automobile Works was established in 1940. The company produced its first motor car in 1958. Production of the BJ212 light utility vehicle started in 1965. Described variously as the Peking or Beijing Jeep and occasionally as the Shanghai Jeep or Overlander, the BJ212 was initially produced with minor detail differences at several locations in China, before production finally settled at the Beijing Jeep Corporation. Aside from the front of the vehicle it could easily be mistaken for the Soviet UAZ-469.

The BJ212 was a light four-wheel drive vehicle intended for both military and civilian use. It was fitted with a four-door body with seating for five. The vehicle was also available as a 600kg/1,323lb two-door truck with transverse seats for six in the rear, designated BJ212A. Both types had a removable canvas top and a folding windscreen. In military service, the BJ212A could also be equipped with a NORINCO 105mm recoilless anti-tank rifle. Other variants subsequently produced included the BJ212F, which was the same as the BJ212A but fitted with a hard-top. The BJ211 was a long-wheelbase 1-ton truck, also available with rear-wheel drive only as the BJ121.

The original engine, which remained available to the end of the production run, was a Chinese-produced 2,445cc four-cylinder petrol unit, driving both axles through a three-speed gearbox and two-speed transfer box. In 1986, the BJ-212E variant was trialled with a US-built AMC four-cylinder petrol engine and a new transmission. The vehicle was finally offered with a 2,520cc Perkins four-cylinder diesel engine.

Aside from its service with the Chinese People's Liberation Army, the vehicle was in service in Chad, Pakistan and elsewhere. Export sales were handled through the State-owned China National Machinery & Equipment Import & Export Corporation.

By the mid-1990s when the BJ212 was superseded by the much-improved BJ2020S and BJ202SA variants, some 460,000 examples had been built.

LEFT: **The truck version of the Beijing Jeep BJ212 was also exported under the name Shanghai and Peking. Aside from the design of the radiator grille, the BJ212 was very similar in appearance to the Soviet-built UAZ-469.**
BELOW: **In utility vehicle or field-car form, the BJ212 was fitted with an open-topped four-door body with seating for five. The vehicle was powered by a 2,445cc four-cylinder water-cooled petrol engine.**

Beijing Jeep BJ212

Type: Truck, light, 4x4
Manufacturer: Beijing Jeep Corporation; Beijing
Production: 1964 on
Powerplant: Beijing; four cylinders in-line; petrol; water-cooled; 2,445cc; overhead valves; power output, 75bhp at 4,000rpm. Perkins 4.154; four cylinders in-line; diesel; water-cooled; 2,520cc; overhead valves; power output, 67bhp at 3,600rpm
Transmission: 3F1Rx2; part-time 4x4
Suspension: Live axles on semi-elliptical multi-leaf springs; double-acting telescopic shock absorbers
Brakes: Hydraulic
Electrical system: 12V
Dimensions: Length – 3,860mm/152in
   Width – 1,750mm/69in
   Height – tilt in place, (BJ212) 1,870mm/74in; (BJ212A) 2,105mm/83in
   Wheelbase – 2,300mm/91in
Weight: Unladen – (BJ212) 1,530kg/3,373lb; (BJ212A) 1,520kg/3,351lb
   Payload – 600kg/1,323lb
Performance: Maximum speed – 98kph/61mph

LEFT: **A Chinese-built Jiefang CA30 truck photographed during a military parade in Phnom Penh, Cambodia, May 1983.**

Jiefang CA30

During the 1950s, the Soviet Union helped the Communist regime in China to establish a motor industry and, as part of this aid, established the Tse Fan "Number 1 Automobile Plant" at Ch'ang-Ch'un, at first building virtual copies of Soviet vehicles. The first product of the factory, introduced in 1956, was the Jiefang ("Liberation") – sometimes, Jay-Fong or Chieh'Fang – CA10, a licence-built

ABOVE: **The Jiefang CA30 "Liberation" truck was effectively a licenced copy of the Soviet ZiL-157K, identifiable by the flattened front mudguards.**

version of the Soviet ZiL/ZIS-151 truck. This was followed in 1958–59 by the Jiefang CA30, based on the more-powerful 2¹/₂-ton ZiL-157K. Although broadly similar, the Chinese truck can easily be identified by squared-off front mudguards, sometimes fitted with integral headlamps.

Like the ZiL the truck was powered by a 5,550cc six-cylinder side-valve petrol engine producing 95bhp, driving all wheels through a five-speed gearbox, with overdrive top gear and two-speed transfer box. The suspension was of the live-axle type on semi-elliptical leaf springs. Large-section cross-country tyres were fitted all round, twinned on the rear wheels.

Production continued for some 28 years, and the truck was widely used by the Chinese People's Liberation Army until well into the 1990s, as well as seeing service with other friendly

LEFT: **The standard variant was a cargo/personnel carrier. There was also a crew-cab variant, and a tractor for semi-trailers.**

nations, including Albania. Standard variants included cargo/personnel carrier, shop van, command post, communications vehicle, compressor, tanker, decontamination vehicle and rocket carrier. Some variants were fitted with a front-mounted winch. There was also a crew-cab variant, and a tractor for semi-trailers.

Jiefang CA30

Type: Truck, 2¹/₂-ton, cargo, 6x6
Manufacturer: Tse Fan "Number 1 Automobile Plant"; Ch'ang-Ch'un, Jilin
Production: 1958 to 1986
Powerplant: Jiefang 120; six cylinders in-line; petrol; water-cooled; 5,550cc; side valves; power output, 95bhp at 2,800rpm
Transmission: 5F1Rx2; part-time 6x6
Suspension: Live axles on semi-elliptical multi-leaf springs; double-acting hydraulic shock absorbers on front axle
Brakes: Air-pressure
Electrical system: 12V
Dimensions: Length – 6,684mm/263in
  Width – 2,320mm/91in
  Height – tilt in place, 2,740mm/108in; minimum, 2,320mm/91in
  Wheelbase – 4,225mm/166in
  Bogie centres – 1,120mm/44in
Weight: Unladen – 5,340kg/11,773lb
  Payload – road, 4,500kg/9,921lb; cross-country, 2,500kg/5,511lb
Performance: Maximum speed – 65kph/40mph

Tatra T128

Tatra was originally established as Nesseldorfer Wagenbau-Fabriks-Gesellschaft in 1899, in what was then Austria. The town of Nesseldorfer came under Czech control following the end of World War I. The company name was changed to Tatra in 1923. Two years later, Tatra introduced an innovative tubular backbone chassis fitted with independently sprung swinging half-axles. This subsequently become something of a company trademark.

Dating from 1951, the Tatra T128 was the Czech Army's standard load carrier for many years. Power is provided by a 9,883cc V8 air-cooled diesel engine driving both axles through a four-speed gearbox and two-speed

Tatra T128

Type: Truck, 3-ton, cargo/prime mover, 4x4
Manufacturer: Ringhoffer Tatra; Národni Podnik
Production: 1951 to 1954
Powerplant: Tatra T108; eight cylinders in V configuration; diesel; air-cooled; 9,883cc; overhead valves; power output, 125bhp at 2,800rpm
Transmission: 4F1Rx2; part-time 4x4
Suspension: Independent suspension, front and rear, using swing axles and quarter-elliptical multi-leaf springs
Brakes: Air-pressure
Electrical system: 24V
Dimensions: Length – 6,540mm/257in
    Width – 2,270mm/89in
    Height – tilt in place, 2,910mm/115in; minimum, 2,580mm/102in
    Wheelbase – 3,950mm/156in
Weight: Unladen – 6,020kg/13,272lb
    Payload – road, 5,500kg/12,125lb; cross-country, 3,000kg/6,600lb
Performance: Maximum speed – 60kph/37mph

transfer box. Independent suspension is provided all round, by means of quarter-elliptical leaf springs. As well as the standard cargo vehicle, there were tanker and shop van variants.

LEFT: **Over a four-year period some 4,000 Tatra T128 vehicles were built, including winch-equipped T128Ns.**

Tatra T805

Despite having been designed in 1953, the steel-cabbed 1¹/₂-ton Tatra T805 did not enter production until two years later, when it was intended to replace the earlier Praga A150 as the Czech Army's standard light truck. However, maintenance difficulties meant that its service career was short-lived.

In typical Tatra fashion, off-road performance was excellent even if the design was far from straightforward. The truck was assembled around a tubular backbone chassis, which enclosed the propeller shafts. Suspension was by torsion bars to all four axles. Power was by a 2,545cc Tatra 603A eight-cylinder air-cooled petrol engine linked to with a four-speed gearbox and two-speed transfer box. All four wheel hubs were fitted with reduction gears.

The T805 was produced in cargo, ambulance and mobile repair variants and saw service with the Czech Army.

Tatra T805

Type: Truck, 1¹/₂-ton, cargo, 4x4
Manufacturer: Ringhoffer Tatra; Národni Podnik
Production: 1955 to 1960
Powerplant: Tatra 603A; eight cylinders in V configuration; 2,545cc; petrol; air-cooled; overhead valves; power output, 75bhp at 4,200rpm
Transmission: 4F1Rx2; part-time 4x4
Suspension: Swing axles front and rear, with independent suspension using torsion bars
Brakes: Hydraulic
Electrical system: 12V
Dimensions: Length – 4,720mm/186in
    Width – 2,190mm/86in
    Height – tilt erected, 2,600mm/102in; minimum, 2,420mm/95in
    Wheelbase – 2,700mm/106in
Weight: Unladen – 2,750kg/6,063lb
    Payload – road, 2,250kg/4,960lb; cross-country, 1,500kg/3,307lb
Performance: Maximum speed – 78kph/48mph

LEFT: **Total production for the T805 was 7,214 vehicles built over a five-year period from 1955.**

Tatra T138

The Tatra 8-ton T138 6x6 military truck was put into production in 1961 as a replacement for the 10-ton T111, which dated from 1945. Although the rounded three-seat steel cab was somewhat "civilian" in appearance, the T138 was nevertheless an extremely versatile and reliable military vehicle. Many remained in service for two or more decades. The truck was powered by an 11,762cc Tatra V8 air-cooled diesel engine in combination with a remotely mounted

five-speed gearbox and two-speed transfer box. This combination provided excellent on-road performance. Off the road, the independent front suspension and lockable rear differentials ensured

BELOW: **The T138 was initially intended for the Czech Army, but was also exported to the Middle East, and to other friendly Soviet Bloc states, including East Germany (DDR). The truck was powered by a typical Tatra air-cooled V8 diesel engine and was produced in a wide range of variants.**

LEFT: **T137VT tractor for semi-trailers. Production continued from 1959 to 1978.**

that the Tatra would not become bogged down in difficult conditions. Most were fitted with a winch mounted under the chassis for self-recovery.

Standard variants included long- and short-wheelbase cargo trucks (designated T138VN and NT, respectively), hydraulic crane carrier (AJ6, AV8), dragline shovel (D013A), 12,000-litre/2,640 gallon tanker (C12 and C) and tipper (S1, S3). There were also 6x6 (T138NT) and 4x4 (T137VT) tractor versions for semi-trailers. Initial production went to the Czech Army, but there were subsequent exports to a number of Middle Eastern nations, as well as to other Soviet satellite states, including East Germany (DDR).

There were 4x2, 4x4, 6x4 and 6x6 versions for commercial use produced between 1961 and 1971. The civilian version could be identified by the absence of the roof hatch that was fitted to the military cab. A total of 48,222 examples of all models were produced. In 1972 the T138 was superseded by the upgraded T148.

Tatra T138

Type: Truck, 8-ton, cargo, 6x6
Manufacturer: Ringhoffer Tatra; Národni Podnik
Production: 1961 to 1972
Powerplant: Tatra T928-12; eight cylinders in V configuration; diesel; air-cooled; 11,762cc; overhead valves; power output, 180bhp at 2,000rpm; also available with a Tatra T928K supercharged diesel engine producing 220bhp
Transmission: 5F1Rx2; part-time 6x6
Suspension: Independent front suspension using swing axles and torsion bars; live axles at rear on semi-elliptical inverted multi-leaf springs
Brakes: Air-pressure
Electrical system: 24V
Dimensions: Length – 8,565mm/337in
Width – 2,450mm/97in
Height – tilt in place, 3,200mm/126in; minimum, 2,440mm/96in
Wheelbase – 4,260mm/168in (T138N); 3,690mm/145in (T138NT)
Bogie centres – 1,320mm/52in
Weight: Unladen – 8,740kg/19,268lb
Payload – road, 12,000kg/26,455lb; cross-country, 8,000kg/17,637lb
Performance: Maximum speed – 70kph/43mph

Tatra T813 *Kolos*

LEFT: The massive Tatra T813 *Kolos* was a cargo/prime mover originally intended for the Czech Army, but was also available on the commercial market. The backbone chassis, a feature of most Tatra designs, was fitted with independent suspension front and rear by means of swing half-axles and longitudinal semi-elliptical leaf springs.

Dating from 1967, the Tatra T813 *Kolos* (Colossus) was an enormous 8-ton 8x8 cargo/prime mover produced primarily for the Czech Army, but also offered on the commercial market. The first prototype, built in 1960, was a 4x4 developed from elements of the company's ubiquitous T138 truck. This was subsequently developed into a powerful and very capable heavy 8x8 forward-control design which offered excellent off-road performance.

Typical of Tatra trucks of the period, the engine was a 17,640cc T930-3E V12 air-cooled direct-injection multi-fuel unit. In effect it was a T928 engine with four cylinders added and was capable of running on diesel fuel, petrol and aviation jet fuel (kerosene). The engine was coupled to a five-speed gearbox and two-speed auxiliary gearbox. There was also a single-speed transfer box and two-speed planetary step-down gearbox mounted between the front and rear axles. A total of 20 forward gears and four reverse were available.

The chassis was of backbone design, with independent suspension at all wheels using swing half-axles and longitudinal semi-elliptical leaf springs. Differential locks were provided in all axles, planetary reduction gears at the hubs and lockable inter-axle differentials. Both front axles were used for steering. There were options for a rear power take-off and winch drive. "Central Tyre-Inflation System" (CTIS) was fitted. Two- and four-door cabs were available, the latter providing seating for seven. The cab was fitted with a circular roof hatch and, for certain applications, could also be armoured. A fuel-burning cab heater was fitted which could also be used to warm the engine.

Standard variants included a cargo/prime mover which could be used as an artillery tractor, crane carrier, 122mm multiple rocket launcher and fire-tender. There was also a 4x4 tractor for semi-trailers. A 6x6 civilian type with tandem front axles and a single rear axle was produced.

A total of 11,751 were completed over a 16-year production period. The vehicle was superseded by the T815 in 1982. Tatra was taken over by the US-based Terex Corporation in 2003, and subsequently sold to the Czech-owned Blue River group in 2006.

LEFT: The cargo/prime mover variant could be used as an artillery tractor. There were also crane carrier, multiple rocket launcher and fire tender versions, as well as a 4x4 tractor for semi-trailers. A 6x6 version was sold on the civilian market.

Tatra T813 *Kolos*

Type: Truck, cargo/prime mover, 8-ton, 8x8
Manufacturer: Ringhoffer Tatra; Národni Podnik
Production: 1967 to 1982
Powerplant: Tatra T930-3E; 12 cylinders in V configuration; diesel; air-cooled; 17,640cc; overhead valves; power output, 257bhp at 2,000rpm
Transmission: 5F1Rx2x2; full-time 8x8
Suspension: Independent suspension at all wheels using swing half-axles and semi-elliptical multi-leaf springs
Brakes: Air-pressure
Electrical system: 24V
Dimensions: Length – 8,800mm/346in
   Width – 2,500mm/98in
   Height – tilt in place, 3,180mm/125in; minimum, 2,780mm/109in
   Wheelbase – 5,400mm/213in
   Bogie centres – 1,650+1,450mm/65+57in
Weight: Unladen – 14,000kg/30,864lb
   Payload – 8,000kg/17,637lb
Performance: Maximum speed – 91kph/56mph

LEFT: **Launched in 1952, with production starting in 1953, the Praga V3S was sold to both military and civilian customers. The distinctive shortened bonnet was fitted because the vehicle had a semi-forward-control driving position. The 7,412cc six-cylinder air-cooled diesel engine was mounted behind the front axle.**

Praga V3S

In 1948, the motor industry in Czechoslovakia was nationalized, with truck production divided between Tatra, Škoda and Praga, the latter being responsible for the design and production of vehicles in the medium weight class.

The Praga V3S was launched in 1952 and was intended for both military and civilian use. The military variants were identified by being fitted with a roof hatch. Despite being odd in appearance, due to the shortened bonnet and semi-forward-control layout, it was a technically interesting and versatile truck rather in the mould of the US-built GMC CCKW of World War II.

Production started in 1953 at the company's Prague factory. During the period 1960 to 1964, this was gradually

transferred to the former Avia aircraft works at Letňany. The vehicle remained in production until the mid-1980s.

The engine was a 7,412cc six-cylinder direct-injection air-cooled diesel of typical Tatra design, producing 98bhp. Drive to all axles was through a four-speed gearbox and two-speed transfer box. In 1981, the engine was upgraded for more power. For maximum ground clearance, the axles were of the portal design, incorporating step-down final drive. Differential locks were fitted in both rear axles. Suspension was by semi-elliptical multi-leaf springs, inverted at the rear.

Aside from the standard wooden-bodied cargo vehicle, variants included a fuel tanker, shop van, rear three-way tipper, twin-boom recovery vehicle,

fire-tender and 130mm rocket launcher. A number of vehicles were fitted with a mechanical winch. The chassis was also used to produce an armoured personnel carrier and a 30mm anti-aircraft gun carriage.

The Praga V3S was widely used by Warsaw Pact nations and was supplied to a number of Middle Eastern nations.

RIGHT: **Standard variants included a wooden-bodied cargo vehicle, fuel tanker, shop van, rear and three-way tipper, twin-boom recovery vehicle, fire-tender and rocket launcher. This surplus tanker has been used as a commercial vehicle.**

Praga V3S

Type: Truck, 3-ton, cargo, 6x6

Manufacturer: Praga, Praha; and Avia Zavody, Letňany

Production: 1953 to mid-1980s

Powerplant: Tatra licence T912, T912-2; six cylinders in-line; direct-injection diesel; air-cooled; 7,412cc; overhead valves; power output, 98bhp (110bhp for T912-2) at 2,100rpm

Transmission: 4F1Rx2; part-time 6x6; differential locks in both rear axles

Suspension: Live portal axles on semi-elliptical multi-leaf springs, inverted at rear

Brakes: Air-pressure

Electrical system: Hybrid 12V/24V

Dimensions: Length – 7,150mm/281in
  Width – 2,320mm/93in
  Height – 2,920mm/115in
  Wheelbase – 3,580mm/141in
  Bogie centres – 1,120mm/44in

Weight: Unladen weight (with winch) 5,470kg/12,059lb
  Payload – road, 5,300kg/11,684lb; cross-country, 3,000kg/6,614lb

Performance: Maximum speed – 60kph/37mph

LEFT: **The distinctive steel wheels of the Škoda RSO-175 were intended to help provide traction in the mud and snow of the Eastern Front, but also had the effect of keeping the top speed down to around 15kph/10mph. Some 200 examples were constructed.**

Škoda RSO-175

In 1859, Emil Škoda established an engineering business in Prague and began truck production in 1924. Early products were based on the British Sentinel steam wagon but, following the acquisition of Laurin & Clement in 1925, the Škoda name began to appear on conventional trucks. The first diesel-powered vehicle was introduced in 1932.

Following the occupation of Czechoslovakia by the Germans in 1939, Škoda was forced to supply trucks to the German war effort. Notable among these was the RSO-175 (*Radschlepper Ost*), a heavy wheeled artillery tractor designed by Porsche for use on the Eastern Front where the roads became impassable either from mud or from being frozen solid. The first prototype was ready by October 1942, with several changes made during the trials period.

It was intended to replace the sophisticated half-tracks which had been produced by Germany since the mid-1930s, but which were proving unreliable under harsh combat conditions. By contrast, the RSO-175 was a straight-forward and somewhat utilitarian machine designed to be produced at minimum cost and in large numbers.

Aside from ungainly height, the main identifying feature was the use of large-diameter (1,500mm/59in) steel wheels with diagonal strakes, but not fitted with conventional rubber tyres. Although lacking a good top speed and satisfactory traction on frozen ground, it was a powerful machine almost in the style of the Austro-Daimler artillery tractor of World War I. The crew were accommodated in a closed, three-seat all-steel cab. A drop-side timber body was mounted at the rear with a removable canvas cover. A V-shaped blade plough could be attached to the truck for digging trenches.

The vehicle was powered by a 6,024cc Porsche four-cylinder engine, either diesel or petrol, driving both axles through a five-speed gearbox. A 565cc auxiliary engine (half of a VW "flat-four") was fitted to assist with engine starting in the extreme cold of the Russian Front. Suspension was by semi-elliptical springs. The use of steel wheels and no tyres made it sensible to reduce the vehicle's maximum speed to 15kmh/10mph.

Between 100 and 200 examples were manufactured between 1942 and 1943. Vehicle production was cancelled in favour of heavy half-tracks also built by Škoda and the lower-cost *Maultier* half-tracks which were based on standard wheeled trucks.

Although Škoda continued to produce trucks after the war, the company was nationalized in 1945 and the vehicles badged as LiAZ (Liberecke Automobile Zavody).

ABOVE: **Dating from 1943, the French-built Latil FTARH was also produced for use on the Eastern Front.**
RIGHT: **The rounded cab gave the truck a modern appearance that was belied by the huge wheels.**

Škoda RSO-175

Type: Tractor, heavy, 4x4
Manufacturer: Škoda-Werke; Plzen
Production: 1942 to 1943
Powerplant: Porsche; four cylinders in-line; 6,024cc; petrol or diesel; air-cooled; overhead valves; power output, 90bhp at 2,000rpm
Transmission: 5F1R; full-time 4x4; centre locking differential
Suspension: Live axles on semi-elliptical multi-leaf springs
Brakes: Mechanical
Electrical system: 12V
Dimensions: Length – 6,220m/245in
    Width – 2,300mm/91in
    Height – 3,065mm/121in
    Wheelbase – 3,000mm/118in
Weight: Unladen – 7,000kg/15,432lb
    Towed load – 5,000kg/11,023lb
Performance: Maximum speed – 15kph/10mph

Sisu KB-45, A-45

Introduced in 1964, the Sisu KB-45 was a 3-ton 4x4 military tactical truck fitted with a high-pressure hydraulic system which could be used to drive the wheels of a suitable two- or four-wheel trailer. This provided significant advantages in mobility and cross-country performance, and allowed an increase in payload to 12 tons.

A Leyland six-cylinder diesel engine was mounted behind the cab, and was accessed via the cargo bay. The power was transmitted through a five-speed gearbox, with overdrive top gear, and a two-speed transfer box, and both axles included differential locks and planetary reduction gears in the hubs. There was a 6½-ton under-chassis winch, and a blowlamp-operated heating system was provided to warm the cooling water and engine oil.

Alongside the standard drop-side cargo/personnel carrier, other variants included artillery tractor, ambulance, fire-tender, radar or communications shelter, command vehicle and workshop. The vehicle could also be supplied as a crew-cabbed tractor for semi-trailers.

Sisu KB-45, A-45

Type: Truck, cargo, 3-ton, 4x4
Manufacturer: OY Suomen Autoteollisuus; Karjaa
Production: 1964 to 1982
Powerplant: Leyland 0.600; six cylinders in-line; diesel; water-cooled; 6,540cc; overhead valves; power output, 135bhp at 2,400rpm
Transmission: 5F1Rx2; part-time 4x4; hydraulic auxiliary trailer drive
Suspension: Live axles on semi-elliptical multi-leaf springs
Brakes: Air-pressure assisted hydraulic
Electrical system: 24V
Dimensions: Length – 5,700mm/240in; Width – 2,300mm/90in; Height – tilt in place, 2,800mm/110in; minimum, 1,753mm/69in; Wheelbase – 3,400mm/134in
Weight: Unladen – 5,000kg/11,023lb; Payload – road, 3,600kg/7,936lb; cross-country, 2,500kg/5,511lb
Performance: Maximum speed – 90kph/56mph

LEFT: **The Sisu KB-45, A-45 was in production from 1964 until 1982 and a total of 500 were delivered.**

Sisu E11T HMTV

Sisu has been producing trucks since 1931. During World War II, the company merged with Vanaja to concentrate on producing military vehicles under the name Yhteissisu. The two companies were de-merged in 1948, but Sisu took over Vanaja in 1967.

The Sisu E11T 6x6 15-ton truck was introduced in May 1998, as the first in a series of off-road vehicles intended for both military and civilian use. Production began in September 1998 with the first 71 trucks delivered to the Finnish Army. The trucks have a Renault-designed tilt cab and were developed using as many components as possible from Sisu's commercial-vehicle range. Power is provided by either an 11,000cc Cummins M380E or M405E six-cylinder diesel engine, driving all axles through a choice of manual or automatic seven-speed gearbox, linked to a two-speed transfer box.

BELOW: **The Sisu E11T HMTV entered service with the Finnish Army in 1998 and remains in production.**

Sisu E11T HMTV

Type: Truck, 15-ton, cargo, 6x6
Manufacturer: Sisu Auto; Karjaa
Production: 1998 on
Powerplant: Cummins M380E or M405E; six cylinders in-line; diesel; water-cooled; 11,000cc; overhead valves; power output, 380–405bhp at 1,900rpm
Transmission: Manual or automatic; 7F1Rx2; full-time 6x6
Suspension: Live axles on parabolic semi-elliptical springs
Brakes: Air-pressure
Electrical system: 24V
Dimensions: Length – 8,636mm/340in; Width – 2,540mm/100in; Height – minimum, 3,150mm/124in; Wheelbase – 4,140mm/163in; Bogie centres – 1,397mm/55in
Weight: Unladen – 10,500kg/23,148lb; Payload – 15,000kg/33,069lb
Performance: Maximum speed – 90kph/56mph

LEFT: Although originally produced as a private venture, some VLRAs have been supplied to the French Army. This example was previously in service with the Irish Defence Force (IDF) which used the VLRA as a tractor for the 105mm light gun. The IDF also had workshop, radio command and recovery versions.

ACMAT VLRA

Although not particularly well known outside France, the Brittany-based company ACMAT (Ateliers de Construction Mécanique de l'Atlantique), has been producing military vehicles since 1958 when the first VLRA (*Véhicule Léger de Reconnaissance et d'Appui*) light reconnaissance and support vehicle was launched.

Superficially, the basic 4x4 vehicle has changed little since the first example was launched 50 years ago. The range has now been expanded to include 6x6 and 8x8 vehicles. The current product range includes 2$\frac{1}{2}$-, 5- and 7-ton trucks, in a range of some 40 variants, including

ambulance, crew bus, command car, tractor for semi-trailer, radio command vehicle, fuel and water tankers, dump truck and DROPS as well as recovery, personnel carrier, missile launcher and flat-bed shelter carrier. There are also armoured versions of both the 4x4 and 6x6 variants. The company boasts an 80 per cent commonality of parts across the product range, including items such as cabs, chassis components, engines and drive-trains.

Early examples used a Ford petrol engine, but this has now been superseded by a 4,390cc Perkins 6.354 diesel, driving all wheels through a four- or five-speed

gearbox (6x6 variants only), and two-speed transfer box which incorporates a lockable differential. The axles are suspended on semi-elliptical springs; these being inverted at the rear on the 6x6 and 8x8 variants, and rubber-mounted radius rods are used for axle location.

Almost in the style of the Dodge Power Wagon of the 1950s, the vehicle has an open cab with a folding windscreen; the cab on the 8x8 variant is a semi-forward control design. Enclosed cabs, with wind-up windows, are also available for all models.

The vehicle has appealed to mining and prospecting companies. The VLRA has been purchased by some armies of North Africa and Asia who could neither afford more expensive vehicles, nor had the maintainance ability. Some VLRAs have also been supplied to the French Army. The Irish Defence Force use the VLRA as a tractor for the 105mm light gun, also as a workshop vehicle, radio command vehicle and recovery vehicle. Since May 2006, ACMAT has been a wholly owned subsidiary of Renault Trucks.

LEFT: The VLRA was produced by the Brittany-based company ACMAT (Ateliers de Construction Mécanique de l'Atlantique), with early prototypes being tested during 1958–59. The basic concept of the vehicle, which was designed to appeal to mining and prospecting companies, as well as to armies which might lack the resources to maintain more sophisticated machinery, has changed little since the early days.

ACMAT VLRA

Type: Truck, 2$\frac{1}{2}$-ton, cargo, 4x4
Manufacturer: Ateliers de Construction Mécanique de l'Atlantique (ACMAT); Saint-Nazaire
Production: 1958 on
Powerplant: Perkins 6.354; six cylinders in-line; diesel; water-cooled; 4,390cc; overhead valves; power output, 120–138bhp at 2,800rpm
Transmission: 4F1Rx2; part-time 4x4
Suspension: Live axles on semi-elliptical multi-leaf springs; hydraulic double-acting shock absorbers
Brakes: Air-assisted hydraulic
Electrical system: 24V
Dimensions: Length – 5,995mm/236in
  Width – 2,070mm/81in
  Height – minimum, 1,826mm/72in
  Wheelbase – 3,600mm/142in; also, 3,300mm/130in, 4,200mm/165in, 4,300mm/169in
Weight: Unladen – 4,300kg/9,480lb
  Payload – 2,500kg/5,511lb
Performance: Maximum speed – 100kph/62mph

ABOVE: **The open cab, with a canvas top and folding screen, is uncompromisingly angular in appearance.** LEFT: **The Berliet GBC8KT equipped as a basic 4-ton cargo truck.**

Berliet GBC8KT

The Berliet GBC8KT was a French replacement for the classic World War II "Jimmy". Development began in the 1950s with the GBC8 Gazelle, a commercial 4x4 truck rated at 3¹/₂-ton. Described as a *porteur moyen à adhérence totale* (all-wheel drive medium load carrier), the Gazelle was adopted by the French Army from 1958. However, the Army was keen to develop the Berliet Gazelle into a more-capable off-road military vehicle and, in late 1959, a militarized prototype was produced which evolved into the purely military 6x6 GBC8KT.

Rated at 4 tons, the GBC8KT may have been derived from the Gazelle, but little of the original vehicle remained. The original curved cab of the civilian vehicle was replaced by a very angular open cab, a canvas top and folding screen. The front mudguards were also angular in shape. The upright radiator grille provided cooling via a series of horizontal slots.

The vehicle was powered by a 5,180cc five-cylinder multi-fuel

(polycarburant) diesel engine, driving through a ZF six-speed manual gearbox. Selectable all-wheel drive was provided by a Herwaythorn two-speed transfer box. Suspension was by conventional semi-elliptical springs, inverted at the rear. The rear bogie mounted on an oscillating pivot. The front axle was a Berliet-Herwaythorn unit, while those at the rear were both Berliet products.

The standard variant was a steel-bodied cargo vehicle, but there were also fuel tanker, light recovery, light recovery, tipper and air-compressor variants. Also the TBC8KT tractor for semi-trailers and recovery vehicle. Some cargo vehicles were fitted with a 5- to 7-ton capacity under-chassis winch.

The GBC8KT quickly became the standard vehicle in its class and a total of almost 18,000 were produced before production came to an end in 1976. Alongside examples supplied to the French Army, the GBC8KT was purchased by Algeria, Austria, China, Iraq and Morocco. The 4x4 variant was supplied to Portugal. The French Army,

in collaboration with Renault, has recently refurbished some 6,000 of these trucks, designating them as the Renault TRM GBC180.

Berliet GBC8KT

Type: Truck, 4-ton, cargo/personnel, 6x6
Manufacturer: Société Automobiles M Berliet; Lyon
Production: 1961 to 1976
Powerplant: Berliet MK-520 or MDU-35MK; five cylinders in-line; multi-fuel diesel; water-cooled; 5,180cc; overhead valves; power output, 125bhp at 2,100rpm
Transmission: 6F1R; part-time 6x6
Suspension: Live axles on semi-elliptical multi-leaf springs, inverted at rear; hydraulic double-acting shock absorbers
Brakes: Air-pressure
Electrical system: 12V, 24V
Dimensions: Length
(cargo vehicles) – 7,280mm/286in;
(long-wheelbase) 8,205mm/323in
Width – 2,400mm/94in
Height – tilt in place, 3,300mm/130in;
minimum, 2,700mm/106in
Wheelbase – 3,950mm/156in or 4,350mm/172in
Bogie centres – 1,280mm/50in
Weight: Unladen – 8,370kg/18,452lb
Payload – road, 5,000kg/11,023lb;
cross-country, 4,000kg/8,818lb
Performance: Maximum speed – 73kph/45mph

LEFT: **The Berliet TBU-15 was a fifth-wheel tractor for use as a 36-ton tank transporter. The transmission for the vehicle was developed by Rochet-Schneider.**

Berliet GBU-15, TBU-15

The Berliet GBU/TBU series was a development of the 6-ton Rochet-Schneider T6 truck from 1951, the company having been absorbed by Berliet in the early 1950s. The innovative transmission which Rochet-Schneider had developed for the T6 was retained, whereby one differential in the forward axle of the rear bogie was used to drive all four rear wheels, but an air-actuated braking system in the second axle was fitted to prevent relative rotation of the wheels on the two axles. In 1955, Berliet redesigned aspects of the truck, notably to accept a multi-fuel diesel engine, produced under licence from the German company MAN, and relaunched it as the T6-15.

Just 10 pilot models were produced before the truck went into series production in 1959 as a 6x6 NATO tactical truck. Three variants were produced. The GBU-15 was a truck/prime mover fitted with an 8-ton under-chassis winch. The vehicle was frequently used as a tractor for the 155mm howitzer. The TBU-15 was a fifth-wheel tractor for use as a 36-ton tank transporter; a 10-ton winch was fitted behind the cab. The TBU-15 CLD (*Camion Lourd de Dépannage*) was equipped as a heavy recovery vehicle, with an Austin-Western hydraulic crane. A 7-ton front winch and a 14-ton rear winch was also fitted.

All three variants used the same type of six-cylinder multi-fuel (polycarburant) engine, driving through a five-speed gearbox and two-speed transfer box. The suspension was by semi-elliptical springs front and rear. The TBU-15 could be specified with reinforced rear suspension which allowed use with a 46-ton trailer.

The GBU-15 CLD was also produced under licence by Alvis in the UK, under the name Alvis-Berliet. Total production was just two vehicles.

BELOW: **The GBU-15 was a 6-ton cargo/prime mover. There was also a heavy recovery variant (TBU-15 CLD) fitted with an Austin-Western crane.**

Berliet GBU-15, TBU-15

Type: Truck, 6-ton, heavy wrecker, 6x6
Manufacturer: Société Automobiles M Berliet; Lyon
Production: 1959 to 1968
Powerplant: MAN-licence Berliet MK640; six cylinders in-line; multi-fuel diesel; water-cooled; 14,750cc; overhead valves; power output, 2,00bhp at 1,800rpm
Transmission: 5F1Rx2; part-time 6x6
Suspension: Live axles on semi-elliptical multi-leaf springs
Brakes: Air-pressure
Electrical system: 24V
Dimensions: (TBU–15 CLD)
    Length – 8,880mm/349in
    Width – 2,500mm/98in
    Height – 3,000mm/118in
    Wheelbase – 4,200mm/165in
    Bogie centres – 1,450mm/57in
Weight: Unladen – 21,200kg/46,737lb
    Maximum load on crane – 10,000kg/22,046lb
Performance: Maximum speed – 68kph/42mph

LEFT: **Often described as the "FOM" (*Forces d'Outre Mer* – Forces Overseas), the Citroën Type 46 was designed to provide exceptional off-road performance, and was intended for the French Army. The standard variant was fitted with a steel drop-side cargo/personnel body with bench seating for 16 troops.**

a five-speed manual gearbox and two-speed transfer box. Unusually for Citroën, who tended to favour unconventional suspension arrangements, the axles were hung on normal semi-elliptical springs with hydraulic shock absorbers. The suspension was capable of extremes of articulation, particularly at the front.

The Type 46F/T differed from the Type 46F by being equipped with a front-mounted 5-ton winch. The standard variant was fitted with a steel drop-side cargo/personnel body, which had bench seats for 16 fully equipped men, and was occasionally fitted with a machine-gun ring mount. Other variants included a container vehicle, refrigerator van, fuel/water tanker, flat-bed truck, recovery and communications vehicles. A long-range "Sahara" version was also built with larger fuel tanks to extend the operating range.

As well as being used by the French Army, the vehicle was supplied to Cameroon, Chad, Ivory Coast, Mauritania, Senegal and Upper Volta. Production ended in 1967.

Citroën Type 46F, 46F/T

Never a company to shy away from innovation, the Citroën Type 46F air-portable cargo truck is typical of the company's approach to design. Originally described as the *Transocéanic*, the first prototype was completed in 1957 and was based on the company's 5-ton Type 55U truck which had been converted to all-wheel drive by Herwaythorn. When production started in 1964, there were both 3-ton and 5-ton variants, the latter identifiable by twinned rear wheels.

Frequently designated "FOM" (*Forces d'Outre Mer*), the truck was designed to provide exceptional off-road performance, and was intended for use by the French Overseas Forces.

Power was provided by a 5,180cc six-cylinder engine, with both petrol and diesel versions available, driving through

BELOW: **The "FOM" demonstrates the vehicle's extraordinary axle articulation. The bumper is designed to move with the front axle.**

Citroën Type 46F, 46FT

Type: Truck, 3- or 5-ton, cargo/personnel, 4x4
Manufacturer: Citroën; Paris
Production: 1964 to 1967
Powerplant: Citroën P38; six cylinders in-line; petrol or diesel; water-cooled; 5,180cc; overhead valves; power output, (petrol) 80–97bhp at 5,200rpm, (diesel) 85bhp at 2,600rpm
Transmission: 5F1Rx2; part-time 6x6
Suspension: Live axles on semi-elliptical multi-leaf springs; dual-action hydraulic shock absorbers
Brakes: Air-pressure assisted hydraulic
Electrical system: 24V
Dimensions: Length – 7,010mm/276in
    Width – 2,480mm/98in
    Height – tilt in place, 2,770mm/109in
    Wheelbase – 4,600mm/181in
Weight: Unladen – 6,340kg/13,977lb
    Payload – 3,000–5,000kg/6,614–11,023lb
Performance: Maximum speed – 100kph/62mph

Citroën Méhari

Citroën introduced the utilitarian 2CV in 1948 and the vehicle remained in production for more than 40 years. Originally described as the TPV (*Trés Petit Voiture*) the 2CV was the basis of a number of similar types,

all sharing the two-cylinder horizontally opposed engine and unique interlinked coil-spring swing-arm suspension. The most interesting of these was the Dyane-based Jeep-like Méhari dating from 1968, which was also produced as a special 24V military version for use in rear areas. There was also a four-wheel-drive version introduced in 1979, although these did not enter military service.

Sharing the chassis, 602cc engine, platform and transmission of the Dyane, the Méhari was fitted with a unique moulded body featuring inner and outer panels of ABS (Acrylonitrile Butadiene Styrene) plastic riveted to a tubular-steel

LEFT: **The Méhari was used in service by the French Army and the Irish Defence Force.**

space frame. The military version was produced as a two-seater with a load area at the rear, or as a four-seater.

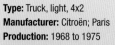

Citroën Méhari

Type: Truck, light, 4x2
Manufacturer: Citroën; Paris
Production: 1968 to 1975
Powerplant: Citroën AK-2; horizontally opposed two-cylinders; petrol; air-cooled; 602cc; overhead valves; power output, 26bhp at 5,500rpm
Transmission: 4F1R; 4x2
Suspension: Swing arms suspended on interlinked lateral coil springs, leading at front, trailing at rear; double-acting hydraulic shock absorbers
Brakes: Hydraulic
Electrical system: 24V
Dimensions: Length – 3,520mm/139in
  Width – 1,530mm/60in
  Height – tilt in place, 1,635mm/64in;
  minimum, 1,050mm/41in
  Wheelbase – 2,370mm/93in
Weight: Unladen – 585kg/1,290lb
  Payload – 405kg/893lb
Performance: Maximum speed – 100kph/62mph

Citroën–Kégresse P2

In 1910, the French engineer Adolphe Kégresse developed a traction system which allowed "travel at all speeds over deep snow and ice, or roads covered with lightly packed snow, or on dry or stony roads". Avoiding the standard crawler tractor approach, which used linked metal plates, Kégresse used an endless flexible-rubber belt track that offered a unique combination of performance, ride quality and reliability.

Returning to France from Russia after the Revolution, Kégresse made contact with André Citroën and sold him sole rights to the design. A Kégresse bogie was fitted to a Citroën B2 motor car to produce the Citroën-Kégresse P2. At military vehicle trials held at Satory (1923, 1924 and 1925) the P2 was the

BELOW: **The Citroën-Kégresse was also trialled by the British War Office.**

only vehicle in its class to be awarded a government subsidy. By 1927, the P2 had been replaced by the P7 with an improved positive drive system, and this led to the P107 of the late 1930s.

Citroën-Kégresse half-tracks were used by the French Army for a variety of roles up to 1940, including ambulance, field car, armoured car, tractor and anti-aircraft.

Citroën-Kégresse P2

Type: Car/tractor, 5-seat, half-track
Manufacturer: La Société Citroën-Kégresse-Hinstin; Paris
Production: 1921 to 1927
Powerplant: Citroën B2; four cylinders in-line; petrol; water-cooled; 1,452cc; side valves; power output, 20bhp at 2,000rpm
Transmission: 3F1R; drive to rear tracks
Suspension: Live axles on semi-elliptical multi-leaf springs
Brakes: Mechanical
Electrical system: 6V
Dimensions: Not available
Weight: Not available
Performance: Maximum speed – 40kph/25mph

Delahaye VLR-D

At the end of World War II, France received supplies of US-built Jeeps. Believing they could improve on the design, in 1947 the French Government began looking into developing a wholly French replacement. The Directorate of Armament Design and Manufacture prepared a specification for an advanced light 4x4 vehicle described as *"Voiture, Légère de Reconnaissance, 4x4, 4 hommes, 1 radio"*. Following an approach to the French motor industry, only Delahaye, who were in financial difficulties, appeared willing to consider the proposal.

Delahaye's original prototype for the project, the VLR Delta (VLR-D), was based on a dual-purpose utility/agricultural vehicle that the company had launched immediately after the war. The vehicle had four seats, simple, open bodywork and a fold-flat windscreen. The engine was at the front; selectable four-wheel drive was fitted. In 1949, an example was delivered to the French Army and put through the usual military trials.

A second series of prototypes followed, at least one of which had a Renault 85 engine, the others being powered by Delahaye's new 1,992cc Type 182 four-cylinder engine fitted with wet-liners, an aluminium crankcase and dry sump lubrication. The gearbox was a four-speed unit with overdrive top gear. A single lever was used for selecting four-wheel drive and the low-ratio gears. The differentials

RIGHT: **The Delahaye VLR-D was a French attempt at improving on the American Jeep. Although it incorporated advanced features such as self-levelling independent suspension, it proved to be unreliable in service, with particular problems in the transfer box and in the general handling.**

could be locked manually by means of a separate lever. The suspension was independent all-round, using adjustable torsion bars and leading/trailing arms, with a self-levelling system on the rear axle.

Further modifications were made as a result of the second round of trials and, finally, on August 1, 1950, the vehicle was standardized. During 1951 production began as the VLR-D Model 51.

Problems arose as soon as the vehicle entered service. The independent suspension created handling difficulties, which resulted in numerous accidents. There were also problems with the locking differentials, which could lock unexpectedly, leading to a loss of control on bends, or causing complete transmission failure.

The French Army had this feature disconnected during the last few years of the vehicle's life.

A slightly improved VLR-D Model 53 was launched in 1953, but by this time, the French Army had begun the search for an interim solution. In 1955, the Delahaye started to be replaced by Hotchkiss licence-built Jeeps.

Total production between 1951 and 1954 was 9,326 of the 24V Models 51 and 53, plus 20 examples of a 12V Air Ministry variant. The civilian variant was designated VLR-C12.

LEFT: **More than 9,000 examples were built between 1951 and 1953 and a civilian version was available. Mechanical and handling problems were never solved and, within a few years, the VLR-D had been superseded by the Hotchkiss M201 – a licence-built version of the Jeep.**

Delahaye VLR-D

Type: Truck, ¼-ton, utility, 4x4
Manufacturer: Société Automobiles Delahaye; Paris
Production: 1951 to 1954
Powerplant: Delahaye Type 182; four cylinders in-line; petrol; water-cooled; 1,992cc; overhead valves; power output, 63bhp at 3,800rpm
Transmission: 4F1Rx2; part-time 4x4
Suspension: Independent suspension on leading/trailing arms, using adjustable torsion bars; self-levelling system on rear axle; telescopic shock absorbers
Brakes: Hydraulic
Electrical system: 12V, 24V
Dimensions: Length – 3,454mm/136in
   Width – 1,626mm/64in
   Height – tilt in place, 1,854mm/73in; minimum, 1,422mm/56in
   Wheelbase – 2,150mm/85in
Weight: Unladen – 1,400kg/3,086lb
   Payload – 990–1,100kg/2,182–2,425lb
Performance: Maximum speed – 110kph/65mph

Hotchkiss M201

Like most of the liberated European nations, France received supplies of surplus US-built Jeeps at the end of World War II. As the vehicles started to deteriorate through age, the Ministry of Defence initiated a largely unsuccessful attempt at producing an all-French replacement in the form of the Delahaye VLR-D. In 1955, a decision was taken to seek a licence from Willys-Overland to build the Jeep in France. Later that year, the Paris-based Hotchkiss company started work on manufacturing 465 examples of the MB, effectively a copy of the Willys MB using French parts wherever possible. This meant that the large proportion of war-surplus parts held by the French Army for the original World War II Jeep could still be used on the French-built replacement.

In 1957, this was followed by the definitive Hotchkiss M201, a 24V version of the original Jeep in which every part was either retooled for manufacture in France or sourced from French manufacturers. Aside from an updated electrical system, this meant that there were no material design changes. The M201 was powered by the same 2,199cc Go-Devil four-cylinder engine as in the original, driving through a three-speed gearbox and two-speed transfer box to live axles which were suspended on semi-elliptical springs. The open bodywork was of the familiar Jeep design, although plastic-coated doors and side curtains were available to provide a full weatherproof enclosure.

Variants included a heavy-duty "Sahara" version, also the SS10, ENTAC and MILAN missile launchers. Another version mounted the US-built 106mm M40 recoilless anti-tank rifle.

Production continued until 1966, by which time 27,628 had been constructed. Hotchkiss also manufactured a civilian Jeep under various designations until 1969.

The M201 remained in service with the French Army and *Gendarmerie* (Police) until the late 1990s.

ABOVE: **The Hotchkiss M201 was a licence-built version of the World War II Jeep, differing only by the use of a 24V electrical system and screened ignition. Although the vehicle was French manufactured, virtually every part was interchangeable with the US original. A total of 27,628 were built.**
LEFT: **An M201 equipped with the M40 106mm recoilless anti-tank rifle. The split windscreen is similar to that on the similarly equipped US-built M38A1 Jeep.**

Hotchkiss M201

Type: Truck, ¼-ton, 4x4
Manufacturer: Hotchkiss-Brandt; Paris
Production: 1957 to 1966
Powerplant: Licence-built Willys Go-Devil Type 442; four cylinders in-line; petrol; water-cooled; 2,199cc; side valves; power output, 52bhp at 3,600rpm
Transmission: 3F1Rx2; part-time 4x4
Suspension: Live axles on multi-leaf semi-elliptical springs; telescopic shock absorbers
Brakes: Hydraulic
Electrical system: 24V
Dimensions: Length – 3,372mm/133in
    Width – 1,575mm/62in
    Height – tilt in place, 1,772mm/70in; minimum, 1,302mm/51in
    Wheelbase – 2,032mm/80in
Weight: Unladen – 1,160kg/2,557lb
    Payload – 400kg/882lb
Performance: Maximum speed – 105kph/65mph

Hotchkiss-Laffly S15T

LEFT: **Variants included a low-profile reconnaissance/prime mover (W15T). Also an ambulance (S15L), powered by a Peugeot engine.**

Laffly was founded in 1849 and started producing trucks at Billancourt in 1912. Although the company is probably best remembered for fire appliances, from the mid-1930s Laffly produced a range of six-wheeled military trucks fitted with an independently sprung rear bogie designed by the Hungarian engineer Hóllos Zsigsmond.

The lightest of these was the S15, for which development started in the mid-1930s, with the first examples entering service in 1936. The chassis was used for an artillery tractor (*auto caisson*), a recovery vehicle, and a personnel carrier, with production undertaken simultaneously by Laffly and Hotchkiss. Power came from a 2,312cc Hotchkiss four-cylinder petrol engine, connected to a four-speed gearbox and two-speed transfer box. There were also hub reduction gears. The front wheels were independently suspended using coil springs and double wishbones, while the rear suspension had swinging half-axles on semi-elliptical leaf springs.

The design featured an overhanging bonnet, with the front axle set back under the engine. Two small free-running wheels were fitted under the radiator to enable the crossing of ditches. Some 411 artillery tractors were in service in 1940 and were used to tow 75mm and 105mm field guns.

Hotchkiss-Laffly S15T

Type: Tractor, light, artillery, 6x6
Manufacturer: Etablissements Laffly; Billancourt. Etablissements Hotchkiss; St Denis
Production: 1936 to 1940
Powerplant: Hotchkiss 486; four cylinders in-line; petrol; water-cooled; 2,312cc; overhead valves; power output, 52bhp at 2,300rpm
Transmission: 4F1Rx2; part-time 6x6
Suspension: Live axle on semi-elliptical multi-leaf springs at front; independent suspension at rear using swing half-axles and semi-elliptical multi-leaf springs
Brakes: Mechanical
Electrical system: 12V
Dimensions: (artillery tractor variant)
Length – 5,550mm/219in
Width – 1,750mm/69in
Height – tilt in place, 2,550mm/100in
Wheelbase – 2,345mm/92in
Bogie centres – 1,000mm/39in
Weight: Unladen – 3,000kg/6,614lb
Payload – 1,500kg/3,307lb
Performance: Maximum speed – 50kph/31mph

Latil TAR

In 1904, Charles Blum established what became Automobiles Industrielles Latil in Suresnes, near Paris to produce powerful four-wheel drive forestry tractors. It was almost inevitable that military vehicles would follow and several thousand of the company's 4x4 heavy trucks and artillery tractors were supplied to the French Army during World War I.

Looking rather like a Renault or a Mack by the shape of the bonnet, the TAR series dated from 1914 and was used for towing the heavy French guns such as the 155mm GPF, the Schneider 220L and the Schneider 280. The tractor was powered by a 4,200cc four-cylinder petrol engine driving through a five-speed gearbox, with separate drive shafts to gear wheels at the hubs. Twinned solid tyres were fitted all round. The truck was equipped with both four-wheel drive and four-wheel steering, and a heavy winch was fitted at the rear.

By 1918, 2,000 Latil tractors were in use, with many remaining in French service throughout the 1920s and into the 1930s. Despite the introduction of the updated TARH in 1932, a few of the originals even survived the opening years of World War II, being captured and used by the *Wehrmacht*. The TAR was also employed by the US Expeditionary Force in France. The last Latil artillery tractor was the low-profile M7Z1 dating from 1938. Latil was taken over by Saviem in 1955 and the name disappeared.

LEFT: **Some TAR tractors were equipped with tracked bogies in place of wheels.**

Latil TAR

Type: Tractor, heavy, artillery, 4x4
Manufacturer: Charles Blum, and then Automobiles Industrielles Latil; Suresnes
Production: 1913 to 1922
Powerplant: Latil; four cylinders in-line; petrol; water-cooled; 4,200cc; side valves; power output, 32bhp at 1200rpm
Transmission: 5F1R; full-time 4x4
Suspension: None
Brakes: Mechanical
Electrical system: Magneto only
Dimensions: Length – 5,900mm/232in
Wheelbase – 3,000mm/118in
Other dimensions not available
Weight: Unladen – 5,800kg/12,787lb
Payload – 2,000kg/4,409lb
Maximum towed load – 3,750kg/8,267lb
Performance: Maximum speed – 10kph/6mph

LEFT: **Powered by a Citroën two-cylinder petrol engine, the LOHR was a lightweight, air-portable vehicle for airborne troops. Some 300 were completed in two variants.**

LOHR FL500, FL501

The LOHR FL500 and FL501 was designed by Victor Bouffort and developed by the French SOFRAMAG company, later to become LOHR. It was

BELOW: **The suspension used the horizontal coil springs and leading/trailing arms of the Citroën Dyane motor car.**

designed to provide a lightweight, air-portable vehicle for airborne troops. Some 300 were delivered to the French Army in 1978–79.

Lacking any conventional bodywork, the vehicle was built around a welded tubular-steel chassis with a simple aluminium chequer-plate flat floor. A roll

hoop was frequently fitted to provide some protection to the driver in the event of an accident.

The engine was a 602cc Citroën A series horizontal two-cylinder unit, mounted crossways in the centre beneath the floor. In the original FL500, the engine was a 29bhp unit, but in the upgraded FL501 the power output was increased to 36bhp, enabling a towing load of 800kg/1,760lb. Separate shaft-driven four-speed transmission units were provided for the front and rear wheels. The swing-arm axles and suspension units from the Citroën Dyane were used. Hydraulic disc brakes were fitted on all four wheels, with an independent hand brake provided for each rear wheel to improve manoeuvrability in tight spaces.

Both variants could be equipped with light machine-guns or to tow a 120mm Brandt mortar. The FL500 was also trialled as a mount for the MILAN anti-tank missile system. A two-stretcher field ambulance and communications variants have also been developed.

Alongside service with the French Army, the vehicle has also been supplied to Argentina, Spain and Tunisia.

LOHR FL500, FL501

Type: Truck, 1/2-ton, air-portable, 4x4
Manufacturer: LOHR; Strasbourg
Production: 1978 to 1979
Powerplant: Citroën AK-2; horizontally opposed two-cylinder; petrol; air-cooled; 602cc; overhead valves; power output, 29–36bhp at 5,500rpm
Transmission: 4F1R; full-time 4x4
Suspension: Swing arms suspended on interlinked lateral coil springs, leading at front, trailing at rear; double-acting hydraulic shock absorbers
Brakes: Hydraulic
Electrical system: 12V
Dimensions: Length – 2,410mm/95in
 Width – 1,500mm/59in
 Height – 1,370mm/54in
 Wheelbase – 1,770mm/61in
Weight: Unladen – 620kg/1,367lb
 Payload – 480kg/1,058lb
Performance: Maximum speed – 44kph/27mph

Renault ADR, AGR

The Renault brothers started building commercial vehicles in 1903, with their first heavy truck following in 1906. Large numbers of military vehicles were manufactured during World War I. Diesel engines were used from around 1930 and, by the mid-1930s, Renault was producing a range of trucks suitable for payloads up to 15 tons.

Falling neatly into the middle of this range, the 3¹/₂-ton ADR, and the shorter-wheelbase 2¹/₂-ton AGR, were bonneted 4x2 trucks for highway use. The ADR was generally fitted with a composite wood and steel cargo body, with a rear tailgate and canvas cover fitted. The AGR could be found with a radio van box-type body.

Both trucks were powered by a 4,025cc four-cylinder petrol engine with magneto ignition driving the rear wheels through a four-

LEFT: **The AGR fitted with a radio van body.**

speed manual gearbox as shared with other Renault trucks of the period.

Both types were in French Army service at the beginning of World War II.

Renault ADR, AGR

Type: Truck, 2¹/₂-ton, radio, 4x2; truck, 3¹/₂-ton, cargo, 4x2

Manufacturer: Renault Frères; Billancourt

Production: 1936 to 1939

Powerplant: Renault 489; four cylinders in-line; 4,025cc; petrol; overhead valves; water-cooled; power output, 65hp at 2,200rpm

Transmission: 4F1R; 4x2

Suspension: Live axles on semi-elliptical multi-leaf springs

Brakes: Mechanical with servo-assistance

Electrical system: 6V

Dimensions: (model ADR)
Length – 6,800mm/268in
Width – 2,250mm/88in
Height – minimum, 2,150mm/85in
Wheelbase – 4,180mm/165in

Weight: (model ADR) Unladen – 4,370kg/9,634lb
Payload – 3,500kg/7,716lb

Performance: Maximum speed – 60kph/37mph

Renault R2060/R2080

The Renault R2060/R2080 series was a development of the company's Model 206E1, a forward-control panel van dating from 1945. In 1947, it was replaced by the much-improved R2060 *Goélette* (Schooner) which the French Army used as an ambulance and general-purpose load carrier. In 1953, Renault introduced

the R2057 and R2064, both 4x4 variants, solely for the French Army. The R2057 had a van body, and the R2064 was produced as a wooden-bodied pick-up, and as a chassis-cab unit. These were replaced by the improved R2068 in 1953 and then by the military/civilian models, R2087 and R2087N in 1956. During its life, the vehicle was fitted with three different types of four-cylinder engine, coupled to a four-speed gearbox and two-speed transfer

box. The French Army used the vehicle in a variety of logistics roles.

Renault R2060/R2080

Type: Truck, ³/₄-ton, cargo, 4x4

Manufacturer: RNU Renault; Boulogne

Production: 1947 to 1965

Powerplant: Renault type 603 85; four cylinders in-line; petrol; water-cooled; 2,383cc; side valves; power output, 46bhp at 2,800rpm; Other engines include: Renault type 668, 1,996cc, overhead valves; Renault type 671, 2,141cc, overhead valves

Transmission: 4F1Rx2; part-time 4x4

Suspension: Live axles on semi-elliptical multi-leaf springs

Brakes: Hydraulic

Electrical system: 24V

Dimensions: (4x4 pick-up variants)
Length – 4,851mm/191in
Width – 1,981mm/78in
Height – tilt in place, 2,489mm/98in; minimum, 1,981mm/78in
Wheelbase – 2,311mm/91in

Weight: Unladen – 1,755kg/3,869lb
Payload – 750kg/1,653lb

Performance: Maximum speed – 83kph/52mph

BELOW: **Two well-restored R2060 ambulances on display at a military vehicle show.**

LEFT: **Powered by a 16,400cc Mack V8 turbocharged water-cooled diesel engine, the Renault TRM 700-100T was designed as the heavy equipment transporter for the French Army's Leclerc main battle tank.**

All three axles were equipped with double-reduction gears. Suspension was by semi-elliptical multi-leaf springs, inverted at the rear and located by torque reaction arms. An auxiliary equalizer spring was fitted at the front, together with hydraulic double-acting shock absorbers.

The truck was fitted with a tiltable four-door crew cab, broadly derived from that used on the TRM 10000 truck, but lengthened to provide seating for a driver and a crew of four. The fifth wheel was placed across the centreline of the rear bogie at a height of 1,640mm/65in. A pair of 15-ton hydraulic winches could be specified for installation behind the cab to assist with loading disabled tanks.

Following an extended period of evaluation, an initial 179 vehicles were ordered for the French Army in March 1994, with deliveries due to begin the following year. A second order was subsequently placed for a further 121 vehicles for delivery in the years 2000 to 2002.

Renault TRM 700-100T

The Renault TRM 700-100 tractor was first shown at the annual Satory defence equipment exhibition in 1987. It was designed to be used as the transporter for France's Leclerc main battle tank in conjunction with a Nicolas SFD A6 70-ton semi-trailer.

In 1987, Renault Véhicules Industriels (RVI) had also acquired a 40 per cent stake in the US company Mack Trucks.

This led to the TRM 700-100 being powered by a 16,400cc Mack E9 V8 diesel, driving through a hydraulic torque converter and six-speed automatic gearbox with electronic control. The transfer case, which provided permanent all-wheel drive in the ratio of 33 per cent to the front and 67 per cent to the rear, was integral with the gearbox. Cross-axle and inter-axle differential locks were also fitted.

ABOVE: **Two 15-ton capacity hydraulic winches are installed behind the crew cab to assist with the recovery and loading of immobilized or damaged tanks.**

Renault TRM 700-100T

Type: Truck-tractor, 70-ton, 6x6
Manufacturer: Renault Véhicules Industriels; Suresnes
Production: 1987 to 2001
Powerplant: Mack (RVI) E9; eight cylinders in V configuration; turbocharged diesel; water-cooled; 16,400cc; overhead valves; power output, 700bhp at 2,500rpm
Transmission: Automatic 6F1R; full-time 6x6; lockable centre and axle differentials
Suspension: Live axles on semi-elliptical multi-leaf springs with auxiliary equalizer spring and hydraulic double-acting shock absorbers at the front
Brakes: Air-pressure
Electrical system: 24V
Dimensions: Length – 8,045mm/317in
　　Width – 2,680mm/106in
　　Height – 3,283mm/129in
　　Wheelbase – 4,325mm/170in
　　Bogie centres – 1,350mm/54in
Weight: Unladen – 12,848kg/28,324lb
　　Gross train weight – 106,000kg/233,686lb
Performance: Maximum speed – 76kph/47mph

Simca F594WML

First produced in 1956, the Simca F594WML was derived from a militarized version of the French-built Ford F59WM truck. Dating from four years earlier, the F294WM had been fitted with a Marmon-Herrington front axle and transfer box in order to provide

four-wheel drive. Ford France was absorbed by Simca in 1954 and truck production was moved from Poissy to the Unic plant at Suresnes. The trucks were then known as Simca-Unic.

The F594WML was powered by a 3,923cc Simca-Ford V8 petrol engine, driving through a four-speed gearbox and two-speed Marmon-Herrington transfer box. The axle and suspension assemblies were thoroughly conventional, with live axles, front and rear, suspended on semi-elliptical springs. The standard body was a composite steel/wood cargo/personnel unit. Other variants included a container body, workshop, compressor, end tipper and fuel tanker. Some vehicles were fitted with a front-mounted winch. There was also a short-wheelbase variant, designated F594WMC.

Simca F594WML

Type: Truck, 3-ton, cargo, 4x4
Manufacturer: FFSA Division Camions Unic; Suresnes
Production: 1956 to 1961
Powerplant: Ford-Simca Type F6CWM; eight cylinders in V configuration; petrol; water-cooled; 3,923cc; side valves; power output, 100bhp at 3,800rpm
Transmission: 4F1Rx2; part-time 4x4
Suspension: Live portal axles on semi-elliptical multi-leaf springs; hydraulic double-acting telescopic shock absorbers
Brakes: Hydraulic with vacuum servo-assistance
Electrical system: 24V
Dimensions: Length – 6,806mm/268in
  Width – 2,286mm/90in
  Height – tilt in place, 3,200mm/126in; minimum, 2,550mm/100in
  Wheelbase – 3,655mm/144in
Weight: Unladen – 4,800kg/10,582lb
  Payload – road, 5,000kg/11,023lb; cross-country, 3,200kg/7,055lb
Performance: Maximum speed – 80kph/50mph

LEFT: **There was also a very similar 4x2 variant, designated F569WML. This example is in French Army service.**

SUMB MH600BS

The SUMB – Simca-Unic-Marmon-Bocquet – MH600BS was developed in France in the late 1950s to replace the ageing Dodge WC63. Designed by Arthur Bocquet of Marmon-Herrington, the design closely followed the specification of the German-built Unimog. Dating from 1957–58, the first prototypes were powered by a 4,184cc Ford-Simca V8 petrol engine but, in 1960, there were trials with a Panhard-built four-cylinder air-cooled engine.

In 1962, after extended trials and modification, the original Ford-Simca powered version was adopted as the French Army's standard 1¹/₂-ton tactical cargo truck. Off-road performance was enhanced by a manual differential lock in the rear axle.

Production started in 1962, with an initial order for 2,150 vehicles, but by the time production ended in 1965, a total of 9,000 examples had been built. Almost all were bodied as cargo/personnel trucks. Other variants included a vehicle-servicing truck, fire tender and light mobile digger. Some examples were

LEFT: **The MH600BS is a popular vehicle with military enthusiasts.**

SUMB MH600BS

Type: Truck, 1¹/₂-ton, cargo, 4x4
Manufacturer: FFSA Division Camions Simca-Unic; Suresnes
Production: 1962 to 1965
Powerplant: Ford-Simca Type F7CWM; eight cylinders in V configuration; petrol; water-cooled; 4,184cc; side valves; power output, 100bhp at 3,200rpm. Late production – fitted with 5,184cc six-cylinder Fiat 8060 diesel engine; in 1996, 564 examples were fitted with a 3,600cc Renault 720-SPC diesel
Transmission: 4F1Rx2; part-time 4x4
Suspension: Live portal axles on coil springs; hydraulic double-acting telescopic shock absorbers
Brakes: Air-pressure assisted hydraulic
Electrical system: 24V
Dimensions: Length – 5,195mm/205in
  Width – 2,305mm/91in
  Height – tilt in place, 2,880mm/113in; minimum, 2,770mm/109in
  Wheelbase – 2,900mm/114in
Weight: Unladen – 3,670kg/8,091lb
  Payload – 1,500kg/3,307lb
Performance: Maximum speed – 85kph/53mph

fitted with removable shelter bodies equipped for the communications role.

A 3-ton long-wheelbase variant was produced from 1974.

LEFT: **The three-cylinder two-stroke Auto-Union DKW MUNGA was one of the first generation of West German military vehicles, and was used by the** Bundeswehr **and the** Grenzschütz**, as well as by the Indonesian and Netherlands armies.**
RIGHT: **A MUNGA 4 leading a convoy of** Bundeswehr **M41 Bulldog tanks.**

Auto-Union DKW F91 MUNGA

In the mid-1950s, the Government of the newly formed West German Federal state was permitted to establish a defence force – the Bundeswehr. No money was available to buy foreign vehicles. Similarly, insufficient funds were available to pay the high maintenance costs of US war-surplus stock. The State authorities approached their automotive industry seeking a range of German designed logistics vehicles in the 1/2-ton, 1-ton, 3-ton, 6-ton and 10-ton weight classifications.

Goliath, Porsche and Auto-Union all provided prototypes in the 1/4-ton category. Porsche produced what they described as the Type 597, Goliath-Werk of Bremen developed the Model 31, and Auto-Union/DKW produced the F91/4, more usually described as the MUNGA (Mehrzweck Universal Geländewagen mit Allradantrieb). After a period of initial testing, contracts were placed with Porsche and Goliath for 50 vehicles each. Auto-Union/DKW received an order for 5,000. The success of Auto-Union was

apparently down to their ability to promise a very short lead time into production.

The MUNGA was an innovative and unusual vehicle with several features setting it apart from the military-vehicle mainstream of the period. For example, the 897cc engine was a three-cylinder two-stroke unit featuring triple coils and contact breaker sets. The engine was upgraded twice during the production of the vehicle. From 1957, the vehicle featured permanent all-wheel drive, with a four-speed gearbox and two-speed transfer box. The front and rear axle units were interchangeable. Independent front and rear suspension by means of transverse leaf springs was standard. The basic model was the four-seat F91/4, or MUNGA 4. There was also the F91/6 MUNGA 6, and F91/8 MUNGA 8. Standard variants included an ambulance,

BELOW: **The angular nose was all its own, but the inspiration for the MUNGA clearly came from the World War II Jeep.**

radio-command vehicle and a mount for the Cobra anti-tank missile. In the autumn of 1957, the vehicle was launched on the commercial market at the 38th International Motor Show, Frankfurt.

The MUNGA served in West Germany with the Bundeswehr and the Grenzschütz (Border Guard), as well as with the armies of Indonesian and the Netherlands.

Production began in 1955 and ended in December 1968. A total of 46,750 vehicles were delivered. Approximately 25,000 F91/4 and 3,000 F91/8s were supplied to the Bundeswehr.

Auto-Union DKW F91 MUNGA

Type: Field car, 4-seat/6-seat/8-seat, 1/4-ton, 4x4
Manufacturer: Auto-Union DKW; Ingolstadt
Production: 1955 to 1968
Powerplant: Auto-Union AU1000; three cylinders in-line; 897cc, 974cc, or 980cc; two stroke petrol; water-cooled; power output, 38bhp at 4,000rpm, 40bhp at 4,250rpm, or 44bhp at 4,250rpm, respectively
Transmission: 4F1Rx2; full-time or part-time 4x4 (1955–56 only)
Suspension: Independent suspension using transverse semi-elliptical multi-leaf springs
Brakes: Hydraulic
Electrical system: 24V
Dimensions: Length – 3,429–3,581mm/135–141in
   Width – 1,702–1,778mm/67–70in
   Height – tilt in place, 1,753–1,930mm/69–76in; minimum, 1,321mm/52in
   Wheelbase – 2,000mm/79in
Weight: Unladen – 1,200–1,810kg/2,645–3,990lb
   Payload – 365kg/805lb
Performance: Maximum speed – 93kph/58mph

Auto-Union Horch 108

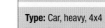

Introduced in 1937, the Auto-Union 108 was one of two chassis types used for the *Schwere Geländegängige Einheits Personenkraftwagen* (sglEPkw) – standardized heavy cross-country car. The other was the Ford EG. All *Typ* A chassis variants were fitted with four-wheel steering, while the *Typ* B had conventional front-wheel steering only. Standard body types included personnel

carrier *Kraftfahrzeug* (Kfz) 18, Kfz 70, command car, ambulance (Kfz 31), amplifier van (Kfz 24), gun mount (Kfz 81) and telephone vehicle (Kfz 23).

Early examples were fitted with a 3,500cc Horch V8 petrol engine, driving through a five-speed gearbox and single-speed transfer box to provide permanent all-wheel drive. Both axles had lockable differentials. The engine was subsequently replaced by a 3,823cc unit. Free-running twin spare wheels were fitted on each side to assist in ditch and trench crossing. Suspension was

LEFT: **A Horch 108; note the spare wheel mounting in the body side.**

by independent coil springs. In 1940, the Horch 108 was replaced by the very similar Horch 40, fitted with a wider body but without the side-mounted spare wheels.

Auto-Union Horch 108

Type: Car, heavy, 4x4
Manufacturer: Auto-Union Horch-Werke; Zwickau
Production: 1937 to 1940
Powerplant: Horch 108; eight cylinders in V configuration; petrol; water-cooled; 3,500cc, 3,823cc; side valves; power output, 80–81bhp at 3,600rpm
Transmission: 5F1R; full-time 4x4; lockable differentials
Suspension: Independent suspension by wishbones and coil springs
Brakes: Hydraulic
Electrical system: 12V
Dimensions: Length – 4,850mm/191in
Width – 2,000mm/79in
Height – tilt in place, 2,040mm/80in
Wheelbase – 3,000mm/118in
Weight: Unladen – 2,300kg/5,070lb
Payload – 2,000kg/4,409lb
Performance: Maximum speed – 80kph/50mph

Borgward B3000

Having already been producing motorcar components, Carl F. Borgward took over Goliath, manufacturers of commercial vehicles under the name Hansa-Lloyd, in 1927. Two years later, Borgward-Goliath took over the car manufacturing side of Hansa and in 1937, renamed the companies Carl F. Borgward Automobil & Motoren-Werke. During the 1930s, Borgward co-produced the *Einheits* 2¹/₂-ton,

standardized 6x6 truck (leglELkw) for the *Wehrmacht*. Between 1939 and 1944 some 30,000 military trucks under the designation B3000 were built.

There were four chassis variants – the 4x2 B3000S/O and B3000S/D were powered by either a 3,745cc petrol or 4,962cc diesel engine, respectively. The equivalent 4x4 chassis were designated B3000A/O and B3000A/D. The engine was attached to a five-speed gearbox and two-speed transfer box. Suspension was by semi-elliptical multi-leaf springs.

In late 1944 the Borgward factory was virtually destroyed by Allied bombing.

LEFT: **A B3000 on the Russian Front in 1942.**

Borgward B3000

Type: Truck, cargo, 3-ton, 4x2, 4x4
Manufacturer: Carl F. Borgward Automobil & Motoren-Werke; Hemelingeny
Production: 1939 to 1944
Powerplant: Borgward D6M5; six cylinders in-line; diesel; water-cooled; 4,962cc; overhead valves; power output, 75bhp at 2,000rpm.
Borgward B3000; six cylinders in-line; petrol; water-cooled; 3,745cc; overhead valves; power output, 78bhp at 3,000rpm
Transmission: 5F1Rx2; part-time 4x4
Suspension: Live axles on semi-elliptical multi-leaf springs
Brakes: Hydraulic
Electrical system: 12V (petrol engine), 24V (diesel engine)
Dimensions: Length – 6,450mm/254in
Width – 2,300mm/91in
Height – tilt in place, 2,930mm/115in; minimum, 2,220mm/87in
Wheelbase – 3,700mm/146in
Weight: Unladen – 6,190–6,646kg/13,618–14,572lb
Payload – 3,125kg/6,889lb
Performance: Maximum speed – 80kph/50mph

Faun SLT50-2 *Elefant*

In the late 1960s, West Germany and the USA embarked on a joint development project for a new main battle tank to be known as MBT-70. At the same time, a joint project was also initiated for the development of a heavy equipment transporter, designated HET-70 or SLT-70. The German partner in the project was Faun-Werke, while work in the USA was entrusted to the Chrysler Corporation. Both projects were eventually cancelled but, in Germany, Faun continued to develop the HET-70 for the *Bundeswehr* and the result was the LH70/420-8 tractor, described by them as the SLT50-2, but often known as *Elefant* (Elephant).

Low and wide, with a huge flat windscreen, the SLT50-2 was a low-profile eight-wheeled tractor powered by a 29,920cc Mercedes-Benz MTU V8 turbocharged diesel engine mounted immediately behind the cab. The transmission was by a four-speed automatic gearbox, having two reverse gears, linked to a two-speed transfer box with a lockable differential. Additionally there were lockable differentials in all four axles. Two 17-ton capacity Rotzler hydraulic winches were installed between the engine compartment and the fifth-wheel coupling; the winches were subsequently upgraded to 18.6-ton capacity. The

ABOVE LEFT AND LEFT: **The Faun SLT50-2 was originally designed as a joint project with the Chrysler Corporation in the USA. Although the project was cancelled, Faun carried on the development of their vehicle resulting in the *Elefant*.**

ABOVE: **Produced for just four years (1976–79), the Faun *Elefant* was intended as the tractor for towing a Leopard, the main battle tank of the *Bundeswehr*. The four-axle trailer was produced by Krupps.**

vehicle went into production in 1976, with 324 produced over a three-year period. A major upgrade programme was initiated in 1984.

A compatible four-axle 52-ton steered semi-trailer was developed by Krupp. The trailers were manufactured under licence by Kassbohrer. A V12-engined "austerity" 8x6 version of the tractor, designated FS42.75/42, was launched in 1981.

Faun SLT50-2 *Elefant*

Type: Heavy equipment transporter, 8x8
Manufacturer: Faun-Werke Karl Schmidt; Lauf
Production: 1976 to 1979
Powerplant: Mercedes-Benz MTU MB837Ea-500; eight cylinders in V configuration; turbocharged diesel; water-cooled; 29,920cc; overhead valves; power output, 730bhp at 2,100rpm
Transmission: Automatic 4F2Rx2; cross-axle differential locks
Suspension: Live axles on semi-elliptical multi-leaf springs with equalizing beams
Brakes: Air-pressure
Electrical system: 24V
Dimensions: (tractor only)
　　Length – 8,830mm/348in
　　Width – 3,070mm/121in
　　Height – 3,000mm/118in
　　Wheelbase – 5,700mm/224in
　　Bogie centres – 1,500+2,700+1,500mm/ 59+106+59in
Weight: Unladen – 22,800kg/50,265lb
　　Gross train weight – 92,000kg/202,822lb
Performance: Maximum speed – 70kph/44mph

Ford G198TS, G398TS

Ford-Werke was founded in Berlin in 1925 to import US-built Ford vehicles. Demand for the vehicles was such that a new assembly plant was built the following year, and within five years, this had been replaced by a new factory in Köln (Cologne), manufacturing cars and trucks for the German market.

When the US-based Ford company introduced a new 3-ton 4x2 truck in 1940, Ford Köln produced the same a

year later. The German truck, designated G198TS, was powered by a 3,923cc V8 petrol engine, driving the rear wheels through a five-speed gearbox. In 1943, the G198TS was superseded by the G398TS, with a deeper radiator and cooling slots in the front. From October that year, shortages of steel saw the standard steel replaced by the utility *Wehrmacht Einheits* cab of compressed cardboard and timber. At the same time, the front mudguards were simplified in shape.

The *Wehrmacht* described the truck as the V3000S. Between 1941 and 1945, some 25,000

LEFT: **A Ford truck with Einheits cab and gas generator equipment.**

were built, 14,000 as the half-track *Maultier* (Mule). During the latter stages of the war, shortages of fuel often led to the use of a wood-gas generator. This system burned air-dried wood or anthracite to produce carbon monoxide gas that was used in place of petrol.

Ford G198TS, G398TS	

Type: Truck, 3-ton, cargo, 4x2
Manufacturer: Ford-Werke; Köln
Production: 1941 to 1945
Powerplant: Ford; eight cylinders in V configuration; petrol; water-cooled; 3,923cc; side valves; power output, 95bhp at 3,500rpm
Transmission: 5F1R; 4x2
Suspension: Live axles on semi-elliptical multi-leaf springs
Brakes: Hydraulic
Electrical system: 12V
Dimensions: Length – 6,390mm/252in
    Width – 2,250mm/89in
    Height – 2,180mm/86in
    Wheelbase – 4,013mm/158in
Weight: Unladen – 2,540kg/5,600lb
    Payload – 3,300kg/7,275lb
Performance: Maximum speed – 85kph/53mph

Ford G398SAM

Dating from 1956, the Ford G398SAM was designed for the German *Bundeswehr* to comply with NATO specifications for medium-weight multi-terrain trucks. It had been developed from a post-war 3-ton 4x4 chassis that Ford had produced for the British and US occupying forces. Like these, and the wartime G198TS/G398TS, the truck was powered by the reliable 3,923cc Ford V8 side-valve engine, driving all four wheels

through a four-speed gearbox and two-speed transfer box.

Frequently nicknamed "Sam" for obvious reasons, it was a curiously angular truck, produced with both open and closed steel cabs. Most were fitted with a steel cargo/personnel body. Other variants included vehicles bodied for the office (*Kofferbau*), field kitchen, ambulance, radar, tipper, workshop, and communications roles.

A chassis variant (G398SAM-S3) was also available for special bodywork. Some examples were

LEFT: **A small number of the Ford G398SAM were supplied to the armies of Greece, Turkey and Israel.**

fitted with a winch. The truck remained in production from 1956 to 1961.

Ford G398SAM	

Type: Truck, 3- to 4-ton, cargo, 4x4
Manufacturer: Ford-Werke; Köln
Production: 1956 to 1961
Powerplant: Ford G29T; eight cylinders in V configuration; petrol; water-cooled; 3,923cc; side valves; power output, 92bhp at 3,500rpm
Transmission: 4F1Rx2; part-time 4x4
Suspension: Live axles on semi-elliptical multi-leaf springs
Brakes: Hydraulic with air servo-assistance
Electrical system: 24V
Dimensions: Length – 7,250mm/285in
    Width – 2,250mm/89in
    Height – tilt in place, 3,180mm/125in; minimum, 2,130mm/84in
    Wheelbase – 4,013mm/158in
Weight: Unladen – 3,970kg/8,752lb; with winch, 4,270kg/9,414lb
    Payload – road, 5,000kg/11,023lb; cross-country, 3,500kg/7,716lb
Performance: Maximum speed – 80kph/50mph

Henschel *Einheitsdiesel*

In 1934, the Nazi party proposed that the German motor industry should be financially supported by the Army to ensure that military interests were adequately represented in the design of motor vehicles. Two years later, the Government announced the implementation of an economic Four Year Plan, under Hermann Göring, designed both to promote the development of key heavy industries, and to encourage increased domestic production of strategic materials such as steel, rubber and petroleum. The Germans believed that an increase in the production of motor vehicles would boost the domestic economy and, at the same time, provide a valuable source of foreign exchange income through export sales. If the vehicles were also suitable for use by the military, then this would be a bonus.

By the middle of the decade there were 36 motor manufacturers in Germany producing military vehicles, or vehicles which could be used by the military should the need arise. This led to a multiplicity of types being available to the

Reichswehr, which obviously presented technical problems. In 1936, in an attempt to rationalize the situation, plans were drawn up for a series of standardized vehicle chassis (*Einheitsfahrgestell*) which were to be developed in conjunction with the *Heereswaffenamt* (Ordnance Department). The plan covered light, medium and heavy cars/personnel carriers, as well as the light, medium and heavy trucks. All of these vehicles were to be provided with all-wheel drive, featuring two, three or four independently sprung and driven axles, according to weight classification.

Curiously, the specifications only laid down broad parameters and did not include any detailed aspects of design. Participating manufacturers were free to interpret the requirements in their own way, and to fit their own engines. As a result, there was little real benefit, and the only truly standardized military truck produced as a result of this programme was a 2$\frac{1}{2}$-ton 6x6 cross-country load carrier, production of which started in 1937.

ABOVE: **Pre-dating the *Einheitsdiesel* by two years, Henschel and Magirus also produced a similar-looking medium 6x4 truck (1934 to 1943), designated 33G1. The two vehicles are not easy to differentiate.**
RIGHT: **The side access door to the rear of the body suggests that this is an engineers' vehicle.**

Described as the *Leicht Geländegängig Einheits Lastkraftwagen* (light cross-country standardized truck), the vehicle was effectively a product of Henschel, who developed the chassis, and the *Heereswaffenamt*. It was eventually produced by seven manufacturers including Borgward, Büssing-NAG, Daimler-Benz, Faun, Henschel, Magirus (Klöckner-Humboldt-Deutz after 1937), and MAN. VOMAG may also have been involved.

The chassis featured independent front and rear suspension by means of swing arms and coil springs as well as permanent six-wheel drive. Power was provided by a 6,234cc six-cylinder diesel engine, based on a design produced by MAN in collaboration with Henschel, driving the wheels through a four-speed gearbox and a two-speed transfer box. Three self-locking differentials were fitted which, in combination with the independent suspension, gave excellent off-road performance.

Most chassis were fitted with an open cab and a steel or timber drop-side cargo body. Different types of standardized body were also available for specific roles including signals,

recovery, field kitchen, snow-blower and others. Until 1943, these body types were indicated by a Kfz (*Kraftfahrzeug*) number. The permitted gross weight of the vehicle was 7,500kg (15,500lb) with an open cargo body and 7,420kg (16,324lb) with a closed body. Production of what was often referred to as the *Einheitsdiesel* continued until 1940. The total number of vehicles produced was around 10,250, with the majority (3,200) built by Büssing-NAG.

Medium (*mittler*) and heavy (*schwere*) standardized vehicles were also planned along similar lines but never made it into production.

ABOVE: **Although it was designed and built by Henschel, the *Einheitsdiesel* was also produced by Borgward, Büssing-NAG, Daimler-Benz, FAUN, Magirus, and MAN.**

LEFT: **The vehicle was large with what was a relatively small payload. It was also bodied for the signals, recovery, field kitchen and as a fire tender. The all-wheel drive and independent suspension on all wheels was standard equipment.**

Henschel *Einheitsdiesel*

Type: Truck, cargo, light, 6x6
Manufacturer: Borgward (Hansa-Lloyd & Goliath Werke); Bremen. Büssing-NAG; Braunschweig. Daimler-Benz; Stuttgart. Faun; Nürnberg. Henschel & Sohn; Kassel. Klockner-Humboldt-Deutz (Magirus); Ulm. Maschinenfabrik Augsburg-Nürnberg (MAN); Augsburg.
Production: 1937 to 1940
Powerplant: HWa526D; six cylinders in-line; 6,234cc; diesel; water-cooled; overhead valves; power output, 85bhp at 2,400rpm
Transmission: 4F1Rx2; full-time 6x6
Suspension: Independent at all six wheels using swing axles and coil springs
Brakes: Air-pressure
Electrical system: Hybrid 12V/24V
Dimensions: Length – 5,850mm/230in
Width – 2,200mm/87in
Height – tilt in place, 2,400mm/94in
Wheelbase – 3,650mm/144in
Bogie centres – 1,100mm/43in
Weight: Unladen – 5,000kg/11,023lb
Payload – 2,500kg/5,511lb
Performance: Maximum speed – 70kph/44mph

Krauss-Maffei KM-m-10, 11

Type: Tractor, medium, 8-ton, half-track

Manufacturer: Carl F. Borgward; Bremen. Krauss-Maffei; München

Production: 1936 to 1944

Powerplant: Maybach HL57 TU; six cylinders in-line; petrol; water-cooled; 5,698cc; overhead valves; power output, 135bhp at 2,600rpm. Maybach HL62 TUK; six cylinders in-line; petrol; water-cooled; 6,191cc; overhead valves; power output, 140bhp at 2,600rpm

Transmission: 4F1Rx2

Suspension: Pivoting front axle suspended on transverse semi-elliptical multi-leaf spring; paired leaf springs for each road wheel at rear

Brakes: Hydraulic

Electrical system: 12V

Dimensions: Length – 8,100mm/319in
Width – 1,940mm/76in
Height – 1,750mm/69in
Track length on ground – KM-m-10, 1,400mm/55in; KM-m-11, 2,235mm/88in

Weight: Unladen – 9,500kg/20,943lb
Payload – 1,500kg/3,307lb
Maximum towed load – 8,000kg/17,637lb

Performance: Maximum speed – 50kph/31mph

Krauss-Maffei KM-m-10, 11

During World War II, the *Wehrmacht* tended to favour large numbers of half-tracked vehicles, particularly for use as prime movers. Following common design principles, the machines were produced in six weight classes ranging from 1–18 tons. First into production was the 8-ton *SonderKraftfahrzeug* (Sd Kfz) 7 "medium" tractor designed for towing heavy artillery including the 17cm and 15cm guns; other variants were fitted with a wooden load-carrying body or were used to mount a 2cm FlaK38 or 43 gun.

Work started in 1933, with early prototypes built by both Krauss-Maffei (KM-m-7) and Büssing-NAG (BN-m-8). Krauss-Maffei was authorized to begin production of the KM-m-8 variant in May 1934. The vehicle was powered by a 5,184cc Maybach HL52 six-cylinder petrol engine driving through a four-speed main gearbox and two-speed auxiliary box. The open coach-type body

had seating for up to 11 men on three rows of bench seats. Stowage for ammunition was at the rear. The vehicle was rated to tow 8,000kg/8 tons. A powerful horizontal-spindle winch was fitted at the rear of the chassis. The winch was eventually superseded by a vertical spindle with a drum design.

In 1935, the KM-m-8 was followed by the KM-m-9, with the definitive KM-m-10 dating from 1936. The original engine gave way to the higher-powered 5,698cc Maybach HL57, followed by the 6,191cc HL62. The final variant dates from March 1938 when Krauss-Maffei and Borgward produced the KM-m-11 (and HL-m-11), which featured longer tracks.

The Sd Kfz 7 was the only one of the German half-tracks to retain the paired leaf-spring suspension for the road wheels a feature from the original prototypes. Torsion-bar suspension was incorporated for the idler wheels. A solid beam axle was

fitted at the front, suspended on a transverse semi-elliptical spring, pivot-mounted on the front cross-member and retained by radius rods.

The KM-m-11 remained in production until 1944, with Krauss-Maffei producing 5,026 examples. In all some 12,000 of these vehicles were built by six manufacturers, including licensed production by Breda of the Type 61 in Milan, Italy. A proposed KM-m-12 of 1939, which was to have been powered by a Maybach HL80 engine was not produced.

ABOVE AND RIGHT: **The medium (8-ton) Sd Kfz 7 tractor was produced by Krauss-Maffei and Borgward. The vehicle was bodied as a personnel carrier/prime mover, gun mount and cargo carrier.**

Krupp L2H, L2H43, L2H143

ABOVE: **The angled bonnet is made possible by the use of a horizontally opposed air-cooled engine. Most of the type were used as artillery tractors.**

Originally established in November 1811, Friedrich Krupp Motoren & Kraftwagen Fabrieken started building trucks, locomotives and agricultural machinery in 1919, the first vehicle being a chain-driven 5-ton truck. Shaft drive was offered in 1925 and, by 1930, Krupp was producing 4x2 and 6x4 forward-control trucks. The company's most significant contribution to the *Wehrmacht* was the Protze (Poseur) light truck, which originated as the L2H in 1933, and entered production the following year as the L2H43, which was also sold commercially. This was eventually superseded by the uprated 1½-ton L2H143 in 1937.

It was an innovative design of 6x4 light truck with independent rear suspension using horizontal coil springs, and was

powered by a 3,308cc Krupp M304 air-cooled flat-four engine which allowed the adoption of a distinctive sloping bonnet. The rear wheels were driven through a four-speed gearbox and two-speed transfer box. Although there was no front-wheel drive, a self-locking differential gave excellent cross-country performance.

The most common role was that of a light artillery tractor (Kfz 69), but many were bodied as a cargo vehicle or personnel carrier (Kfz 70). Others were fitted with a searchlight (Kfz 83) or FlaK gun (Kfz 81), or carried a closed signals telephone body (Kfz 68). Production continued until 1941, by which time some 7,000 examples had been built.

The company also produced 3-ton and 6½-ton trucks until the factory

was affected by heavy bombing in September 1942. In December 1943, the company Friedrich Krupp AG reverted back to sole ownership being transferred to the eldest son, Alfried Krupp von Bohlen und Halbach. The company's manufacturing activities were then relocated to areas less vulnerable to bombing.

LEFT: **A column of *Wehrmacht* troops in Krupp L2H143 vehicles pass through a village in Poland, September 1939. The vehicle was used extensively by troops of the *Legion Kondor* (Condor Legion) during the Spanish Civil War from July 17, 1936 to April 1, 1939.**

Krupp L2H, L2H43, L2H143

Type: Truck, light, 6x4
Manufacturer: Friedrich Krupp Motoren & Kraftwagen Fabrieken; Essen
Production: 1933 to 1941
Powerplant: Krupp M304; four cylinders, horizontally opposed; petrol; water-cooled; 3,308cc; side valves; power output, 60bhp at 2,500rpm
Transmission: 4F1Rx2; 6x4
Suspension: Live front axle on semi-elliptical multi-leaf springs; independent rear suspension using trailing arms and horizontal coil springs
Brakes: Hydraulic
Electrical system: 12V
Dimensions: Length – 5,100mm/201in
 Width – 1,960mm/77in
 Height – tilt in place, 1,620mm/64in; minimum, 1,485mm/58in
 Wheelbase – 2,905mm/114in
 Bogie centres – 910mm/36in
Weight: Unladen – 2,450kg/5,401lb
 Payload – 1,150kg/2,535lb
Performance: Maximum speed – 70kph/43mph

Magirus-Deutz M178D15A

In 1938, the Köln (Cologne) based Klöckner-Deutz Motoren company, which manufactured tractors, took over Conrad Dietrich Magirus, a fire appliance manufacturer based in Ulm. Although the company's origins went back to 1903, Magirus had not started manufacturing trucks until 1916. In 1933, Magirus launched a range of specialized military vehicles powered by a 7,500cc diesel engine. Subsequent diesel engines included a 12-cylinder horizontally opposed unit, but the distinctive Deutz air-cooled engines started to be used from the middle years of World War II. Between 1937 and 1940, Magirus was one of the manufacturers commissioned to build the standardized 6x6 *Einheits* truck, but the company's most significant *Wehrmacht* vehicles included some 18,000 examples of the 3-ton A3000/S3000 as both 4x2 and 4x4.

The company's factory was badly damaged during the latter years of the war. In 1946, production resumed and the company continued to prosper,

specializing in heavy vehicles, including tank transporters. The A6500 Jupiter was announced in 1951. Conservatively rated at 7 tons, it was powered by a 10,644cc Deutz F8L V8 air-cooled multi-fuel diesel engine driving through a six-speed gearbox and two-speed transfer box. In 1958, the original engine was replaced by a more-powerful 12,667cc unit, and the designation was changed to A7500. The 4x4 was replaced by a 6x6 variant in 1962. In 1964, the name Jupiter was deleted and the truck carried the designation M178D15A.

On all models, the suspension was by semi-elliptical multi-leaf springs, inverted at the rear. There were both open- and closed-cab designs. Standard variants included a steel drop-side cargo body, dump, workshop, crane carrier and multiple rocket launcher; also as a snow plough,

BELOW: **A winch-equipped M178D15A recovery tractor fitted with a World War II-style canvas-covered cab.**

ABOVE: **The Magirus Jupiter (M178D15A) was introduced in 1951 and was widely used by the** *Bundeswehr*. **Aside from the multiple rocket launcher, standard variants included cargo, dump, workshop, crane carrier, snow plough, airfield fire tender, fuel tanker, recovery and tractor for semi-trailer.**

airfield fire tender, fuel tanker, recovery and tractor for semi-trailer. A total of 7,800 were produced, and widely used by the *Bundeswehr*. Many were also used by the British Army in Germany. The M178D15A was widely exported. In 1975, Magirus-Deutz AG was merged into the Fiat Iveco Group.

Magirus-Deutz M178D15A

Type: Truck, cargo, 7-ton, 4x4, 6x6
Manufacturer: Klöckner-Humboldt-Deutz; Ulm
Production: 1951 to 1967
Powerplant: Deutz F8L-614; eight cylinders in V configuration; multi-fuel diesel; air-cooled; 10,644cc; overhead valves; power output, 170bhp at 2,300rpm.
Deutz F8L-714A; eight cylinders in V configuration; diesel; air-cooled; 12,667cc; overhead valves; power output, 178bhp at 2,300rpm
Transmission: 6F1Rx2; part-time 4x4
Suspension: Live axles on semi-elliptical multi-leaf springs, inverted at the rear
Brakes: Air-pressure assisted hydraulic
Electrical system: 24V
Dimensions: Length – 7,520mm/296in, 8,000mm/315in
Width – 2,500mm/98in
Height – tilt in place, 3,240mm/128in; minimum, 2,500mm/98in
Wheelbase – 4,410mm/174in, 4,820mm/190in
Bogie centres (6x6 variant only) – 1,280mm/50in
Weight: Unladen – typical, 14,600kg/32,187lb
Payload – 10,000kg/22,046lb
Performance: Maximum speed – 75kph/47mph

LEFT: **The diesel-powered MAN ML4500 was produced as a 4x4 (ML4500A) and also the 4x2 (ML4500S) variant. The vehicle was among the largest trucks used by the *Wehrmacht* during World War II. It was also manufactured by ÖAF in Austria.**

MAN ML4500A, ML4500S

In 1897, Maschinenfabrik Augsburg-Nürnberg (MAN) worked with Dr Rudolf Diesel on the design and development of the compression-ignition engine which was to bear his name. The company began building Saurer trucks under licence from 1915, before production of trucks under the MAN badge began in 1920. The name was changed to Kraftwagenwerke MAN-Saurer in 1916, with Saurer trucks being built until 1918. MAN produced the first diesel-engined truck in 1923 and the company's products manufactured during the 1930s were generally available with either diesel or petrol engines. MAN was also responsible for the design of the diesel engine which powered all of the light 6x6 German military vehicles.

Since the 1930s the company had tended to specialize in heavier trucks, becoming a major supplier to the *Wehrmacht*. Typical of these were the 4¹/₂-ton ML4500S (4x2) and ML4500A (4x4), both of which were built in relatively large numbers between 1940 and 1945. The truck was of conventional design and was powered by a 7,980cc six-cylinder direct-injection diesel engine driving through a five-speed gearbox with overdrive top gear. The 4x4 variant was also fitted with a two-speed transfer box. The suspension was by semi-elliptical springs carrying live axles.

Production was at MAN in Nürnberg (until the factory became too busy building submarine engines) and at the ÖAF factory in Wien, Austria. The ÖAF company was purchased in 1936. Some 10,000 were built, with most bodied as cargo vehicles. The ML4500A was discontinued in 1944 and the ML4500S continued until 1945.

MAN ML4500A, ML4500S

Type: Truck, heavy, 4¹/₂-ton, 4x2, 4x4
Manufacturer: Maschinenfabrik Augsburg-Nürnberg (MAN); Nürnberg. Österreichische Automobil-Fabriks (OAF); Wien
Production: 1940 to 1945
Powerplant: MAN D1040G; six cylinders in-line; direct-injection diesel; water-cooled; 7,980cc; overhead valves; power output, 1,10bhp at 1,900rpm
Transmission: (ML4500A) 5F1Rx2; part-time 4x4. (ML4500S) 5F1R; 4x2
Suspension: Live axles on semi-elliptical multi-leaf springs
Brakes: Air-pressure
Electrical system: 12V
Dimensions: Length – 7,500mm/295in
  Width – 2,350mm/93in
  Height – tilt in place, 3,350mm/132in; minimum, 2,610mm/103in
  Wheelbase – 4,600mm/181in
Weight: Unladen – 5,050–5,550kg/11,113–12,235lb
  Payload – road, 4,950kg/10,890lb; cross-country (ML4500A only), 4,350kg/9,590lb
Performance: Maximum speed – 63kph/39mph

139

MAN HX2000, SX2000

ABOVE: **An eight-wheel-drive DROPS-equipped SX2000 being driven around the MAN company's test facility in Germany.**

In the mid-1960s, the German truck manufacturer Maschinenfabrik Augsburg-Nürnberg (MAN) started work on the second generation of logistics trucks for the *Bundeswehr*. Assistance came from Klöckner-Humboldt-Deutz (KHD), Rheinstahl-Henschel, Krupp and Büssing. By late 1965, vehicles had been demonstrated in the 4-, 7- and 10-ton weight classes, using what was basically an identical chassis. Following extensive trials, the series was officially accepted for production in April 1975. The first production vehicle was the 10-ton cargo truck, designated Kat 1. Deliveries began in January 1977, with the last of almost 9,000 vehicles delivered on May 18, 1983.

In 1985, work started on an improved version in collaboration with the US Army. Designated Kat 2, some were delivered to the USA, France and Canada. At the same time, work was in progress building the Kat 3 variant, and a total of 1,594 of these were purchased by Algeria, Ireland, Oman, Peru, Singapore and Venezuela. The Kat 1-A1 variant entered production in 1987, and was an improvement on the original Kat 1 with a wider, tilting cab and improved performance. In 1989, drawing on the experience gained in service since the launch of the original Kat 1 trucks, the range was rationalized into what MAN described as the improved medium-mobility SX, the medium-mobility HX and LX, and the militarized civilian FX. The trucks were available with a choice of power units, and with 4x4, 6x6 and 8x8 drive configurations. The range also included tractor variants. All shared the MAN-originated modular three-man tilting cab. An appliqué armour kit was available for fitting when operating in hazardous areas.

ABOVE: **British Army high-mobility 8x8 recovery vehicle.** RIGHT: **In 2001, the British Ministry of Defence awarded a contract to MAN for 4,851 high-mobility cargo vehicles in three drive configurations. The bodies were to be built by Marshall Specialist Vehicles Ltd., Cambridge.**

LEFT: **The four-wheel-drive cargo vehicle will replace existing Leyland-DAF and Bedford trucks in service with the British Army. All the trucks are fitted with the same low-profile cab first seen on the *Bundeswehr* Kat 1 trucks in the mid-1960s.**

MAN acquired ERF, a British company, in March 2000, forming MAN-ERF in 2004. A year later it was announced that the Ministry of Defence had awarded MAN-ERF a contract worth 1.5 billion Euros covering 4,851 4x4, 6x6 and 8x8 high-mobility cargo vehicles, plus 314 high-mobility recovery tractors. All were to use the HX and SX chassis. Deliveries began in 2007 and are scheduled to continue until 2014, replacing a variety of existing, in many cases ageing, vehicles including Leyland-DAF and Bedford MJ, Bedford TM4-4 and TM6-6 models, as well as Foden and Scammell recovery vehicles.

The trucks are powered by an 11,967cc MAN six-cylinder turbocharged diesel engine driving all wheels through an eight- or twelve-speed (8x8 variants) semi-automatic gearbox and two-speed transfer box. Suspension is by live axles suspended on coil springs, with radius rods.

Bodies and associated equipment for the UK trucks come from Marshall Specialist Vehicles (MSV), EKA, Fluid Transfer, Andover Trailers and Atlas Cranes.

BELOW: **The manufacturer's six-wheel drive demonstrator for the cargo-bodied truck. The vehicle is painted in the distinctive UN white livery.**

MAN HX2000, SX2000

Type: Truck, cargo, 8- to 10-ton, 4x4
Manufacturer: MAN Nutzfahrzeuge Altiengesellschaft; München
Production: 1989 on
Powerplant: MAN D2866; six cylinders in-line; turbocharged diesel; water-cooled; 11,967cc; overhead valves; power output, 400bhp at 2,000rpm
Transmission: Semi-automatic 8F2R; full-time 4x4
Suspension: Live axles on coil springs with axle location by radius rods; hydraulic double-acting shock absorbers at front
Brakes: Air-pressure
Electrical system: 24V
Dimensions: Length – 7,711mm/304in
Width – 2,550mm/100in
Height – top of cab, 3,308mm/130in
Wheelbase – 4,500mm/177in
Weight: Unladen – 7,950kg/17,526lb
Payload – 8,000-10,000kg/17,637-22,046lb
Performance: Maximum speed – 88kph/55mph

**Mercedes-Benz G4
W31, W131**

Type: Car, heavy, six-seat, 6x4, 6x6
Manufacturer: Mercedes-Benz; Stuttgart
Production: 1933 to 1939
Powerplant: Mercedes-Benz M24; eight cylinders in-line; petrol; water-cooled; 5,018, 5,252 or 5,401cc; overhead valves; power output, 110–115bhp at 3,400rpm
Transmission: 4F1Rx2; 6x4 (W31), 6x6 (W131)
Suspension: Live axles, front and rear on semi-elliptical multi-leaf springs; hydraulic vane shock absorbers
Brakes: Vacuum servo-assisted hydraulic
Electrical system: 12V
Dimensions: Length – 5,400mm/213in
    Width – 1,890mm/74in
    Height – top erected, 1,800mm/71in
    Wheelbase – 2,530mm/100in
    Bogie centres – 9,50mm/37in
Weight: Unladen – 3,566kg/7,826lb
Performance: Maximum speed – 60kph/37mph

Mercedes-Benz G4

Often described as "Hitler's Mercedes", the G4 was a six-seater heavy staff car (*schwere Personnenkraftwagen*) built for senior ministers, military officers and officials of the Third Reich. Despite much evidence to the contrary, it was a product of the belief that three axles offered the best off-road performance. The design only remained in production because it was favoured by the *Führer*.

ABOVE: **The Mercedes-Benz G4 6x4 heavy motor car was much favoured by Hitler and his senior staff. Just 57 examples were produced between 1933 and 1934. Although equipped for the purpose, the vehicle was hardly ever used for cross-country travel.**

The G4 had a Mercedes-Benz M24 straight-eight cylinder petrol engine, coupled to a four-speed main gearbox and two-speed auxiliary transfer box.

The W31 was driven by the rear wheels only, while the W131 was fitted with six-wheel drive. Despite an impressive power output of 110–115bhp, the unladen weight of 3,566kg/7,826lb restricted top speed to 60kph/37mph. Just 57 were completed between 1933 and 1939.

Mercedes-Benz G5

Announced in 1937 the Mercedes-Benz G5 first appeared in public at the 1938 British Motor Show at Olympia. Based on the 200V passenger car, the G5 was not the company's first all-wheel-drive vehicle, nor was it an entirely new design. Mercedes-Benz built an all-wheel-drive vehicle in 1904.

The car was powered by a 2,006cc four-cylinder petrol engine, driving both axles via a unitary five-speed gearbox/transfer box, the fifth gear being an overdrive. The differentials were located so that the drive-shafts passed through the chassis side members for increased ground clearance. The suspension was independent at front and rear, using cast wishbones and heavy-duty coil springs, together with double-acting shock absorbers. In normal use, the vehicle was steered by means of the front wheels, with the rear wheels locked in the straight-ahead position. The driver could select all-wheel drive and steering.

LEFT: **The prototype G5 Mercedes-Benz. Note the all-wheel steering.**

Mercedes-Benz G5

Type: Car, medium, 4x4
Manufacturer: Mercedes-Benz; Stuttgart
Production: 1937 to 1940
Powerplant: Mercedes-Benz M149; four cylinders in-line; petrol; water-cooled; 2,006cc; overhead valves; power output, 48bhp at 3,700rpm
Transmission: 5F1R; part-time 4x4
Suspension: Independent front and rear, using coil springs; hydraulic vane shock absorbers
Brakes: Hydraulic
Electrical system: 12V
Dimensions: Length – 3,990mm/157in
    Width – 1,680mm/66in
    Height – 1,900mm/75in
    Wheelbase – 2,530mm/100in
Weight: Unladen – 1,880kg/4,145lb
Performance: Maximum speed – 80kph/50mph

Three body styles were built – a strictly military *Kübelwagen* with steel half doors, a four-door convertible known as the *Kommandeurwagen*, and an open-sided vehicle with side curtains.

LEFT: **Like the 4¹/₂-ton MAN truck, the Mercedes-Benz L4300 was produced in 4x4 (L4500A) and 4x2 (L4500S) variants. There was also a half-tracked *Maultier* (Mule) conversion, designated L4500R. The truck was introduced in 1939 and produced until 1944. It was then was put back into production for the post-war commercial market.**

Mercedes-Benz L4500A, L4500S

The Mercedes-Benz L4500 was the standard heavy truck in the *Wehrmacht* during the later years of World War II and was produced in both 4x2 and 4x4 configurations. The road-going L4500S 4x2 variant was launched in 1939 and remained in production until 1944. The off-road L4500A 4x4 was introduced in 1941 and continued to be built until 1944. The Austrian company Saurer also produced the L4500A during 1944 and 1945, and the total number of both types built by the two companies was some 9,000.

Power was provided by a 7,274cc six-cylinder diesel engine driving the rear wheels through a five-speed gearbox with overdrive top gear. For the all-wheel drive variant, there was a two-speed auxiliary gearbox that included the transfer gears. Suspension was by semi-elliptical leaf springs.

In original form, the truck was fitted with an all-steel enclosed cab. But from around 1943, continued shortages of materials led to the adoption of the *Einheits* cab, made from pressed cardboard and timber. Most were bodied as cargo vehicles but there were also other body types, including shop vans. The chassis was used

as a mounting for 3-, 5- and 8-ton cranes. The vehicle was used as a self-propelled mount for the 37cm FlaK gun. Some 1,480 were adapted for use as a heavy *Maultier* (Mule) by fitting a tracked bogie at the rear. This was designated L4500R.

The L4500S was put back into production after the war for civilian customers and another 1,500 of the vehicle were manufactured.

BELOW: **The *Maultier* (Mule) Mercedes-Benz 4500R fitted with a 7,274cc six-cylinder diesel engine.**

Mercedes-Benz L4500A, L4500S

Type: Truck, cargo, 4¹/₂-ton, 4x4
Manufacturer: Daimler-Benz; Stuttgart
Production: 1939 to 1944
Powerplant: Daimler-Benz OM67/4; six cylinders in-line; diesel; water-cooled; 7,274cc; overhead valves; power output, 112bhp at 2,250rpm
Transmission: L4500S, 5F1R; 4x2. L4500A, 5F1Rx2; part-time 4x4
Suspension: Live axles on semi-elliptical multi-leaf springs, inverted at the rear
Brakes: Hydraulic front, air-pressure rear
Electrical system: 12V
Dimensions: Length – 7,860mm/309in
   Width – 2,350mm/93in
   Height – L4500S, 3,215mm/127in;
   L4500A, 3,345mm/132in
   Wheelbase – 4,600mm/181in
Weight: Unladen – L4500S, 4,930kg/10,846lb;
   L4500A, 5,715kg/12,573lb
   Payload – L4500S, 4,950kg/10,913lb;
   L4500A, road 4,685kg/10,328lb,
   cross-country 4,085kg/9,006lb
Performance: Maximum speed – 66kph/41mph

Mercedes-Benz G Class

The military vehicle that is universally known as the G-Wagen was first manufactured by the Austrian company Gelaendewagenfahrzeug Gessellschaft (GFG) in 1979. Although it was originally sold on the civilian market, the design had been inspired by proposals for a military vehicle by Shah Mohammad Reza Pahlavi of Iran in the early 1970s.

At the time, GFG was part-owned by Mercedes-Benz and Steyr-Daimler-Puch. When GFG closed down in the early 1980s, Steyr-Daimler-Puch continued to produce the vehicle under direct contract to Mercedes-Benz. In 1980, Peugeot entered the vehicle in a competition held by the French Army to find a replacement for the ageing Hotchkiss M201 Jeep. The Peugeot entry was selected against competition from Citroën and Renault, and entered service as the Peugeot licence-built P4 in 1982.

The Austrian-built original is generally now described as the Mercedes-Benz G Class and has undergone continuous development since it was first launched. The vehicle was originally produced in a choice of two wheelbases – 2,400mm/94in and 2,850mm/112in – but the original shorter wheelbase has been discontinued and a new 3,428mm/135in wheelbase has been added. There are currently four body variations: station wagon, van, open cargo vehicle (which can also be configured as a weapons mount) and chassis-cab for special body-work, including an ambulance for forward areas. A crew cab is also available, as are armoured variants. The engine is a 2,874cc five-cylinder turbocharged common-rail diesel driving both axles through a four-speed automatic gearbox and two-speed transfer box. Suspension is by live axles on coil springs located by longitudinal and transverse links. Both the front and rear axles include differential locks.

Since its launch, more than 60,000 Mercedes G Class have been supplied to more than 24 nations, including Germany, USA and Ireland.

The G Class is produced also under licence by the Hellenic Vehicle Industry in Greece as the 290GD.

Mercedes-Benz G Class

Type: Truck, personnel/cargo, 4x4
Manufacturer: Daimler; Stuttgart
Production: 1979 on
Powerplant: Mercedes-Benz OM602/DE29LA; five cylinders in-line; turbocharged diesel; water-cooled; 2,874cc; overhead valves; power output, 156bhp at 3,800rpm
Transmission: Automatic 5F1Rx2; part-time 4x4; differential locks front and rear
Suspension: Live axles on coil springs with longitudinal and transverse links; double-acting telescopic shock absorbers
Brakes: Vacuum servo-assisted hydraulic
Electrical system: 12V, 24V
Dimensions: Length – 4,165mm/164in
　Width – 1,700mm/75in
　Height – tilt in place, 2,005mm/86in
　Wheelbase – 2,400mm/94in, 2,850mm/112in, 3,428mm/135in
Weight: Unladen – typical, 2,100kg/4,630lb
　Payload – 500–2,000kg/1,102–4,409lb
Performance: Maximum speed – 138kph/86mph

Unimog U25, U402

The Unimog – the name is a contraction of *Universal Motor Gerät* (Universal Power Plant) – was designed by Albert Friedrich, former chief engineer of aviation engine research at Daimler-Benz. However, because Germany was not permitted to produce four-wheel drive vehicles, the pre-production models were assembled by Erhard & Söhn in Schwäbisch Gmünd. During 1949 and 1950

initial production was carried out by Gebr. Boehringer in Goppingen under a licence agreement. It was only in 1951 that Daimler-Benz received consent to build the Unimog and found space for a production line at Gaggenau.

Development had started in 1945 with the first prototype, powered by a 1,697cc petrol engine, ready by the end of 1947. The vehicle was unveiled to the public at Frankfurt am Main in August 1948, with deliveries beginning the following year. The first production model

was designated 70200 by Boehringer but by 1950 this had been changed to U25.

The vehicle was assembled around a steel channel-section ladder chassis. All production machines were diesel powered, at first utilizing the 1,697cc engine of the Mercedes-Benz 170. By 1951, there was a choice of either 1,720cc or 2,120cc engine.

The engine was coupled via an extended bell housing to a centre-mounted combined gearbox and transfer box. Short drive-shafts conveyed power to portal axles at front and rear. The axles incorporated self-locking differentials, and were suspended on coil springs. A power take-off on the side of the gearbox was used to drive a flat pulley situated on the right-hand side of the vehicle.

The intention was to produce a universal tractor/truck which could be used for industrial, agricultural and forestry work, but the Unimog was equally suitable for military usage. In 1950–51, the French Army became the first military customer, placing an order for 400 for use in the French-occupied zones of Germany. The *Bundeswehr* also acquired some early examples following the formation of the post-war German Army in 1955.

In 1953, the model designation was changed to U401 for the short-wheelbase model and U402 for the long-wheelbase. These models remained in production until 1956, by which time 16,250 had been built.

Unimog U25, U402

Type: Truck, 1-ton, prime mover, 4x4
Manufacturer: Daimler-Benz Unimog; Gaggenau
Production: 1949 to 1956
Powerplant: Mercedes-Benz; four cylinders in-line; diesel; water-cooled; 1,697cc, 1,720cc, 2,120cc; overhead valves; power output, 34–45bhp at 2,500rpm
Transmission: 6F2Rx2; part-time 4x4
Suspension: Live portal axles on coil springs; hydraulic shock absorbers
Brakes: Hydraulic
Electrical system: 12V
Dimensions: Length – 3,520mm/139in
  Width – 1,630mm/64in
  Height – tilt in place, 2,050mm/81in; minimum, 1,600mm/63in
  Wheelbase – 1,720mm/68in
Weight: Unladen – 1,700kg/3,740lb
  Payload – 1,000kg/2,240lb
Performance: Maximum speed – 65kph/40mph

ABOVE: **Following its formation in 1955, the West German Army (*Bundeswehr*) acquired some early Unimogs. Note how the portal-type axles provide high ground clearance.** RIGHT: **The original Unimog was designed as a dual-purpose universal tractor/truck for both industrial and agricultural use but was equally suitable for military usage. The first military versions were supplied to the French Army.**

Unimog S404

The 1½-ton Unimog Model S was effectively an enlarged and improved version of the original civilian-based U25/U402. The S404 was designed as a military machine, originally intended for the embryonic *Bundeswehr*, at that time restricted to the role of internal security. Daimler-Benz had started to produce development models as early as 1953, but the vehicle did not enter production until 1955, the first production variant being the military S404.

There were strong visual and technical similarities with the original U25/U402. However, where, for example, early prototypes for the Model S had retained the rather flat, angular front of the original U25/U402 models, extended to accommodate the larger engine, on the production version the windscreen was moved forward and the bonnet shortened. At the same time, the front was made more rounded with a stylized full-width radiator grille carrying the distinctive Mercedes three-pointed star.

Under NATO pressure, the diesel of the original design was removed in favour of the Daimler-Benz M180, a 2,195cc six-cylinder overhead-camshaft petrol engine. Although it was down-rated for use in this vehicle, specifically having a lower compression ratio and a single carburettor, it was essentially the same as that in the Mercedes-Benz 220 and 230 cars of the 1950s and 1960s. Transmission was by a six-speed all-synchromesh gearbox driving through a two-speed transfer box with selectable four-wheel drive. Both axles had manual differential locks and these, as well as the front-wheel drive, could be selected on the move in any gear. A crucial feature of the first Unimog design has always been the high ground clearance achieved by the use of portal-type axles and large wheels.

LEFT: **Unlike the original diesel-engined U25, the S404 was powered by a 2,195cc Mercedes-Benz M180 water-cooled petrol engine.**

The S404 was effectively hand-built and offered with a choice of engine, body and cab options as well as a wide range of additional equipment. The basic cab options included the open-cabbed S404 and the metal-cabbed S404.1. The latter was often fitted with a roof hatch. There were also single and crew-cab configurations. As regards the body, users could choose the standard 1½-ton cargo or box (*Kofferbau*) body, as well as special bodies such as ambulance, fire appliance, radio shelter and maintenance or decontamination unit. There was also a choice of engine-driven compressor, generator and winch, as well as auxiliary equipment, including a rear stabilizer bar, larger wheels and tyres, raised air-intake, sound insulation, power-assisted brakes, auxiliary fuel pump, steering-protection plate, larger generator and engine/battery heater. During the production run, the truck was made available in a choice of two standard wheelbase lengths – the S404, S416 and S421 had a 2,900mm/114in wheelbase, while the equivalent length for the S406 and S411 was 1,720mm/68in.

Once again, it seems that the French were the first military customers for the U404s, ordering 1,100. Throughout the life of the vehicle, the *Bundeswehr* was a dedicated user. Other military buyers included the British and US armies (for use in West Germany) as well as Argentina, Austria, Belgium, Finland, Greece, India, Jordan, Netherlands, Switzerland and Turkey. The Unimog was also a popular choice with the German civil authorities and was frequently equipped as a fire tender or rescue vehicle. In 1963, a steel-cabbed variant, the S406, was made available for civilian customers.

ABOVE: **The S404 was available with a choice of open and closed cabs and also cargo and box bodies. This example also has a front-mounted winch.**

An "Armoured-Personnel Carrier" (APC) variant was produced by the Swedish company Landsverk between 1956 and 1960 for the Belgian Army. In 1960, the Swedish Government stopped delivery of the last 15 when civil war erupted in the Belgian Congo. Following a period in storage, they were supplied to the Irish Defence Force in 1971–72.

With a production run of 64,242 units over nearly 20 years, the Unimog S was the most numerous and successful of the type.

LEFT: **Despite the use of live axles, suspended on nothing more sophisticated than coil springs, the Unimog was always capable of negotiating the most extreme terrain.**

Unimog S404

Type: Truck, 1½-ton, cargo, 4x4
Manufacturer: Daimler-Benz Unimog; Gaggenau
Production: 1955 to 1972
Powerplant: Mercedes-Benz M180; six cylinders in-line; petrol; water-cooled; 2,195cc; overhead valves; power output, 80bhp at 4,850rpm
Transmission: 6F2Rx2; part-time 4x4
Suspension: Live portal axles on coil springs; hydraulic shock absorbers
Brakes: Hydraulic
Electrical system: 12V
Dimensions: Length – 4,925mm/194in
Width – 2,141mm/84in
Height – tilt in place, 2,540mm/100in; minimum, 2,190mm/86in
Wheelbase – 2,900mm/114in
Weight: Unladen – 2,000kg/4,409lb
Payload – 1,500kg/3,307lb
Performance: Maximum speed – 95kph/60mph

Opel *Blitz S*

Opel was founded in Rüsselsheim in 1862, at first producing sewing machines and bicycles but moving into motor car production in 1899. The company's first trucks appeared in 1912. General Motors acquired all of the stock of Opel between 1928 and 1931. By 1937, GM-Opel was the largest German truck manufacturer. Three years later, Opel had built a total of one million vehicles and supplied 31,674 *Blitz* (Lightning) trucks to the *Wehrmacht*.

Launched in 1930, the original *Blitz* range was a family of trucks covering load ratings of 1, 1^1/$_2$ and 2 tons. In 1934, Opel started building a new factory at Brandenburg on the Havel river. The first new product of the factory was a replacement for the 1930 *Blitz*.

The new vehicle, known as the *Blitz S*, was a modern truck with an all-steel two-door cab, very much in the American style. It was powered by the original 3,417cc engine, driving the rear axle through a new five-speed gearbox. In 1937, the original engine was replaced by a new 3,626cc unit. By this time, the *Blitz* was being offered as the 3-ton Model 3.6-36, which was favoured by the *Wehrmacht* in the "medium" truck category, together with the Models 3.6-42 and 3.6-47. In 1938, the 1^1/$_2$-ton Model 2.5-32 was added to the range, remaining in

production until 1942, and used by the military in the "light" category.

Most military types were fitted a standard general-purpose wooden cargo body. There were other standardized variants including a fire-fighter, tanker, radio van, shop or office van and water-purification plant (*Wasseraufbereitungs*). A bus which could be used as a troop carrier or large ambulance was also built.

In 1940, a military all-wheel-drive variant was added to the range. Designated Model 3.6-6700 Typ A – or simply 6700A – the "A" indicating *Allradantrieb* (all-wheel drive), the vehicle was fitted with a two-speed transfer box which used a single control to both select the low ratios and engage the front axle.

In 1940, the government took control of the Opel factories and all civilian production ceased, but the *Blitz* continued to be produced for the *Wehrmacht*. From October 1943, shortages of raw materials

led to the replacement of the steel cab with the utility *Einheits* cab made from pressed cardboard and timber.

More than 120,000 *Blitz* were built before production ceased in 1944. The chassis was also selected for conversion to the 2-ton half-tracked *Maultier* (Mule).

ABOVE AND LEFT: **More than 120,000 Opel *Blitz* were manufactured between 1937 and 1944, with 4x2 and 4x4 variants produced.**

Opel *Blitz S*

Type: Truck, medium, cargo, 4x2 or 4x4
Manufacturer: Adam Opel; Rüsselsheim
Production: 1937 to 1944
Powerplant: Opel; six cylinders in-line; petrol; water-cooled; 3,417cc (1936 only) or 3,626cc; overhead valves; power output, 75bhp at 3,000rpm
Transmission: Model 3.6-36, 5F1R, 4x2; Model 3.6-6700A, 5F1Rx2; part-time 4x4
Suspension: Live axles suspended on semi-elliptical multi-leaf springs
Brakes: Hydraulic
Electrical system: 12V
Dimensions: Length – 3,450mm/136in
  Width – 2,265mm/89in
  Height – tilt in place, 2,825mm/111in; minimum, 2,175mm/86in
  Wheelbase – Model 3.6-36, 3,330mm/131in; Model 3.6-6700A, 3,450mm/136in
Weight: Unladen – 2,710kg/5974lb
  Payload – road, 3,500kg/7,716lb; cross-country, 3,000kg/6,614lb
Performance: Maximum speed – 85kph/53mph

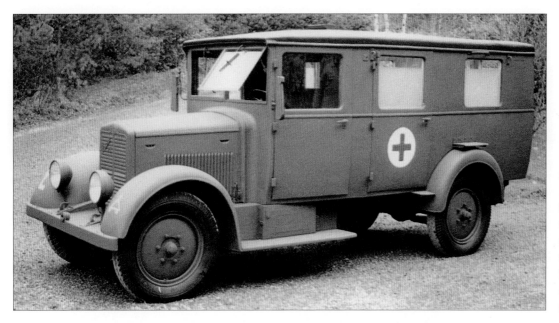

LEFT: **The Phänomen** *Granit* **25H dates from the mid-1930s and was essentially a commercial truck chassis. It was replaced in 1940 by the updated** *Granit* **1500, built as a 4x2 and 4x4.**

Phänomen *Granit* 1500S, 1500A

The Phänomen-Werke, Zittau, was established by Gustav Hiller in 1888, at first to produce bicycles and motorcycles. The Phänomobil motor car was launched in 1907. From 1927 onwards, when the company name was changed to Phänomen, only commercial vehicles were produced. The company specialized in lightweight trucks, at first powered by a 1,550cc V2 air-cooled petrol engine, but soon

upgraded to 2,678cc. The trucks acquired a reputation for reliability and were widely used as mail vans and civilian ambulances, as well as being supplied to the German Army.

The updated *Granit* range, now with four-cylinder air-cooled engine, was introduced in 1940, replacing the earlier 25H. Rated at 1½ tons, it was available with two-wheel drive (1500S) and from 1942 and more rarely, with all-wheel drive (1500A). The two-wheel-drive variant was fitted with twinned rear wheels, but larger single wheels were used on the 1500A. Both types had a four-speed gearbox.

The all-wheel-drive variant was fitted with a two-speed transfer box.

Both cargo and box van types were procured by the *Wehrmacht* in relatively large numbers from 1940, the 4x2 and 4x4 van being widely used as a field ambulance (*Krankenwagen*).

After the end of World War II, Phänomen-Werke, Zittau, was in the Soviet Zone. But vehicles continued to be produced under the IFA Robur *Granit* name until 1956.

BELOW: **The standard variant was fitted with a drop-side timber cargo body, but the chassis was also often used for an ambulance or box van.**

Phänomen *Granit* 1500S, 1500A

Type: Truck, 1½-ton, 4x2, 4x4
Manufacturer: Gustav Hiller, Phänomen-Werke; Zittau
Production: 1940 to 1944
Powerplant: Phänomen Granit 27; four cylinders in-line; petrol; air-cooled; 2,678cc; side valves; power output, 50bhp at 2,800rpm
Transmission: Model 1500S, 4F1Rx2; 4x2 (1500S); Model 1500A, part-time 4x4
Suspension: Live axles on semi-elliptical multi-leaf springs
Brakes: Hydraulic
Electrical system: 12V
Dimensions: Length – 5,490mm/216in
 Width – 1,980mm/78in
 Height – 2,160mm/85in
 Wheelbase – 3,270mm/129in
Weight: Unladen – 2,215kg/4,883lb
 Payload – 1,400–1,600kg/3,086–3,527lb
Performance: Maximum speed – 80kph/50mph

Stoewer R200 *Spezial*

Stoewer-Werke manufactured the R180 *Spezial* (Special) four- to five-seat cross-country car between 1936 and 1938, when it was replaced by the larger engined R200 which remained in production until 1940. Between 1937 and 1940, similar vehicles were also produced by BMW (*Typ* 325) and Hanomag (*Typ* 20B). Although the products of each manufacturer differed, both in detail and in the choice of power unit, the vehicle was designed on what was described as the *Einheits Leicht*

Geländegangige Personenkraftwagen chassis – "standardized light field car".

Unfortunately, the intended interchangeability of power units was compromised by details such as differing fuel supply and exhaust outlet positions. From 1940, the introduction of the *Typ* 40 AW2 variant saw all production moved to the Stoewer factory and the adoption of the Stoewer 1,997cc engine as the standard power unit.

Regardless of origin, the engine was linked to the wheels via a five-speed

gearbox and single-speed transfer box. Self-locking differentials were fitted in both axles as well as in the transfer box. Suspension was independent on all four wheels, using upper and lower wishbones and coil springs. The earliest examples had four-wheel steering and four-wheel drive, but this proved to offer no particular advantage in off-road use and was eventually abandoned as being dangerous.

Alongside the four- to five-seat field car (Kfz 1), standard variants included a communications vehicle (Kfz 2), maintenance/repair vehicle (Kfz 2/40) and surveillance vehicle (Kfz 3). In all cases, the bodies were built by Ambi-Budd Stanzerie, Berlin.

Some problems arose when the vehicle was operated under the extreme conditions encountered on the Eastern Front, but it was generally a useful and reliable vehicle. Total production amounted to some 13,000 vehicles over an almost eight-year period.

LEFT: Early examples of the vehicle were fitted with a four-wheel steering system which was intended to be locked out at speeds above 25kph/16mph. The feature was eventually abandoned as being dangerous.

Stoewer R200 *Spezial*

Type: Car, light, four seat, 4x2; Kfz 1
Manufacturer: Stoewer-Werke; Stettin
Production: 1936 to 1943
Powerplant: Stoewer AW2; four cylinders in-line; petrol; water-cooled; 1,997cc; overhead valves; power output, 48bhp at 3,600rpm. Up to 1940, alternative engines include BMW (six cylinders, 1,957cc), and Hanomag (four cylinders, 1,991cc)
Transmission: 5F1R; part-time 4x4; axle and inter-axle self-locking differentials
Suspension: Independent suspension at all four wheels using twin wishbones and coil springs
Brakes: Mechanical
Electrical system: 12V
Dimensions: Length – 3,900mm/154in
    Width – 1,690mm/67in
    Height – tilt in place, 1,900mm/75in
    Wheelbase – 2,400mm/94in
Weight: Unladen – 1,780kg/3,924lb
    Payload – 420kg/926lb
Performance: Maximum speed – 80kph/50mph

LEFT: **A G1200 built to *Wehrmacht* specifications. The vehicle was fitted with four-wheel drive and selectable all-wheel steering. A revolving spare wheel was mounted on each side to prevent gounding.**

Tempo G1200

Tempo G1200

Type: Car, light, four seat, 4x4
Manufacturer: Vidal & Söhn, Tempo-Werke; Hamburg
Production: 1936 to 1939
Powerplant: ILO; two cylinders in-line; 2x 596cc; petrol; two-stroke; air-cooled; power output, 2x 19bhp
Transmission: 4F1R; part-time 4x4
Suspension: Independent suspension front and rear, by swing axles and coil springs
Brakes: Mechanical
Electrical system: 6V
Dimensions: Length – 4,000mm/157in
   Width – 1,680mm/66in
   Height – minimum, 1,500mm/59in
   Wheelbase – 2,830mm/111in
Weight: Unladen – 1,060kg/2,332lb
Performance: Not available

Tempo began manufacturing motorcycles in 1926. Following the acquisition of the manufacturing rights to the Vidal & Söhn three-wheeler in 1928, they turned to producing motor cars. Dating from 1936, the G1200 car designed by Ing Otto Daus was developed as a private venture for military use. By any standards, it was one of the most unusual vehicles of the period, by virtue of using two engines to provide four-wheel drive.

Each of the two axles was driven by a 596cc two-cylinder air-cooled engine through a four-speed gearbox. The drive could select to run one or both engines. There was also selectable four-wheel steering. The suspension was independent, front and rear, by means of swing axles and coil springs. Most of the vehicles were fitted with a four-seat open body, but a small number had doors. The G1200 was supplied to the *Wehrmacht* and to the armies of Sweden, Romania, Argentina and Mexico.

Tempo-Rover

Tempo-Rover

Type: Car, six seat, 4x4
Manufacturer: Vidal & Söhn, Tempo-Werke; Hamburg
Production: 1953 to 1954
Powerplant: Rover; four cylinders in-line; 1,997cc; petrol; water-cooled; overhead inlet valves, side exhaust; power output, 52bhp at 4,000rpm
Transmission: 4F1Rx2; part-time 4x4
Suspension: Live axles on semi-elliptical multi-leaf springs; hydraulic double-acting shock absorbers
Brakes: Hydraulic
Electrical system: 12V
Dimensions: Length – 3,700mm/147in
   Width – 1,550mm/61in
   Height – tilt in place, 1,930mm/76in; minimum, 1,420mm/56in
   Wheelbase – 2,030mm/80in, 2,180mm/86in
Weight: Unladen – 1,422kg/3,138lb
   Payload – 625kg/1,375lb
Performance: Maximum speed – 89kph/55mph

Although Tempo stopped making motor cars in 1940, the company continued to produce light trucks after the war. In 1952, the West German Army's *Grenzschütz* (Border Guard) invited bids for a six-seat cross-country vehicle for patrolling the country's eastern border. The most satisfactory of the vehicles trialled for the role was the Land Rover Series I, but the service was obliged to purchase a German vehicle. Tempo approached Rover for a licence to assemble the Land Rover in Germany and the result was the Tempo-Rover.

Between April and August 1953, approximatley 100 to 189 vehicles were assembled at Tempo-Werke, Hamburg, using complete rolling 2,030mm/80in chassis and bulkheads supplied from the UK. Although broadly resembling the

LEFT: **A radio-equipped Tempo of the *Grenschütz*. Storage lockers were also incorporated in the front wings.**

standard Land Rover, the bodies were built by Herbert Vidal & Söhn and differed in many respects, most notably in the use of steel rather than aluminium. In 1954, up to 187 further examples were assembled using the 2,180mm/86in wheelbase chassis which had replaced the original 2,030mm/80in in the UK.

Volkswagen *Typ* 82 *Kübelwagen*

The Volkswagen *Kübelwagen* – "Bucket" or "Cube" car because of its simple bodywork – was the closest vehicle the *Wehrmacht* had to the US-built Jeep during World War II. The *Kübelwagen* had independent suspension which ensured a high standard of road-holding and the vehicle's light weight meant that it could perform equally well on most surfaces. Despite the use of special balloon tyres, it was never particularly good on loose sand due to the lack of four-wheel drive. On the road fuel economy was very good.

The *Kübelwagen* or, the correct military designation, *leicht Kraftpersonenwagen*, Kfz 1, was effectively a militarized version of Ferdinand Porsche's iconic "Beetle". Work on the design of a military "Beetle" had begun in 1938 and the first prototype was ready by the end of the year. Early pre-production models were available in December 1939 in time for the invasion of Poland. The first standard production examples – described by Porsche as the *Typ* 82 – were manufactured during February 1940, with the first 25 vehicles being built in Stuttgart. From May 1940 onwards, production took place at the Fallersleben factory. The vehicle was first used in action in Russia and North Africa in 1941, the air-cooled engine ensuring rugged reliability in either climatic extreme.

The *Kübelwagen* had a backbone-and-platform chassis used on the standard "Beetle" and, with some modification,

ABOVE: **Based on the backbone-and-platform chassis of the standard VW "Beetle" and sharing many mechanical components, the Porsche-designed *Typ* 82 *Kübelwagen* was the closest vehicle the *Wehrmacht* had to the US-built Jeep. Although the vehicle lacked all-wheel drive, the light weight and an air-cooled engine were distinct benefits in harsh conditions.**

most of the mechanical components from the same vehicle. Power came from a 985cc four-cylinder horizontally opposed air-cooled engine mounted in a fork between the chassis members, low down at the rear. The engine was bored out to 1,131cc in March 1943, increasing output from 23.5bhp to 25bhp. The drive from the engine was transmitted through a single dry-plate clutch to a four-speed non-synchromesh gearbox with an overdrive top gear. Drive to the rear wheels was through a limited-slip ZF differential. Reduction gears were used in the rear hubs.

Suspension was independent at all four wheels by means of laminated torsion bars; at the front these were contained within the tubular cross members.

The angular, flat-panelled four/five-seat open body was built by the American-owned company Ambi-Budd Stanzerie at their Johannesthall factory, Berlin. The body was little more than a rectangular tub of ribbed pressed steel, with curved projecting wings to cover the wheels at the four

ABOVE: **The simple, flat-panelled body that gave the vehicle its nickname (Kübelwagen – "Bucket" or "Cube" car) provided reasonably comfortable accommodation for four. Other variants were produced, including radio, survey and maintenance/repair vehicles.**

corners. A simple, top-hinged flat cover was provided for the engine compartment at the rear. The spare wheel was placed on top of the sloping front compartment, either in a recess or on a boss. Four un-trimmed steel doors, hinged on the centre pillar, provided access. The body was strengthened by means of a transverse beam across the door pillars which also served as a grab rail for the occupants. Small headlamps were mounted on the front wings, with the inevitable Notek blackout light on the front panel. Inside, there were four thinly upholstered seats covered with coated cloth, and wooden duckboards covered the floor.

Instrumentation was minimal. A canvas hood, supported on a folding frame, provided weather protection. Sidescreens were designed to be attached to the door tops to make a complete enclosure.

During its six years of production 48,454 were built. Along with the basic four-seat personnel car, standard variants included a three-seat command car (Kfz 3), radio communications vehicle (Kfz 2) and an automotive repair car (Kfz 2/40). There were experimental variants produced as a dummy tank. In the manner of the Jeep, there was also a field ambulance conversion. Some work was done on two four-wheel-drive prototypes (*Typ* 86 and *Typ* 87); also on an experimental half-tracked version (*Typ* 155). None entered production.

ABOVE: **Unlike the US-built Jeep, which was not provided with satisfactory weather protection, the Kübelwagen had shoulder-high doors fitted with sidescreens and a weatherproof roof.**

Volkswagen *Typ 82* *Kübelwagen*

Type: Car, light, four seat, 4x2; Kfz 1
Manufacturer: KDF Volkswagen; Wolfsburg
Production: 1940 to 1945
Powerplant: VW; four cylinders horizontally opposed; 985cc or 1,131cc; petrol; overhead valves; air-cooled; power output, 23.5–25hp at 3,000rpm
Transmission: 4F1R; 4x2; limited-slip differential
Suspension: Independent suspension by swing axles and torsion bars
Brakes: Mechanical
Electrical system: 6V
Dimensions: Length – 3,740mm/147in
  Width – 1,600mm/63in
  Height – tilt erected, 1,650mm/65in; minimum, 1,111mm/44in
  Wheelbase – 2,400mm/96in
Weight: Unladen – 685kg/1,510lb
  Payload – 450kg/992lb
Performance: Maximum speed – 80kph/50mph

RIGHT: **The VW** *Typ* **166** *Schwimmwagen* **was effectively a four-wheel drive amphibious version of the** *Kübelwagen.* **With all-wheel drive, the vehicle had excellent off-road performance.**

Volkswagen *Typ* 166 K2s

The *Schwimmwagen* – or, simply *Schwimmer* – was an amphibious version of the standard *Kübelwagen* light field car, sharing the same basic rear-engined layout as well as engine and suspension components. It was originally intended for use on the Eastern Front where, unlike the *Kübelwagen*, conditions called for four-wheel drive. Design work started in July 1940, with the first prototype – the *Typ* 128 – available for testing in September of that year. The inevitable teething problems meant that the vehicle was not approved for production until March 1942 but, by the end of the war, some 14,250 examples had been constructed.

As in the *Kübelwagen*, the engine was the familiar horizontally opposed

air-cooled four-cylinder unit of the VW "Beetle". Aside from the first 150 vehicles – designated *Typ* 138 – which were constructed by Porsche for extended field trials, all of the production *Typ* 166 *Schwimmwagen* used the more powerful 1,131cc version of the engine. There was a new five-speed gearbox, in combination with selectable all-wheel drive through a single-speed transfer box. With independent suspension at all four wheels using swing arms and torsion bars, combined with the use of self-locking differentials, the vehicle offered almost unstoppable cross-country performance even where amphibious operation was not required. However, the use of mechanical brakes was an oddly archaic touch.

The mechanical components were assembled into a boat-shaped welded-steel watertight hull fabricated by Ambi-Budd, which provided accommodation for a driver and three passengers. Access to the rear-mounted engine was via a horizontal hinged cover, and there were twin fuel tanks in the front. The windscreen could be folded forward and there was a simple canvas roof which could be erected to provide weather protection.

LEFT: **The** *Schwimmwagen's* **propeller was lowered manually to engage with a dog clutch attached to a power take-off from the engine.**

Propulsion in the water was achieved via a hinged propeller unit manually swung down and locked to engage with a drive dog on the front of the engine crankshaft. No reverse gear was available in the water, and when afloat the vehicle was steered by the front wheels.

Prototypes were initially produced by both Porsche and Volkswagen, but most of the production vehicles were produced by Volkswagen at Wolfsburg.

Volkswagen *Typ* 166 K2s

Type: Car, light, amphibious, 4x4
Manufacturer: KDF Volkswagen; Wolfsburg. Porsche; Stuttgart
Production: 1942 to 1944
Powerplant: VW; four cylinders horizontally opposed; 1,131cc; petrol; overhead valves; air-cooled; power output, 25hp at 2,500rpm
Transmission: 5F1R; part-time 4x4; self-locking differentials; amphibious operation by hinged propeller
Suspension: Independent suspension by swing axles and torsion bars
Brakes: Mechanical
Electrical system: 6V
Dimensions: Length – 3,825mm/151in
  Width – 1,480mm/58in
  Height – tilt erected, 1,615mm/64in;
  minimum, 960mm/37in
  Wheelbase – 2,000mm/79in
Weight: Unladen – 910kg/2,006lb
Performance: Maximum speed – 74kph/46mph; in water – 12kph/7.5mph

VEB G-5, G-5/2

Produced by the Ernst Grübe factory of the East German VEB (Volkseigener Betriebe or People's Enterprises), the 3¹/₂-ton G-5 6x6 was introduced in 1957 and quickly became the standard truck of the East German Army.

The design was entirely conventional, with a front-mounted six-cylinder diesel engine driving all axles through a five-speed gearbox, with overdrive on top gear, and a two-speed transfer box. Suspension was by means of leaf springs all round. Early examples had an open cab, but this was replaced by an all-steel type in the G-5/2.

In the most numerous cargo form, the truck was fitted with a drop-side timber body but there were also many other variants.

The G-5 was superseded by the upgraded G-5/2 in 1958, but the planned air-cooled G-5/3 was not produced.

LEFT: **VEB G-5 trucks at an East German May Day parade.**

VEB G-5, G-5/2	
Type:	Truck, 3¹/₂-ton, cargo, 6x6
Manufacturer:	VEB Kraftfahrzeugwerk Ernst Grübe; Sachsen
Production:	1957 to 1961
Powerplant:	EMb W6 (G-5) or W6-20 (G-5/2); six cylinders in-line; diesel; water-cooled; 9,036cc (G-5) or 9,840cc (G-5/2); overhead valves; power output, 120–150bhp at 2,000rpm
Transmission:	5F1Rx2; part-time 6x6
Suspension:	Live axles on multi-leaf semi-elliptical springs
Brakes:	Air pressure
Electrical system:	24V
Dimensions:	Length – 7,170mm/282in Width – 2,500mm/98in Height – tilt in place, 3,000mm/118in; minimum, 2,600mm/102in Wheelbase – 4,420mm/174in Bogie centres – 1,250mm/49in
Weight:	Unladen – 7,850kg/17,306lb Payload – road, 5,000kg/11,023lb; cross-country, 3,500kg/7,716lb
Performance:	Maximum speed – 105kph/65mph

Trabant P601A

After the end of World War II, the East German provinces came under Soviet control, and the former Auto Union factory at Zwickau, which had produced Horch and Audi cars, became part of the State-owned IFA (Industrie-Vereinigung Volkseigner Fahrzeugwerke), an administrative group of nationalized manufacturers.

In 1948, car production commenced with the two-cylinder two-stroke F8, later renamed P70. Shortages of steel meant that the body was moulded from a composite of phenolic resin reinforced with linen, wool or cotton fibres known as Duroplast. In 1959, the same technology was incorporated into the Trabant P50, a small four-seat car. In 1962, the design was modified and the vehicle was renamed P60. Two years later, the familiar Trabant P601 was launched, still with a Duroplast body.

Trabant P601A	
Type:	Field car, four seat, 4x2
Manufacturer:	VEB Sachsenring Automobilwerke; Zwickau
Production:	1964 to 1988
Powerplant:	P60; two-cylinders in-line; two-stroke petrol; air cooled; 595cc; power output, 26bhp at 4,200rpm
Transmission:	4F1R; freewheel on top gear; 4x2
Suspension:	Independent suspension using transverse leaf spring at front and swing axles with coil-over shock absorber struts at rear
Brakes:	Hydraulic
Electrical system:	12V
Dimensions:	Length – 3,480mm/137in Width – 1,498mm/59in Height – 1,498mm/59in Wheelbase – 2,006mm/79in
Weight:	Unladen – 645kg/1,422lb
Performance:	Maximum speed – 100kph/62mph

ABOVE: **An open field car, military designation P601A (known as the *Grentztrabant*), was used by the East German Border Police.**

Csepel 130

The Csepel Engineering Works was established in Budapest in 1950, to manufacture commercial and military vehicles for the domestic market. Exports were handled through the Hungarian state-owned Mogurt organization.

The 1-ton Csepel 130, which dates from 1951, was a purpose-designed military vehicle with more than a passing resemblance to the Dodge WC series. Standard variants included an open cargo vehicle, available with or without a winch, as well as a box-bodied van and ambulance.

Sharing mechanical components with the company's militarized D350 truck, the Csepel 130 used a petrol version of the company's D413

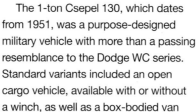

LEFT: **The Csepel 130 is very similar looking to the Dodge WC series of World War II.**

diesel engine, driving both axles through a five-speed gearbox. Suspension was by multi-leaf semi-elliptical springs. In the late 1970s, the company name was changed to Csepel Autogyar.

Csepel 130	
Type: Truck, 1-ton, cargo, 4x4	
Manufacturer: Csepel Engineering Works; Budapest	
Production: 1951 on	
Powerplant: Csepel; four cylinders in-line; petrol; water-cooled; 5,322cc; overhead valves; power output, 85bhp at 2,200rpm	
Transmission: 5F1R; part-time 4x4	
Suspension: Live axles on semi-elliptical multi-leaf springs; hydraulic double-acting telescopic shock absorbers	
Brakes: Hydraulic	
Electrical system: 12V	
Dimensions: Length – 4,840mm/191in	
Width – 2,150mm/85in	
Height – minimum, 2,070mm/81in	
Wheelbase – 3,000mm/118in	
Weight: Unladen – 3,500kg/7,716lb	
Payload – 1,300kg/2,867lb	
Performance: Maximum speed – 80kph/50mph	

Rába Botond

Rába Magyar Vagon és Gépgyár (MAVAG) started producing trucks in 1904, acquiring a licence to build the Praga 5-ton model in 1912. During World War I, the company built 2- and 3-ton 4x2 trucks under Praga licence and, by 1920, was licence-building Krupp models.

The Botond A was a 1¹⁄₂-ton 6x4 anti-aircraft gun tractor. It was designed by

Dezsö Winkler in 1936–37 and entered production at MAVAG and four other companies in 1938. The truck was powered by a 3,770cc engine driving two worm-gear axles at the rear, through a five-speed gearbox. It was replaced by

BELOW: **Production continued after the war, but only five vehicles were built between 1948 and 1950.**

the Botond B in 1942, which used a 4,330cc engine and had self-locking differentials but was otherwise similar.

The timber rear body provided accommodation for a two-man crew together with a gun crew of 14.

Rába Botond	
Type: Truck, 1¹⁄₂-ton, tractor, 6x4	
Manufacturer: Rába Magyar Vagon és Gépgyár (MAVAG); Györ	
Production: 1938 to 1948	
Powerplant: Rába; four cylinders in-line; petrol; water-cooled; 3,770cc, 4,330cc; overhead valves; power output, 65–70bhp at 3,800rpm	
Transmission: 5F1Rx2; part-time 4x4	
Suspension: Live front axle on semi-elliptical multi-leaf springs; independent suspension at rear using balancing beam and coil springs	
Brakes: Hydraulic	
Electrical system: 12V	
Dimensions: Length – 5,746mm/226in	
Width – 2,080mm/82in	
Height – tilt in place, 2,550mm/100in	
Wheelbase – 3,030mm/119in	
Weight: Unladen – 3,950kg/8,708lb	
Payload – 1,500kg/3,307lb	
Performance: Maximum speed – 60kph/37mph	

Mahindra CJ3B

In 1947, Mahindra began assembling Willys CJ2A Jeeps under licence at their Mumbai (Bombay) engineering works. By the early 1950s, they were manufacturing their own versions. The first of these was the CJ3B Universal Jeep which had been launched in the USA in 1953 and which Mahindra started to manufacture under licence from 1954. Both military and civilian versions were produced.

Although the CJ3B was probably Jeep's first really new post-war product, in truth, it differed little from the World War II original. The most significant change was the use of the Willys Hurricane F-head engine in place of the side-valve Go-Devil. The gearbox was a three-speed unit, installed in conjunction with a two-speed transfer box, and a 4x2 variant was also produced. There were live axles, front and rear, hung on multi-leaf semi-elliptical springs.

The vehicle was also used as a mount for the US-built 106mm M40 recoilless rifle. Mahindra continued to offer the CJ3B alongside the exclusively Indian CJ4 into the 1970s.

Mahindra CJ3B	
Type: Truck, ¼-ton, utility, 4x4	
Manufacturer: Mahindra & Mahindra; Mumbai	
Production: From 1954 on	
Powerplant: Licence-built Willys Hurricane; four cylinders in-line; petrol; water-cooled; 2,199cc; overhead inlet valves, side exhaust; power output, 72bhp at 4,000rpm. Diesel engine option also available	
Transmission: 3F1Rx2; part-time 4x4, or 4x2	
Suspension: Live axles on semi-elliptical multi-leaf springs	
Brakes: Hydraulic	
Electrical system: 12V	
Dimensions: Length – 3,330mm/131in; Width – 1,750mm/69in; Height – minimum, 1,680mm/66in; Wheelbase – 2,030mm/80in	
Weight: Unladen – 1,077kg/2,374lb; Payload – 545kg/1,201lb	
Performance: Maximum speed – 100kph/62mph	

LEFT: **An Indian Army CJ3B with a US-built 106mm M40 recoilless rifle.**

Shaktiman 415 L1AR

In 1958, the Indian State Ordnance Factory, Jabalpur acquired a licence to build MAN 415 L1AR 4-ton trucks. By 1963 a total of some 5,000 had been built. Early production used a high proportion of imported components, but this was gradually reduced until the trucks were almost entirely of Indian origin.

The vehicle was powered by a 5,880cc MAN multi-fuel engine, driving both axles through a five-speed gearbox and two-speed transfer box. A lockable torque-splitter was included in the transfer box, and the rear axle was fitted with a differential lock. Suspension was by multi-leaf semi-elliptical springs.

A simple, robust and reliable vehicle, it remained in service for more than four decades, eventually being replaced by Indian-built Ashok-Leyland and Tata vehicles.

BELOW: **The distinctive front of the Shaktiman 415 L1AR, powered by a 5,880cc MAN multi-fuel engine.**

Shaktiman 415 L1AR	
Type: Truck, 3- to 5-ton, cargo, 4x4	
Manufacturer: Indian State Ordnance Factory; Jabalpur	
Production: 1958 to 2003	
Powerplant: Licence-built MAN D0026M1; six cylinders in-line; multi-fuel diesel; water-cooled; 5,880cc; overhead valves; power output, 110bhp at 2,500rpm	
Transmission: 5F1Rx2; part-time 4x4	
Suspension: Live axles on semi-elliptical multi-leaf springs	
Brakes: Air-assisted hydraulic at front, hydraulic at rear	
Electrical system: Hybrid 12V/24V	
Dimensions: Length – 7,163mm/282in; Width – 2,275mm/90in; Height – minimum, 2,413mm/95in; Wheelbase – 4,191mm/165in	
Weight: Unladen – 2,540kg/5,600lb; Payload – road, 5,000kg/11,023lb; cross country, 3,000kg/6,614lb	
Performance: Maximum speed – 72kph/45mph	

Timoney 8x8

The Irish company, Timoney Technology, produced a series of technically advanced "Armoured Personnel Carriers" (APCs) for the Irish Defence Force in the 1970s, and has long been involved in the development of high-mobility suspension systems and related technology. Under the name Timoney High Mobility Vehicles, the company has also developed a high-mobility 8x8 truck as a demonstrator for a heavy-duty independent suspension system. The truck is effectively a front-engined development of an airfield crash/rescue truck, and was the first such vehicle with independent suspension to be supplied to the US Air Force.

Aside from the Timoney suspension system, the truck was of conventional design, using a Volvo six-cylinder turbocharged diesel engine driving through a Volvo six-speed automatic gearbox and Steyr two-speed transfer box. All-wheel steering was offered as an option. The cab was a Volvo commercial forward-control design with seating for a crew of two or three.

The use of independent suspension remains unusual for a truck of this size. The patented Timoney axle units, which were initially developed for the company's APC in 1972, were separate axle units rigidly attached directly to the chassis. The suspension is by double wishbones at each wheel, with twin variable-rate coil springs and concentric dampers allowing more than 400mm/16in of travel. A version of this system, which is also manufactured under licence in the US by Rockwell, was fitted to a high-mobility 6x6 carrier produced by the British Defence

ABOVE: **Timoney's heavy-duty suspension and chassis technology has been licensed to Volvo. Under this agreement the Swedish company took over manufacturing and marketing the Timoney high-mobility truck range.**

Equipment Research Agency (DERA). The same system was used on the TACOM 10x10 technology demonstrator, which was based on the Oshkosh 10x10 "Palletized Load System" (PLS) truck.

The standard body was a flat platform with removable drop-down side panels. The vehicle could also be equipped with a Multilift demountable rack (DROPS) load-handling system.

Other variants, none of which has progressed beyond the demonstrator stage, included 10x10, 6x6 and 4x4 truck chassis, and a 6x6 tractor.

ABOVE AND LEFT: **The Timoney independent suspension system is by double wishbones on each wheel, with twin variable-rate coil springs and concentric dampers. A version of this system was trialled on this 6x6 high-mobility cargo carrier produced by the British Defence Equipment Research Agency (DERA).**

Timoney 8x8

Type: Truck, cargo, 18-ton, 8x8
Manufacturer: Timoney High Mobility Vehicles; Navan, Co Meath
Production: 2000
Powerplant: Volvo D12A4220; six cylinders in-line; turbocharged diesel; water-cooled; 12,100cc; overhead valves; power output, 420bhp at 1,900rpm
Transmission: Automatic 6F2Rx2; cross-axle differential locks
Suspension: Independent at all eight wheels using double wishbones and twin variable-rate coil springs
Brakes: Air-pressure
Electrical system: 24V
Dimensions: Length – 9,155mm/360in
Width – 2,500mm/98in
Height – 3,200mm/125in
Wheelbase – 7,898mm/311in
Bogie centres – 1,524mm/60in
Weight: Unladen – 13,630kg/30,048lb
Payload – 18,370kg/40,498lb
Performance: Maximum speed – 105kph/65mph

ABOVE: **The Alfa-Romeo 430RE was effectively a medium version of the 800RE, with which it shared the same cab design. Although usually diesel-powered, this truck has been fitted with a wood-burning gas producer plant.** ABOVE LEFT: **The Alfa-Romeo 800RE was a 6$^{1}/_{2}$-ton standardized heavy truck produced between 1940 and 1944.**

Alfa-Romeo 800RE

Although best known for sporting motor cars, (much favoured by Benito Mussolini) the Italian manufacturer Alfa-Romeo first started producing trucks in 1930. The earliest designs were based on German designs by Büssing-NAG, but by the end of the decade the company had developed its own vehicles. Alfa-Romeo became a significant supplier of military vehicles to the Italian Army during World War II. The 800RE was

a 4x2 cargo truck introduced in 1940. It was allocated to the standardized 6$^{1}/_{2}$-ton "heavy" class (*Autocarro Unificato Pesante*), one of three standardized vehicle classes introduced in 1932 – light, medium and heavy – which laid down gross vehicle weights, payloads and basic dimensions.

Power came from an Alfa-Romeo six-cylinder diesel engine, driving the rear axle through a four-speed gearbox, together with a two-speed rear axle. Essentially a conventional road-going truck, it had live axles carried on semi-elliptical springs. Although the doors lacked windows, the all-steel cab and deep windscreen

were surprisingly modern in appearance for the period.

As well as the standard cargo variant, there was a fire appliance. The truck was also used as the basis for an experimental half-track conversion. There was also a medium version (430RE) of similar appearance.

The truck remained in production until 1944, and was reintroduced after the war in a slightly modernized form, notably with a window in the cab door. Designated CP48, it remained in production until 1950. Alfa-Romeo terminated truck production in 1967.

BELOW: **Most examples were fitted with a wooden cargo body, but there was also a fire tender variant. The chassis was also used for an experimental half-track conversion.**

Alfa-Romeo 800RE

Type: Truck, 6$^{1}/_{2}$-ton, cargo, 4x2

Manufacturer: Alfa-Romeo (Societa Anonima Lombarda Fabbrica Automobili); Milano

Production: 1940 to 1944, 1950

Powerplant: Alfa-Romeo AR800; six cylinders in-line; diesel; water-cooled; 8,725cc; overhead valves; power output, 108–115bhp at 2,000rpm

Transmission: 4F1Rx2; 4x2

Suspension: Live axles on semi-elliptical multi-leaf springs

Brakes: Air-assisted hydraulic

Electrical system: 12V

Dimensions: Length – 6,840mm/269in
Width – 2,350mm/93in
Height – tilt in place, 2,850mm/112in
Wheelbase – 3,800mm/150in

Weight: Unladen – 5,500kg/12,125lb
Payload – 6,500kg/14,330lb

Performance: Maximum speed – 65kph/40mph

Alfa-Romeo 1900M *Matta*, AR51, AR52

The prototype for the Alfa-Romeo *Matta* (Crazy) field car was produced in 1950 under the designation 1900R. It went into production from 1951 as the 1900M, in two variants –

the AR51 was intended for the Italian Army, the AR52 for the Air Force.

Typical of post-war Jeep-type utility vehicles, with steel doors, folding two-piece windscreen and hinged rear tailgate, the prototype resembled the British Land Rover. However, the four-cylinder twin-cam dry-sump engine was considerably more advanced than anything used by Land Rover. Independent front suspension was standard using torsion bars. The production vehicle used the same components of the prototype. Production ended in 1955 after some 2,200 had been built, 50 of which were sold to civilians.

LEFT: **The 1900M retained a post-war Jeep-like styling.**

**Alfa-Romeo 1900M
Matta, AR51, AR52**

Type: Truck, ¼-ton, utility, 4x4
Manufacturer: Alfa-Romeo (Societa Anonima Lombarda Fabbrica Automobili); Milano
Production: 1951 to 1955
Powerplant: Alfa-Romeo AR1307; four cylinders in-line; petrol; water-cooled; 1,884cc; overhead valves; power output, 65bhp at 4,500rpm
Transmission: 4F1Rx2; 4x2
Suspension: Independent suspension using wishbones and torsion bars at front; live axles on semi-elliptical multi-leaf springs at rear
Brakes: Hydraulic
Electrical system: 12V
Dimensions: Length – 3,520mm/139in
  Width – 1,575mm/62in
  Height – tilt in place, 1,820mm/72in
  Wheelbase – 2,200mm/87in
Weight: Unladen – 1,425kg/3,141lb
  Payload – 470kg/1,036lb
Performance: Maximum speed – 100kph/62mph

Fiat *Tipo* 508C *Militare*

The Italian company Fiat was established in 1899 and started to manufacture trucks in 1903, supplying the Italian Army during

the Italian–Turkish conflict in Libya in 1911 and World War I. The company remained a significant supplier of trucks of up to 6-ton capacity to the Italian forces during World War II. Among the smallest of these was the *Tipo* 508C *Militare*, a light truck which went into production in 1939, using the chassis of the 1937 Fiat Balilla 1100.

The steel bonnet and wings of the original Balilla were combined with

timber half-doors and a timber pick-up body rated for a 350kg/772lb payload. The running gear

ABOVE LEFT AND LEFT:

The 508C *Militare* was based on the Balilla 1100, which was also supplied as a canvas-topped staff car.

Fiat *Tipo* 508C *Militare*

Type: Truck, cargo, 4x2
Manufacturer: Fabbrica Italiana d'Automobili (Fiat); Torino
Production: 1939 to 1945
Powerplant: Fiat 108C; four cylinders in-line; petrol; water-cooled; 1,089cc; overhead valves; power output, 32bhp at 2,800rpm
Transmission: 4F1R; 4x2
Suspension: Independent at front; live axle at rear on semi-elliptical multi-leaf springs
Brakes: Hydraulic
Electrical system: 12V
Dimensions: Length – 4,005mm/158in
  Width – 1,510mm/59in
  Height – 2,150mm/85in
  Wheelbase – 1,920mm/76in
Weight: Unladen – 2,710kg/5,974lb
  Payload – 2,500kg/5,511lb
Performance: Maximum speed – 80kph/50mph

was all derived from the Balilla and included a 1,089cc four-cylinder engine and four-speed gearbox. Independent suspension was fitted at the front, combined with a live axle and semi-elliptical springs at the rear.

An extended wheelbase variant was produced under the designation *Tipo* 508 LRM.

LEFT: Rated for a 6-ton payload, the Fiat 665 was among the heaviest trucks used by the Italian Army. The 665NM was fitted with differential locks to improve off-road performance.

Fiat *Tipo* 665NL, 665NM

Produced by Fiat's truck division – Fiat Veicoli Industriali – which had been established in 1929, the *Tipo* 665 was a heavy road-going military cargo truck rated for a 5-ton payload. It entered service from 1942. Fitted with a forward-control steel cab it was a modern-looking vehicle, and was effectively a militarized version of the civilian *Tipo* 665 announced in 1939.

The truck was also produced with an armoured (*Blindato*) cab.

Like all of the *Tipo* 600 series trucks, power came from a 9,365cc six-cylinder diesel engine, driving the rear wheels through a four-speed main gearbox and two-speed auxiliary gearbox. A reduction gear was fitted between the clutch and gearbox. The suspension was by semi-elliptical

multi-leaf springs. In common with other Italian military vehicles, the cab was equipped with a right-hand driving position which was felt to be safer on narrow Alpine passes. The *Tipo* 665NL – the N suffix indicates *Nafta* (diesel fuel) – had steel cab doors with wind-up windows. The *Tipo* 665NM (*Nafta Militare*) had half doors and was fitted with a differential lock to improve performance on rough tracks.

Military production continued until 1944, although it would appear that the truck was built only in small numbers. There were many more examples produced of the militarized long-wheelbase *Tipo* 666, rated at 6 tons. This chassis was developed into the *Tipo* A10000 with a 10-ton payload in 1945.

The series was put back into production after the war for commercial customers and the cab remained standard on Fiat trucks until a new design was introduced in 1952. Fiat Veicoli Industriali merged with the German Klöckner-Humboldt-Deutz in 1974 and although the company continues to produce trucks, they are now badged Iveco. The Fiat name was dropped in 1982.

MIDDLE: **Production of the *Tipo* 665 continued in small numbers until 1944. The vehicle was put back into production after the war for the civilian market. The modern-looking all-steel cab remained a standard on Fiat trucks until a new design was introduced in 1952.**
LEFT: **The *Tipo* 665 was also produced with an armoured (*Blindato*) cab. Firing ports in the rear body suggest that this vehicle has been adapted for use as an armoured personnel carrier.**

Fiat *Tipo* 665NL, 665NM

Type: Truck, heavy, 5-ton, 4x2
Manufacturer: Fiat Veicoli Industriali; Torino
Production: 1942 to 1944
Powerplant: Fiat 365; six cylinders in-line; diesel; water-cooled; 9,365cc; overhead valves; power output, 110bhp at 2,200rpm
Transmission: 4F1Rx2; 4x2; differential lock on Tipo 665NM
Suspension: Live axles on semi-elliptical multi-leaf springs
Brakes: Air-pressure assisted hydraulic
Electrical system: 24V
Dimensions: Length – 7,095mm/279in
   Width – 2,670mm/105in
   Height – tilt in place, 3,210mm/126in
   Wheelbase – 3,760mm/148in
Weight: Unladen – 7,200kg/15,873lb
   Payload – road, 5,140kg/11,332lb;
   cross-country, 4,140kg/9,127lb
Performance: Maximum speed – 55kph/34mph

Fiat AR51, AR55, AR59 *Campagnola*

LEFT: Introduced in 1951, the military version of the Fiat *Campagnola* was designated AR51, and was produced especially for the Italian Army and the police service. The vehicle was typical of post-war efforts to improve on the US-built Jeep.

The Fiat *Campagnola* (Country) was a civilian multi-purpose utility vehicle very much in the mould of the World War II Jeep. Launched in 1951, the civilian variant was soon followed by the military AR51 *Autovettura da Ricognizione* (reconnaissance vehicle), which was produced especially for the

Italian Army. In 1955, the original AR51 was replaced by the improved AR55. The AR59, which was modified to conform with various NATO requirements, including the use of a 24V electrical system, followed in 1959.

Suspension at the front was independent using upper and lower wishbones with coil springs enclosed in an oil-bath housing. At the rear, there was a live axle on conventional multi-leaf semi-elliptical springs. The vehicle was powered by a four cylinder 1,901cc

petrol engine driving both axles through a four-speed gearbox and two-speed transfer box. In 1953, the civilian version was also made available with the option of a diesel engine. The original petrol-engined version was then identified as *Campagnola* A, while the diesel version was designated *Campagnola* B and C.

The body was typical of such vehicles, with a removable canvas cover and folding windscreen. The half-height steel doors could be secured in the open position, folded back against the body sides.

Alongside service with Italian forces, the vehicle was also exported, for example to Mexico, Venezuela and Bolivia, as well as various African countries. A licence-built version, the Zastava AR51, was produced in Yugoslavia.

BELOW: The Fiat *Campagnola* was originally introduced for civilian usage and was aimed at the market which had been developed by Land Rover and Jeep since the end of the war.

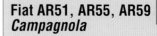

Fiat AR51, AR55, AR59 *Campagnola*

Type: Truck, ¼-ton, utility, 4x4
Manufacturer: Fabbrica Italiana d'Automobili (Fiat); Torino
Production: 1951 to 1959
Powerplant: Fiat 105B017; four cylinders in-line; petrol; water-cooled; 1,901cc; overhead valves; power output, 56–63bhp at 4,000rpm
Transmission: 4F1Rx2; part-time 4x4
Suspension: Independent front suspension using upper and lower wishbones and fully-enclosed coil springs in oil-bath housing; live axle at rear on semi-elliptical multi-leaf springs
Brakes: Hydraulic
Electrical system: 12V, (AR59) 24V
Dimensions: Length – 3,600mm/142in
Width – 1,570mm/62in
Height – tilt in place, 1,800mm/71in; minimum, 1,370mm/54in
Wheelbase – 2,250mm/89in
Weight: Unladen – 1,430kg/3,153lb
Payload – 487kg/1,074lb
Performance: Maximum speed – 100kph/62mph

Moto-Guzzi *Mulo Meccanico*

During the inter-war years and into World War II, the Italian Army made widespread use of commercial motor tricycles, typically the front end of a motorcycle attached to a two-wheeled rear sub-frame on which was mounted a cargo box. The narrow width made the machines particularly useful on the restricted roads of the Alpine passes.

In 1959, Moto-Guzzi started the design work for the ultimate purpose-designed military load-carrying tricycle, which was described as the *Mulo Meccanico* (Mechanical Mule).

Although the rider was presented with a steering wheel, which turned the front wheel through a reduction gearbox, rather than a pair of handlebars, the *Mulo Meccanico* was clearly derived from a motorcycle. The vehicle was assembled around a tubular-steel duplex frame and was powered by a 745cc V2 fan-cooled engine installed transversely beneath the saddle. The front suspension was by coil springs. The rear axle, on which the track was adjustable on the move between 1,300mm/51in and 850mm/33in, was carried on rubber-sprung trailing arms.

All three wheels were driven, through a six-speed gearbox. A torque-dividing locking differential at the centre split the power between the front and rear wheels (80 per cent rear, 20 per cent front). A locking differential on the cross-shaft and bevels translated the power to the separate rear wheels. The front wheel was shaft-driven through a bevelled box at the steering head. Demountable caterpillar tracks, which were tensioned by drop-down idler wheels, were available for the rear wheels.

A single front seat was mounted ahead of bodywork which housed the battery, fuel tank and spare wheel.

At the rear, there was a small load platform with a capacity of 500kg/1,102lb, which also included simple mudguards. Around 500 were built during 1961 and 1962.

Moto-Guzzi *Mulo Meccanico*

Type: Motor tricycle, cargo, 3x3
Manufacturer: Moto-Guzzi; Mandello del Lario
Production: 1961 to 1962
Powerplant: Moto-Guzzi; V2; petrol; forced air cooled; 745cc; overhead valves; power output, 20bhp at 5,500rpm
Transmission: 6F1R; 3x3; lockable differentials, front and rear
Suspension: Coil-sprung friction-damped front forks; trailing arms at rear with rubber suspension
Brakes: Hydraulic
Electrical system: 12V
Dimensions: Length – 3,000mm/117in
Width – maximum, 1,570mm/62in
Height – 1,420mm/56in
Wheelbase – 2,030mm/80in
Weight: Unladen – 1,000kg/2,200lb
Payload – 500kg/1,102lb
Performance: Maximum speed – 50kph/31mph

ABOVE: **With the rear tracks in place, the Moto Guzzi *Mulo Meccanico* provides wall-climbing performance.**

ABOVE: **All three wheels on the machine are driven. The rear track width can be adjusted on the move, between 1,300mm/51in and 850mm/33in.**

IVECO 320-45 WTM

LEFT: The Iveco 320-45 WTM tractor-truck was put into production in 1981 for use as a heavy equipment transporter to carry a Leopard, the Italian Army's main battle tank. At the time, it was the largest military vehicle built by IVECO.

In 1975, Magirus-Deutz and Fiat established the Industrial Vehicle Corporation (IVECO), a joint company headquartered in the Netherlands, to develop and manufacture trucks for the civilian and defence markets in competition with other leading world manufacturers such as Mercedes-Benz. The intention was that the heavy trucks would be produced in the former Fiat plant in Turin, while the medium and lighter vehicles were produced at the Magirus-Deutz plant in Ulm. The 320-45 WTM tractor-truck was prototyped in 1978 to satisfy an Italian Army requirement for a heavy equipment transporter to tow a semi-trailer carrying a Leopard main battle tank. The truck began to enter service in 1981 and, at the time, it was the largest IVECO military vehicle in production.

Powered by a 17,174cc V8 turbocharged diesel engine, the 320-45 WTM was described by the manufacturer as being suitable for transporting tanks up to 60 tons both on-road and across country. The engine was coupled to all six wheels through a torque converter, eight-speed gearbox and single-speed transfer box, the latter including a lockable torque divider. Suspension was by semi-elliptical leaf springs. The truck could be specified with single or twin rear wheels, and the rear axles were fitted with differential locks. Both open- and closed-cab and left- and right-hand drive versions were available. The open cab was fitted with a canvas top and was designed to allow the side windows to be removed and the screen to be folded forward. Two 20-ton winches were fitted behind the cab to assist with loading disabled or damaged tanks. The standard 60-ton four-axle semi-trailer was designed by OTO Melara and produced by Bartoletti. Magirus-Deutz left IVECO in 1980, and in 1986 IVECO merged with the truck division of Ford UK.

LEFT: The standard 60-ton semi-trailer was a four-axle design by OTO Melara. Production trailers were manufactured by Bartoletti. Two 20-ton capacity winches on the tractor were used to assist in loading and unloading disabled or damaged tanks.

IVECO 320-45 WTM

Type: Truck-tractor, heavy equipment, 60-ton, 6x6
Manufacturer: IVECO, Defence Vehicle Division; Bolzano
Production: 1981 to 2001
Powerplant: IVECO 8280.22; eight cylinders in V configuration; turbocharged diesel; water-cooled; 17,174cc; overhead valves; power output, 450bhp at 2,400rpm
Transmission: 8F1R; full-time 6x6; differential locks at rear
Suspension: Live axles on semi-elliptical multi-leaf springs
Brakes: Air-pressure
Electrical system: 24V
Dimensions: Length – 7,520mm/296in
Width – 2,775mm/109in
Height – 3,051mm/120in
Wheelbase – 3,600mm/142in
Bogie centres – 1,380mm/54in
Weight: Unladen – 15,400kg/33,950lb
Gross train weight – 93,420kg/205,525lb
Performance: Maximum speed – 65kph/40mph

OM *Tipo* 32, 35, 36, 37

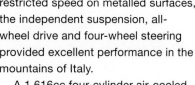

OM *Tipo* 32, 35, 36, 37

Type: Truck, light, 4x4
Manufacturer: Officine Meccaniche (OM);
   Brescia, Eritrea
Production: 1932 to 1937
Powerplant: OM; four cylinders in-line; petrol;
   air-cooled; 1,616cc; side valves;
   power output, 23bhp at 2,400rpm
Transmission: 4F1R, 4F1Rx2; full-time 4x4;
   lockable centre differential
Suspension: Independent suspension by parallel
   transverse semi-elliptical multi-leaf springs
Brakes: Mechanical
Electrical system: 6V
Dimensions: Length – 3,600mm/142in
   Width – 1,360mm/54in
   Height – tilt in place, 2,150mm/85in
   Wheelbase – 2,000mm/79in
Weight: Unladen – 1,615kg/3,535lb
   Payload – 800kg/1,764lb
Performance: Maximum speed – 50kph/31mph

Prototyped by Ansaldo and originally introduced in 1932 as the *Tipo* 32, the OM *Autocarretta da Montagne* (mountain vehicle) was an unusual forward-control short-wheelbase light truck. Although the solid tyres of the original model, combined with the use of an engine of less than 2,000cc, restricted speed on metalled surfaces, the independent suspension, all-wheel drive and four-wheel steering provided excellent performance in the mountains of Italy.

A 1,616cc four-cylinder air-cooled engine was permanently coupled to both axles incorporating a lockable differential through a four-speed gearbox. Independent suspension was fitted on all four wheels using transverse leaf springs. Development

LEFT: **A parade of *Autocarretta* 32s of the Italian Army in Abyssinia.**

continued through the life of the vehicle with improvements such as pneumatic tyres (*Tipo* 36M), electric lighting and auxiliary gearbox introduced into subsequent models, which were designated by the year of introduction.

Pavesi P4-100

Pavesi P4-100

Type: Tractor, heavy, artillery, 4x4
Manufacturer: Societa Ligure Piemontese
   Automobili (Fiat-SPA); Torino
Production: 1936 to 1942
Powerplant: Fiat P4/1; four cylinders in-line; petrol;
   water-cooled; 4,724cc; overhead valves; power
   output, 55bhp at 2,800rpm
Transmission: 4F1R; 4x4; locking differentials
Suspension: Live axles on semi-elliptical
   multi-leaf springs
Brakes: Mechanical
Electrical system: 6V
Dimensions: Length – 4,155mm/164in
   Width – 2,045mm/80in
   Height – 1,650mm/65in
   Wheelbase – 2,425mm/95in
Weight: Unladen – 4,800kg/10,582lb
   Payload – Not available
Performance: Maximum speed – 22kph/14mph

Designed by Ugo Pavians, the Pavesi P4 articulated agricultural tractor was first produced in 1914. Exceptional off-road abilities, and particularly a small turning circle assisted by articulated steering, made the vehicle ideal for military usage. The type was adopted by the Italian Army as an artillery tractor. In 1923, the Italian Army began trials for a high-performance artillery tractor. In June 1924, a heavy version of the P4 was ordered, with series production starting in 1926.

Three different models were deployed during World War II, both produced by Fiat-SPA. The TL-31 (L140) *Trattore Leggero* (light tractor), entered service with Italian artillery units in 1931–32. The P4-100 *Trattore Pesante* (heavy tractor) appeared in 1936, followed by the P4-110. At first, the P4-100 ran on dual solid tyres, but these were

LEFT: **The Pavesi P4-100 began life as an agricultural tractor.**

replaced by pneumatics in 1938. The Italian Army continued to experiment with the design, even building an armoured version. The Pavesi was trialled in Britain and was used by Bulgaria, Denmark and Finland.

SPA AS37

SPA AS37	
Type: Truck, light, 1- to 2-ton, 4x4	
Manufacturer: Societta Ligure Piemontese Automobili (Fiat-SPA); Torino	
Production: 1937 to 1948	
Powerplant: Fiat 18TL; four cylinders in-line; petrol; water-cooled; 4,053cc; side valves; power output, 57bhp at 2,000rpm	
Transmission: 5F1R; part-time 4x4; lockable centre differential	
Suspension: Independent front suspension using twin wishbone links and coil springs; live axle at rear on semi-elliptical springs	
Brakes: Mechanical	
Electrical system: 6V	
Dimensions: Length – 4,700mm/185in	
Width – 2,100mm/83in	
Height – 2,120mm/84in	
Wheelbase – 2,500mm/98in	
Weight: Unladen – 3,500kg/7,716lb	
Payload – 1,000kg/2,205lb	
Performance: Maximum speed – 80kph/50mph	

Societta Ligure Piemontese Automobili (SPA) started producing trucks in 1910 and was taken over by Fiat in 1925. In the years immediately following the takeover, Fiat produced lighter vehicles. SPA tended to concentrate on trucks with a payload rating above 5 tons.

Dating from 1937, the AS37 (*Autocarro Sahariano*) was a short-wheelbase, high-mobility truck for use in North Africa. Features included four-

ABOVE: **Production of the AS37 finally ended in 1948 after some 3,000 had been built.**

wheel drive and four-wheel steering together with independent front suspension using wishbones and coil springs. A 4,053cc four-cylinder petrol engine drove the wheels through a five-speed gearbox, with a lockable centre differential and separate drive-shafts to each wheel. The standard variant was

fitted with a 1-ton cargo body, and the chassis was also used as the TL37 – *Trattore Leggero* (artillery tractor), and as a self-propelled gun mount and desert reconnaissance vehicle.

SPA *Dovunque Tipo* 35

The *Autocarro Dovunque* ("go anywhere truck") was prototyped at the beginning of the 1930s and put into production at Fiat's SPA division in 1933 as the *Tipo* 33. Subsequent service proved that the design was underpowered and, in 1935, it was replaced by the improved *Tipo* 35, which remained in production until 1948.

The engine was a 4,053cc four-cylinder petrol unit, driving the rear wheels through a four-speed main gearbox and two-speed auxiliary box. The suspension was by rigid axles on semi-elliptical multi-leaf springs; a single spring was fitted transversely at the front, with inverted longitudinal springs at the rear. Early production used air-pressure brakes, but later models had hydraulic operation. Most were bodied as cargo vehicles, but other variants included an anti-aircraft gun mount and integral signals van.

SPA *Dovunque Tipo* 35	
Type: Truck, medium, 2- to 3-ton, 6x4	
Manufacturer: Societta Ligure Piemontese Automobili (Fiat-SPA); Torino	
Production: 1935 to 1948	
Powerplant: Fiat 18D; four cylinders in-line; petrol; air-cooled; 4,053cc; side valves; power output, 60bhp at 2,000rpm	
Transmission: 4F1Rx2; 6x4	
Suspension: Live axles on transverse semi-elliptical multi-leaf spring at front, longitudinal inverted springs at rear	
Brakes: Air-pressure or hydraulic	
Electrical system: 6V	
Dimensions: Length – 5,030mm/198in	
Width – 2,070mm/81in	
Height – tilt in place, 2,905mm/114in	
Wheelbase – 3,200mm/126in	
Bogie centres – 1,000mm/39in	
Weight: Unladen – 4,490kg/9,899lb	
Payload – 2,670kg/5,886lb	
Performance: Maximum speed – 50kph/31mph	

LEFT AND FAR LEFT: **The SPA *Tipo* 35 was the Italian Army's all-terrain vehicle – *Dovunque*.**

SPA *Dovunque Tipo* 41

The development of the SPA *Autocarro Dovunque Tipo* 41 started in 1941, with production taking place between 1942 and 1948. Rated for a 5- to 6-ton payload, the vehicle was described as a "medium" 6x6 truck, and was assembled using a large number of Fiat components.

The engine was a 9,365cc six-cylinder diesel unit, which gave the vehicle a top speed of 80kph/50mph on metalled

BELOW: **The *Tipo* 41 was also fitted with an open-topped artillery tractor body. This provided accommodation for the gun crew and space for stores, equipment and ammunition.**

surfaces. The engine was coupled to all six wheels through a five-speed gearbox and two-speed transfer box, with a reduction gear interposed between the clutch and the main gearbox. Lockable centre and axle differentials were also fitted to assist in cross-country performance. Front suspension was by a single transverse multi-leaf semi-elliptical spring; inverted longitudinal springs were used at the rear. In common with other *Dovunque* trucks, two free-running spare wheels were fitted to either side of the chassis, immediately behind the cab, to prevent the vehicle from grounding during ditch crossings.

Standard variants included a general-service load carrier and an open-topped artillery tractor. Both variants were fitted with a 6-ton capacity under-chassis winch. The standard cargo truck shared the same all-steel forward-control cab with other Fiat trucks built since 1939, although the radiator panel was different. In 1950, the *Dovunque Tipo* 41 was replaced by the uprated *Tipo* 50.

SPA *Dovunque* Tipo 41

Type: Truck, medium, 5- to 6-ton, 6x6
Manufacturer: Societta Ligure Piemontese Automobili (Fiat-SPA); Torino
Production: 1942 to 1948
Powerplant: Fiat 366; six cylinders in-line; diesel; water-cooled; 9,365cc; overhead valves; power output, 110bhp at 2,000rpm
Transmission: 5F1Rx2; part-time 6x6; lockable centre and axle differentials
Suspension: Live axle on transverse semi-elliptical multi-leaf spring at front, longitudinal inverted springs at rears
Brakes: Air-pressure assisted hydraulic
Electrical system: 6V
Dimensions: Length – 7,040mm/277in
  Width – 2,350mm/93in
  Height – tilt in place, 3,150mm/124in; minimum, 2,800mm/110in
  Wheelbase – 3,900mm/154in
  Bogie centres – 1,360mm/54in
Weight: Unladen – 9,210kg/20,304lb
  Payload – 5,270kg/11,618lb
Performance: Maximum speed – 80kph/50mph

Isuzu Type 94A (TU10)

ABOVE: **A captured Isuzu Type 94A in storage at the Aberdeen Proving Grounds in Maryland, USA.**

The name Isuzu was first used on the Type 94 military truck produced by Ishikawajima Dockyard & Engineering – the number indicates the year of its introduction (1934, or 2594 in the Japanese system). Ishikawajima had started building cars in 1918, and had been assembling Wolseley trucks for military use under licence since 1922. In 1933, Ishikawajima merged with the truck division of Dat Auto Manufacturing and, in 1937, merged with Tokyo Gas & Electric to form the Tokyo Jidosha Kogyo Group (TJKG). A new factory for manufacturing heavy trucks was constructed at Kawasaki in 1938, and the name Isuzu was subsequently applied to all of the vehicles produced by the TJKG.

Based heavily on European 6x4 truck designs of the mid-1930s, the Type 94 was developed to support the Japanese invasion of China. The truck was

produced in perhaps as many as 40 variants, including cargo truck, prime mover, refueller, aircraft-starting unit, searchlight truck and armoured car. The standard design used an open cab with a canvas top and steel half-doors, but there were also closed-cab variants, as well as short-wheelbase and forward-control designs. A 4x2 chassis was also produced which simply lacked the rear bogie.

Power for the Type 94A was provided by a 4,390cc six-cylinder side-valve engine, connected to the worm-drive rear axle(s) through a four-speed gearbox. Smaller numbers of the Type 94B were produced, equipped with a 4,800cc four-cylinder diesel engine. For both models, live axles were suspended on semi-elliptical springs, inverted at the rear.

The truck was also manufactured under other names, and subsequently

supplied under a "subsidy" scheme to civilian users as the TU10, when it was rated for a 3-ton load.

Isuzu Type 94A (TU10)

Type: Truck, 1½-ton, cargo, 6x4
Manufacturer: Tokyo Jidosha Kogyo; Tokyo
Production: 1934 to 1945
Powerplant: Isuzu XA; six cylinders in-line; petrol; water-cooled; 4,390cc; side valves; power output, 70bhp at 2,800rpm
Transmission: 4F1R; 6x4
Suspension: Live axles on semi-elliptical multi-leaf springs, inverted at rear
Brakes: Mechanical
Electrical system: 12V
Dimensions: Length – 5,430mm/214in
  Width – 2,500mm/77in
  Height – 2,680mm/106in
  Wheelbase – 3,550mm/140in
  Bogie centres – 1,100mm/43in
Weight: Unladen – 3,400kg/7,496lb
  Payload – 1,900kg/4,189lb
Performance: Maximum speed – 60kph/37mph

Nihon Nainenki Kurogane

**Nihon Nainenki
Kurogane**

Type: Car, light, 4x4
Manufacturer: Nihon Nainenki; Tokyo
Production: 1935 to 1944
Powerplant: Nihon Nainenki; two cylinders in V-formation; petrol; air-cooled; 1,399cc; overhead valves; power output, 33bhp at 3,300rpm
Transmission: 3F1R; part-time 4x4
Suspension: Independent front suspension, using wishbones and coil springs; live axle at rear using semi-elliptical multi-leaf springs
Brakes: Mechanical, rear wheels only
Electrical system: 12V
Dimensions: Length – 3,550mm/140in
Width – 1,250mm/49in
Height – 1,500mm/59in
Wheelbase – 2,000mm/79in
Weight: Unladen – 1,060kg/2,337lb
Payload – 190kg/419lb
Performance: Maximum speed – 80kph/50mph

The smallest of the Imperial Army's staff cars during World War II, and the only entirely Japanese product, the small Type 95 Kurogane was designed by Tetsushi Makita. A lightweight 4x4 open-bodied reconnaissance vehicle, it was the first all-wheel-drive vehicle produced in Japan. As with all Japanese military vehicles, the

ABOVE: **The Kurogane was the most widely used vehicle of its type in the Japanese Imperial Army. The total produced was some 4,800. There were several body types, including a small truck.**

designation "Type 95" indicated the year of development, in this case 1935 (2595 in the Japanese system).

Power came from a V-twin magneto-ignition air-cooled petrol engine, with a three-speed gearbox and single-speed transfer box. The suspension was independent at the front by double wishbones and coil springs, with a live axle at the rear on semi-elliptical springs.

Mitsubishi Type 73 Kogata

**Mitsubishi Type 73
Kogata**

Type: Truck, cargo, 1¹/₂-ton, 4x4
Manufacturer: Mitsubishi Motors; Tokyo
Production: 1996 to date
Powerplant: Mitsubishi 4M40; four cylinders in-line; turbocharged diesel; water-cooled; 2,835cc; overhead valves; power output, 125bhp at 4,000rpm
Transmission: 4F1Rx2 automatic; part-time 4x4; lockable centre differential
Suspension: Live axles on coil springs; double-acting telescopic shock absorbers
Brakes: Hydraulic with vacuum-servo assistance
Electrical system: 24V
Dimensions: Length – 4,140mm/163in
Width – 1,765mm/69in
Height – tilt in place, 1,970mm/78in
Wheelbase – 2,420mm/95in
Weight: Unladen – 1,940kg/4,277lb
Payload – 1,500kg/3,307lb
Performance: Maximum speed – 105kph/65mph

Mitsubishi Shipbuilding & Engineering Company had started to build trucks during the 1920s. During World War II, the company built tanks, ships and armaments. In 1950, under US control, the company was split into three – Mitsubishi Shipbuilding & Engineering Company, Mitsubishi Heavy Industries (Reorganized), and Mitsubishi Nippon Heavy Industries, the latter continuing to build Mitsubishi Fuso trucks. Mitsubishi Motors was formed in 1970 from the automotive division of Mitsubishi Heavy Industries.

Originally introduced in 1973, the first Type 73s, known as Kyus in Japanese, were based on the Jeep CJ3B that Mitsubishi had been producing under licence since 1953. The current Kogata variant was introduced in 1996 and is derived from the Mitsubishi Pajero. It is powered by a 2,835cc four-cylinder diesel engine, driving all four wheels through a four-speed automatic transmission

LEFT: **The Type 73 is used by the Japanese Self Defense Force. Earlier versions were supplied to the Philippines, Burma and South Vietnam.**

and two-speed transfer box, with a lockable centre differential. Suspension is by coil springs and dampers.

Nissan 4W73 Carrier

Type: Truck, ³/₄-ton, cargo, 4x4
Manufacturer: Nissan Motor Company; Yokohama
Production: 1959 on
Powerplant: Nissan P; six cylinders in-line; petrol;
    water-cooled; 3,956cc; overhead valves;
    power output, 125–140bhp at 3,200rpm
Transmission: 4F1R; part-time 4x4
Suspension: Live axles on semi-elliptical multi-leaf
    springs; double-acting hydraulic shock
    absorbers
Brakes: Hydraulic
Electrical system: 24V
Dimensions: Length – 4,770mm/188in
    Width – 2,045mm/81in
    Height – 2,320mm/85in
    Wheelbase – 2,800mm/110in
Weight: Unladen – 2,730kg/6,018lb
    Payload – road, 1,500kg/3,307lb;
    cross-country, 840kg/1,852lb
Performance: Maximum speed – 90kph/56mph

Nissan 4W73 Carrier

The Nissan Motor Company can trace its origins back to 1912 when Masujiro Hashimoto established the Kwaishinsha Motor Works and built the Dat light car. In 1925, Kwaishinsha changed its name to the Dat Motor Company and, following more than one subsequent change of ownership, was finally renamed Nissan in 1933. The company's first trucks were manufactured in 1937.

In 1958, Nissan developed the 4W72, a ³/₄-ton 4x4 short-wheelbase truck

intended for the Japanese Self Defense Force. It was initially based on the Dodge WC52 weapons carrier. The more-powerful 4W73 followed in 1959, taking its body cues from the post-war Dodge M37. Where the 4W72 had been powered by a 3,670cc four-cylinder side-valve engine of the contemporary Nissan Patrol, in the 4W73, this was replaced by a 3,956cc overhead-valve engine with power output subsequently increased from 125bhp to 140bhp. There was also

a diesel-engined version designated 4W73(U). The engine was coupled to a four-speed gearbox and single-speed transfer box. The live axles were suspended on semi-elliptical springs with dampers.

As well as the weapons carrier, standard variants included an integral-bodied ambulance and a fire vehicle. Both variants were also available commercially under the name "Carrier". A version of the 4W73 was built under licence in India at the Jabalpur Ordnance Factory. Similar vehicles were also produced by Toyota.

ABOVE: **Clearly based on the design of the Dodge WC series of World War II, also the post-war Dodge M37 and "Power Wagon". The 4W73 was produced as a weapons carrier, integral-bodied ambulance and a fire tender. An optional front-mounted winch was available.** RIGHT: **The 4W73 was introduced in 1959, and was available on the civilian market as the "Carrier". A version was built under licence in India.**

LEFT: **Post-war DAF military vehicles were part funded by US aid and, for this reason, were powered by US-built Hercules engines. Unusual features included World War II type free-running spare wheels and independent torsion-bar front suspension.**

DAF YA328

DAF had already started work on a range of innovative-design military vehicles in 1949–50. One of the first vehicles to appear was the 3-ton YA318 6x6, approved for production in 1952. Some 300 examples were built before it was decided that it was underpowered. It was superseded by the improved YA328 in 1952, with the vehicles coming off the production line in 1953.

Although manufactured at DAF's Eindhoven factory, the vehicle was partly the product of the post-war Marshall Plan that had sought to re-establish the

BELOW: **The artillery tractor (above) was the first variant to be produced. Other types included a 3-ton cargo truck, fire/crash tender (below), also an aviation oil-service truck for the Air Force.**

shattered European economies. For this reason, it was powered by a Hercules six-cylinder engine. A JXC unit, with a four-speed gearbox was used in the original YA318, and the more-powerful JXLD, together with a five-speed gear box, in the YA328.

Unusually for a soft-skin vehicle, the drive-line was laid out in an H pattern, with a centrally mounted transfer box and differential from which individual drive-shafts transferred the power to worm-gear casings at the wheels. Suspension was independent on all six wheels, using trailing arms and torsion bars at the front, with a walking beam and leaf springs at the rear.

The artillery tractor was the first to enter production, but the most common variant

was the 3-ton cargo truck. There was also a fire/crash tender (YC328), and an aircraft oil-service truck (YF318). Modifications to the cargo vehicle included anti-aircraft gun mount, workshop, mobile store, crane truck, communications vehicles and field canteens among others.

Production continued until 1958–59, by which time DAF had delivered around 4,825 vehicles. Three hundred were the YA318, (210 artillery tractors and 90 others). A total of 4,525 of the YA328 variant were built.

The vehicles remained in service until the mid-1970s, when disposals began. Nevertheless, many were used for a further two decades by which time vehicle performance was becoming outdated. It was planned that 600 would be upgraded by replacing the JXLD with a White G-3000 overhead-valve petrol engine, with a 15 per cent power increase. For some reason, the modification was not a success and was abandoned after only a few vehicles had been converted in 1976.

DAF YA328

Type: Truck, 3-ton, cargo, 6x6
Manufacturer: Van Doorne's Automobielfabriek (DAF); Eindhoven
Production: 1953 to 1959
Powerplant: Hercules JXLD; six cylinders in-line; 5,556cc; petrol; water-cooled; side valves; power output, 131bhp at 3,200rpm
Transmission: 5F1Rx2; part-time 6x6
Suspension: Independent front suspension using parallel trailing arms and transverse torsion bars; walking-beam rear suspension using parallel arms and semi-elliptical multi-leaf springs; telescopic hydraulic shock absorbers
Brakes: Vacuum hydraulic
Electrical system: 24V
Dimensions: Length – 6,130mm/241in
    Width – 2,400mm/95in
    Height – 2,650mm/104in
    Wheelbase – 3,400mm/134in
    Bogie centres – 1,300mm/52in
Weight: Unladen – 6,140kg/13,536lb
    Payload – 3,000kg/6,614lb
Performance: Maximum speed – 80kph/50mph

DAF YA126

Dating from 1952, the DAF YA126 was a 1-ton 4x4 cargo vehicle designed to replace the Dodge WC Series, many of which had been supplied to the Dutch Army. Like the larger YA328, it was powered by a US-built Hercules six-cylinder engine and production was partly funded with US money from the Marshall Plan.

Suspension was independent on all four wheels, using trailing arms and torsion bars. The drive-line was laid out in an H pattern, using a centrally mounted transfer box and differential with longitudinal drive-shafts running to worm-gear casings at the wheel stations. Some examples were fitted with a 2½-ton horizontal-spindle winch mounted between the chassis rails at the rear and driven by a power take-off from the gearbox.

DAF YA126	
Type: Truck, 1-ton, cargo, 4x4	
Manufacturer: Van Doorne's Automobielfabriek (DAF); Eindhoven	
Production: 1952 to 1960	
Powerplant: Hercules JXC; six cylinders in-line; 4,620cc; petrol; water-cooled; overhead inlet valves, side exhaust; power output, 102bhp at 3,200rpm	
Transmission: 4F1Rx2; part-time 4x4	
Suspension: Independent at all four wheels by means of trailing arms suspended on lateral torsion bars; hydraulic double-acting shock absorbers	
Brakes: Vacuum hydraulic	
Electrical system: 24V	
Dimensions: Length – 4,550mm/179in	
Width – 2,100mm/83in	
Height – 2,180mm/86in	
Wheelbase – 2,830mm/111in	
Weight: Unladen – 3,400kg/7,496lb	
Payload – 1,000kg/2,205lb	
Performance: Maximum speed – 84kph/52mph	

Production continued until 1960, and most of the 7,200 produced were bodied for the cargo (weapons carrier) role.

LEFT: **The DAF YA126 only saw service with the Dutch Army.**

DAF YT514

Introduced in 1961, the 5-ton DAF YT514 was a militarized version of the standard civilian-type DS256 road tractor. With the flat-panelled soft-top cab and folding windscreen, it was clearly a product of the same thinking which had produced other post-war DAF military trucks. The cab was the same as fitted to the YA314 and YA324.

The YT514 was a multi-terrain truck designed for use with the DAF YF101 and YAF1014 fuel tankers, together with a range of other standardized military semi-trailers. Power came from a DAF six-cylinder supercharged diesel engine

BELOW: **A DAF YT514 with a standardized Dutch Army military-pattern semi-trailer.**

DAF YT514	
Type: Truck, 5-ton, tractor, 4x4	
Manufacturer: Van Doorne's Automobielfabriek (DAF); Eindhoven	
Production: 1961 to 1966	
Powerplant: DAF DS575; six cylinders in-line; 5,750cc; supercharged diesel; water-cooled; overhead valves; power output, 165bhp at 2,400rpm	
Transmission: 5F1Rx2; part-time 4x4	
Suspension: Live axles on semi-elliptical multi-leaf springs	
Brakes: Air pressure	
Electrical system: 24V	
Dimensions: Length – 6,130mm/241in	
Width – 2,350mm/92in	
Height – tilt in place, 2,620mm/103in; minimum, 2,090mm/82in	
Wheelbase – 3,580mm/141in	
Weight: Unladen – 5,200kg/11,464lb	
Gross train weight – 36,650kg/80,798lb	
Performance: Maximum speed – 80kph/50mph	

driving both axles through a five-speed gearbox and two-speed transfer box. Suspension was by semi-elliptical springs at the front and rear.

LEFT: **Although very similar to the US-built CJ5 and military M38A1, the NEKAF can be identified by its smaller headlamps and by the small reflectors mounted on the front wing panels.**

NEKAF M38A1 (MD)

Between 1951 and 1953, the Dutch Army had purchased around 600 Willys CJ3A Jeeps. However, the Army also had more than 3,000 war-surplus Jeeps. To replace these, they had tested the DAF YA054, Willys CJ3B, Land Rover, French Delahaye VLR-D and Fiat AR59 *Campagnola*. A prototype of the US-built M422 "Mighty Mite" was also trialled. The DAF was the obvious choice, but production could not be approved because US funding was not available. The CJ3B was selected as second choice and an order for 2,000 issued in 1953. A year later, this order was cancelled when the US State Department agreed to approve assembly of the Willys M38A1 (or MD) Jeep in the Netherlands.

The M38A1 had been introduced as a replacement for the MC (M38) in 1952, with the almost identical civilian CJ5 and the military equivalent, the CJ5M, following in 1954. Although the CJ5M was available to qualifying nations under the Marshall Aid Plan, the Dutch Army preferred the original military M38A1 and it was agreed that production would be undertaken by Rotterdam-based Nederlandse Kaiser-Frazer Fabrieken (NEKAF). The company had been building Kaiser cars in the Netherlands since 1947, as well as the CJ3B, some of which had already been supplied to the Dutch Air Force.

A contract for 4,000 vehicles was awarded to NEKAF in January 1955, with the first M38A1 to be delivered in May of

that year. All of the major components were supplied from the USA. Dutch content was restricted to tyres, electrical equipment and upholstery, which comprised 25 per cent.

The NEKAF version was little more than the US-built M38A1 with changes made to comply with Dutch traffic regulations; for example, white reflectors were attached to the front wing panels, and flashing indicator signals were mounted to the body sides. Blackout lights were fitted to the grille. Like the original, the vehicle was powered by a Willys Hurricane four-cylinder engine, driving live axles through a three-speed gearbox and two-speed transfer box. Suspension was by semi-elliptical leaf springs.

The total number manufactured by NEKAF was 5,674, under three contracts. After the NEKAF contracts were complete, a further 2,237 were constructed, during 1959–63, by Kemper & Van Twist of Dordrecht. The vehicles remained in service with the Dutch Army from 1955 into the late 1990s.

LEFT: **In 1955, production of the NEKAF M38A1 started in Rotterdam. A total of 7,911 were built over a nine-year period. By the time production came to an end in 1963, 25 per cent of the vehicle was assembled from Dutch components.**

NEKAF M38A1 (MD)

Type: Truck, $^1/_4$-ton, utility, 4x4
Manufacturer: Nederlandse Kaiser-Frazer Fabrieken (NEKAF); Rotterdam. Kemper & Van Twist; Dordrecht
Production: 1955 to 1963
Powerplant: Willys Hurricane; four cylinders in-line; 5,556cc; petrol; water-cooled; side inlet valves, overhead exhaust; power output, 72bhp at 4,000rpm
Transmission: 3F1Rx2; part-time 4x4
Suspension: Live axles on semi-elliptical multi-leaf springs; telescopic hydraulic shock absorbers
Brakes: Hydraulic
Electrical system: 24V
Dimensions: Length – 3,510mm/138in
  Width – 1,550mm/61in
  Height – 1,900mm/75in
  Wheelbase – 2,060mm/81in
Weight: Unladen – 1,225kg/2,700lb
  Payload – road, 544kg/1,199lb; cross-country, 363kg/800lb
Performance: Maximum speed – 90kph/56mph

FSC Lublin L-51

In 1950, FSC was established in the Polish town of Lublin to produce Soviet trucks under licence for the Polish Army. The company's first product was the 2½-ton L-51, the

first of which was completed on November 7, 1951.

The L-51 was based on the GAZ-51, the design of which dated back to 1938, although it did not enter production in the Soviet Union until 1946. It was widely used in most Soviet Bloc countries, both for military and civilian use. The L-51 was identical in almost every respect, and used the same 3,485cc six-cylinder engine as the Soviet original, driving the twinned rear wheels through a four-speed gearbox. Suspension was by means of conventional semi-elliptical leaf springs. As well as a fabricated-timber cargo body, a six-stretcher ambulance was also produced.

FSC Lublin L-51	
Type: Truck, 2½-ton, cargo, 4x2	
Manufacturer: Fabryka Samochodów Ciężarowych (FSC); Lublin	
Production: 1951 to 1959	
Powerplant: FSC; six cylinders in-line; petrol; water-cooled; 3,485cc; side valves; power output, 70bhp at 2,800rpm	
Transmission: 4F1Rx2; 4x2	
Suspension: Live axles on semi-elliptical multi-leaf springs	
Brakes: Hydraulic	
Electrical system: 12V	
Dimensions: Length – 5,550mm/219in	
Width – 2,200mm/87in	
Height – 2,150mm/85in	
Wheelbase – 3,300mm/130in	
Weight: Unladen – 2,710kg/5,974lb	
Payload – 2,500kg/5,511lb	
Performance: Maximum speed – 73kph/45mph	

LEFT: **An FSC Lublin L-51 fitted with the standard timber-type cargo body.**

Polski-Fiat 508/518 Mazur

Polski-Fiat was established in Warsaw in 1932 following an agreement between the Polish and Italian governments. The company's first product was a version of the Fiat Balilla, slightly re-engineered by Zygmunt Okolow, and assembled from knocked-down kits.

BELOW: **A 518 with canvas covers erected. Note the side-mounted anti-grounding revolving spare wheel.**

In 1935, a licence was granted for the new Fiat 508, with practically the complete vehicle produced in Poland.

The 508/518 Mazur was a specialized military vehicle using components of both the Ballila 508 and the *Ardita* 518. The original engine was a 1,758cc unit but, in 1937, was replaced by the more powerful 1,994cc of the Fiat *Ardita* (Daring). Drive was through a four-speed gearbox with optional auxiliary gear. Rotating spare

wheels were fitted to help prevent bellying on ditch crossings. The rear axle was fitted with a differential lock.

Some 400 were produced between 1935 and 1939, with variants including a field car, radio van, telephone line layer, pick up and an artillery tractor for anti-tank guns.

Polski-Fiat 508/518 Mazur	
Type: Truck, light, 4x2	
Manufacturer: Polski-Fiat (PZInz); Warsaw	
Production: 1935 to 1939	
Powerplant: Fiat/PZInz 118A or 157; four cylinders in-line; petrol; water-cooled; 1,758cc or 1,944cc; side valves; power output, 36–45bhp at 3,600rpm	
Transmission: 4F1R plus auxiliary gear; 4x2	
Suspension: Live axles on semi-elliptical multi-leaf springs	
Brakes: Hydraulic	
Electrical system: 12V	
Dimensions: Length – 3,695mm/145in	
Width – 1,580mm/62in	
Height – 1,870mm/74in	
Wheelbase – 2,300mm/100in	
Weight: Unladen – 1,500kg/3,307lb	
Payload – 400kg/882lb	
Performance: Maximum speed – 100kph/62mph	

GAZ-64, 67, 67B

Work on designing the GAZ-64 started in February 1941. The vehicle was based on the four-wheel drive chassis of the GAZ-61 and powered by a licence-built version of the Ford Model A four-cylinder engine, identical to that used in the GAZ-AA truck. The vehicle was little more than a pre-production prototype, designed over a very short timescale by Vitaliy Grachev. Nevertheless, the GAZ-64 was the Soviet Union's first attempt at building an off-road vehicle in the style of the Jeep, thousands of which had been supplied to the Red Army under the Lend-Lease arrangements.

The open bodywork, of decidedly crude appearance, was clearly derived from the Jeep. However, the resemblance ended there because, although part-time four-wheel drive was included in the design, there were no low-ratio gears. Out-of-date features such as the mechanical brakes and front quarter-elliptical springs must have seriously restricted performance when compared to the original. Live axles were fitted at front and rear, the latter suspended on more conventional semi-elliptical springs. Special 6.50-16 tyres were developed for the vehicle, but shortages often led to road tyres being used. This further reduced the off-road performance.

The first vehicle was assembled in just 51 days before being turned over to the Red Army for trials. Production started in August 1941, with just 646 having been built by the summer of 1942 when it was superseded by the improved GAZ-67. This was followed, soon after, by the wider-tracked and more-powerful GAZ-67B.

There were no variants, but the GAZ BA-64 armoured car was built on the chassis of the original GAZ-64, while the chassis of the GAZ-67B was used for the BA-64B armoured car.

The design remained in production until 1953, by which time a total of 63,489 had been built of all three types. The vehicle was used by the Soviet Union and by a number of Soviet satellite states.

GAZ-64, 67, 67B

Type: Car, 4 seat, 4x4
Manufacturer: Gorkiy Auto Zavod; Gorkiy
Production: 1941 to 1953
Powerplant: GAZ-M1; four cylinders in-line; petrol; water-cooled; 3,285cc; side valves; power output, 50bhp at 2,800rpm (54bhp for GAZ-67B)
Transmission: 4F1R; part-time 4x4
Suspension: Live axles on quarter-elliptical multi-leaf springs at front, semi-elliptical at rear; single- or double-acting hydraulic shock absorbers
Brakes: Mechanical
Electrical system: 6V
Dimensions: Length – 3,350mm/132in
Width – 1,685mm/66in
Height – tilt in place, 1,700mm/67in; minimum, 1,300mm/51in
Wheelbase – 2,100mm/83in
Weight: Unladen – 1,200kg/2,645lb
Payload – 400kg/882lb
Performance: Maximum speed – 75kph/47mph

ABOVE: **In 1934, an improved version of the the GAZ-AA 6x4 entered service, designated GAZ-AAA. At the same time, ZIS produced an almost identical ZIS-6. The vehicles are carrying multiple machine-gun anti-aircraft mounts.** LEFT: **The GAZ-AA was a licence-built version of a US 1930 Ford Model AA. The Ford Motor Company assisted GAZ with the design of the factory and production line. The GAZ-AA remained in production until 1938.**

GAZ-AA, AAA	

Type: Truck, 1½-ton, cargo, 4x4; truck, 2-ton, cargo, 6x4
Manufacturer: Gorkiy Auto Zavod; Gorkiy
Production: 1932 to 1943
Powerplant: GAZ-A or GAZ-M1; four cylinders in-line; 3,285cc; petrol; water-cooled; side valves; power output, 40–50bhp at 2,800rpm
Transmission: 4F1Rx2; 4x2 or 6x4
Suspension: Live axles on semi-elliptical multi-leaf springs, cantilevered at the rear
Brakes: Mechanical
Electrical system: 6V
Dimensions: Length – 5,335mm/210in
     Width – 2,040mm/80in
     Height – 1,970mm/121in
     Wheelbase – GAZ-AA, 3,340mm/131in; GAZ-AAA, 3,200mm/118in
     Bogie centres – GAZ-AAA, 940mm/37in
Weight: Unladen – GAZ-AA, 1,810kg/3,990lb; GAZ-AAA, 2,475kg/5,456lb
     Payload – GAZ-AA, 1,700kg/3,748lb; GAZ-AAA, 2,200kg/4,850lb
Performance: Maximum speed – 70kph/44mph

GAZ-AA, AAA

The GAZ-AA was a 1½-ton 4x2 road-going cargo truck which went into production at the Soviet Gorkiy Auto Zavod motor plant in 1932. It was effectively a licence-built copy of the 1930 Ford Model AA. The Ford company had provided assistance with designing the factory and the production line. In 1934, the GAZ-AA was joined by an upgraded 6x4 variant, GAZ-AAA – also known as GAZ-3A or GAZ-Timken – which was fitted with a Timken-designed tandem-drive rear bogie. This allowed the payload to be increased to 2,032kg/4,480lb. Prototypes for the latter, which had no US equivalent, were assembled by the Soviet NAMI (National Automobile Research Institute) and in the workshops of the Soviet Army.

In both trucks, the engine was a Soviet-built version of the 3,285cc Ford four-cylinder side-valve unit, upgraded in 1936 to give an additional 10bhp. Drive to the rear wheels was through a four-speed gearbox, with a two-speed auxiliary box on the 6x4 variant. The rear axles were of the worm-drive type, and all axles were suspended on semi-elliptical springs. The rear wheels were twinned. The brakes on the vehicle were mechanically operated.

Alongside the basic drop-side cargo truck, standard variants included communications vehicle, searchlight mount, recovery vehicle, anti-aircraft gun mount, bus and command vehicle.

The GAZ-AA remained in production until 1938. The GAZ-AAA survived until 1943 by which time the factory had

produced 37,373. A low-cost utility variant of the AAA was produced between 1941 and 1943 which had a simplified front, no front bumper, one headlamp, no front brakes and single rear wheels.

LEFT: The GAZ-69 replaced the GAZ-67B in 1952. In 1956, the production line was moved to Ulyanovsk, when the vehicle became known as the UAZ-69. The vehicle is powered by a 2,438cc four-cylinder water-cooled petrol engine.

GAZ-69, UAZ-69

In 1952, the GAZ-69 field car was introduced to replace the wartime GAZ-67B. At first production took place at the Molotov plant of Gorkiy Auto Zavod but, in December 1954, Ulyanovsk Auto Zavod also began to assemble the vehicle, using parts supplied by GAZ. In the summer of 1956, the entire production line was moved to Ulyanovsk, at which time the designation officially became UAZ-69.

Standard variants included a four-door field car, identified as GAZ-69A or UAZ-69A, and a two-door cargo vehicle, designated simply GAZ-69 or UAZ-69. There was also a modification allowing it to be used as a launch vehicle for the Soviet *Schmel* wire-guided anti-tank missile.

The open-topped cargo or five-seat bodywork was typical of a field car or utility vehicle of the period. It was a robust and simple vehicle, powered by a 2,112cc four-cylinder side-valve engine, driving both axles through a three-speed gearbox and two-speed transfer box. The primitive quarter-elliptical springs of the earlier GAZ-67 were replaced by semi-elliptics. In 1957, a more powerful 2,438cc engine producing an additional 10bhp was fitted. The designation was amended by the use of an "M" suffix, for example GAZ-69AM.

By 1959, the vehicle was being exported to more than 22 countries across the world and was widely used by the Red Army and other nations within the Soviet Bloc. Production continued into the early 1970s, when it was replaced by the improved UAZ-469. A four-speed variant designated M461 was produced by MICM-UMM in Romania.

LEFT: By 1959, the GAZ/UAZ-69 had been exported to more than 22 countries across the world and was widely used by the Red Army and by other Warsaw Pact nations. This example has been equipped as a communications vehicle for the East German Army.

GAZ-69, UAZ-69

Type: Truck, cargo, 4x2

Manufacturer: Gorkiy Auto Zavod; Gorkiy. Ulyanovsk Auto Zavod; Ulyanovsk

Production: 1952 to 1971

Powerplant: GAZ-69B/UAZ-69B; four cylinders in-line; petrol; water-cooled; 2,112cc (GAZ-69A/UAZ-69A), 2,438cc (UAZ-69AM); side valves; power output, 55–68bhp at 3,800rpm

Transmission: 3F1Rx2; part-time 4x4

Suspension: Live axles on semi-elliptical multi-leaf springs

Brakes: Mechanical

Electrical system: 12V

Dimensions: Length – 3,850mm/152in
Width – 1,750mm/69in
Height – tilt in place, 1,950mm/112in
Wheelbase – 2,300mm/91in

Weight: Unladen – 1,535kg/3,384lb
Payload – 425kg/937lb

Performance: Maximum speed – 95kph/59mph

GAZ-46

ABOVE: **The GAZ-46 was an almost identical copy of the US-built Ford GPA.**

The Soviet Army used large numbers of Ford GPA amphibians during World War II. Between 1944 and 1945, after US production had ceased, GAZ produced a licence-built version designated GAZ-011, which used the engine, transmission and components of the GAZ-67B.

After the war, the GAZ-46, a larger version of the GAZ-011, was developed using the engine and transmission of the GAZ/UAZ-69. Like the GPA, the vehicle had a welded-steel hull with a steeply raked bow and sloped rear to aid entry and exit from rivers. A folding windscreen was fitted across the foredeck and a canvas roof could be erected over the crew compartment. The hull provided seating for five. Power was provided by a four-cylinder engine installed immediately above the front

axle, driving either the wheels, or a small three-blade propeller, via a three-speed gearbox and two-speed transfer box. Suspension was by semi-elliptical springs. Production started in 1952 and was terminated around 1956.

GAZ-46

Type: Car, 5-seat, amphibious, 4x4
Manufacturer: Gorkiy Auto Zavod; Gorkiy
Production: 1952 to 1956
Powerplant: GAZ-69B; four cylinders in-line; petrol; water-cooled; 2,112cc; side valves; power output, 55bhp at 2,800rpm
Transmission: 3F1Rx2; part-time 4x4; selectable propeller drive
Suspension: Live axles on semi-elliptical multi-leaf springs
Brakes: Hydraulic
Electrical system: 24V
Dimensions: Length – 4,930mm/194in
Width – 1,735mm/68in
Height – tilt in place, 1,790mm/70in
Wheelbase – 2,300mm/91in
Weight: Unladen – 1,850kg/4,078lb
Payload – 400kg/822lb
Performance: Maximum speed – on land, 83kph/52mph; in water, 10kph/6mph

GAZ-39371 Vodnik

Nicknamed Vodnik, the GAZ-39371 is an amphibious four-wheel drive high-mobility multi-purpose vehicle developed from the GAZ-2975 Tigr. The hull is of welded construction and is made up of separate front and rear modules. The front contains the power

unit and driving position. The rear, which is interchangeable, allows the vehicle to be used for different roles, for example as a passenger-carrying vehicle with seats for up to ten personnel, or as a cargo vehicle.

Power comes from a mid-mounted GAZ six-cylinder diesel engine driving through a five-speed gearbox. Other engine options include Caterpillar 3114, JaMZ-460 or HINO JO7C diesels. Suspension is independent on all four wheels

LEFT: **A civilian version of the Vodnik is available under the designation GAZ-3937.**

GAZ-39371 Vodnik

Type: Truck, cargo/personnel, amphibious, 1½- to 2½-ton, 4x4
Manufacturer: Gorkiy Auto Zavod; Gorkiy
Production: 1999 on
Powerplant: GAZ-562; six cylinders in-line; turbocharged diesel; water-cooled; 6,230cc; side valves; power output, 55bhp at 2,800rpm
Transmission: 5F1Rx2; full-time 4x4
Suspension: Independent suspension using upper and lower wishbones and torsion bars
Brakes: Vacuum servo-assisted hydraulic
Electrical system: 24V
Dimensions: Length – 5,380mm/212in
Width – 2,600mm/102in
Height – 2,150–2,570mm/85–101in
Wheelbase – 3,000mm/118in
Weight: Unladen – 6,600–7,500kg/14,550–16,534lb
Payload – 1,500–2,500kg/3,307–5,511lb
Performance: Maximum speed – on land, 112kph/76mph; in water, 4–5kph/2.5–3mph

by the use of upper and lower wishbones and torsion bars.

Entering service in 1999, the GAZ-39371 is in use with the Russian Army, and is available for export; Uruguay ordered 48 vehicles in 2006.

YaAZ-214, KrAZ-214

YaAZ-214, KrAZ-214

Type: Truck, cargo, 7-ton, 6x6
Manufacturer: Yaroslav'l Auto Zavod; Yaroslav'l. Kremenchug Auto Zavod; Kremenchug
Production: 1956 to 1967
Powerplant: YaAZ M206B; six cylinders in-line; two-stroke diesel; 6,972cc; power output, 205bhp at 2,000rpm
Transmission: 5F1Rx2; part-time 6x6
Suspension: Live axles on semi-elliptical multi-leaf springs
Brakes: Air-pressure
Electrical system: 12V (early production), 24V
Dimensions: (cargo vehicles)
    Length – 8,530mm/336in
    Width – 2,700mm/106in
    Height – tilt in place, 3,170mm/125in; minimum, 2,880mm/113in
    Wheelbase – 5,300mm/209in
    Bogie centres – 1,400mm/55in
Weight: Unladen – 12,300kg/27,060lb
    Payload – 7,000kg/15,400lb
Performance: Maximum speed – 55kph/34mph

The YaAz-214 – or JAAZ-214 – was a heavy-duty 7-ton 6x6 truck first produced at the Yaroslav'l Auto Plant in 1956. In 1959, production was moved to the Kremenchug plant in Ukraine and the designation changed to KrAZ-214.

Power was provided by a 6,972cc six-cylinder two-stroke diesel engine driving all six wheels through a five-speed

ABOVE: **In 1967 the YaAZ-214 model was replaced by the similar, but improved KrAZ-255.**

gearbox (with overdrive on top gear) and a two-speed transfer box. An inter-axle differential was fitted. Suspension was provided by basic multi-leaf semi-elliptical springs, inverted at the rear. The standard variant was a steel-bodied cargo vehicle

and was probably the most numerous vehicle of the class in the Soviet Army. Other variants included a tractor for a semi-trailer, bridge-layer, multiple rocket launcher, crane carrier and shovel. The chassis was fitted with a 12-ton winch and many vehicles were also equipped with a "Central Tyre Inflation System" (CTIS).

LuAZ 967M

LuAZ 967M

Type: Truck, cargo, amphibious, 4x4
Manufacturer: Lutskiy Auto Zavod; Lutskiy
Production: 1961 to 1975
Powerplant: MeMZ-967A; four cylinders in V configuration; petrol; air-cooled; 887cc; overhead valves; power output, 37bhp at 2,250rpm
Transmission: 4F1Rx2; part-time 4x4
Suspension: Independent suspension all round using semi-trailing arms and coil springs
Brakes: Hydraulic
Electrical system: 12V
Dimensions: Length – 3,682mm/145in
    Width – 1,712mm/67in
    Height – maximum, 1,580mm/62in
    Wheelbase – 1,800mm/71in
Weight: Unladen – 950kg/2,094lb
    Payload – 450kg/992lb
Performance: Maximum speed – 75kph/47mph

The LuAZ 967M was an airborne amphibious vehicle intended for ferrying supplies to the front line across difficult terrain. It could also be adapted for casualty evacuation, with stretchers carried on either side of the driver.

The first prototype was developed at the Moskvitch (MeMZ) factory in 1958, and constructed around a steel chassis

with permanent all-wheel drive and independent torsion-bar suspension using semi-trailing arms. Power came from a MD-65 motorcycle engine and the open body was of composite glass-fibre construction. The second prototype used front-wheel drive with selectable rear axle drive. The engine was a MeMZ air-cooled V4 as used in the ZAZ motor car.

The body was now of steel construction, with a central driving position which allowed the driver to also operate the vehicle from a prone position. The torsion bars were replaced by coil springs. In 1961, the vehicle went into production at the Ukranian Lutskiy factory.

LEFT: **The LuAZ 967 also provided the basis for the civilian LuAZ 969A, a small four-wheel-drive vehicle intended for agricultural use.**

LEFT: **A MAZ-537A coupled to a semi-trailer loaded with an unidentifiable Soviet surface-to-surface missile. The white trim to the tractor and wheels has been applied as decoration for the May Day Parade in Moscow.**

MAZ-535, 537

Design work for the MAZ-535 and 537 began at the end of the 1950s. The intention was to produce a heavy load carrier and civilian construction vehicle that could be used in even the most remote and inhospitable terrain. Prototypes date from 1958, with the truck entering production around 1960. It was first seen by Western military observers at the 1964 May Day parade in Moscow.

There were three variants. Firstly, the original MAZ-535 cargo vehicle. The later, more-powerful, MAZ-537 was built both as a cargo/prime mover vehicle for heavy artillery, and as a fifth-wheel tractor (MAZ-537A) for use as a heavy equipment transporter. The latter was typically seen towing a Soviet ChMZAP-5247 or ChMZAP-5247G semi-trailer carrying an armoured fighting vehicle, or a missile, such as the SS-5 (Skean), SS-8 (Sasin), SS-N-6 (Sawfly), SS-X-10 (Scrag), or the ABM-1 (Galosh) – all are

NATO reporting names. Finally, there was the MAZ-537D, a 75-ton tractor-truck with a power generator mounted behind the engine compartment.

Both variants were built on the same chassis and were powered by effectively the same V12 diesel engine. For the MAZ-535, the engine was down-rated to 375bhp, while that used in the MAZ-537 produced 525bhp and was used in Soviet tanks of the period. The engine was mounted at high level behind the cab, and drove all eight wheels through a torque converter and three-speed planetary gearbox, the latter incorporating a smooth-start device on both first and reverse gears. A manual two-speed transfer box and an auxiliary

BELOW: **Typical of the Russian approach to military-vehicle design, the MAZ-535/537 is massive, powerful and unsophisticated. Power comes from an 18,300cc V12 water-cooled diesel engine.**

reduction gear incorporating an inter-axle self-locking differential were fitted.

Suspension on the first two axles – and on the rear axles of the MAZ-535 – was independent using torsion bars. The two rear axles of the MAZ-537 had no conventional springing but incorporated what was described as a "suspension equalizer". There was hydraulic power steering on axles one and two, together with air-hydraulic brakes all round. The first series of the MAZ-537 was produced at the Minsk Automobile Plant in Byelorussia until 1964. Production was subsequently moved to the KAVZ factory at Kurgan in the Urals.

MAZ-535, 537

Type: Truck, tractor, heavy equipment transporter, 8x8

Manufacturer: Minsk Auto Zavod; Minsk. Kurgan Auto Zavod; Kurgan

Production: 1960 to 1968

Powerplant: D-12-A-525; 12 cylinders in V formation; diesel; water-cooled; 18,300cc; overhead valves; power output, 375–525bhp at 2,100rpm

Transmission: 3F1Rx3; 8x8

Suspension: Independent suspension by torsion bars on forward two axles; no suspension on rear axles; hydraulic double-acting shock absorbers

Brakes: Air-assisted hydraulic

Electrical system: 24V

Dimensions: Length – 8,960mm/353in
Width – 2,885mm/113in
Height – 2,885mm/113in
Wheelbase – 1,800+2,650mm/71+104in

Weight: Unladen – 21,600kg/47,619lb
Gross train weight (MAZ-537A) – 112,500kg/248,016lb

Performance: Maximum speed – 60kph/37mph

263 UXR

LEFT: Introduced in 1958 to replace the earlier ZiL-151 range, the ZiL-157 was a versatile 6x6 truck adapted for a wide range of military roles. Like many Soviet trucks of the period, it was equipped with a "Central Tyre Inflation System" (CTIS). BELOW: Although superseded by the ZiL-157 from 1962, the ZiL-151 remained in production until 1966. The vehicle was also available to civilian users. Many were later fitted with the ZiL-157KD diesel engine.

ZiL-151, 157

Unashamedly based on the US Army 6x6 trucks of World War II, thousands of which had been supplied to the Soviet Union under the Lend-Lease arrangements, the ZiL-151 – originally described as the ZIS-151 – was a multi-terrain military load carrier which was the "workhorse" of the early post-war Red Army.

Introduced in 1948, it was to remain in production at the Likhachev Automobile Plant, Moscow, until 1958. It was then superseded by the broadly similar, ZiL-157, which was fitted with a more-powerful engine and larger-section single rear tyres in place of the original twins.

The engine was a 6,550cc six-cylinder side-valve petrol unit producing 92 or 104bhp, according to variant. Transmission was by five-speed gearbox (overdrive top gear) and a two-speed transfer box. The suspension arrangements were thoroughly conventional, with live axles on semi-elliptical leaf springs.

Both trucks were rated at a nominal 2^1/$_2$ tons, although the chassis was perfectly capable of carrying 4^1/$_2$ tons on surfaced roads. As well as a standard fixed-side wooden cargo body, there were crane, fuel-tanker, fuel service, water and oil service, multiple rocket launcher and tractor variants. It could also be equipped with various types of shop van-type bodies to cover the workshop, signals and stores roles. The ZiL-157 was equipped with a "Central Tyre Inflation System" (CTIS) which could be operated with the truck on the move. Both vehicles could be fitted with a front-mounted drum winch.

Production ended in 1966 with the introduction of the ZiL-131.

ZiL-151, 157

Type: Truck, 2^1/$_2$-ton, cargo, 6x6
Manufacturer: Likhachev Auto Zavod; Moscow. Ulyanovsk Auto Zavod; Ulyanovsk
Production: 1948 to 1966
Powerplant: ZiL-121; six cylinders in-line; petrol; water-cooled; 6,550cc; side valves; power output, 92bhp (ZiL-151) or 104bhp (ZiL-157) at 2,600rpm
Transmission: 5F1R; part-time 6x6
Suspension: Live axles on semi-elliptical multi-leaf springs; double-acting hydraulic shock absorbers on front axle
Brakes: Air-pressure
Electrical system: 12V
Dimensions: Length – 6,930mm/273in
Width – 2,320mm/91in
Height – tilt in place, 2,740mm/108in; minimum, 2,320mm/91in
Wheelbase – 4,225mm/166in
Bogie centres – 1,120mm/44in
Weight: Unladen – 5,540kg/12,213lb
Payload – road, 4,500kg/9,920lb; cross-country, 2,500kg/5,511lb
Performance: Maximum speed – 65kph/40mph

ZiL-135L4

In the early 1960s, the Likhachev factory in Moscow started the development work on what became the ZiL-135L4 – the vehicle is also sometimes described as the BAZ-135 to reflect the Bryansk factory where it was produced.

Although the truck was also supplied for heavy civilian usage, there were three major military variants. The 9P113 "Transporter-Erector-Launcher" (TEL) for the 9K52 Luna-M missile system (NATO name: "Frog 7") carried a single surface-to-surface artillery rocket on a hydraulically raised launch rail; a crane was fitted to the right-side of the vehicle to assist with reloading. The 9T290 was a resupply vehicle carrying three Luna-M missiles. There was also a 10-ton cargo/prime mover variant with a fixed-side cargo body and drop tailgate. With a different cab, the same chassis was also used to produce a transporter-launcher for the S-35, SSC-1a (Shaddock) surface-to-surface missile.

The truck was powered by two 7,000cc V8 petrol engines mounted

ABOVE: **Powered by two V8 diesel engines, each driving the wheels on one side of the truck, the ZiL-135L4 was produced both as a 10-ton cargo vehicle, and as a missile loading vehicle (shown). The vehicle was also used as a missile "Transporter-Erector-Launcher" (TEL) unit.**

behind the cab. Each engine drove the wheels on one side of the vehicle through a hydro-mechanical transmission system. There was torsion-bar suspension on the first and fourth axles; both provided steering. The centre axles were mounted as a fixed bogie unit without suspension. For military use, the truck was equipped with a "Central Tyre Inflation System" (CTIS).

This massive forward-control truck, with eight huge wheels, was fitted with a wide two-door glass-fibre composite cab providing seating for a crew of four or five. It could easily be recognized by the triple windscreen, which could be shuttered to protect against blast as the rocket was fired. The truck began to enter service in 1964 and was used by the Soviet Army and other Warsaw Pact countries as well as by other nations friendly to the Soviet Union. A number were captured from Iraqi forces during the First Gulf War.

ABOVE: **A ZiL-135L4 missile "Transporter-Erector-Launcher" (TEL) with a Luna-M (NATO name: "Frog 7") missile in the ready-to-launch position. A number of TEL vehicles were captured from Iraqi forces.**

ZiL-135L4

Type: Truck, missile "Transporter-Erector-Launcher" (TEL), 10-ton, 8x8

Manufacturer: Bryansk Auto Zavod; Bryansk

Production: 1964 on

Powerplant: 2x ZiL-375; each of eight cylinders in V configuration; petrol; water-cooled; 7,000cc; overhead valves; power output, 150bhp at 1,800rpm

Transmission: Hydro-mechanical; full-time 8x8

Suspension: Independent suspension by upper and lower wishbones and torsion bars on first and fourth axles; no suspension on centre axles

Brakes: Air-pressure

Electrical system: 24V

Dimensions: Length – 9,270mm/365in
　　Width – 2,800mm/110in
　　Height – to top of cab, 2,530mm/100in; missile in place, 3,375mm/133in
　　Wheelbase – 6,300mm/248in
　　Bogie centres – 2,415+1,500+2,415mm/ 95+59+95in

Weight: Unladen – 9,000kg/19,8041lb
　　Payload – 10,000kg/22,046lb

Performance: Maximum speed – 65kph/40mph

ABOVE AND LEFT: **The ZiL-167E was effectively a high-mobility 6x6 version of the ZiL-135. It was originally intended as a civil engineering vehicle, but the Soviet authorities believed it could be easily adapted into an all-terrain heavy artillery tractor or prime mover.**

ZiL-167E

Dating from the mid-1960s, the ZiL-167E was an experimental version of the 8x8 BAZ-135/ZiL-135. Although not specifically designed for military usage, since it was eminently suitable for use as a heavy tractor for civil engineering, it was believed that the truck could be developed into a high-mobility artillery tractor or prime mover that would be capable of providing exceptional performance in extremely difficult terrain.

Like the BAZ-135/ZiL-135, it was powered by two ZiL 7,000cc V8 petrol engines, although for this vehicle the engines were mounted at the extreme rear. Each engine was arranged to drive the wheels on one side of the vehicle through a hydro-mechanical transmission system located between the first and second axles. The axles were not selectable and the truck had full-time six-wheel drive. Torsion-bar suspension was fitted on the first and third axles, both of which provided steering. The centre axle was not fitted with suspension.

BELOW: **It is thought that a single example was produced and that there was no series production.**

At least for early prototypes, the truck shared the same two-door glass-fibre composite cab of the BAZ-135/ZiL-135. A covered crew accommodation area was located between the driving and the engine compartments.

It is not known whether there was any series production, but there is some evidence to believe that the same chassis was used on a 6x6 "Transporter-Erector-Launcher" (TEL) for the Soviet SA-8A (NATO name: "Gecko") surface-to-air missile.

ZiL-167E	

Type: Truck-tractor, high mobility, 5-ton, 6x6
Manufacturer: Likhachev Auto Zavod; Moscow
Production: 1967
Powerplant: 2x ZiL-375; each of eight cylinders in V configuration; petrol; water-cooled; 7,000cc; overhead valves; power output, 180bhp at 1,800rpm
Transmission: Hydro-mechanical; full-time 6x6
Suspension: Independent suspension by upper and lower wishbones and torsion bars on first and third axles; no suspension on centre axle
Brakes: Air-pressure assisted hydraulic
Electrical system: 24V
Dimensions: Length – 9,260mm/365in
  Width – 3,130mm/123in
  Height – to top of cab, 3,060mm/120in
  Wheelbase – 3,150+3,150mm/248+248in
Weight: Unladen – 7,000kg/15,432lb
  Payload – 5,000kg/11,023lb
Performance: Maximum speed – 65kph/40mph

LEFT: Rated at a nominal 10 tons, the Pegaso model 3055 entered service in March 1982. The vehicle was a further development of Pegaso's earlier 3046. Many components were common to both vehicles. The model 3046 had originally been a joint development by Pegaso and DAF.

Pegaso model 3055

In 1946, the Spanish state-owned Empresa Nacional de Autocamiones (ENASA) acquired the Barcelona-based truck-building operation of Hispano-Suiza and relaunched the products under the name Pegaso. The Hispano-based models were discontinued in 1958 and a range of entirely new vehicles was launched. In 1960, Leyland acquired an interest in ENASA which led to the widespread adoption of Leyland engines and running gear. In 1981, International-Harvester acquired a 35 per cent stake, but withdrew a year or so later. At this time, ENASA acquired Seddon-Atkinson, which had also been previously owned by International-Harvester.

DAF had also been under International-Harvester control for a while and, in the late 1960s, had designed trucks for Pegaso. ENASA maintained design links with DAF following the withdrawal of International. The model 3055, dating from 1982, is a good example of this shared development process. It was effectively a 6x6 development of the Pegaso 3046 which, in turn, had been based on the DAF-designed 3045. There was considerable commonality of components between the types.

Rated at a nominal 10 tons, the 3055 was powered by a six-cylinder turbocharged diesel engine driving through a six-speed gearbox and two-speed, pneumatically operated, transfer box. Suspension was by semi-elliptical multi-leaf springs.

The truck shared a canvas-topped cab with the 3046. A hard-top cab variant was also available. Standard variants included a cargo/personnel carrier, artillery tractor, multiple rocket launcher, fuel tanker, water tanker, heavy crane carrier, tipper, fire tender, workshop and refrigerated van. There was also a tractor for semi-trailers which could be used as a tank transporter. In 1987, the model 3055 was replaced by the longer-wheelbase model 7323.

LEFT: A canvas cover could be erected over the cab. With the cover removed, the profile of the vehicle could be further reduced by folding down the windscreen and the side window frames.

Pegaso model 3055

Type: Truck, cargo, 6- to 10-ton, 6x6
Manufacturer: Empresa Nacional de Autocamiones (ENASA); Madrid
Production: 1982 to 1987
Powerplant: Pegaso 9220/10; six cylinders in-line; turbocharged diesel; water-cooled; 10,581cc; overhead valves; power output, 200–220bhp at 2,000rpm
Transmission: 6F1Rx2; part-time 6x6
Suspension: Live axles on semi-elliptical springs; double-acting hydraulic shock absorbers at front
Brakes: Air-pressure
Electrical system: 24V
Dimensions: Length – chassis-cab, 6,956mm/274in
Width – 2,400mm/94in
Height – top of cab, 2,710mm/107in
Wheelbase – 3,245mm/128in
Bogie centres – 1,484mm/58in
Weight: Unladen – 9,000kg/19,841lb
Payload – road, 10,000kg/22,046lb;
cross-country, 6,000kg/13,228lb
Performance: Maximum speed – 80kph/50mph

LEFT: **The S-2000 could be considered a Spanish version of the British-built Land Rover 101 forward-control model.**

Santana S-2000	
Type: Truck, cargo, 2-ton, 4x4	
Manufacturer: Metalúrgica de Santa Ana; Madrid	
Production: 1978 on	
Powerplant: Six cylinders in-line; petrol; water-cooled; 3,429cc; overhead valves; power output, 100bhp at 4,000rpm	
Transmission: 4F1Rx2; part-time 4x4	
Suspension: Live axles on semi-elliptical springs	
Brakes: Hydraulic	
Electrical system: 24V	
Dimensions: Length – 4,918mm/194in	
Width – 1,925mm/76in	
Height – 2,235mm/88in	
Wheelbase – 2,565mm/101in	
Weight: Unladen – 2,360kg/5,203lb	
Payload – 2,000kg/4,409lb	
Performance: Maximum speed – 90kph/56mph	

Santana S-2000

In 1956, the Santana company began building Land Rovers in Spain, and by 1981 was producing 18,000 vehicles a year. Early production matched the Solihull product but, once the Spanish Army became a customer, Santana vehicles started to develop along different lines to those produced in the UK.

Dating from 1978, and intended for both military and civilian users, albeit rated at 2 tons. The vehicle was powered by a six-cylinder petrol engine, although a diesel option was also available, driving through a four-speed gearbox and two-speed transfer box. Suspension was by live axles on semi-elliptical multi-leaf springs.

The distinctive flat-panelled cab shared little with the Solihull product. Standard variants included a drop-side truck, personnel carrier, workshop, command/communications vehicle and shelter carrier. The Spanish Army also used the vehicle as a mount for a 20mm Oerlikon anti-aircraft cannon. The company name was changed to Land Rover Santana in 1981, although the relationship with Land Rover ended in 1983.

Volvo TP21 P2104

Nicknamed *Sugga* (Sow) in recognition of its snout-shaped front, the Volvo TP21 was a field command car very much in the mould of the World War II $^3/_4$-ton Dodge WC series. The vehicle was introduced in 1953 and was built on the chassis of the Volvo TL11 four-wheel drive truck on to which the bodyshell of the PV830 taxi had been mounted. The military bonnet and front wings were similar to those used on TL11 trucks of the same period. The TP21 was designed to replace the wartime TPV command car and was produced in two variants – a five-seat radio car and a seven-seat command car. The same chassis was also used to mount a station wagon body.

The engine was a six-cylinder side-valve unit, coupled to a four-speed gearbox and two-speed transfer box. Live axles were suspended on semi-elliptical springs.

Vacuum-operated differential locks were fitted to both axles. Total production was 720 vehicles over six years.

LEFT: **The vehicle used a light truck chassis and a taxi body.**

Volvo TP21 P2104	
Type: Car, 5/7 seat, command/radio, 4x4	
Manufacturer: Volvo; Göteborg	
Production: 1953 to 1958	
Powerplant: Volvo ED/90; six cylinders in-line; petrol; water-cooled; 3,650cc; side valves; power output, 90bhp at 3,600rpm	
Transmission: 4F1Rx2; part-time 4x4	
Suspension: Live axles on semi-elliptical multi-leaf springs	
Brakes: Hydraulic	
Electrical system: 12V	
Dimensions: Length – 4,500mm/177in	
Width – 1,900mm/75in	
Height – 1,950mm/77in	
Wheelbase – 2,680mm/106in	
Weight: Unladen – 2,600kg/5,732lb	
Payload – 600kg/1,323lb	
Performance: Maximum speed – 105kph/65mph	

Volvo TL31

ABOVE: **The Volvo TL31 was developed from the company's L395 truck of the early 1950s.**

Volvo's TL31 6x6 was developed from the company's L395 Titan truck in the early 1950s and entered production in 1956. Designed specifically for the military, the original cab of the Titan was replaced by a strictly functional all-steel type fabricated by Nyström of Umea. Standard variants included cargo/prime mover (L3154), recovery (L3164), and fire-crash-rescue (L3154S).

The cargo and recovery variants were powered by a six-cylinder diesel engine, while the variants produced for the Swedish Air Force used a turbocharged version of the same power unit with an additional 35bhp. The engine was coupled to double-reduction axles via a five-speed gearbox (overdrive top) and a two-speed transfer box. Suspension was by live axles on semi-elliptical leaf springs, inverted at the rear. An 8-ton capacity winch was fitted under the chassis. A total of 921 had been built when production ended in 1962.

Volvo TL31	
Type: Truck, cargo, 3-ton, 6x6	
Manufacturer: Volvo; Göteborg	
Production: 1956 to 1962	
Powerplant: Volvo D96As, TD96AS; six cylinders in-line; diesel (TD96AS, turbocharged); water-cooled; 9,586cc; overhead valves; power output, 150bhp at 2,200rpm (185bhp for TD96AS)	
Transmission: 5F1Rx2; part-time 6x6	
Suspension: Live axles semi-elliptical multi-leaf springs	
Brakes: Air-pressure assisted hydraulic	
Electrical system: 24V	
Dimensions: (cargo vehicles) Length – 7,150mm/281in Width – 2,150mm/85in Height – tilt in place, 2,950mm/116in Wheelbase – 3,920mm/154in Bogie centres – 1,250mm/49in	
Weight: Unladen – 7,320kg/16,138lb Payload – 3,000kg/6,614lb	
Performance: Maximum speed – 73kph/45mph	

Volvo Laplander L3314

Nicknamed *Valp* (Pup or Cub), the Laplander was a small utility vehicle based largely on the Amazon motor car and designed to replace the Swedish Army's ageing Willys Jeeps.

Following a run of 91 of the pre-production L2304 version during 1959 and 1960, building of the definitive L3314 began in 1961.

Where the L2304 had been powered by Volvo's B16 four-cylinder engine, this was replaced by the iconic B18 and then the B20 for the L3314. The engine drove both axles through a four-speed gearbox and two-speed transfer box. Suspension was by live axles on semi-elliptical leaf springs. The combination of a forward-control driving position, differential locks, flexible suspension and large low-pressure tyres, provided excellent off-road performance.

Standard variants included personnel/cargo carrier, missile carrier, radio vehicle, ambulance and fire tender.

LEFT: **Over a ten-year period 7,737 of the Laplander L3314 and 1,116 of the L3315 were built.**

Volvo Laplander L3314	
Type: Truck, personnel/cargo, 4x4	
Manufacturer: Volvo; Göteborg	
Production: 1961 to 1970	
Powerplant: Volvo B18A, B20A; four cylinders in-line; petrol; water-cooled; 1,778cc, 1,978cc; overhead valves; power output, 65–82bhp at 4,500rpm	
Transmission: 4F1Rx2; part-time 4x4; differential locks, front and rear	
Suspension: Live axles on semi-elliptical multi-leaf springs	
Brakes: Vacuum servo-assisted hydraulic	
Electrical system: 12V, 24V	
Dimensions: Length – 4,050mm/159in Width – 1,660mm/65in Height – tilt in place, 2,100mm/83in Wheelbase – 2,100mm/83in	
Weight: Unladen – 1,600kg/3,527lb Payload – 850kg/1,874lb	
Performance: Maximum speed – 90kph/56mph	

There was also a fully enclosed variant designated L3315. Total production, over a ten-year period, amounted to 7,737 examples of the L3314, plus 1,116 of the L3315.

Volvo Laplander L4140, L4141

ABOVE: **In the mid-1960s, Volvo's chief designer of off-road vehicles, Nils Magnus 'Måns' Hartelius, began work on a replacement for the Volvo L3314 Laplander. Early prototypes were fitted with the Volvo B20A four-cylinder engine as used in the L3314. On production vehicles this was replaced by the B30A six-cylinder engine. Variants included the L4140 (open-topped) and the L4141 (enclosed cab).**

In 1966, Volvo started the development work on a replacement for the L3314 Laplander. Early prototypes were powered by the B20A four-cylinder engine as used in the earlier vehicle but by 1974, when the truck went into production, this had been replaced by the B30A six-cylinder unit. Designated L4140 in open form and L4141 when fitted with an enclosed body, the new Laplander all-terrain vehicle had been designed under the direction of Mans Hartelius. It was manufactured at the company's "A Plant" at Lundby, which had previously been used for the P1800 and Duett motor cars. The chassis was identified as the C300 series, and there were long- (C304) and short-wheelbase (C303) versions.

Like the earlier L3314, the truck was fitted with a forward-control driving position, which ensured excellent visibility. The use of reduction-gear portal-type axles improved the ground clearance, and vacuum-operated differential locks made it unlikely that the truck would become immobilized in even the roughest terrain. The engine was a down-rated version of the company's B30 six-cylinder twin-carburettor unit, driving both axles through a four-speed gearbox and two-speed transfer box. Suspension was by live axles on semi-elliptical multi-leaf springs with hollow rubber assisters.

The vehicle was intended for use by the Swedish and Norwegian defence forces and also for public utilities and fire services. Standard variants included a hard-topped personnel cargo carrier (Swedish Army TGB 111A MT), the C404 open-topped mount for an anti-tank gun (PVP JTGB 1111A) and a hard-topped radio communications vehicle (RATGB 1112A MT). There was also a three-axle 6x6 variant designated L4143 (C306). An 8x8 was prototyped, but not put into production. Total production, over an 11-year period, amounted to 8,718 of all variants.

A civilian version was launched in 1976, and production of the old L3314 was transferred to Hungary where it was designated as the C202.

Volvo Laplander L4140, L4141

Type: Truck, personnel/cargo, 1-ton, 4x4
Manufacturer: Volvo; Göteborg
Production: 1974 to 1984
Powerplant: Volvo B30A; six cylinders in-line; petrol; water-cooled; 2,980cc; overhead valves; power output, 117bhp at 4,000rpm
Transmission: 4F1Rx2; part-time 4x4; differential locks front and rear
Suspension: Live portal axles on semi-elliptical multi-leaf springs; double-acting telescopic shock absorbers
Brakes: Vacuum servo-assisted hydraulic
Electrical system: 24V
Dimensions: Length – 4,350mm/171in
Width – 1,900mm/75in
Height – tilt in place, 2,170mm/86in
Wheelbase – 2,300mm/91in, 2,530mm/100in
Weight: Unladen – 2,400kg/5,291lb
Payload – 1,250kg/2,756lb
Performance: Maximum speed – 120kph/75mph

MOWAG GW4500

In 1950, MOWAG Motorwagenfabriek was established in Kreuzlingen, Switzerland. The company's first product was the GW4500, a purpose-designed ³/₄-ton 4x4 cross-country military truck.

Despite the use of a forward-control driving position, and the company's proud boast of employing a "patented framework chassis", the vehicle was very much the same type as the

T214-engined WC Dodge trucks of World War II, even to the extent of being powered by a similar engine and transmission.

The engine was a Dodge T137 six-cylinder, driving both axles through a four-speed crash gearbox, with synchromesh being introduced during the production run. The vehicle was subsequently upgraded to 1 ton and then 1¹/₂ tons, using a 103bhp version of the engine giving a useful increase in top speed. Final drive was via a two-speed transfer box. The live axles were suspended on conventional semi-elliptical leaf springs.

Standard variants included an open-cabbed weapons/personnel carrier, for which there was also a bolt-on hardtop, box-bodied five-stretcher ambulance, radio command vehicle, civil-defence vehicle, fire-tender and police vehicle. The chassis was also used as the basis for a tank-training vehicle. Like all Swiss military vehicles, it had a right-hand steering position.

A total of 1,688 were built, with production taking place between 1950 and 1956. Production restarted with the upgraded version in 1962.

MOWAG remains in defence manufacturing and is now part of the General Dynamics Group.

ABOVE: **A steel-bodied ambulance variant of the GW4500 with the canvas cab roof rolled back.**
LEFT: **Other variants of the GW4500 included an open-bodied weapons carrier. The vehicle was also built with a fully enclosed body which could be used as a radio command, civil-defence or police vehicle. A crew cab fire-tender body was available for the Swiss Air Force.**

MOWAG GW4500

Type: Truck, ³/₄- to 1¹/₂-ton, cargo, 4x4
Manufacturer: MOWAG Motorwagenfabriek; Kreuzlingen
Production: 1950 to 1956, 1962
Powerplant: Dodge T137; six cylinders in-line; water-cooled; petrol; 3,770cc; side valves; power output, 91–103bhp at 3,600rpm
Transmission: 4F1Rx2; part-time 4x4
Suspension: Live axles on semi-elliptical multi-leaf springs
Brakes: Hydraulic
Electrical system: 6V, 12V
Dimensions: Length – 4,740mm/187in
  Width – 1,830mm/72in
  Height – soft-top variants, 2,215mm/87in; hard-top variants, 2,480mm/98in
  Wheelbase – 2,600mm/102in
Weight: Unladen – 3,200kg/7,055lb
  Payload – 750–1,500kg/1,653–3,307lb
Performance: Maximum speed – 90kph/55mph

MOWAG DURO

The high-mobility multi-role DURO (*Dauerhaft, Unabhängig, Robust, Oekonomisch* – durable, self-reliant, robust, economical) was developed in the late 1980s to replace the Swiss Army's ageing logistics fleet. After a period of extensive trials, an initial order for 2,000 vehicles was placed in 1993 with deliveries commencing in 1994. Initially manufactured by a consortium of Swiss engineering companies led by Bucher-Guyer, from 2003 the truck has been marketed under General Dynamics MOWAG, with recent upgrades designated DURO II and DURO III.

The DURO is available as a standard- and long-wheelbase 4x4, and as a 6x6, with a high degree of component commonality across the configurations. Early examples were powered by a VM six-cylinder diesel engine, but this was subsequently replaced by a Cummins six-cylinder unit, driving all axles through a four- or five-speed automatic gearbox, and two-speed transfer box. All axles are fitted with self-locking differentials to provide enhanced mobility and an inter-axle differential lock. The torsion-free underslung chassis is of tubular design and incorporates swing-arm independent suspension with an integral roll-stabilizing system.

All soft-skin variants use the same forward-control tilt-cab of aluminium/composite construction. Variants include cargo, personnel, shelter carrier, ambulance, communications, command, fire tender and police command. An armoured variant (DURO 4x4SP, 6x6SP) is available for cargo, personnel and ambulance roles. There is also an armoured variant based on the standard 4x4 and 6x6 chassis.

The DURO is in widespread service, including the Swiss, German, Danish, and Irish armies. Also the British Army and RAF.

ABOVE: **The DURO was initially manufactured by a consortium of Swiss engineering companies led by Bucher-Guyer. From 2003 the vehicle has been marketed under General Dynamics MOWAG. Both 4x4 and 6x6 versions have been produced.**

LEFT: **The armoured DURO 4x4SP, and the similar 6x6SP, are intended for the cargo, personnel and ambulance roles. The type is in widespread service, including with the armed forces of Venezuela and Malaysia. The German Army also uses the DURO IIIP 6x6 ballistic and mine-protected version.**

MOWAG DURO

Type: Truck, 2-ton, cargo, 4x4
Manufacturer: MOWAG Motorwagenfabrik; Kreuzlingen
Production: 1993 on
Powerplant: VM-642 LM; six cylinders in-line; direct-injection turbocharged diesel; water-cooled; 4,171cc; overhead valves; power output, 160bhp at 3,000rpm Cummins ISBe 185; six cylinders in-line; direct-injection turbocharged diesel; water-cooled; 5,883cc; overhead valves; power output, 185bhp at 2,500rpm
Transmission: 4F1Rx2 or 5F1Rx2; automatic; full-time 4x4
Suspension: Independent suspension using leading and trailing arms with coil springs, twinned at the rear
Brakes: Hydraulic
Electrical system: 24V
Dimensions: Length – 5,200mm/205in, 6,350mm/250in
  Width – 1,990mm/78in
  Height – to top of cab, 2,600mm/102in
  Wheelbase – 3,230mm/127in, 3,880mm/153in
Weight: Unladen – 3,800kg/8,377lb
  Payload – 2,970–3,100kg/6,548–6,834lb
Performance: Maximum speed – 110kph/68mph

ABOVE: **By 1918, AEC had built 8,821 Y Types.
The truck was also used by US forces in France.**

AEC Y Type

The Associated Equipment Company Limited (AEC) was originally founded at Walthamstow in June 1912 to manufacture and repair buses for the London General Omnibus Company (LGOC). By 1913, AEC employed more than 1,200 workers, and by the outbreak of World War I, the company had also turned its hand to manufacturing motor lorries for the War Office. A sales agreement signed in 1912 meant that, at first, these were marketed by Daimler, as had been the early buses, and were also identified with that company's brand.

The Y Type dated from March 1915 and was actually little more than a lower-geared version of the earlier X Type, which, had been a development of the W Type with heavy-duty rear hubs. At the

end of June 1916, the AEC factory was placed under direct Government control and from that date the trucks were identified as AEC, although the distinctive Daimler radiator remained. A moving production line was installed in 1917 when the factory was extended and this helped to raise output to 130 chassis per week.

The original Y Type was powered by a 5,700cc four-cylinder 40bhp Daimler sleeve-valve engine, driving the rear wheels, which were shod with solid rubber tyres, through a four-speed gearbox to a worm-drive rear axle. By 1917, the Daimler engine had been replaced by a 7,700cc Tylor four-cylinder unit, with the model designation becoming YA to signify the change. The YB was similar but used a pressed-steel frame and the YC used a David Brown worm-gear final drive.

Mounting a fixed-side timber body combined with a canvas-covered open cab, the Y Type was the typical military cargo vehicle of the period and was used by the British and US armies during World War I.

By the time of the armistice in 1918, AEC had built 8,821, of which

5,200 were fitted with the Tylor engine. The War Office purchased a further 822 Y Types during 1919, and the vehicle remained in production for commercial customers into the early 1920s.

After the war, many Y Types passed to civilian operators, where the standard military body was often removed to convert the vehicle to an omnibus.

AEC Y Type

Type: Truck, 3-ton, cargo, 4x2
Manufacturer: Associated Equipment Company; Walthamstow
Production: 1915 to 1922
Powerplant: Y Type – Daimler; four cylinders in-line; petrol; water-cooled; 5,700cc; sleeve valves; power output, 40bhp at 1,300rpm. YA, YB, YC Type – Tylor JB4; four cylinders in-line; water-cooled; petrol; 7,700cc; side valves; power output, 49bhp at 1,300rpm
Transmission: 4F1R; 4x2
Suspension: Live axles on semi-elliptical multi-leaf springs
Brakes: Mechanical, rear wheels only
Electrical system: Magneto only
Dimensions: Length – 7,163mm/282in
Width – 2,108mm/83in
Height – tilt in place, 3,099mm/122in
Wheelbase – 4,343mm/171in
Weight: Unladen – 4,277kg/9,492lb
Payload – 3,048kg/6,720lb
Performance: Maximum speed – 19kph/12mph

LEFT: **The 3-ton timber cargo body was typical of those fitted to vehicles of the period.**

LEFT: **The Matador was widely considered to be the best British-built truck of World War II. Many remained in military service into the 1960s.**

AEC Model O853 Matador

Design work on what became the Matador medium artillery tractor was carried out by Charles Cleaver of the Four Wheel Drive Motor Company (FWD), in conjunction with Hardy Motors who were working on a 4-ton 4x4 chassis for the War Department. AEC purchased FWD of Southall, Middlesex, and Cleaver completed the work. The first prototype, which was petrol-engined and designated Model 853, was trialled in 1938. Following the successful conclusion of the trials, AEC received a Ministry of Supply contract for 200 vehicles. By the time World War II was over, almost 10,500 Matadors had been supplied, the majority of which were diesel-engined, designated Model O853, with the "O" indicating the "oil" engine.

Powered by AEC's own 7,580cc A173 six-cylinder diesel engine, the forward-control layout placed the engine between the driver and passenger seat. The engine was coupled to a four-speed unitary gearbox and a remote two-speed transfer box, driving both axles.

The most numerous variant was the artillery tractor, which was fitted with a composite wood and steel body, with seating for a gun crew of nine or ten. Shell carriers attached to rails in the floor were intended to make it easy to offload the ammunition. Most vehicles were fitted with a 5- or 7-ton underfloor winch. Alongside the artillery tractor, there was also a cargo variant used by the RAF, as well as a range of specialized bodies including an armoured command post. Matador mechanical components were also used to develop the AEC heavy armoured car.

The Matador was the first all-wheel-drive truck to be produced in Britain in quantity. It served all through the war, and right into the 1950s and 1960s. Indeed, in 1953, with problems being encountered in the development of a post-war replacement, a further 1,800 Matadors were purchased, with an uprated A187 engine.

Rugged and powerful, the Matador was used over all types of terrain. This reputation for reliability also made the vehicle a popular choice with fairground operators, and round-timber and heavy-haulage contractors.

BELOW: **An early production Matador; note that the vehicle does not have the distinctive double-skin domed roof on the cab.**

AEC Model O853 Matador

Type: Tractor, medium artillery, 4x4
Manufacturer: AEC Motors; Southall
Production: 1938 to 1953
Powerplant: AEC A173 or A187; six cylinders in-line; direct-injection diesel; water-cooled; 7,580cc; overhead valves; power output, 95bhp (105bhp for A187) at 1,800rpm
Transmission: 4F1Rx2; part-time 4x4
Suspension: Live axles on semi-elliptical multi-leaf springs
Brakes: Air-assisted hydraulic or air-pressure
Electrical system: 12V
Dimensions: Length – 6,325mm/249in
Width – 2,426mm/95in
Height – tilt in place, 3,099mm/122in; minimum, 2,946mm/116in
Wheelbase – 3,848mm/151in
Weight: Unladen – 7,190kg/15,850lb
Payload – 3,833kg/8,450lb
Performance: Maximum speed – 61kph/38mph

LEFT: **Produced in cargo, artillery tractor, tipper and crane carrier variants, the AEC Militant was developed from the AEC Matador of World War II.**

AEC Militant Mk 1

Development work on the AEC Militant started in 1951, with the vehicle entering production the following year. Rated at 10 tons, the chassis was derived from the 6x6 Model O854 which the company had produced for the RAF during World War II. The Militant was produced in both 6x6 (Model O860) and 6x4 (Model O859) configurations, also in two wheelbase lengths. It was offered both as a military and commercial vehicle and was widely exported, with a total of 3,200 examples produced during 13 years in production. British Army variants included a medium/heavy artillery tractor, cargo vehicle, three-way tipper and a crane carrier.

The standard engine was an 11,310cc AEC A223 six-cylinder direct-injection diesel unit driving the rear, or front and rear, axles through a five-speed gearbox and separately mounted two-speed auxiliary gearbox which also contained the front axle selector for 6x6 vehicles. Suspension was entirely conventional, using semi-elliptical leaf springs, inverted at the rear.

Although it had originally been designed as a cargo truck and most of those produced were bodied for this role, a total of 349 artillery tractors were built between 1954 and 1964. The artillery tractor was intended to be used as a prime mover for artillery pieces weighing up to 16 tons, for example the 5.5 or 7.2in howitzer. It was a replacement for the similar Matador and Mack vehicles from World War II. A fixed-side wood and steel composite body was fitted, produced by Crossley Motors. This could accommodate a crew of nine together with stowage space for 4,491kg/9,900lb of stores and ammunition. A 5- or 7-ton Turner chain-driven winch was mounted behind the auxiliary gearbox.

A multi-fuel engined Mk 2 version was produced in 1962 and, although, this did not enter series production, it provided a useful test-bed for further development work. The original Militant was eventually superseded in the cargo role by the much updated Mk 3.

LEFT: **The cargo variant was fitted with a fabricated steel dropside body. The side panels were removable to provide a flat bed for containers. The truck was also available to civilian customers and was popular in foreign markets. A total of 3,200 were produced.**

AEC Militant Mk 1

Type: Tractor, medium/heavy artillery, 10-ton, 6x4, 6x6; FV11001, FV11002
Manufacturer: AEC Motors; Southall
Production: 1952 to 1964
Powerplant: AEC A223; six cylinders in-line; diesel; water-cooled; 11,310cc; overhead valves; power output, 150bhp at 1,800rpm
Transmission: 5F1Rx2; 6x4 or part-time 6x6
Suspension: Live axles on semi-elliptical multi-leaf springs, inverted at the rear
Brakes: Air-pressure
Electrical system: 24V
Dimensions: Length – 7,353mm/289in
Width – 2,438mm/96in
Height – tilt in place, 2,946mm/116in; minimum, 2,807mm/111in
Wheelbase – 3,924mm/154in, and (cargo variants only) 4,880mm/192in
Bogie centres – 1,372mm/54in
Weight: Unladen – 10,304–10,558kg/ 22,715–23,276lb
Payload – 5,100kg/11,220lb
Performance: Maximum speed – 40kph/25mph

Albion CX22S

ABOVE: **Only 532 Albion CX22S vehicles were built between November 1943 and June 1945.**

Albion Motors was founded in Glasgow in 1899 and began building trucks in 1910. The company produced 6,000 trucks for the British Army during World War I and remained an important supplier of military vehicles throughout the 1930s and into World War II.

Dating from late 1943 and designed to supplement the Scammell R100 Pioneer (which was never available in large enough numbers) the Albion CX22S was a heavy artillery tractor for towing the 7.2 or 6in howitzers. Developed from the company's CX23N 10-ton truck, it was powered by a six-cylinder diesel engine driving the rear wheels through a four-speed gearbox and two-speed auxiliary gearbox.

The cab provided bench seating for two/three, while the rear body had a bench seat for four, together with folding seats for another two. There was also stowage for ammunition, tools and equipment. An 8-ton capacity Scammell vertical-spindle winch was fitted under the rear body.

Albion CX22S

Type: Tractor, heavy artillery, 6x4
Manufacturer: Albion Motors; Scotstoun
Production: 1943 to 1945
Powerplant: Albion EN244; six cylinders in-line; diesel; water-cooled; 9,060cc; overhead valves; power output, 100bhp at 1,750rpm
Transmission: 4F1Rx2; 6x4
Suspension: Live axles on semi-elliptical multi-leaf springs
Brakes: Air-assisted mechanical, rear wheels only
Electrical system: Hybrid 12V/24V
Dimensions: Length – 7,777mm/306in
 Width – 2,669mm/105in
 Height – 3,162mm/124in
 Wheelbase – 4,474mm/176in
 Bogie centres – 1,372mm/54in
Weight: Unladen – 10,605kg/23,379lb
 Payload – 5,216kg/11,500lb
Performance: Maximum speed – 45kph/28mph

Albion WD66N

In 1951, Albion Motors took over the contract for the FV1300, a 3-ton 6x6 chassis originally developed by Vauxhall and, in June of that year, received an order for 6,000 vehicles. In May 1953,

BELOW: **The WD66N was a promising vehicle, but was cancelled after only nine chassis had been completed.**

before any had been built, the contract was cancelled but, in 1955, Albion was asked to produce a prototype for a 5-ton 6x6 semi-forward control vehicle which would take its place.

Aside from the Rolls-Royce eight-cylinder engine, the vehicle was based on an existing Albion chassis, and was fitted with a five-speed gearbox and two-speed transfer box. The rear axles were of the worm-drive type, while that at the front was fitted with spiral bevel gears. Hub reduction gears were fitted at front and rear. Suspension was by semi-elliptical springs. Just nine chassis were built, some of which were fitted with a steel drop-side cargo body (FV14001).

Albion WD66N

Type: Truck, 5-ton, cargo, 6x6; FV14000 series
Manufacturer: Albion Motors; Scotstoun
Production: 1955 to 1956
Powerplant: Rolls-Royce B80 Mk 1D; eight cylinders in-line; petrol; water-cooled; 5,675cc; overhead inlet valves, side exhaust; power output, 165bhp at 3,750rpm
Transmission: 5F1Rx2; part-time 6x6
Suspension: Live axles on semi-elliptical multi-leaf springs
Brakes: Air-assisted hydraulic
Electrical system: 24V
Dimensions: Length – 7,163mm/282in
 Width – 2,438mm/96in
 Height – 3,277mm/129in
 Wheelbase – 3,180mm/125in
 Bogie centres – 1,372mm/54in
Weight: Unladen – 7,069kg/15,584lb
 Payload – 5,480kg/12,078lb
Performance: Maximum speed – 56kph/35mph

LEFT: **The prototype for the Alvis Stalwart was based on the company's Salamander, a rear-engined fire tender.**

Alvis Stalwart

The amphibious Stalwart was the last of four vehicles to use the Rolls-Royce-powered Alvis 6x6 chassis; this had already been used for the Salamander airfield fire tender, the Saladin heavy armoured car and the Saracen armoured personnel carrier. Although it was said to have been developed from the front-engined Salamander, initially

as a private venture, on the Stalwart the engine was mounted in the centre of the vehicle. A prototype was proposed to the War Office as a possible contender for the cargo-carrying tracked vehicle role for which the FV431 was being considered. Following a series of trials, it was concluded that the Stalwart offered comparable performance at lower cost and further development work was undertaken.

With permanent six-wheel drive, independent suspension on all six wheels, and "Hydrojet" propulsion for the amphibious role, the Stalwart was an impressive vehicle which offered performance equal to tracked vehicles, but without the maintenance requirements. The Corten steel hull was a monocoque fitted with a cab and drop-side cargo bay, which was fitted with a waterproof cover. The driver sat centrally in the cab, for which there were no doors; the crew was required to enter through roof hatches. A typical load comprised 5,080kg/ 5 tons of cargo or 38 fully equipped troops. The engine and transmission were installed beneath the cargo bay floor.

The vehicle was powered by a Rolls-Royce B81 eight-cylinder petrol engine with a five-speed gearbox driving six

BELOW: **In production form, the Stalwart was mid-engined, with the 6,516cc Rolls-Royce power unit installed beneath the cargo bay. The deep corner windows identify this as a Stalwart Mk 2.**

large, equally spaced wheels. There was a single-speed unitary transfer box, which allowed the use of all five gears in forward or reverse and also incorporated a limited-slip differential. Final drive to the wheels was transmitted by bevel-geared boxes and epicyclic reduction gears. This subsequently proved to be something of a weakness, and if the vehicle was driven on hard surfaces for too long, the fact that there was just one differential could lead to transmission stresses causing failure of the bevel-geared boxes and drive shafts. A power take-off on the transfer box was linked to the two Dowty "Hydrojet" units which provided propulsion and directional control when afloat.

Suspension was independent on all six wheels using twin wishbones and longitudinal torsion bars; there were two double-acting hydraulic shock absorbers at each wheel station. Steering was through the front and centre axles.

The first prototypes were submitted for trials in 1960. Two years later, in August 1962, Alvis received contracts for 250 Mk 1 Stalwarts, designated FV620. In 1966, the Mk 1 was replaced by the Mk 2 which offered increased power and mobility, particularly in the water. It also required less maintenance. Alongside the basic cargo vehicle, now designated FV622, there were the FV623 artillery tractor and the FV624 REME fitters' vehicle, both of the latter with an Atlas 3-ton hydraulic crane mounted behind the cab. Field modifications saw the Stalwart fitted with the EMI Ranger anti-personnel mine-laying system, and with "Unit Bulk Replenishment Refuelling Equipment" (UBRE).

The production total for the Mk 2 was 1,322, of which 117 were the FV623 variant and 120 were the FV624. The vehicle saw service with British Army units in West Germany

ABOVE: **A Mk 1 Stalwart, designated FV620. Propulsion in the water was by Dowty "Hydrojet" units at the rear of the vehicle.**

and was sold to the armies of Austria, Sweden and Switzerland. A scheme to allow the vehicle to be built under licence by Berliet in France, under the name Auroch, never progressed beyond the prototype stage.

Changing attitudes towards amphibious vehicles within NATO led to the "Hydrojet" units being removed in 1985, but the Stalwart remained in service until the early 1990s.

Alvis Stalwart

Type: Truck, 5-ton, high-mobility load carrier, 6x6; FV620, FV622, FV623, FV624

Manufacturer: Alvis; Coventry

Production: 1962 to 1971

Powerplant: Rolls-Royce B81 Mk 8B; eight cylinders in-line; petrol; water-cooled; 6,516cc; overhead inlet valves, side exhaust; power output, 195bhp at 3,750rpm

Transmission: 5F5R; full-time 6x6; "Hydrojet" propulsion when afloat

Suspension: Independent at all six wheels by double wishbones and torsion bars; double-acting hydraulic shock absorbers

Brakes: Air-assisted hydraulic

Electrical system: 24V

Dimensions: Length – 6,400mm/252in
Width – 2,600mm/102in
Height – tilt in place – 2,640mm/104in; minimum, 2,400mm/94in
Wheelbase – 1,524+1,524mm/60+60in

Weight: Unladen – 8,408-9,932kg/18,575-21,863lb
Payload – 5,239kg/11,550lb

Performance: Maximum speed – on land, 48-64kph/30-40mph; in water, 6.4-9.7kph/4-6mph

ABOVE: **The FV623 artillery tractor and the FV624 REME vehicle were both equipped with an Atlas hydraulic arm-type crane mounted behind the cab bulkhead.**

Austin K2

Although it is probably best known in K2/Y ambulance form, a total of 27,800 of the 2-ton Austin K2 were built during World War II, of which approximately half (13,102) were bodied as an ambulance. In this form it was the most widely used ambulance in World War II, and as well as being used by the British Army, it was supplied to France, Norway, Russia and the USA.

Described as a "heavy ambulance", the standardized body of the K2/Y variant was produced by Mann Egerton coachbuilders and was designed to accommodate four stretchers or ten seated casualties, together with a medical attendant. The body was of lightweight construction, by way of painted leathercloth fabric stretched over a timber frame; insulation was incorporated in the body and a heater was fitted. A connecting door gave access from the rear body to the cab. Other roles for what was essentially the same vehicle included mobile office and loudspeaker van. The same body, designated No 2 Mk I/L, was also fitted to the Bedford ML chassis.

The K2 dates from 1940 and was derived from the company's K30, a 30cwt open-cabbed military truck.

ABOVE: **Austin K2/Y ambulance ready for shipment to the Soviet Union, a charitable gift from the people of Scarborough, North Yorkshire.**

In turn, this had been based on the civilian vehicle with which the company had re-entered the commercial vehicle market in 1939. The truck was powered by a 3,462cc six-cylinder petrol engine driving the rear axle through a four-speed gearbox. There were live axles fitted at front and rear, carried on semi-elliptical leaf springs.

Other roles for this chassis included a general-service cargo vehicle, as well as a workshop and power equipment vehicle. In 1944, the K2/A variant was produced for the RAF and equipped as a fire tender.

Austin K2

Type: Truck, 2-ton, ambulance, 4x2
Manufacturer: Austin Motor Company; Longbridge
Production: 1940 to 1945
Powerplant: Austin; six cylinders in-line; petrol; water-cooled; 3,462cc; overhead valves; power output, 60bhp at 3,000rpm
Transmission: 4F1R; 4x2
Suspension: Live axles on semi-elliptical multi-leaf springs; hydraulic shock absorbers
Brakes: Hydraulic
Electrical system: 6V
Dimensions: Length – 5,486mm/216in
Width – 2,210mm/87in
Height – 2,743mm/108in
Wheelbase – 3,404mm/134in
Weight: Unladen – 8,426–9,917kg/18,575–21,863lb
Payload – 1,016kg/2,240lb
Performance: Maximum speed – 88kph/55mph

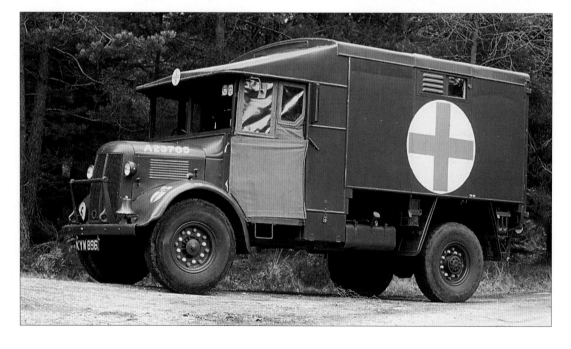

RIGHT: **The four-stretcher, insulated and heated rear body, manufactured by Mann Egerton, was of lightweight construction. A connecting door allowed access from the rear body to the cab. Side doors were not fitted, only canvas sidescreens.**

Austin WN1 "Champ"

Towards the closing years of World War II, the Austin Motor Company had been asked by the War Office to investigate the possibility of producing an all-British replacement for the Jeep. Nothing is known of Austin's reply in this respect but, in 1946, Nuffield Mechanizations produced a number of prototypes for a Jowett-powered vehicle identified as the "Gutty". It is said that Alec Issigonis was involved. In 1949, this was superseded by the FV1801 Wolseley "Mudlark". Retaining very little of the "Gutty" beyond the suspension, the "Mudlark" was powered by a Rolls-Royce B Series four-cylinder engine as used in a range of new British combat vehicles.

Following an almost three-year trials period, the production contract for this vehicle, described as FV1801A, was awarded to Austin. Between 1952 and 1955, some 13,500 were produced in two types – a standard cargo vehicle and a "Fitted For Wireless" (FFW) version intended for the communications role.

It was an advanced vehicle for the time, with a licence-built Rolls-Royce four-cylinder engine, five forward and reverse gears and independent torsion-bar suspension, and of unitary (chassis-less) construction. Screened and waterproofed 24V electrical equipment was fitted. Unfortunately, the WN1 was also expensive and unreliable and was quickly superseded by the cheaper Land Rover.

There were also field ambulance, cable layer and recoilless-rifle mount versions produced as well as a special forces version in the style of the Land Rover "Pink Panther". Few of these special vehicles were produced, and even fewer appear to have been used in action. The FV1801A was used only by the armies of Britain and Australia.

The name "Champ" was actually only officially assigned to the Austin A90-engined civilian version (chassis designation WN3), but was adopted by the National Servicemen who had a love-hate relationship with this advanced but unreliable vehicle. There was also an A90-engined military variant designated WN2.

ABOVE: **The Rolls-Royce engined FV1801 Austin "Champ" was intended as a replacement for the Jeep, but in service it was too expensive, complex and unreliable. The Land Rover proved to be an adequate and cheaper alternative.**

LEFT: **The "Champ" began to enter service in 1952 and was used during the Suez Crisis. By 1966, all had been disposed of with some being used by the Territorial Army.**

Austin WN1 "Champ"

Type: Truck, 1/4-ton, cargo (or FFW), 4x4; FV1801A
Manufacturer: Austin Motor Company; Longbridge
Production: 1952 to 1955
Powerplant: Licence-built Rolls-Royce B40 Mk 2A or Mk 5A; four cylinders in-line; petrol; water-cooled; 2,880cc; overhead inlet valves, side exhaust; power output, 52bhp at 3,600rpm
Transmission: 5F5R; part-time 4x4
Suspension: Independent suspension using wishbones and torsion bars; telescopic shock absorbers
Brakes: Hydraulic
Electrical system: 24V
Dimensions: Length – 3,670mm/144in
Width – 1,559mm/61in
Height – tilt in place, 1,880mm/74in; minimum, 1,372mm/54in
Wheelbase – 2,134mm/84in
Weight: Unladen – 1,660kg/3,660lb
Payload – 363kg/800lb
Performance: Maximum speed – 97kph/60mph

Bedford MW

During 1935, the British Army issued a specification for a 15cwt 4x2 "General Service" (GS) military truck inviting manufacturers to supply vehicles to take part in the annual comparative trials in north Wales. The trials were repeated, for various classes of vehicle, in 1936 and 1937.

In May 1937, one of Bedford's contributions to the trials was a short, square-fronted vehicle identified as WD-1 and assembled mainly from off-the-shelf components. It performed well in the trials, and did even better the following year by which time it was designated MW and fitted with a more powerful 3,519cc six-cylinder engine producing 72bhp. Although lacking four-wheel drive and thus not suitable for off-road use, the powerful engine, combined with a short wheelbase, low centre of gravity and relatively light weight, gave the vehicle excellent acceleration and almost sportscar-like handling.

Between 1939 and 1945 the company supplied more than 66,000 vehicles equipped for many different roles. The earliest examples were equipped with aero-type screens and canvas doors, but on later models there was a full windscreen, together with

steel doors, which resulted in a 150mm/6in increase in height. The vehicle was always open-cabbed, and the unusually wide bonnet was necessitated by the need for a special WD-type air cleaner. This was never actually fitted to production vehicles.

Alongside the standard cargo bodied vehicle (MWD), anti-aircraft gun tractor (MWT), machinery truck, water tanker (MWC), "Fitted For Wireless" (FFW) communications

ABOVE: **Although never fitted with four-wheel drive, the 15cwt Bedford MW was one of the best British trucks of World War II. It remained in production until 1945, by which time some 66,000 had been produced.**

truck (MWR) and radio van (MWV), there were even armoured versions. During production, the MW was supplied to all three British services as well as other Government departments and overseas customers.

ABOVE: **A Bedford MW being refuelled from a drum using a hand pump. Like all early MWs, the vehicle is fitted with folding aero-type screens.**

Bedford MW

Type: Truck, 15cwt, cargo, 4x2
Manufacturer: Vauxhall Motors; Luton
Production: 1939 to 1945
Powerplant: Bedford; six cylinders in-line; petrol; water-cooled; 3,519cc; overhead valves; power output, 72bhp at 3,000rpm
Transmission: 4F1R; 4x2
Suspension: Live axles on semi-elliptical multi-leaf springs
Brakes: Hydraulic
Electrical system: 12V
Dimensions: Length – 4,369mm/172in
　Width – 1,981mm/78in
　Height – tilt in place, 2,286mm/90in; minimum, 1,600mm/63in
　Wheelbase – 2,515mm/99in
Weight: Unladen – 2,146kg/4,730lb
　Payload – 1,361kg/3,000lb
Performance: Maximum speed – 64kph/40mph

ABOVE: Dating from 1941, and remaining in production until the end of the war, the QL was Bedford's first 4x4 truck. A total of more than 52,000 were produced.

ABOVE: A QLR signals office van at the headquarters of Field Marshal Montgomery, Commander-in-Chief of 21st Army Group, spring 1945.

Bedford QL

While Bedford's MW and OY trucks had basically been militarized versions of civilian types, the forward-control QL was a purpose-built military vehicle. Discussions about the design of such a vehicle had begun in 1938, with the War Department indicating that it might be interested in a four-wheel drive Bedford in early 1939. Development work started in September of that year and by November was considered to be of the utmost importance. The first prototype, QL-1, was available for trials in February 1940 and further prototypes followed as teething troubles were

BELOW: A Bedford QLC 4x4 truck/tractor with a 6-ton semi-trailer.

eliminated. There were particular problems with cracks appearing in the chassis. Full-scale production finally started in February 1941.

The engine was the same 3,519cc six-cylinder unit as used in the smaller MW, driving all four wheels through a four-speed gearbox and two-speed transfer box, with front axle disconnect. The front and rear axles were similar in design, incorporating spiral bevel gears. The sound of the intermediate gears, particularly when the low ratios were engaged, earned the QL the nickname "Screamer". The suspension was by conventional semi-elliptical leaf springs.

By the end of World War II, Bedford had produced 52,247 QLs, most of which

were fitted with the GS cargo body (chassis version QLD). Other standard variants included a radio/communications van (QLR and QLC), troop carrier (QLT), kitchen (QLD), battery storage (QLD), machinery (QLD), petrol tanker (QLC), fire-fighter (QLC), a tractor for the Bofors light anti-aircraft gun (QLB), winch-equipped air-portable tipper (QLW) and tractor for semi-trailer (QLC).

The QL was a reliable vehicle and was supplied to all three British services, remaining in use well into the post-war years. It was finally succeeded by the Bedford RL.

Bedford QL

Type: Truck, 3-ton, cargo, 4x4
Manufacturer: Vauxhall Motors; Luton
Production: 1941 to 1945
Powerplant: Bedford; six cylinders in-line; petrol; water-cooled; 3,519cc; overhead valves; power output, 72bhp at 3,000rpm
Transmission: 4F1Rx2; part-time 4x4
Suspension: Live axles on semi-elliptical multi-leaf springs
Brakes: Hydraulic with vacuum servo-assistance
Electrical system: 12V
Dimensions: Length – 5,994mm/236in
   Width – 2,261mm/89in
   Height – tilt in place, 3,048mm/120in; minimum, 2,591mm/102in
   Wheelbase – 3,632mm/143in
Weight: Unladen – 3,277kg/7,225lb
   Payload – 3,708kg/,8,175lb
Performance: Maximum speed – 60kph/38mph

Bedford RL

In 1950, Bedford introduced the S-Type, or so-called "Big Bedford", a range of new forward-control trucks taking the marque into the 7-ton class. The design and development of a military variant to replace the QL started in December the same year, and the first prototype was delivered to the Fighting Vehicles Research & Development Establishment (FVRDE) in May 1951.

Designated RL and assigned the classification FV13100 series, the vehicle was powered by the new 4,927cc six-cylinder engine first used in the S-Type, driving through a four-speed gearbox and two-speed transfer box. By April 1952, it had been approved for production and over the next 17 years, some 73,135 examples were built in a very wide range of body types.

Although not strictly a military vehicle, the best-known RL variant

LEFT: **A Bedford RL equipped as a missile launcher.**

is probably the RLHZ "Green Goddess" Civil Defence emergency fire pump.

The four-wheel-drive RL was offered to civilians from October 1953. It was also built under licence in Denmark.

Bedford RL	
Type: Truck, 3-ton (later 4-ton), cargo, 4x4; FV13100 series	
Manufacturer: Vauxhall Motors; Luton	
Production: 1952 to 1969	
Powerplant: Bedford 300; six cylinders in-line; petrol; water-cooled; 4,927cc; overhead valves; power output, 110–130bhp at 3,200rpm	
Transmission: 4F1Rx2; part-time 4x4	
Suspension: Live axles on semi-elliptical multi-leaf springs	
Brakes: Hydraulic with air-pressure or vacuum-servo-assistance	
Electrical system: 24V	
Dimensions: Length – 6,350mm/250in Width – 2,390mm/94in Height – tilt in place, 2,995mm/118in; minimum, 2,591mm/102in Wheelbase – 3,353mm/132in or 3,962mm/156in	
Weight: Unladen – 4,001kg/8,820lb Payload – 3,493kg/7,700lb; subsequently uprated to 3,992kg/8,800lb	
Performance: Maximum speed – 64kph/40mph	

Bedford MK, MJ

Introduced in 1971, the Bedford M-Type has been the workhorse of the British Army for more than three decades. Design of the truck was derived from Bedford's TK series and started in the early 1960s, with the first example, designated RL Mk 2, demonstrated in 1962. It was powered by a new 5,408cc normally aspirated multi-fuel diesel engine. There was also a new transfer case, giving four-wheel drive in both high and low gears, and a new braking system. Although most were fitted with a steel 4- to 5-ton cargo body like the earlier RL, the MK and MJ were equipped for a very wide range of roles.

In 1981, after 24,000 had been built, the original engine was superseded by a turbocharged unit, and was designated MJ.

BELOW: **The Bedford MJ remains in service with the British Army to this day.**

Bedford MK, MJ	
Type: Truck, 3-ton (later 4-ton), cargo, 4x4; FV 13800 series	
Manufacturer: Vauxhall Motors; Luton	
Production: 1971 to 1985	
Powerplant: Bedford 330D; six cylinders in-line; multi-fuel diesel (MJ, turbocharged); water cooled; 5,408cc; overhead valves; power output, 98–108bhp at 2,600rpm	
Transmission: 4F1Rx2; part-time 4x4	
Suspension: Live axles on semi-elliptical multi-leaf springs; direct-acting hydraulic shock absorbers	
Brakes: Hydraulic with air-pressure servo-assistance	
Electrical system: 24V	
Dimensions: Length – 6,570mm/259in Width – 2,490mm/98in Height – tilt in place, 3,403mm/134in Wheelbase – 3,353mm/132in or 3,962mm/156in	
Weight: Unladen – 5,118kg/11,284lb Payload – 3,493kg/7,700lb; subsequently uprated to 3,992kg/8,800lb	
Performance: Maximum speed – 80kph/50mph	

Total production was around 50,000, and the truck has been exported widely, notably to Ireland and the Netherlands.

Commer Q4

During the 1950s, the British Army replaced most of its wartime 3-ton 4x4 trucks with the new Bedford RL. Whether Bedford could not manage to produce the trucks fast enough or for some other reason, similarly rated types were also purchased from Commer, Ford and Thornycroft.

Commer's contribution was the Q4 FV13200 series, and several thousand were built from 1952. The vehicle was effectively a militarized version of the company's civilian "Superpoise" range, with extended wheel arches being used to cover the wider-track axles. Power was by a Commer 4,752cc six-cylinder petrol engine, driving through a four-speed gearbox and two-speed transfer box. Alongside the standard "General Service" (GS) cargo vehicle, there were signals, tipper,

LEFT: **Two Commer Q4s fitted with the signals-type body.**

photographic processing and workshop variants. The Q4 was also used by the Home Office as a pump carrier and hose layer with Civil Defence mobile columns of the 1950s.

Commer Q4

Type: Truck, 3-ton, 4x4; FV13200 series
Manufacturer: Rootes Group, Commer-Karrier Division; Dunstable
Production: 1952 to 1956
Powerplant: Commer; six cylinders in-line; petrol; water-cooled; 4,752cc; overhead valves; power output, 95bhp at 3,000rpm
Transmission: 4F1Rx2; part-time 4x4
Suspension: Live axles on semi-elliptical multi-leaf springs
Brakes: Hydraulic with vacuum servo-assistance
Electrical system: 12V
Dimensions: Length – 6,985mm/275in
Width – 2,440mm/96in
Height – tilt in place, 3,175mm/125in
Wheelbase – 4,242mm/167in
Weight: Unladen – 4,725kg/10,416lb
Payload – 2,876kg/6,340lb
Performance: Maximum speed – 68kph/42mph

Crossley Q-Type

Crossley Motors were established in the late 19th century, producing Otto engines under licence and from 1904 building motor cars. Armoured cars were produced during the inter-war period, and the company started to manufacture trucks in 1932, eventually abandoning car production in 1937. Crossley trucks were supplied to the British Army and the RAF throughout the 1930s.

During World War II, the company produced some 11,000 of the Q-Type, the majority of which were supplied to the RAF. The standard body was a 3-ton cargo type. Other variants included a ballast-bodied tractor for semi-trailers, used by the RAF for towing the "Queen Mary" low-loader trailer, as well as a mobile workshop. The truck was powered by a Crossley 5,266cc four-cylinder petrol engine driving through a four-speed gearbox and two-speed transfer box.

Crossley never resumed truck manufacture after the war and was absorbed into the AEC-controlled

Associated Commercial Vehicles (ACV) group in 1948. The name was retained by ACV for some export markets.

Crossley Q-Type

Type: Truck, 3-ton, 4x4
Manufacturer: Crossley Motors; Manchester
Production: 1940 to 1945
Powerplant: Crossley 30/100; four cylinders in-line; petrol; water-cooled; 5,266cc; side valves; power output, 90bhp at 2,500rpm
Transmission: 4F1Rx2; part-time 4x4
Suspension: Live axles on semi-elliptical multi-leaf springs
Brakes: Hydraulic with air servo-assistance; vacuum brakes for trailer
Electrical system: 12V
Dimensions: Length – 6,172mm/243in
Width – 2,286mm/90in
Height – tilt in place, 3,353mm/132in; minimum, 2,743mm/108in
Wheelbase – 3,505mm/138in; 2,591mm/102in for tractor
Weight: Unladen – 4,750kg/10,472lb
Payload – 3,048kg/6,720lb
Performance: Maximum speed – 45kph/28mph

LEFT: **A Crossley Q-Type 4x4 fire tender fitted with foam-making equipment.**

Fordson WOT2

In 1939, the Ford Motor Company started to produce a series of "War Office Trucks", designated WOT1 to WOT6. The smallest of these was the 15cwt WOT2. This was almost certainly derived from the Fordson 7V, a 2- to 3-ton forward-control commercial vehicle available in a choice of wheelbase lengths. Two basic variants were produced – a GS truck and a closed van. The first production vehicles were designated as WOT2A and this progressed through seven variants to WOT2H each incorporating various changes. There was no WOT2G.

Power was by a Ford V8 side-valve petrol engine, driving the rear axle through a four-speed gearbox. Following Ford's standard practice, the propeller shaft was enclosed in a rigid torque tube that provided location for the rear axle. The suspension was by conventional semi-elliptical springs. At the front, the axle was supported on a single transverse-leaf spring carried on two radius rods which, in turn, were attached to a ball joint on a chassis cross-member.

Initially, the vehicle was fitted with an open cab with roll-up canvas doors and aero-type screens. A semi-enclosed cab was fitted from the WOT2E onwards, with a full-height windscreen, hinged metal doors and side-screens.

The GS truck was fitted with a steel-framed, fixed-sided timber body with a drop-down tailgate. Later examples were provided with a canvas tilt supported on tubular hoops; on the WOT2F variant the rear body was steel-panelled. The van variant (WOT2B, WOT2D) was not dissimilar in appearance, but the body was enclosed at the rear with a fixed canvas cover stretched across wooden panels. There were also house-bodied variants equipped as office, radio communications and fire service vehicles, the latter used by the National Fire Service and the Home Office. Some were converted to light "Anti-Aircraft" (AA) trucks mounting a 20mm Polsten or Hispano cannon, while others included provision for mounting an anti-aircraft Bren gun above the passenger roof.

Almost 60,000 were produced under 36 or more contracts over a six-year period, and the vehicle remained in service into the 1950s.

ABOVE: **Ford's smallest truck of World War II was the WOT2, which was produced in two basic variants – a GS truck and a closed van.** BELOW: **While the earliest examples were fitted with an open cab that had roll-up canvas doors and aero-type screens, an enclosed cab was fitted from the WOT2E type onwards.**

Fordson WOT2

Type: Truck, 15cwt, cargo, 4x2
Manufacturer: Ford Motor Company; Dagenham
Production: 1939 to 1945
Powerplant: Ford; eight cylinders in V configuration; petrol; water-cooled; 3,621cc; side valves; power output, 60bhp at 2,840rpm
Transmission: 4F1R; 4x2
Suspension: Live axles on semi-elliptical multi-leaf springs; hydraulic shock absorbers
Brakes: Mechanical
Electrical system: 6V, 12V
Dimensions: Length – 4,500mm/177in
    Width – 2,000mm/79in
    Height – 2,295mm/90in;
    minimum, 1,803mm/71in
    Wheelbase – 2,692mm/106in
Weight: Unladen – 2,050kg/4,520lb
    Payload – 748kg/1,650lb
Performance: Maximum speed – 80kph/50ph

Fordson WOT1

Fordson WOT1

Type: Truck, 3-ton, cargo, 6x4
Manufacturer: Ford Motor Company; Dagenham
Production: 1940 to 1945
Powerplant: Ford; eight cylinders in V configuration; petrol; water-cooled; 3,621cc; side valves; power output, 85bhp at 3,800rpm
Transmission: 4F1R, 4F1Rx2; 6x4
Suspension: Live axles on semi-elliptical multi-leaf springs
Brakes: Hydraulic (WOT1A/1 with vacuum servo-assistance)
Electrical system: 6V
Dimensions: Length – 7,087mm/279in
　　Width – 2,134mm/84in
　　Height – 3,099mm/122in
　　Wheelbase – 4,470mm/176in; 4,191mm/165in
　　Bogie centres – 1,090mm/43in
Weight: Unladen – 3,352kg/7,390lb
　　Payload – 3,361kg/7,410lb
Performance: Maximum speed – 72kph/45mph

Rated at 3 tons, and with a Sussex conversion to allow a 6x4 drive line, the Fordson WOT1 was the largest of Ford's "War Office Trucks". It was introduced in 1940, with the majority being supplied to the RAF. The standard variant was a GS truck, but there were also special bodies produced, including parachute drying, power and charging equipment, dental surgery, searchlight carrier, crew coach, and

ABOVE: **A restored WOT1 equipped as an RAF fire/crash tender, painted in desert camouflage.**

office variants. An airfield crash tender equipped with pumping equipment was supplied to the RAF.

The engine was the Ford V8 side-valve, driving the middle axle through a four-speed gearbox; a second crown-wheel and pinion set in this axle conveyed the drive to the rear axle.

Suspension was by semi-elliptical springs, inverted at the rear.

A total of 9,154 Fordson WOT1 vehicles were built, with two chassis variants – the WOT1A had a longer wheelbase, while the WOT1A/1 was equipped with vacuum servo-assisted brakes.

Fordson WOA2

Fordson WOA2

Type: Car, heavy utility, 4x2
Manufacturer: Ford Motor Company; Dagenham
Production: 1941 to 1944
Powerplant: Ford; eight cylinders in V configuration; petrol; water-cooled; 3,621cc; side valves; power output, 85bhp at 3,600rpm
Transmission: 3F1R; 4x2
Suspension: Live axles on transverse semi-elliptical multi-leaf springs; hydraulic shock absorbers
Brakes: Mechanical
Electrical system: 6V, 12V
Dimensions: Length – 4,395mm/173in
　　Width – 1,905mm/75in
　　Height – 1,778mm/70in
　　Wheelbase – 2,742mm/108in
Weight: Unladen – 1,613kg/3,555lb
　　Payload – 565kg/1,245lb
Performance: Maximum speed – 80kph/50ph

Introduced in May 1941, the Fordson WOA2 was a six-seat heavy utility vehicle derived from the company's WOA1 staff car, a militarized version of the Ford Model 62 sedan. There was a folding map table behind the front seats, and the rear seats could be folded down to provide a load-carrying area. A number were converted to open cars in the field, by cutting through the door pillars at window level.

Power was by a Ford V8 engine driving the rear wheels through a three-speed gearbox. Suspension was by live axles at front and rear, each suspended on a single transverse semi-elliptical spring. The rear axle was located on a torque tube. The WOA2 model was fitted with 9.00x13 tyres, while the WOA2/A used narrow-section 6.50x16 tyres.

LEFT: **A WOA2/A with narrow-section tyres.**

The vehicle remained in production until 1944, and around 5,000 examples were built. It was widely used by all three of the British services as a staff and command car.

FWD R6T (AEC Model 850)

In 1928, Guy, Leyland, Scammell and FWD were requested by the War Office to submit six-wheel drive tractors as a possible replacement for the Thornycroft "Hathi". This tractor had been developed by Thornycroft and the Royal Army Service Corps, but was proving not powerful enough to tow heavy anti-aircraft guns on wheeled trailer mounts. The War Office required that the new tractors be capable of producing a drawbar pull of 5,443–6,804kg/12,000–15,000lb.

FWD's contribution to this project was the R6T, which had been introduced in 1927 by the company's predecessors. Four Wheel Drive Motors – generally known as FWD – had been formed in 1929, in Slough, as the successor to the British Four Wheel Drive Tractor-Lorry Company and the Four Wheel Drive Tractor-Lorry Engineering Company Limited. The R6T was the company's first

six-wheel drive chassis and was powered by a Dorman JUP six-cylinder side-valve engine, driving all wheels through a four-speed gearbox, two-speed transfer box and spur-gear axles with reduction hubs. Front suspension was by a novel centre-pivoted beam with steel sliders at the spring ends to ensure axle location.

A military prototype was supplied to the War Office for trials in 1929 and was judged to be satisfactory. The prototype was returned to FWD and fitted with a new body. At the end of the year, a contract was issued for a further nine vehicles. This batch of vehicles were modified in various respects, with the most significant change being the replacement of the original Dorman engine and gearbox with an 6,126cc AEC A136 overhead-valve engine driving through an AEC gearbox. Changes were also made to both the cab and the body, notably by

the provision of seating for six in the rear, with two more seats alongside the driver.

In mid-1932, FWD was taken over by AEC and the R6T became the AEC Model 850. A total of 24 R6Ts were built by FWD at Slough, and a further 33 were built by AEC at Southall between 1932 and 1936. This gave a combined production total of 57.

As well as being used as an artillery tractor, a number were equipped for the recovery role and were used by the Royal Army Ordnance Corps. It was not unknown for the vehicle to be used as temporary tank transporter tractor units.

FWD R6T, (AEC Model 850)

Type: Tractor, heavy artillery, 6x6
Manufacturer: FWD Motors; Slough. AEC Motors; Southall
Production: 1929 to 1936
Powerplant: Prototype – Dorman JUL; six cylinders in line; petrol; water-cooled; 6,597cc; side valves; power output, 78bhp
Production vehicles – AEC A136; six cylinders in line; water-cooled; 6,126cc; overhead valves; power output, 95bhp
Transmission: 4F1Rx2; part-time 6x6
Suspension: Live axles on semi-elliptical multi-leaf springs, transverse at front
Brakes: Air-pressure
Electrical system: 6V
Dimensions: Length – prototype, 5,740mm/226in; production vehicles, 5,867mm/231in
Width – 2,286mm/90in
Height – tilt in place, 2,642mm/104in
Wheelbase – 3,048mm/120in
Bogie centres – 1,220mm/48in
Weight: Unladen – 8,687kg/19,152lb
Performance: Maximum speed – 32kph/20mph

ABOVE: **The FWD R6T was an all-wheel-drive heavy artillery tractor. Following the take-over of FWD by AEC in mid-1932, the vehicle became known as the AEC Model 850. A total of 58 were produced between 1929 and 1936.** LEFT: **An R6T recovery tractor. A total of 57 were built; 24 by FWD at Slough and 33 by AEC at Southall.**

Humber FWD

During World War II, Humber produced a range of small military vehicles based on a common 4x4 chassis, fitted with independent front suspension and a six-cylinder side-valve engine. The chassis was developed from that used for the company's "Super Snipe" saloon car and was introduced in 1940, remaining in production throughout World War II. There was a heavy utility vehicle, nicknamed "The Box" because of the vehicle's square appearance, an 8cwt truck, and an ambulance. A version of the same chassis was also used as the basis for an armoured scout car, an armoured reconnaissance vehicle and a light armoured car.

The front suspension used a semi-elliptical transverse multi-leaf spring as the top link, combined with wishbones at the bottom to provide basic independent suspension. All-wheel drive allowed drivers the benefit of excellent off-road performance. The 4,086cc six-cylinder petrol engine was connected to a four-speed gearbox and two-speed transfer box, the latter including the front axle disconnect.

Most examples were fitted with a steel-panelled four-door heavy utility body equipped with six seats. During

1940–41, a small pick-up truck was also produced with a removable body which could be used as a tent by folding down telescopic legs. Finally, there was an enclosed field ambulance with a steel-panelled body built by Thrupp & Maberly. The BBC operated a fleet of these Humbers for use by war correspondents, using both utility- and ambulance-bodied variants, the latter converted into recording vans. There was also a plan to produce

ABOVE: **The Humber FWD was a well-designed and reliable vehicle. The Humber chassis was also bodied as an 8cwt pick-up truck and as a field ambulance.**

a 4x4 staff car on the same chassis, but it does not appear that any were actually produced.

Total production amounted to 5,199 units, of which the majority (3,960) were of the heavy utility type.

ABOVE: **The Humber FWD 8cwt cargo/personnel truck; the same chassis was also used as the basis for an ambulance, staff car, and wireless vehicle.**

Humber FWD

Type: Car, heavy utility, 4x4
Manufacturer: Humber; Coventry
Production: 1940 to 1945
Powerplant: Humber; six cylinders in-line; petrol; water-cooled; 4,086cc; side valves; power output, 85bhp at 3,400rpm
Transmission: 4F1Rx2; part-time 4x4
Suspension: Independent front suspension using transverse semi-elliptical multi-leaf spring and wishbone links; live axle at rear on semi-elliptical multi-leaf springs
Brakes: Hydraulic
Electrical system: 12V
Dimensions: (heavy utility variant)
    Length – 4,293mm/169in
    Width – 1,880mm/74in
    Height – 1,956mm/77in
    Wheelbase – 2,845mm/112in
Weight: Unladen – 2,413kg/5,320lb
    Payload – 533kg/1,176lb
Performance: Maximum speed – 80kph/50mph

Humber FV1600

During World War II, the 15cwt truck was the most widely used by the British Army, with vehicles supplied by Ford, Morris-Commercial, Humber and Commer. During the re-equipping of the British Army which followed the end of the war, this class of truck was upgraded to 1-ton capacity. At the same time, current military thinking divided British military vehicles into three broad types. The most sophisticated of these, designated CT or "combat", was a purpose-designed truck incorporating features such as all-wheel drive, built-in waterproofing and radio suppression, independent suspension and common electrical equipment. All CT vehicles were powered by a Rolls-Royce B Series engine, which was produced as a four-, six- or eight-cylinder unit.

The 1-ton CT truck, always known simply by the Fighting Vehicles Development Establishment (FVDE) designation FV1600, was developed by the Rootes Group and was badged Humber. Prototypes were produced during 1951 to an FVDE specification which laid down various performance parameters. Following a series of extensive trials, the FV1600 was assembled at the company's Ryton-on-Dunsmore plant during 1952–53, with a total of 3,700 built.

Humber FV1600

Type: Truck, 1-ton, cargo, 4x4; FV1601
Manufacturer: Rootes Group; Ryton-on-Dunsmore
Production: 1952 to 1953
Powerplant: Rolls-Royce B60 Mk 2A, Mk 5A; six cylinders in-line; petrol; water-cooled; 4,256cc; overhead inlet valves, side exhaust; power output, 109bhp at 3,750rpm
Transmission: 5F1R; part-time 4x4
Suspension: Independent suspension using double wishbones and adjustable torsion bars; double-acting hydraulic shock absorbers
Brakes: Vacuum servo-assisted hydraulic
Electrical system: 24V
Dimensions: (FV1601) Length – 5,054mm/199in
  Width – 2,083mm/82in
  Height – tilt in place, 2,362mm/193in; minimum, 2,114mm/83in
  Wheelbase – 2,743mm/108in
Weight: Unladen – 3,811kg/8,402lb
  Payload – 1,384kg/3,051lb
Performance: Maximum speed – 88kph/55mph

The engine was the six-cylinder B60 unit, driving both axles through a five-speed gearbox and single-speed transfer box. Suspension was independent on all wheels by double wishbones and longitudinal torsion bars. The prototypes had featured an open cab, but production machines had a modern all-steel enclosed cab incorporating drop-down windows and a top-hinged windscreen. The cargo body had fixed sides and a hinged tailgate.

Most of the production total was bodied as the FV1601 cargo vehicle. Other standard variants included the FV1602, a version of the cargo vehicle which was "Fitted For Wireless" (FFW). The FV1604 was fitted with a Marshalls of Cambridge "radio house" body. Around 1960, a small number designated FV1621 and FV1624 were converted as test and support vehicles for trials of Malkara, an anti-tank missile.

Many of those produced were put directly into store, and when demand arose in the mid-1950s for an armoured truck and armoured personnel carrier, the cargo bodies were removed and the chassis were rebodied for the armoured role. In this form, and nicknamed "Pig", the Humber became a common sight on the city streets of Northern Ireland.

ABOVE: **The Humber FV1600 series was powered by a Rolls-Royce six-cylinder engine and fulfilled the 1-ton "combat" role in the post-war inventory of British military vehicles. The steel-bodied cargo variant was designated FV1601, and there was a similar "Fitted For Wireless" (FFW) variant.**
LEFT: **FV1604 with a house-bodied radio truck.**

Hunting-Percival Harrier

In 1957, the Hunting-Percival Aircraft Company built four prototype folding cars for air-drop trials with the British Army. The vehicle was produced to a design which had been patented by J. Dolphin of Marlow in 1953. It was powered by a front-mounted 649cc BSA two-cylinder motorcycle engine, driving the rear wheels via a four-speed transmission and roller chain. For ease of transport, the vehicle could be folded down to a box-shaped unit measuring

3,150x533x914mm/124x21x36in and easily lifted by four men. The vehicle could be made ready for use in around one minute. The Harrier had a conventional steering wheel, and was fitted with four seats. Independent suspension was fitted front and rear, using semi-elliptical springs and

BELOW LEFT AND BELOW: **The Hunting-Percival Harrier was a four-seat lightweight folding vehicle intended for air-dropping.**

wishbones. The springs were located by coil-sprung struts and formed the upper link on which the stub axles were mounted. There was no series production.

Karrier K6

The Rootes Group started production of the 3-ton Karrier K6 in December 1940. It was bodied as a fixed-side GS cargo vehicle with both fixed and split-waist cabs, the latter intended to be air-portable. Approximately 2,500 of the total

produced were fitted with a 4½-ton capacity vertical-spindle winch, mounted just forward of the rear axle and driven from a power take-off on the transfer

BELOW: **The Karrier K6 entered service with the British Army in December 1940.**

box. A short-wheelbase artillery tractor, KT4, was built for the Indian Army.

The engine was the same six-cylinder side-valve unit as installed in the Humber FWD range, fitted with a four-speed gearbox and two-speed transfer box. Unusually for the period, four-wheel drive was available in both the high and low ratios. A total of 4,500 were produced.

RIGHT: **The Wolf Defender can be traced directly to the Series I of 1948. Here members of No. 4001 Armoured Car Flight of the RAF Regiment are on patrol in the Canal Zone, Egypt, in a Series I Land Rover in 1953. The Land Rover is followed by a Humber Mk III airfield-defence armoured car.**

Land Rover Wolf Defender XD

The Land Rover was the brainchild of Maurice Wilks, a director of Rover, who had purchased a military-surplus Jeep in 1946 and found it useful on his farm in Wales. As the vehicle began to wear out, Wilks reasoned that there might be sufficient market for a similar dual-purpose machine to carry the Rover company through the difficult post-war years. The first prototype was based on a Jeep chassis, and used Jeep axles and transfer case. Aluminium was used for the body panels because Rover could not obtain licences to buy sufficient steel. Following the completion of 48 pre-production prototypes, the Series I was launched at the Amsterdam Motor Show in 1948. It was an immediate success.

Although there was no intention for the Land Rover to be used as a military vehicle, it was not long before the British Army realized that the vehicle could provide a low-cost replacement for the inventory of ageing Jeeps. At the same time, it could also be operated alongside the expensive Austin "Champ" which was still in development. The first military purchases came in 1948 and have continued to this day.

BELOW: **A Wolf TUM bogged down in the mud of Iraq. Some vehicles which served in that country carried a small air-conditioning unit installed in the locker ahead of the rear wheel.**

In 1951, the original 1,595cc petrol engine was replaced by a 1,997cc unit. In 1958, the Series I was superseded by the wider and more powerful Series II, which was fitted with a 2,286cc petrol engine. By this time, the original 2,032mm/80in wheelbase had been lengthened to 2,182mm/86in, and then to 2,235mm/88in. A 2,718mm/107in long-wheelbase chassis was introduced in 1954 and lengthened to 2,768mm/109in in 1957. Three years later, the Series IIA was launched and, in 1971, this was replaced by the Series III, still powered by the 2,286cc engine and still fitted with a body that was not dissimilar to that used 20 years earlier. The British Army continued to purchase Land Rovers in their thousands and the vehicle was also widely exported.

At the Geneva Motor Show in March 1983, Land Rover announced the replacement of the Series III by the short-wheelbase "Ninety" and the longer-wheelbase "One-Ten", later to be renamed Defender 90 and Defender 110. For the first time the vehicle featured permanent all-wheel drive and coil-spring suspension, and a V8 petrol engine was offered alongside the standard petrol and diesel options. The body could still be recognized as a Land Rover, but there was a one-piece windscreen and extensions over the wheel arches.

The Defender remains in production at the time of writing, and thousands are in service with the British Army and elsewhere, but it was effectively superseded, at least in British service, by the purpose-designed military Wolf Defender XD.

A specification for a more capable replacement for the Defender was drawn up by the Ministry of Defence in 1988 and Land Rover, IVECO and Pinzgauer all expressed interest in the project which would culminate in a contract for 8,000 vehicles. IVECO and Pinzgauer were eliminated. In late 1991, Land Rover was asked to prepare prototype vehicles in the "light" (short-wheelbase) and "medium" (long-wheelbase) classes. The vehicles which Land Rover produced were based on the then-current Defender but failed to meet the performance parameters.

LEFT: **A Wolf Defender variant with the British Army "Weapons Mount Installation Kit" (WMIK) which allows weapons to be fitted on the roll cage. The photograph shows troopers from the 3rd Battalion, Parachute Regiment, in training with a MILAN anti-tank missile equipped vehicle.**

The trials were called off in 1993. A second prototype, far more radical in its engineering, and now identified as Wolf 2, was more successful. Following the trials, Land Rover was awarded the contract and the Wolf Defender XD – "extra duty" – was first shown to the public in 1995. Production started in late 1996.

The vehicle was powered by a Land Rover 300 Tdi direct-injection turbocharged diesel engine, giving a top speed in the order of 129kph/80mph. The drive-line was by a five-speed gearbox and two-speed transfer box, connected permanently to the four wheels through a lockable centre differential. Suspension was by long-travel coil springs, with the axles located by a Panhard rod at the front and an A frame at the rear.

Two standard variants were produced – the "Truck, Utility, Light" (TUL) on a 2,286mm/90in wheelbase, rated for a payload of 508kg/½ ton, and the "Truck, Utility, Medium" (TUM) on which the wheelbase was extended to 2,794mm/110in and the payload increased to 1,016kg/1 ton. Both hard- and soft-top types were produced and all of the vehicles were fitted with a substantial roll cage. By fitting the "Weapons Mount Installation Kit" (WMIK), any Wolf Defender could be converted to a weapons platform,

typically mounting two 7.62mm general purpose machine-guns or a .50in Browning heavy machine-gun. All of the vehicles were equipped with a 24V electrical system and half of the total produced were "Fitted For Radio" (FFR). There was also a 3,226mm/127in wheelbase variant, which has been used as the basis for a battlefield ambulance.

Production was ended in October 1998 after 7,996 vehicles had been built. Of these, 1,411 were the TUL variant, the remainder being the TUM. Most were supplied to the British Army. The Royal Dutch Marines ordered the TUM and 71 were delivered in 1997.

BELOW: **Soldiers of the Heavy Machine-Gun Platoon of the 1st Battalion Royal Irish Regiment in Iraq during Operation Desert Storm.**

Land Rover Wolf Defender XD

Type: Truck, utility, light, ½-ton, 4x4; truck, utility, medium, 1-ton, 4x4
Manufacturer: Land Rover; Solihull
Production: 1996 to 1998
Powerplant: Land Rover 300 Tdi; four cylinders in-line; direct-injection turbocharged diesel; water-cooled; 2,506cc; overhead valves; power output, 111bhp at 4,000rpm
Transmission: 5F1Rx2; full-time 4x4; lockable centre differential
Suspension: Live axles on coil springs; axle location by Panhard rod at front, A-frame at rear
Brakes: Vacuum servo-assisted hydraulic
Electrical system: 24V
Dimensions: Length – 3,840mm/151in, 4,550mm/179in
Width – 1,800mm/70in
Height – tilt in place, 2,030mm/80in
Wheelbase – 2,286mm/90in, 2,794mm/110in
Weight: Unladen – 1,996kg/4,400lb, 2,595kg/5,720lb
Payload – 599kg/1,320lb, 1,143kg/2,520lb
Performance: Maximum speed – 129kph/80mph

Land Rover 101

The 1-ton forward-control Land Rover – generally described as the 101 – was developed as a heli-portable light artillery tractor which could also carry the gun's crew and a quantity of ammunition.

In 1967, Rover started building five forward-control 1-ton military prototypes, the first of which appeared in 1969. Although it generally resembled the production 101, there was a short bonnet projection, required to house the Rover P5 six-cylinder engine. A General Statement of Requirements (GSR 3463) was issued in June 1968, clarifying the role of the vehicle, stating that it should be capable of towing the new 105mm light gun, or a load of up to 1,814kg/ 4,000lb. Other possible roles included command post, Rapier and MILAN missile launcher, missile test/repair vehicle, signals office, radio repair vehicle, computer exchange unit, dry-air generator, power-supply vehicle, battery-charging truck, line layer, load carrier, and battlefield ambulance. Demountable body panels allowed vehicle weight to be reduced for lifting by a Wessex helicopter. It was also to be air-portable in Andover and Britannia aircraft. The specification also stated that the vehicle be capable of towing a powered-axle trailer via a special coupling and detachable propshaft.

In 1970, Rover produced 10 prototypes for trials, this time using the Buick-designed Rover 3,528cc V8 petrol engine, mated to a Range Rover gearbox with a

permanent four-wheel drive transfer box. There were heavy-duty Salisbury axles incorporating larger half-shafts than normal. An inter-axle differential lock was also fitted. Suspension was by live axles on semi-elliptical tapered multi-leaf springs, with an anti-roll bar at front. Double-acting telescopic shock absorbers were fitted to all four wheels.

Tested in trials against the Volvo-Ailsa 4140 series Laplander, the Land Rover emerged as the clear winner and went into production in 1975 as the FV19000 series. There were four production variants in all – GS, ambulance, and two types of signals body. Both right- and

BELOW: **The 101 was originally intended to be coupled to a powered-axle Scottorn trailer to provide improved mobility. Shown, here, is a Land Rover prototype.**

ABOVE: **The Vampire was a special signals-bodied variant of the 1-ton Land Rover forward-control intended for the re-broadcast or relay role.**

left-hand drive vehicles were produced. The vehicle remained in production until 1978, with 2,669 vehicles manufactured. Of these, 127 went to the RAF and 2,129 went to the British Army. The 101 was also supplied to the armies of Australia, Egypt, Iran and Luxembourg, and evaluated by Canada and others.

Land Rover 101 forward control

Type: Truck, 1-ton, GS, forward control, 4x4; FV19000 series
Manufacturer: Land Rover; Solihull
Production: 1975 to 1978
Powerplant: Rover; eight cylinders in V configuration; water-cooled; petrol; 3,528cc; overhead valves; power output, 128bhp at 5,000rpm
Transmission: 4F1Rx2; full-time 4x4; positive lock on inter-axle differential
Suspension: Live axles on semi-elliptical multi-leaf springs
Brakes: Hydraulic
Electrical system: 12V, 24V
Dimensions: Length – 4,115mm/162in
Width – 1,830mm/72in
Height – soft-top variants, 2,133mm/84in; hardtop variants, 2,388mm/94in
Wheelbase – 2,565mm/101in
Weight: Unladen – 1,920kg/4,233lb
Payload – 1,179kg/2,600lb
Performance: Maximum speed – 98kph/62mph

Leyland Hippo Mk II

As well as producing tanks and tank engines during World War II, Leyland Motors also supplied trucks, including the 3-ton Retriever, the 3-ton Lynx, and the 10-ton Hippo. The original Hippo Mk I, or WSW17, was essentially a pre-war commercial truck fitted with a military-type open cab and timber GS body, with some 330 examples supplied during 1939–40. The Mk II, introduced in 1944, was an altogether more capable vehicle.

During the planning for D-Day, it became obvious that 10-ton vehicles offered a considerable logistic advantage compared to smaller vehicles and, although Leyland had little spare capacity for producing new trucks, design work on the 10-ton Hippo Mk II started in 1943. Series production began in late 1944, which means that these vehicles were not used in the early days following the invasion. However, some 1,000 examples were in service by VE Day and the vehicle remained in use by both the Army and the RAF well into the 1950s.

The new vehicle used few components from the Mk I. It was powered by a Leyland 7,399cc

RIGHT: **The Leyland Hippo Mk II was a 10-ton 6x4 cargo vehicle intended for transporting supplies in Europe after D-Day. Production began in 1944 and around 1,000 had been shipped to Europe by the end of the war.** BELOW: **The Hippo was fitted with a fabricated-steel body as standard. For the signals/command role a house-type body was fitted. The Mk IIB had dual rear wheels and smaller-section tyres at the front.**

six-cylinder diesel engine driving the rear wheels through a five-speed gearbox and two-speed auxiliary box. The rear axles were of the full-floating worm-drive type. Suspension was by semi-elliptical springs, inverted at the rear. Large bar-grip tyres were fitted, with singles at the rear, although the Mk 2B reverted to twin rears.

The two-man steel-panelled cab was an all-new, enclosed design with

pull-down windows. The cab could be split to reduce shipping height. A circular observation hatch was provided in the roof above the passenger seat to allow the use of an anti-aircraft machine-gun on a pintle mount. The steel-framed timber GS body was of the well type, incorporating wheel arches to provide a reduced loading height. Various van bodies were fitted during the post-war years.

Leyland Hippo Mk II

Type: Truck, 10-ton, cargo, 6x4
Manufacturer: Leyland Motors; Leyland
Production: 1944 to 1945
Powerplant: Leyland L6; six cylinders in-line; diesel; water-cooled; 7,399cc; overhead valves; power output, 100bhp at 1,800rpm
Transmission: 5F1Rx2; 6x4
Suspension: Live axles on semi-elliptical multi-leaf springs, inverted at rear
Brakes: Hydraulic with vacuum servo-assistance
Electrical system: Hybrid 12V/14V
Dimensions: Length – 8,306mm/327in
  Width – 2,464mm/97in
  Height – tilt in place, 3,327mm/131in; minimum, 2,921mm/115in
  Wheelbase – 4,674mm/184in
  Bogie centres – 1,397mm/55in
Weight: Unladen – 8,433kg/18,592lb
  Payload – 11,583kg/25,536lb
Performance: Maximum speed – 48kph/30mph

Leyland Martian

LEFT: The FV1100 series Rolls-Royce-engined Leyland Martian was the largest production vehicle in the British Army's "combat" range. This is the prototype for the FV1103 heavy artillery tractor. The vehicle was also exhibited at the Commercial Motor Show in 1954, fitted with a Leyland 0.600 diesel engine, where it was offered to civilian users.

Produced in long- and short-wheelbase cargo, artillery tractor and recovery-tractor variants, the FV1100 series Leyland Martian was one of the purpose-designed Rolls-Royce-engined "CT" (combat) rated British military vehicles of the 1950s. Nominally rated at 10 tons, with six-wheel drive, it was the largest production vehicle in the "CT" series.

Development work began in 1950, with the first entering series production around 1953. This was the crew-cabbed FV1103 medium artillery tractor, intended to replace the AEC Matador as a towing vehicle for the 5.5, 7.5 and 8in howitzer and for the 40mm anti-aircraft gun. This was followed by the FV1110 cargo truck using a longer wheelbase, and later by the FV1119 recovery vehicle, which was fitted with Royal Ordnance/Thornycroft recovery equipment. A short-wheelbase cargo vehicle was also subsequently produced, based on the chassis of the artillery tractor.

The first 25 production vehicles used a Rolls-Royce B80 eight-cylinder petrol engine, but this was changed later for the more-powerful B81. In all cases, the transmission was by a four-speed gearbox and three-speed transfer box; the lowest of the transfer box gears could only be engaged when all-wheel drive was selected. Drive from the rear axle was conveyed to the wheels via a walking-beam gearcase, while at the front, the kingpins were used to drive the wheels through bevel gears as used on Mack trucks of World War II. The front suspension was similar to that used by Scammell with a single transverse leaf spring, allowing the live axle to pivot across the frame from a perch bar mounted further back on the chassis. At the rear, the bogie was suspended on semi-elliptical multi-leaf springs. The recovery vehicle was fitted with additional "helper" springs and the suspension could

be locked out during lifting operations. Production continued over an almost 10-year period, finally ending in 1964. Total production was 1,380, of which 60 were bodied as artillery tractors and 280 as recovery vehicles; the remainder were the cargo type. The vehicle was also offered to civilian users and exhibited at the Commercial Motor Show in 1954, but was far too expensive to market.

BELOW: The Martian was built as an artillery tractor, and also as long- and short-wheelbase cargo vehicles. The heavy recovery vehicle was fitted with Royal Ordnance/Thornycroft recovery equipment.

Leyland Martian

Type: Truck, 10-ton, medium artillery tractor; FV1103
Manufacturer: Leyland Motors; Leyland
Production: 1953 to 1964
Powerplant: Rolls-Royce B80 Mk 2H (first 25 vehicles), or B81 Mk 2H, 5H or 5K; eight cylinders in-line; petrol; water-cooled; 5,675cc (B80), 6,516cc (B81); overhead inlet valves, side exhaust; power output, 165bhp (B80) or 220bhp (B81) at 3,750rpm; civilian version offered with Leyland 0.600 diesel engine
Transmission: 4F1Rx3; part-time 6x6
Suspension: Front suspension by transverse semi-elliptical multi-leaf spring and centre-pivoted axle; walking-beam gearcase at rear, suspended on semi-elliptical multi-leaf springs
Brakes: Air-pressure
Electrical system: 24V
Dimensions: Length – 8,185mm/322in
 Width – 2,591mm/102in
 Height – 3,073mm/121in
 Wheelbase – 4,420mm/174in; FV1110 cargo vehicle, 5,140mm/202in
 Bogie centres – 1,397mm/55in
Weight: Unladen – 14,301kg/31,528lb
 Payload – 8,464kg/18,660lb
Performance: Maximum speed – 42kph/26mph

Morris-Commercial CD Series

In 1924, William Morris established Morris-Commercial at Soho, Birmingham, initially to build light trucks which were based on the company's heavier motor car chassis. In 1930, the company moved to the former Wolseley factory at Adderley Park and, by 1933, had added heavier vehicles to the range. The War Office was soon listed among the company's customers and the military CD 6x4 was introduced in 1933. This replaced the civilian D Type of 1927 in military service.

Utilizing a standard War Department rear bogie, the CD was powered by a 3,519cc Morris EB four-cylinder side-valve engine, driving overhead worm axles at the rear through a five-speed gearbox. Suspension was by semi-elliptical multi-leaf springs, inverted at the rear. The hydraulic brakes were modern for the period, albeit only acting on the front and centre axles.

Standard variants included the CD six-seat open-topped command car, of which 80 were built, also a 30cwt truck and field ambulance. The CDF, and the winch-equipped CDFW variants, were of the semi-forward control pattern and fitted with GS cargo, office and breakdown bodies. All of the truck variants were fitted with a canvas-covered cab; the CDF and CDFW models lacked a windscreen.

ABOVE: **The last variant to be built on the Morris-Commercial CD 30cwt chassis was the CDSW breakdown/recovery vehicle.**

Production of the CD ceased in 1939, but the CDF and CDFW continued to be produced into 1940. In 1935, the range was extended by the addition of the CDSW which shared a military-pattern cab with the smaller military Morris-Commercials of the period.

LEFT: **Produced from 1939, the second version of the Morris-Commercial CDSW was intended as a tractor for the Bofors light anti-aircraft gun. The rear body provided covered accommodation for the gun crew, as well as including stowage lockers for tools, equipment and ammunition.**

Morris-Commercial CD Series

Type: Truck, cargo, 30cwt, 6x4
Manufacturer: Morris-Commercial; Adderley Park, Birmingham
Production: 1933 to 1940
Powerplant: Morris EB; four cylinders in-line; petrol; water-cooled; 3,519cc; side valves; power output, 55bhp at 2,750rpm
Transmission: 5F1R; 6x4
Suspension: Live axles on semi-elliptical multi-leaf springs, inverted at the rear
Brakes: Hydraulic
Electrical system: 6V
Dimensions: (CDF variant) Length – 5,232mm/206in
Width – 1,880mm/74in
Height – tilt in place, 2,642mm/104in
Wheelbase – 3,251mm/128in
Bogie centres – 1,016mm/40in
Weight: Unladen – 2,743kg/6,048lb
Payload – 1,930kg/4,256lb
Performance: Maximum speed – 60kph/37mph

Morris-Commercial CS8

Morris-Commercial CS8

Type: Truck, cargo, ³/₄-ton, 4x2
Manufacturer: Morris-Commercial Cars;
  Adderley Park, Birmingham
Production: 1934 to 1941
Powerplant: Morris OH; six cylinders in-line;
  petrol; water-cooled; 3,485cc; sided valves;
  power output, 60bhp at 2,800rpm
Transmission: 4F1R; 4x2
Suspension: Live axles on multi-leaf
  semi-elliptical springs
Brakes: Mechanical
Electrical system: 12V
Dimensions: Length – 4,216mm/166in
  Width – 1,981mm/78in
  Height – tilt in place, 2,261mm/89in;
  minimum, 1,676mm/66in
  Wheelbase – 2,489mm/98in
Weight: Unladen – 2,041kg/4,500lb
  Payload – 1,007kg/2,220lb
Performance: Maximum speed – 64kph/40mph

The Morris-Commercial CS8 went into production in 1934 and became the most numerous ³/₄-ton 4x2 truck in British service during the years leading up to World War II. The engine was a six-cylinder side-valve unit driving the rear axle through a four-speed gearbox. Suspension was by live axles mounted on semi-elliptical leaf springs. Mechanical brakes were used throughout the production run.

Early production featured an open cab with aero screens and roll-up doors. This was eventually replaced by a full windscreen and half-doors. Most were bodied for the GS cargo role but there were also water tank, fire tender, wireless truck, fuel tanker, and office variants. There was also a portee for a 2pdr anti-tank gun. Captured examples were used by the *Wehrmacht*, occasionally with their own bodywork fitted. The CS8 remained in production until 1941.

BELOW: **Many CS8s were abandoned at Dunkirk only to be used by the *Wehrmacht*. Some were even fitted with German military-pattern bodies.**

Morris-Commercial MRA/1

Morris-Commercial MRA/1

Type: Truck, cargo, 1-ton, 4x4; FV16101
Manufacturer: Morris-Commercial Cars;
  Adderley Park, Birmingham
Production: 1952 to 1954
Powerplant: Morris SEA/5; six cylinders in-line;
  petrol; water-cooled; 4,196cc; overhead valves;
  power output, 72bhp at 2,750rpm
Transmission: 4F1Rx2; part-time 4x4
Suspension: Live axles on multi-leaf semi-
  elliptical springs; hydraulic double-acting
  shock absorbers
Brakes: Hydraulic
Electrical system: 12V
Dimensions: Length – 5,372mm/212in
  Width – 2,083mm/82in
  Height – tilt in place, 2,654mm/105in;
  minimum, 2,235mm/88in
  Wheelbase – 3,124mm/123in
Weight: Unladen – 3,239kg/7,140lb
  Payload – 1,293kg/2,850lb
Performance: Maximum speed – 80kph/50mph

The FV16100 series Morris-Commercial MRA/1 was an all-wheel-drive 1-ton military truck based on the company's civilian 3- and 5-ton NVS chassis. Prototypes were produced in 1950, and the first of a total of 7,238 was delivered in 1952. The all-steel cab was the same as that on the civilian NSV range, and featured pull-up lockable side windows and a rubber glazed two-piece fixed windscreen.

Power came from a 4,966cc overhead-valve petrol engine, driving all four wheels via a four-speed gearbox and two-speed transfer box. Live axles at front and rear were suspended on semi-elliptical multi-leaf springs with double-acting telescopic shock absorbers.

Of the total number built, 5,624 were fitted with a steel cargo/personnel body. The remaining 1,614 were supplied in chassis-cab form to be fitted with a 900-litre/200-gallon steel water tank and ancillary pumping equipment.

LEFT: **The Morris-Commercial MRA/1 was produced for only two years.**

Reynolds–Boughton RB-44

Originally produced as a private venture by the Boughton Group in 1978, when it was designated RB-510, the Renault-cabbed RB-44 was purchased by the British Army as a replacement for the Land Rover forward-control 1-ton truck. It was to be a tractor for the 105mm light gun.

The vehicle featured a bolted chassis in three wheelbase lengths, with the axles suspended on conventional semi-elliptical springs. A 3,000cc Perkins Phaser diesel engine drove all four wheels through a five-speed manual gearbox and two-speed transfer box. Automatic transmission was also offered as an option.

The standard British Army variant was the 2-ton cargo/prime mover. Other possible roles included transporter-launcher for the Swingfire anti-tank or Rapier surface-to-air missiles, and lubrication servicing and electronics communications vehicles. The company has also produced demonstrators for an ambulance, light recovery and command vehicles.

Production finally began in 1992, with the British Army purchasing some 846.

**Reynolds-Boughton
RB-44**

Type: Truck, 2-ton, cargo/prime mover, 4x4
Manufacturer: Reynolds-Boughton; Amersham
Production: 1992 to 1993
Powerplant: Perkins Phaser 110MT; four cylinders in-line; direct-injection diesel; water-cooled; 3,000cc; overhead valves; power output, 109bhp at 2,800rpm
Transmission: 5F1Rx2; full-time 4x4
Suspension: Live axles on semi-elliptical multi-leaf springs with rubber assisters; double-acting hydraulic shock absorbers
Brakes: Servo-assisted hydraulic
Electrical system: 12V, 24V
Dimensions: Length – 5,060mm, 5,650mm, 6,030mm/199in, 222in, 237in
Width – 2,100mm/83in
Height – minimum, 2,348mm/92in
Wheelbase – 3,226mm, 3,680mm, 4,060mm/ 127in, 145in, 160in
Weight: Unladen – 2,994kg/6,600lb
Payload – 2,041kg/4,500lb
Performance: Maximum speed – 109kph/68mph

LEFT: **The RB-44 was beset by reliability problems requiring a lengthy modifications programme.**

Rotinoff Atlantic, Super Atlantic GR7

George A. Rotinoff, a White Russian émigré to Britain, started his post-war career converting Sherman tanks into bulldozers. By 1955, his company was building a heavy tank-transporter tractor. Available with either a ballast body or fifth wheel, the Atlantic GR7 was powered by a Rolls-Royce six-cylinder supercharged (later turbocharged), diesel engine driving through a 12- or 15-speed transmission. In 1957, the Super Atlantic GR7 was launched, with an eight-cylinder turbocharged diesel engine and 15-speed transmission. Automatic transmission and all-wheel drive were optionally available on both trucks.

The British War Office trialled an Atlantic in 1955. The Swiss Army purchased 10 ballast tractors in 1958; 18 went to the Iraqi Army and one to the South African Army. In 1960, the company name changed to Lomount.

In 1962, the models were taken over by Atkinson. Total production was approximately 35–50 vehicles.

LEFT: **The Rotinoff Atlantic was used by the Swiss, Iraqi and South African armies.**

**Rotinoff Atlantic,
Super Atlantic GR7**

Type: Truck, 35-ton, tractor, 6x4
Manufacturer: Rotinoff Motors; Colnbrook
Production: 1955 to 1963
Powerplant: Rolls-Royce C6TFL, C6SFL, C8TFL; six or eight cylinders in-line; supercharged or turbocharged diesel; water-cooled; 12,170cc, 16,227cc; overhead valves; power output, 250–366bhp at 2100rpm
Transmission: 4F1Rx3, 5F1Rx3; 6x4
Suspension: Live axles on semi-elliptical multi-leaf springs
Brakes: Air-pressure
Electrical system: 24V
Dimensions: Length – 8,738mm/344in; 8,992mm/354in
Width – 2,972mm/117in
Height – 3,400mm/134in
Wheelbase – 5,258mm/207in
Bogie centres – 1,730mm/68in
Weight: Unladen – 17,600kg/38,800lb; 18,280kg/40,300lb
Gross train weight – 142,249kg/313,600lb; 203,213kg/448,000lb
Performance: Maximum speed – 64kph/40mph

Scammell Pioneer

ABOVE: Dating from 1935, and used by the British Army well into the 1950s, the Scammell Pioneer R100 was a heavy artillery tractor.

Design work on the Pioneer began in 1925 with Percy G. Hugh working under the direction of Oliver Danson North at the Scammell factory, Tolpits Lane, Watford. The vehicle was originally developed for use in the oilfields of the Middle East and, although it lacked all-wheel drive, the combination of Oliver North's superb walking-beam gearcase at the rear and a transversely pivoted front axle meant that it was useful over rough terrain. The original engine was a Scammell four-cylinder petrol unit, but this was eventually replaced by a Gardner diesel engine. The Pioneer acquired a reputation for providing a reliable, if somewhat slow, performance on the road. The first vehicles were produced in 1927, and although it was not originally intended for military service, more than 3,500 Pioneers were used by the British Army over three or more decades.

The Pioneer entered service in 1932 when the British War Office purchased a single example, powered by a petrol engine and equipped for use as a tank transporter. Rated at 16–18 tons, it was a six-wheeled tractor unit permanently coupled to an 18-ton semi-trailer. Loading was by removing the rear bogie of the trailer; mechanical screw jacks were provided for raising and lowering the trailer which must have been laborious. The vehicle was quickly assigned to a training unit, and it was not until 1937 that further tank transporters were purchased.

In 1935, a second Pioneer variant was specified and purchased, this time as a heavy artillery tractor. Designated R100, the Scammell engine of the 1932 prototype had been replaced by the Gardner. The vehicle was fitted with a large steel body which provided accommodation for the gun's crew as well as providing space for stowing tools, ammunition and other equipment. A tow hitch at the rear allowed the tractor to be coupled to the heavy guns of the period, typically the 60pdr and the 6 or 7.2in howitzer. A year later, deliveries began of the first production batch of 114 vehicles. By the time the war was over, Scammell had produced 980 of these heavy gun tractors.

The third Pioneer variant, dating from 1936, was a heavy recovery vehicle. There were three versions – the first two, designated SV/1S and SV/1T, were fitted with a collapsible 3-ton jib. After just 43 had been built, a redesigned extending jib was

LEFT: Introduced in 1936, the Pioneer SV/2S was a heavy recovery vehicle and was fitted with an under-chassis winch and a sliding jib crane.

fitted and the vehicle designation became SV/2S. Deliveries of the SV/2S began in 1938 and continued throughout the war. By 1945, a total of 1,975 had been produced.

Despite having first been supplied in 1932, series purchases of the tank transporter did not begin until 1937, using what was effectively a longer-wheelbase version of the chassis that had been adopted for the artillery tractor and recovery vehicles. By this time the vehicle had been uprated to 20 tons and was designated TRMU20. The trailer, which still required the bogie to be removed for loading, was designated TRCU20. The trailer was soon redesigned to allow loading by means of rear ramps. However, by the time 115 examples of this version had been built, a new rear-loading version appeared, rated at 30 tons and designated TRMU30/TRCU30. With some small changes, this version remained in production throughout World War II, and the total number manufactured was 459.

With the exception of the original 1932 tank transporter, all of the military Pioneers were powered by a Gardner 6LW six-cylinder direct-injection diesel engine driving the rear wheels through a six-speed constant-mesh gearbox fitted with a power take-off for an under-chassis winch. The winch was fitted to all variants to help with loading, and to provide a means for self-recovery. The single rear axle, which was attached to the chassis by semi-elliptical multi-leaf springs, incorporated walking-beam gearcases which allowed the

wheels on either side of the vehicle to rise and fall independently by as much as 300mm/12in. At the front, the axle was mounted on a single inverted transverse semi-elliptical spring pivoted in a fulcrum bracket. The axle was located by means of an A frame, the apex of which was attached to a perch bar further back on the chassis.

Although the Pioneer was almost certainly obsolete for most of the war years, and was never available in sufficient numbers, it was a reliable vehicle held in much affection by its crews. The tank-transporter variant was effectively superseded by the US-built Diamond T Model 980/981 from 1941 onwards. The artillery tractor and recovery vehicles continued to see service with the British Army through the 1950s into the 1960s. The Pioneer remained in the Scammell catalogue into the 1950s, but the War Office made no further purchases after 1945.

BELOW: **An R100 artillery tractor in typical blue and sand camouflage of the Western Desert. The towed load is a British 5.5in howitzer.**

Scammell Pioneer

Type: Tractor, heavy artillery, 6x4
Manufacturer: Scammell Lorries; Watford
Production: 1936 to 1945
Powerplant: Gardner 6LW; six cylinders in-line; diesel; water-cooled; 8,396cc; overhead valves; power output, 102bhp at 1,700rpm
Transmission: 6F1R; 6x4
Suspension: Pivoting front axle suspended on inverted transverse semi-elliptical multi-leaf spring with axle location by A frame; pivoting walking-beam gearcases at rear suspended on semi-elliptical multi-leaf springs
Brakes: Air-pressure assisted mechanical, rear wheels only
Electrical system: Hybrid 12V/24V
Dimensions: Length – 6,176mm/243in
    Width – 2,593mm/102in
    Height – top of cab, 2,974mm/117in
    Wheelbase – 3,708mm/146in
    Bogie centres – 1,302mm/51in
Weight: Unladen – 7,938kg/17,500lb
    Payload – 2,994kg/6,600lb
    Maximum towed load – road, 19,958kg/44,000lb; 9,979kg/22,000lb
Performance: Maximum speed – 38kph/24mph

Scammell S25 Commander

The Scammell Commander was the fourth-generation tank transporter used by the British Army. The development extended across 16 years and was in danger of cancellation more than once but the Commander finally started replacing the Thornycroft Antar in 1984, serving for 17 years and used during Operation Desert Storm and in Kosovo.

Development started in 1968 when Thornycroft and Scammell, both part of the Leyland Group, were asked to investigate producing a new 55-ton tank transporter tractor which was being described as the Antar Mk 4. It was anticipated that production would begin in 1971. By 1973, nothing had happened except that Scammell and Thornycroft had been merged and had produced a feasibility study. In 1976, a wood and fibreglass mock-up was produced which set down the basic shape of the vehicle. In 1978, this was followed by two engineering prototypes, one powered by

a Cummins engine, the other using a version of the 26,110cc Rolls-Royce CV12 as was fitted in the Challenger tank. The Rolls-Royce engine was selected and by mid-1980, the initial trials had been completed.

In 1982, the contract was cancelled as part of a programme of sweeping defence cuts, but by the end of that year was reinstated. Three new tractors were to be produced, now rated at 62 tons, for trials. Full-scale production was started in 1983, before acceptance trials were complete. The first Commander was delivered in February 1984.

The Commander was effectively an amalgamation of the design thinking which had created the Thornycroft Antar Mk 3 and the Scammell Contractor. It was an ultra-heavy fifth-wheel tractor for tank-transporter duties, what is currently termed a "Heavy Equipment Transporter" (HET), and was powered by a 26,110cc V12 twin turbocharged diesel engine driving the rear wheels through a GM

ABOVE: **It took almost 15 years before the Rolls-Royce-engined Scammell Commander began to replace the Thornycroft Antar Mk 3 in 1984. The Commander was used in the first Gulf War (Operation Desert Storm) and in Kosovo.**

Allison six-speed semi-automatic gearbox. Suspension was by semi-elliptical springs with shock absorbers at the front only.

A total of 122 were manufactured, and three of the trials vehicles were reworked making a total of 125. The Commander was replaced by the Oshkosh M1080E1 from 2001 and the surplus vehicles were sold to a Middle Eastern nation.

Scammell S25 Commander

Type: Tractor, wheeled, semi-trailer, 98-ton, 6x4
Manufacturer: Leyland Specialised Vehicles, Scammell Motors Plant; Watford
Production: 1983 to 1985
Powerplant: Rolls-Royce CV12-TCE; 12 cylinders in V configuration; turbocharged diesel; water-cooled; 26,110cc; overhead valves; power output, 625bhp at 2,100rpm
Transmission: 6F1R; semi-automatic; 6x4
Suspension: Live axles on semi-elliptical multi-leaf springs, inverted at rear; double-acting hydraulic shock absorbers at front
Brakes: Air-pressure
Electrical system: 24V
Dimensions: Length – 9,011mm/355in
 Width – 3,150mm/124in
 Height – 3,356mm/132in
 Wheelbase – 5,029mm/198in
 Bogie centres – 1,600mm/63in
Weight: Unladen – 21,755kg/47,960lb
 Gross train weight – 101,189kg/223,080lb
Performance: Maximum speed – 64kph/40mph

LEFT: **Both Cummins and Rolls-Royce engines were trialled. The production vehicle had a down-rated version of the Rolls-Royce CV12 power unit as used in the Challenger main battle tank.**

Thornycroft J-Type

In 1895, John I. Thornycroft commenced production of steam wagons in Chiswick and moved to a new site in Basingstoke in 1898. Thornycroft steam wagons were used during the Boer War, but the J-Type truck was the company's first vehicle supplied to the military in significant numbers.

The J-Type was designed to meet a 1911 British War Office specification for a 3-ton "subsidy scheme" cargo truck. Such schemes lowered the price of civilian trucks, but allowed them to be requisitioned by the military should this prove necessary. Thornycroft supplied the War Office with 24 H-, J- and K-Type chassis between August 1912 and May 1913. Further mixed orders followed but, after August 1914, the War Office settled on the J-Type. Approximately 5,000 were

Thornycroft J-Type	
Type: Truck, 3-ton, cargo, 4x2	
Manufacturer: John I. Thornycroft & Company; Basingstoke	
Production: 1911 to 1926	
Powerplant: Thornycroft M4; four cylinders in-line; petrol; water-cooled; 6,256cc; side valves; power output, 45bhp at 1,800rpm	
Transmission: 4F1R; 4x2	
Suspension: Live axles on semi-elliptical multi-leaf springs	
Brakes: Mechanical	
Electrical system: 6V	
Dimensions: Length – 6,756mm/266in Width – 2,210mm/87in Height – tilt in place, 3,174mm/125in Wheelbase – 4,166mm/164in	
Weight: Unladen – 4521kg/9,968lb Payload – 2,994kg/6,600lb	
Performance: Maximum speed – 19kph/12mph	

delivered over the next four years. Typical of the "subsidy A" trucks of the period, the J-Type was powered by a Thornycroft M4 6,256cc four-cylinder petrol engine driving a worm axle at the rear through a four-speed gearbox.

LEFT: **Ex-military J-Types proved very popular with civilian transport companies after 1918.**

Thornycroft Nubian TF/AC4

A pilot model for the Thornycroft Nubian TF was produced in June 1940, with the vehicle entering production in February 1941. By the time production ended in 1945, the company had built 3,824 vehicles.

Although it was mostly used by the RAF, the forward-control Nubian 3-ton 4x4 was typical of British military cargo vehicles developed during World War II. The engine was the manufacturer's AC4/1, a 3,865cc four-cylinder petrol unit dating from 1934, driving both axles through a four-speed gearbox and two-speed transfer box. The hubs incorporated epicyclic reduction

Thornycroft Nubian TF/AC4	
Type: Truck, 3-ton, cargo, 4x4	
Manufacturer: John I. Thornycroft & Company; Basingstoke	
Production: 1941 to 1945	
Powerplant: Thornycroft AC4/1; four cylinders in-line; petrol; water-cooled; 3,865cc; overhead valves; power output, 85bhp at 2,500rpm	
Transmission: 4F1Rx2; part-time 4x4	
Suspension: Live axles on semi-elliptical multi-leaf springs	
Brakes: Hydraulic with vacuum servo-assistance	
Electrical system: 6V	
Dimensions: Length – 6,098mm/244in Width – 2,286mm/90in Height – tilt in place, 3,124mm/123in Wheelbase – 3,658mm/144in	
Weight: Unladen – 4,826kg/10,640lb Payload – 2,994kg/6,600lb	
Performance: Maximum speed – 63kph/39mph	

LEFT: **A Nubian at the Thornycroft factory, finished in World War II vehicle camouflage.**

gears. Production resumed between 1950 and 1953, the vehicle being fitted with a Rolls-Royce B80 engine.

LEFT: The first civilian "Mighty Antar" was a diesel-engined fifth-wheel tractor intended for oilfield use. When the vehicle entered military service in 1951, the Mk 1 military Antar was fitted with a petrol engine and equipped with a steel ballast body for use with a draw-bar trailer.

Thornycroft Antar

The Thornycroft Antar – it was never "Mighty Antar" in military service – was originally produced for the civil engineering contractor George Wimpey in 1949. Powered by an 18,012cc Rover Meteorite diesel engine, it was intended for hauling steel pipeline sections across the Iraqi deserts, where Wimpey was laying the Homs to Kirkuk pipeline for the Iraq Petrol Company. At around the same time, the War Office had been trying to develop a new prime mover to replace the Diamond T Model 980/981 which had been in service since 1940. It was felt that the Diamond T would not be sufficiently powerful to deal with the 65-ton Conqueror tank which was about to enter service. It was thought that the Antar might represent a low-cost option which would allow time while development of a "more suitable" vehicle continued.

In 1951, the Ministry of Supply agreed to purchase 15 Antars at a price of £8,177 each for use as a tank transporter tractor. A steel ballast box was installed over the rear axle to allow the tractor to be used with a 50-ton drawbar trailer. The Meteorite engine of the civilian vehicle was replaced by a petrol version which offered better torque. The engine was coupled to a four-speed gearbox and three-speed auxiliary box.

In 1952, Thornycroft started work on the military Mk 2 and Mk 2A variants, the former with a fifth-wheel coupling to allow use with a 60-ton semi-trailer, the latter with a wooden ballast box. The engine and transmission were unchanged. The Mk 2 remained in production until 1957 when it was superseded by the Mk 3 and Mk 3A, with the Rolls-Royce C8SFL diesel engine and a simplified six-speed transmission and overdrive top gear. A new cab was fitted and, again, there were versions for semi-trailer (Mk 3) and drawbar trailer (Mk 3A).

Some 700 Antars were produced, of which 590 were supplied to the British Army and the RAF. The Antar was replaced in British service by the Scammell Commander in 1984. The vehicle was used by the armies of Burma, Kuwait, Pakistan and South Africa.

LEFT: By 1961, the vehicle had evolved into the Mk 3 and Mk 3A, powered by a Rolls-Royce C8SFL diesel-engine. The Mk 3 (shown) was fitted with a fifth wheel. The Mk 3A had a ballast body.

Thornycroft Antar	

Type: (Mk 1 variant) Tractor, 30-ton, GS, 6x4; FV12001

Manufacturer: Transport Equipment Thornycroft; Basingstoke

Production: 1951 to 1964

Powerplant: (Mk 1, Mk 2) Rover Meteorite Mk 204; eight cylinders in V configuration; petrol; water-cooled; 18,012cc; overhead valves; power output, 260bhp at 2,300rpm. (Mk 3) Rolls-Royce C8SFL/843; six cylinders in-line; super-charged diesel; water-cooled; 16,200cc; overhead valves; power output, 333bhp at 3,250rpm

Transmission: (Mk 1, Mk 2) 4F1Rx3, (Mk 3) 6F1R; 6x4

Suspension: Live axles on multi-leaf semi-elliptical springs

Brakes: Air-pressure

Electrical system: 24V

Dimensions: (Mk 1 variant)
Length – 8,440mm/332in
Width – 2,820mm/111in
Height – 3,050mm/120in
Wheelbase – 4,720mm/186in
Bogie centres – 1,580mm/62in

Weight: Unladen – 20,058kg/44,220lb
Gross train weight – 142,253kg/313,610lb

Performance: Maximum speed – 45kph/28mph

American Motors "Mighty Mite"

Officially designated M422, but generally known as the "Mighty Mite", this American Motors product is probably the smallest practical Jeep-type military vehicle ever produced. The design was by some of the original team that had been responsible for designing the Bantam BRC40 in 1940. It was produced for the US Marine Corps and light weight was important to allow transportation by helicopter.

Development began in the early 1950s at the Mid-American Research Corporation (MARCO). The first prototype weighed just 680kg/1,503lb and was powered by a Porsche four-cylinder air-cooled engine. Eventually, MARCO handed the final development and production over to American Motors Corporation (AMC) who replaced the engine with a 1,770cc V4 air-cooled engine of their own design. The vehicle was finally accepted for production in April 1958, when it was agreed that AMC would produce seven pre-production vehicles followed by a further 50 production models. If these were satisfactory then a further 243 would be built. By December 1959, AMC had started assembling the first of 1,250 examples of the M422.

In original M422 configuration, the vehicle had a 1,651mm/65in wheelbase, was just 2,718mm/107in long and weighed 679kg/1,496lb. On the later M422A1, the wheelbase was increased to 1,805mm/71in and the length increased to 2,870mm/113in. The weight increased to 771kg/1,700lb. In order to help save weight, only the M422A1 was provided with a canvas top and spare wheel.

The AMC four-cylinder engine was coupled to a four-speed gearbox, and single-speed transfer box. Drive was to all four wheels. The latter included a third differential. Prototype vehicles had utilized a tubular-steel chassis to give the maximum possible strength to weight ratio, but this was subsequently replaced by a conventional channel-section ladder design. However, all of the body parts were of aluminium, and many components were drilled (or "skeletonized") to keep the weight to a minimum. Independent suspension was fitted on all four wheels by means of leading and trailing arms on quarter-elliptical leaf springs. The brakes were inboard. Production continued until early 1963 by which time some 4,000 vehicles had been built, of which 1,250 were the original M422 variant.

American Motors "Mighty Mite"

Type: Truck, utility, lightweight, ¼-ton, 4x4; M422, M422A1

Manufacturer: American Motors Corporation; Detroit, Michigan

Production: 1960 to 1963

Powerplant: AMC AV-108-4; four cylinders in V configuration; petrol; air-cooled; 1,770cc; overhead valves; power output, 55bhp at 3,600rpm

Transmission: 4F1Rx2; part-time 4x4

Suspension: Independent suspension by leading and trailing arms and quarter-elliptical multi-leaf springs

Brakes: Hydraulic

Electrical system: 24V

Dimensions: Length – (M422) 2,718mm/107in; (M422A1) 2,870mm/113in
Width – 1,550mm/61in
Height – tilt in place, 1,473mm/58in; minimum, 1,195mm/47in
Wheelbase – (M422) 1,651mm/65in; (M422A1) 1,805mm/71in

Weight: Unladen – 679–771kg/1,496–1,700lb
Payload – road, 453kg/1,000lb; cross-country, 386kg/850lb

Performance: Maximum speed – 76kph/47mph

ABOVE: **The wheelbase of the M422A1 was lengthened to 1,805mm/71in; subsequently the overall length increased to 2,870mm/113in. Of 4,000 vehicles completed some 2,750 were the M422A1 variant.**

AM-General M998 Series (HMMWV)

Development of the vehicle that was to replace the M151 began in 1978 when the US Army created a requirement for a go-anywhere "High Mobility Multi-purpose Wheeled Vehicle" (HMMWV) for use as a cargo truck, communications vehicle, weapons platform, personnel carrier and command/reconnaissance vehicle. A detailed specification was published in 1980 and the Chrysler Corporation, Teledyne Continental and AM-General (AMG) submitted vehicles for trials. The AMG vehicle was selected for production and in March 1983, the US Army's Tank, Automotive and Armaments Command (TACOM) awarded AM General a $1.2 billion contract to produce 55,000 vehicles over a five-year period.

The vehicle was officially designated as the M998 Series and was nicknamed both "Humvee" and "Hummer". Subsequent agreements between AM-General and General Motors have attempted to rationalize the use of the two names, assigning one to the military vehicle and one to its civilian counterpart. Production vehicles began to enter service in 1983, and by 1996, more than 100,000 had been built. By the beginning of 2004, more than

160,000 HMMWVs had been delivered to the US Army and to 30 other armies.

The original M998 Series was powered by a 6,200cc Detroit-Diesel V8, driving through a three-speed automatic transmission, incorporated full-time four-wheel drive, and independent coil-spring suspension. Although there were initially five basic models, these were developed into 15 different configurations, allowing the chassis to be used for weapons systems, command and control systems and field ambulance, as well as ammunition, troop and general cargo transport.

In 1992, the M1097 "Heavy Hummer Variant" (HHV) was introduced. The frame and suspension were reinforced to accommodate a payload of 2,000kg/ 4,400lb. Subsequent improvements led to the A1 variants in 1994, and a year later, the A2 series was introduced using a more powerful 6,500cc diesel engine, and electronically controlled four-speed automatic transmission, allowing the payload to be increased to 2,000kg/ 4,400lb. The M1113 "Expanded Capacity Vehicle" (ECV, sometimes ECH) was also introduced in 1995, fitted with a turbocharged version of the engine,

improved differentials, brakes, cooling system and a stronger chassis. This allowed the payload to be increased further to 2,313kg/ 5,100lb. The chassis is also the basis for the O'Gara-Hess & Eisenhardt uparmoured M1114 HMMWV.

As of 2006, the M1113 became the base vehicle for future HMMWV orders.

AM-General M998 Series HMMWV

Type: Truck, weapons carrier, 1-ton, 4x4; M1025, M1026
Manufacturer: AM-General Corporation; South Bend, Indiana
Production: 1983 on
Powerplant: Detroit-Diesel; eight cylinders in V configuration; diesel; water-cooled; 6,200cc; overhead valves; power output, 150bhp at 3,600rpm
Transmission: Automatic 3F1Rx2; full-time 4x4
Suspension: Independent suspension by upper and lower wishbones and coil springs
Brakes: Hydraulic
Electrical system: 24V
Dimensions: Length – 4,570mm/180in
Width – 2,180mm/86in
Height – to top of cab, 1,880mm/74in; minimum, 1,830mm/72in
Wheelbase – 3,300mm/130in
Weight: Unladen – 2,703kg/5,960lb
Payload – 1,016kg/2,240lb
Performance: Maximum speed – 113kph/70mph

American Bantam 40BRC

In mid-1940, Karl Probst, a freelance automotive designer, undertook a project for the ailing American Bantam company which was to change history. Working from little more than a scribbled sketch and a written specification setting out basic parameters, Probst and his team designed and built what was effectively the first Jeep in a matter of days.

Bantam had been one of three companies to respond to a US Quartermaster Corps (US QMC) request for bids for a new lightweight 4x4 reconnaissance vehicle. The timescale dictated that Bantam's prototype was little more than a new chassis and body to which had been bolted an assembly of existing components. The engine was from Continental, the axles and transfer case from Spicer, and the transmission from Warner. By September 1940, the Model 60, as the prototype was called, was driven to Maryland and delivered to the US QMC for trials.

Unable to break the vehicle, US QMC told Bantam to go ahead and build 60 vehicles. This was rapidly followed by a second contract for 1,500 production vehicles, now designated the 40BRC.

American Bantam 40BRC

Type: Truck, ¼-ton, 4x4, command reconnaissance
Manufacturer: American Bantam; Butler, Pennsylvania
Production: 1940 to 1941
Powerplant: Continental BY-4112; four cylinders in-line; petrol; water-cooled; 1,835cc; side valves; power output, 48bhp at 3,150rpm
Transmission: 3F1Rx2; part-time 4x4
Suspension: Live axles on semi-elliptical multi-leaf springs
Brakes: Hydraulic
Electrical system: 6V
Dimensions: Length – 3,200mm/126in
  Width – 1,372mm/54in
  Height – tilt in place, 1,816mm/72in; minimum, 1,245mm/49in
  Wheelbase – 2,019mm/79.5in
Weight: Unladen – 954kg/2,103lb
  Payload – 250kg/551lb
Performance: Maximum speed – 96kph/60mph

LEFT: **A total of 2,675 Bantams were built before production switched to the Willys Jeep.**

Aqua-Cheetah XAC-1, 2, 3

Aqua-Cheetah XAC-1, 2, 3

Type: Truck, ½- or ¾-ton, 4x4, amphibian
Manufacturer: Amphibian Car Corporation; Buffalo, New York
Production: 1941 to 1942
Powerplant: Dodge T214 or T215; six cylinders in-line; petrol; air-cooled; 3,772cc; side valves; power output, 92–99bhp at 3,200rpm
Transmission: 4F1Rx1; part-time 4x4; selectable propeller drive
Suspension: Independent suspension using trailing arm chaincases on coil springs
Brakes: Hydraulic
Electrical system: 12V
Dimensions: Length – 4,978mm/196in
  Width – 2,286mm/90in
  Height – tilt in place, 1,525mm/64in
  Wheelbase – 2,438mm/96in
Weight: Unladen – 2,500kg/5,512lb
  Payload – 500–750kg/1,102–1,653lb
Performance: In water – 11kph/6.6mph

The Aqua-Cheetah was designed by Roger W. Hofheins, president of the Amphibian Car Corporation in mid-1941. The XAC-1 was an amphibious ½-ton vehicle originally powered by a mid-mounted Ford V8 engine driving a single propeller or all four wheels through trailing-arm chaincases. Independent suspension was fitted on all four wheels. Performance in the water was good, but less so on land.

In May 1942, Hofheins produced the XAC-2, using a rear-mounted Dodge T214 engine, with a mid-mounted gearbox coupled to a chain-driven transfer case. The differential housings were welded to the hull and connected to the chaincases by axles. The prototype was followed by seven pre-production vehicles for evaluation.

By mid-1942, the design had evolved into the XAC-3 using a Dodge T215 engine. Only 12 Aqua-Cheetah amphibians were built before the project was cancelled in late 1942.

BELOW: **The XAC-1 was fitted with a Ford V8 petrol engine. The XAC-2 had a Dodge T214 and the final version, XAC-3, a Dodge T215 petrol engine.**

Autocar U-4144T, U-7144T

The Autocar U-4144T was a 2½-ton 4x4 tractor, manufactured during 1940 and 1941. In 1941, it was superseded by the 4- to 5-ton U-7144T. Both were derived from a civilian vehicle, and were intended for use with a 6-ton (10-ton gross), or 9,092-litre/2,000-gallon fuel-servicing semi-trailer. The earliest examples were fitted with a civilian-type two-door cab. In 1942, this was replaced by a standard open-cab design with a canvas top and side-screens. A folding windscreen was fitted.

The U-4144T was powered by an Autocar six-cylinder petrol engine, while the U-7144T used a Hercules RXC unit, in combination with a five-speed gearbox and two-speed transfer box. The suspension was by live axles hung on semi-elliptical springs. Total production amounted to 274 of the U-4144T and 13,856 of the U-7144T.

Autocar U-4144T, U-7144T
Type: Truck, 2½- or 4- to 5-ton, tractor, 4x4
Manufacturer: Autocar Company; Ardmore, Pennsylvania. White Motor Company; Cleveland, Ohio
Production: 1940 to 1945
Powerplant: U4144-T – Autocar D358; six cylinders in-line; petrol; water-cooled; 5,866cc; side valves; power output, 100bhp at 2,200rpm. U-7144T – Hercules RXC-529; six cylinders in-line; petrol; water-cooled; 8,669cc; side valves; power output, 112bhp at 2,200rpm
Transmission: 5F1Rx2; part-time 4x4
Suspension: Live axles on semi-elliptical multi-leaf springs
Brakes: Air-pressure
Electrical system: Dual 6V/12V
Dimensions: (U-7144T) Length – 5,182mm/204in Width – 2,413mm/95in Height – tilt in place, 2,870mm/113in; minimum, 2,337mm/92in Wheelbase – 3,429mm/135in
Weight: Unladen – 5,264kg/11,606lb Payload – 4,536kg/10,000lb
Performance: Maximum speed – 64kph/40mph

LEFT: **An Autocar U-4144T fitted with a civilian-type two-door cab, coupled to a 7,600-litre/2,000-gallon fuel-servicing semi-trailer.**

Autocar U8144, U8144T

The Autocar U8144 was a 5- to 6-ton 4x4 truck produced in two major variants. Of the total of approximately 3,300 manufactured between 1941 and 1945, 2,700 were of the U8144T variant. This was equipped as a fifth-wheel tractor intended for use with bridging equipment semi-trailers.

A large equipment locker for construction tools was fitted behind the cab, and there was a 7½-ton capacity mechanical winch. The remainder, some 600, were fitted with a large van body built by York-Hoover and were assigned to the US Air Force for the transport of radar and signals equipment.

The engine was an 8,669cc Hercules RXC 8, six-cylinder unit, producing 112bhp, driving either the rear wheels or both axles through a five-speed gearbox with overdrive

Autocar U8144, U8144T
Type: Truck, tractor, 5- to 6-ton, 4x4
Manufacturer: Autocar; Ardmore, Pennsylvania
Production: 1941 to 1945
Powerplant: Hercules RXC; six cylinders in-line; petrol; water-cooled; 8,669cc; side valves; power output, 112bhp at 2,200rpm
Transmission: 5F1Rx2; part-time 4x4
Suspension: Live axles on semi-elliptical multi-leaf springs, inverted at the rear
Brakes: Air-pressure
Electrical system: Hybrid 6V/12V
Dimensions: (U8144T variant) Length – 6,273mm/247in Width – 2,489mm/98in Height – to top of cab, 2,921mm/115in Wheelbase – 4,166mm/164in
Weight: Unladen – 7,530kg/16,600lb Payload – 5,321kg/11,730lb
Performance: Maximum speed – 76kph/47mph

LEFT: **An Autocar U8144 tractor unit fitted to the all-metal cab.**

top gear, and a two-speed transfer box. On late production vehicles, the steel cab was replaced by a standardized open-topped cab with a folding windscreen and canvas cover.

Willys M274 "Mechanical Mule"

LEFT: **Although not road legal, the "Mechanical Mule" is ideal for operating on military bases. The vehicle can be driven in the conventional manner or pedestrian-controlled.**

In 1944–45, Willys built a small motorized platform vehicle which was described as the "jungle burden carrier", and intended for use by airborne infantry. Developed from the chassis of the MB Jeep, it consisted of little more than a flat load-carrying bed on four wheels, with the driver placed at the very front. The engine and transmission were under the floor and both the driver's seat and the steering column could be folded down to provide a completely flat platform which allowed easy stacking. There was no series production, but in the mid-1950s the concept was revisited as the XM274, generally described as the "Mechanical Mule".

The main departure from the earlier version was that the steering column was arranged to tilt forward and the clutch and accelerator were duplicated to allow the operator to either drive the machine in the conventional manner, or to walk along behind using the tilted wheel to steer. The platform was of magnesium-alloy on all variants except the M274A5.

Early versions went into production as the M274, powered by a Willys-Continental AO53 horizontally opposed four-cylinder engine placed at the rear under the floor. In the M274A1 variant, this was replaced by the AO53-1 power unit. Subsequent variants (M274A2, A3, A4 and A5) were fitted with a standard military Continental-Hercules AO42 two-cylinder engine. Permanent four-wheel drive through a three-speed gearbox and two-speed transfer box was fitted, also four-wheel steering (not on A5 variant). No suspension was fitted,

but the over-sized tyres provided some degree of cushioning against road shocks.

Initial production was at Willys' Toledo factory but, from 1965, was moved to Baifield Industries in Texas. From 1970, production was shared between the Brunswick Corporation and Bowen-McLaughlin-York.

Although intended for use as a load carrier, M274s deployed to Vietnam were used as stretcher carriers. It was also equipped with a 106mm anti-tank recoilless rifle or TOW missile system. A similar vehicle was produced in the Netherlands by DAF, described as the YM500 "Pony". In 1965, this was trialled as a possible replacement for the M274.

ABOVE: **The "Mule" also provides a useful weapons platform for a recoilless anti-tank rifle.**

Willys M274 "Mechanical Mule"

Type: Truck, 1/2-ton, platform, utility, 4x4
Manufacturer: Baifield Industries; Carrollton, Texas. Bowen-McLaughlin-York; York, Pennsylvania. Brunswick Corporation; Lake Forest, Illinois. Willys-Overland/ Kaiser-Jeep; Toledo, Ohio.
Production: 1956 to 1972
Powerplant: (M274, M274A1) Willys-Continental AO53, A053-1; four cylinders, horizontally opposed; petrol; air-cooled; 877cc; overhead valves; power output, 17bhp at 3,200rpm (M274A2, A3, A4, A5) Continental-Hercules AO42; two cylinders, horizontally opposed; petrol; air-cooled; 688cc; overhead valves; power output, 14bhp at 3,000rpm
Transmission: 3F1Rx2; full-time 4x4
Suspension: Live portal axles, no suspension
Brakes: Mechanical acting on drive shaft
Electrical system: Magneto only
Dimensions: Length – 2,980mm/117in
  Width – 1,780mm/70in
  Height – maximum, 1,193mm/47in;
  minimum, 686mm/27in
  Wheelbase – 1,448mm/57in
Weight: Unladen – 420kg/925lb
  Payload – 500kg/1,102lb
Performance: Maximum speed – 40kph/25mph

Caterpillar M520, M553, M559 "Goer"

During the late 1950s, the US Army started to investigate the possibility of adapting some of the concepts used in the design of all-terrain engineering plant to produce high-mobility military vehicles. Early trials were conducted with commercial vehicles from companies such as Caterpillar, Euclid and International, which were steered by articulation and which used large balloon tyres in place of conventional suspension.

In 1960–61, LeTourneau-Westinghouse, Caterpillar and Clark Equipment were asked to produce prototypes for what was being described as the "Goer" range. Caterpillar developed the 8-ton chassis, LeTourneau's contribution was a 15-ton vehicle and Clark built a 5-ton variant.

In all cases, the vehicles were built of two separate components – a forward-control cab unit which incorporated the engine and transmission, and a separate load-carrying unit, each component carried on its own axle. The two units were coupled together in such a way as to allow them to roll independently. Hydraulic rams between the two units allowed 60 degrees of lateral movement to provide steering; this was sufficient

to allow the vehicles to be swung from side to side across soft terrain.

In the 8-ton series, the engine was a Caterpillar six-cylinder turbocharged diesel or multi-fuel diesel unit. On early prototypes the front axle, which incorporated hub-reduction gears, was driven through a five-speed main gearbox and two-speed auxiliary box. Later prototypes used an automatic six-speed gearbox. The standard drive configuration was to use the front axle. The rear wheels were driven by electric motors mounted in the hubs, and could only be used in the two lowest of the gear ratios.

Prototypes were eventually produced for an 8-ton cargo vehicle (XM520E1), wrecker (XM553) and tanker (XM559E1) – all were amphibious. The performance during trials was exceptional and, in 1971, the Army Material Command invited bids from industry for a total

ABOVE: **Caterpillar "Goer" fitted as a "Transporter-Erector-Launcher" (TEL) for the US Army's Nike Hercules anti-aircraft missile.**

of 1,300 vehicles – 812 cargo trucks (M520 and M877), the latter being fitted with a handling crane, 371 tankers (M559) and 117 10-ton wreckers (M553). The $61.5 million contract was awarded to Caterpillar and production began in 1972.

A 15-ton 6x6 "Goer" prototype was produced in the early 1970s.

Caterpillar M520, M553, M559 "Goer"

Type: Truck, cargo, 8-ton, 4x4; M520
Manufacturer: Caterpillar Tractor Company; Peoria, Illinois
Production: 1972 to 1974
Powerplant: Caterpillar D333 or D333C; six cylinders in-line; multi-fuel diesel (D333C, diesel only); water-cooled; 10,455cc; overhead valves; power output, 192bhp at 2,200rpm
Transmission: Automatic, 6F1Rx2; part-time 4x4; rear-wheel drive by electric motors
Suspension: None, balloon tyres only
Brakes: Air-pressure
Electrical system: 24V
Dimensions: (M520 variant)
   Length – 6,273mm/247in
   Width – 2,743mm/108in
   Height – tilt erected, 2,997mm/118in; minimum, 2,565mm/101in
   Wheelbase – 5,969mm/235in
Weight: Unladen – 10,864kg/23,950lb
   Payload – 7,258kg/16,000lb
Performance: Maximum speed – road, 48kph/30mph; in still water, 13kph/8mph

LEFT: **The articulated two-component assembly helped to ensure that the wheels remained on the ground regardless of the terrain and the steering was by hydraulic rams between the two components. The "Goer" lacked conventional suspension, relying instead on balloon tyres.**

LEFT: **The Chevrolet G4113/G7113 tractor and semi-trailer was used by the US Army on the "Red Ball Express" supply routes after D-Day.**

Chevrolet G4100, G7100 series

First appearing in 1940 and designated as the G4100 series, the normal-control 1$\frac{1}{2}$-ton Chevrolet became the US Army's standard 4x4 vehicle in this weight class throughout World War II. The G4100 was superseded in 1942 by the more militarized G7100.

The truck was derived from a civilian vehicle of the same rating, and incorporated all-wheel drive. The two-man cab was the same as on the GMC CCKW 6x6, but, unlike the GMC, there was no open cab variant. Power was provided by a Chevrolet six-cylinder petrol engine, driving both axles through a four-speed gearbox and two-speed transfer box. The front axle could be disengaged

when not required. GM "banjo"-type hypoid axles were fitted, front and rear, suspended on semi-elliptical leaf springs. The brakes were hydraulic, with vacuum servo power assistance. A Warner electric brake hand controller was fitted in the cab to allow the trailer brakes to be operated separately.

Most of the total production was the steel-bodied cargo vehicle. Other standard variants included panel van, airfield crash tender, bomb servicing

BELOW: **The Chevrolet G4112 tipper truck was fitted with a hydraulically operated steel-fabricated body produced by Heil or Hercules Steel Products. The designation changed to G7116 from 1942.**

vehicle, oil servicing vehicle, telephone and maintenance vehicle. There were also tractor variants (G4113 and G7113), of which just 169 were produced, designed for use in conjunction with a range of 6-ton (gross) semi-trailers. Some 168,603 vehicles were built, representing 30 per cent of Chevrolet's total World War II output. The design was widely used by the US Signal Corps and remained in production until 1945.

Chevrolet G4100, G7100 series

Type: Truck, 1$\frac{1}{2}$-ton, cargo, 4x4
Manufacturer: Chevrolet Motor Division, General Motors Corporation; Detroit, Michigan
Production: 1940 to 1945
Powerplant: Chevrolet BV1001-UP; six cylinders in-line; water-cooled; 3,859cc; overhead valves; petrol; power output, 84bhp at 3,000rpm
Transmission: 4F1Rx2; part-time 4x4
Suspension: Live axles on semi-elliptical multi-leaf springs
Brakes: Hydraulic with vacuum servo-assistance; electric connection for trailer brakes on tractor variants
Electrical system: 6V
Dimensions: Length – 5,232mm/206in
Width – 2,185mm/86in
Height – tilt in place – 2,692mm/106in; minimum, 2,210mm/87in
Wheelbase – 3,683mm/145in
Weight: Unladen – 3,422kg/7,545lb
Payload – road, 5,389kg/11,880lb; cross–country, 1,497kg/3,300lb
Performance: Maximum speed – 77kph/48mph

LEFT: The "Gama Goat" was powered by a 2,610cc Detroit-Diesel 3-53 three-cylinder supercharged water-cooled engine mounted behind the cab bulkhead. The proximity and noise from the engine required the crew to wear ear defenders.

Condec M561, M792 "Gama Goat"

The "Gama Goat" 6x6 was one of the more unusual US military vehicles of the post-war period. The idea for an articulated twin-bodied high-mobility truck, where the two components were able to pitch and roll relative to one another, was based on a hydraulically suspended vehicle produced by the Swiss Meili Company, tested in the USA in 1961. Development work on what was the XM561 was initiated at the Chance-Vought Aircraft Corporation around 1962. Early prototypes were powered by a Chevrolet Corvair air-cooled engine and featured front- and rear-wheel steering, as well as being amphibious.

The name was derived from Roger L. Gamaunt, the designer of the articulating coupling which transmitted power between the two components.

Production was entrusted to the Consolidated Diesel Electric Corporation in 1969. By this time, the Corvair engine had been replaced by a Detroit Diesel 3-53, a three-cylinder supercharged two-stroke engine which was so noisy that the crew were obliged to wear ear defenders. The transmission was a four-speed unit, with a two-speed transfer box. Propulsion and steering in the water was achieved through the wheels alone. The truck was also fitted with

outboard brakes using "O" rings in the drums to maintain a water seal.

Suspension was by a centre swing axle suspended on a single transverse leaf spring. Independent coil-spring suspension was fitted on the front and rear axles. In normal road use the centre axle provided drive, but six-wheel drive was also available.

It would be true to say that the "Gama Goat" was not popular with drivers. The curious handling characteristics led to roll-over accidents. The vehicle was also considered difficult to enter and exit. These characteristics were additional to a reputation for poor reliability and high noise levels.

There were two standard variants, M561 cargo vehicle and the M792 field ambulance. A total of 14,000 were built over a five-year period. Some vehicles were fitted with a front-mounted winch which made the vehicle very nose-down in the water.

Condec M561, M792 "Gama Goat"

Type: Truck, 1¼-ton, 6x6; M561, M792
Manufacturer: Consolidated Diesel Electric Corporation (Condec); Schenectady, New York
Production: 1969 to 1973
Powerplant: Detroit Diesel 3-53; three cylinders in-line; supercharged two-stroke diesel; water-cooled; 2,610cc; overhead inlet valves; power output, 103bhp at 2,800rpm
Transmission: 4F1Rx2; part-time 6x6; amphibious capability via the road wheels
Suspension: Centre swing axle on transverse leaf spring; independent suspension front and rear using coil springs and wishbones; hydraulic double-acting shock absorbers
Brakes: Hydraulic
Electrical system: 24V
Dimensions: Length – 5,490mm/216in
    Width – 2,311mm/91in
    Height – 2,075mm/82in
    Wheelbase – 2,050+2,154mm/81+85in
Weight: Unladen – 3,308kg/7,293lb
    Payload – 1,313kg/2,895lb
Performance: Maximum speed – 88kph/55mph

ABOVE: The M561 was made up of two separate units – the tractor and carrier – both of which were able to roll and pitch relative to one another. The vehicle was also amphibious.

Condec, LeTourneau-Westinghouse LARC-5

The 5-ton "Lighter, Amphibious, Resupply, Cargo, 5" – also described as LARC-5 and LARC-V – dates from the end of the 1950s, and was among the final vehicles directly attributable to the design concept which had originated with the GMC DUKW in 1942. While the rated payload of 5,080kg/11,200lb was twice that of the DUKW, the LARC was intended for ferrying supplies from ship to shore in the same way that the DUKWs had been used during various amphibious landings in World War II.

The vehicle was developed by the Ingersoll-Kalamazoo Division of Borg-Warner during 1958 and 1959 under the direction of the US Transportation Engineering Command (USTEC) at Fort Eustis, Virginia. Early production vehicles used a Ford V8 engine, but most of the production run was installed with a Cummins V8 engine combined with a single-speed transmission, fitted with a lock-up hydraulic retarder. The vehicle lacked conventional suspension, relying on low-pressure sand tyres to absorb road shocks. This led to claims of unacceptable "pitching" on the road when approaching the vehicle's maximum speed of 45kph/28mph.

The hull was fabricated from aluminium sheet, with the engine compartment at the rear, the cargo bay placed centrally and the control position at the front. Propulsion in the water was provided by a combination of propeller and water jet,

ABOVE: **Although probably too large and cumbersome to be used as a road-going truck, the 5-ton LARC-5 was really intended for ferrying supplies from ship to shore. The lack of conventional suspension gave rise to claims of unacceptable "pitching" on the road when approaching maximum speed.**

both systems operating in a tunnel through the hull.

The first production contract was awarded to the Adams Division of LeTourneau-Westinghouse in June 1961, with a second contract going to Consolidated Diesel Electric Corporation (Condec). A total of 950 vehicles were built between 1962 and 1968. In mid-2004 it was announced that Power Dynamics had been awarded a contract to refurbish 37 LARC-5s, with delivery of the first craft in October 2006.

LARC-5s were used during the Vietnam War, operating across the beach at Cam Ranh Bay, Nha Trang and Phan Rang, Phan Thiet and Vung Ro Bay. Similar vehicles produced around the same time include the 10-ton LARC-XI, the 15-ton LARC-XV, which

was fitted with a bow ramp, and the 60-ton LARC-LX. This was also known as the BARC-LX or "Barge, Amphibious, Resupply, Cargo".

Condec, LeTourneau-Westinghouse LARC-5

Type: Lighter, amphibious, resupply, cargo, 5-ton, 4x4
Manufacturer: Consolidated Diesel Electric Corporation; Waterbury, Connecticut. LeTourneau-Westinghouse, Adams Division; Peoria, Illinois
Production: 1962 to 1968
Powerplant: Cummins V-903; eight cylinders in V configuration; diesel; water-cooled; 14,798cc; overhead valves; power output, 295bhp at 2,600rpm
Transmission: 1F1R; part-time 4x4
Suspension: None
Brakes: Air-pressure
Electrical system: 24V
Dimensions: Length – 10,675mm/420in
    Width – 3,150mm/124in
    Height – 3,048mm/120in
    Wheelbase – 4,877mm/192in
Weight: Unladen – 4,082kg/9,000lb
    Payload – 4,536kg/10,000lb
Performance: Maximum speed – road, 45kph/28mph; in water, 11kph/7mph

LEFT: **In the water, the LARC-5 was probably more useful than the DUKW. The LARC was used in the Vietnam War where it was used to ferry supplies across the beach at Cam Ranh Bay, Nha Trang, Phan Rang and other areas. Despite the LARC-5 being 50 years old, 37 were refurbished for USTEC between 2004 and 2006.**

Diamond T Models 980, 981

Considered by many to be the best-looking truck of World War II, at least in original closed-cab form, the Diamond T Models 980 and 981 were developed for the British Army to supplement a shortage of Scammell Pioneer tank transporters. The project began in late 1940, when the British Purchasing Commission approached several US manufacturers of heavy trucks with a specification for a 40-ton diesel-engined tractor. One of the prime considerations was that the chosen vehicle could be put into production immediately.

Diamond T proposed a conventional bonneted 6x4 truck based on their civilian 12-ton Model 512, a design which had already been militarized for the Canadian Diamond T Models 967–975. Under the huge bonnet there was a Hercules DFXE six-cylinder diesel engine – despite running counter to US Army practice at that time, the diesel engine was chosen to provide fuel compatibility with the Gardner-engined Scammell. The transmission was a four-speed unit with a two-speed transfer box. The cab was Diamond T's standard civilian design with a steep 30-degree V-shaped windscreen. At the rear was a steel ballast box designed to allow weight to be placed over the rear axles to provide traction when loaded.

The first production variant was the Model 980, designed for use with either the British 40-ton multi-wheeled trailer, typified by the products of Cranes and British Trailers, or the 45-ton US Army

LEFT: The Model 981 can be identified by the use of winch fairlead rollers in the front bumper. The vehicle has a ballast body for towing a semi-trailer.

equivalent produced by Fruehauf, Winter-Weiss and others. The Model 981 followed in 1942–43, the only difference being the provision of winch fairlead rollers in the front bumper to allow the vehicle to be used for tank recovery vehicle. In August 1943, the all-steel closed cab was replaced by a standard open cab designed to save materials and reduce the shipping height.

The Diamond T remained in production until 1945, by which time approximately 6,500 had been built. Of these, 2,255 were used by the British Army. Although it was classified as "substitute standard", the vehicle was also used by the US Army who designated it the M20. The tank-transporter train, including trailer, was the M19.

Large numbers of Diamond Ts remained in British service into the post-war years. It was re-engined in the mid-1950s with a Rolls-Royce C6NFL-143 six-cylinder water-cooled diesel engine.

LEFT: The Diamond T Models 980, 981 were developed for the British War Office and were used to supplement Scammell Pioneer tank transporters. Although also used by the US Army, the use of a diesel engine meant that it was never considered acceptable. The US Army designated it as "substitute standard".

Diamond T Models 980, 981

Type: Truck, 12-ton, 6x4; M20
Manufacturer: Diamond T Motor Car Company; Chicago, Illinois
Production: 1941 to 1945
Powerplant: Hercules DFXE; six cylinders in-line; diesel; water-cooled; 14,500cc; overhead valves; power output, 201bhp at 1,800rpm. Rolls-Royce C6NFL-143; six cylinders in-line; diesel; water-cooled; 12,170cc; overhead valves; power output, 175bhp at 2,100rpm
Transmission: 4F1Rx2; 6x4
Suspension: Live axles on multi-leaf semi-elliptical springs
Brakes: Air-pressure
Electrical system: Hybrid 6V/12V/24V
Dimensions: Length – 9,144mm/360in
    Width – 2,896mm/114in
    Height – 1,575mm/62in
    Wheelbase – 4,553mm/179in
    Bogie centres – 1,321mm/52in
Weight: Unladen – 12,117kg/26,712lb
    Gross train weight – 80,777kg/178,079lb
Performance: Maximum speed – Hercules engine, 37kph/23mph; Rolls-Royce engine – 47kph/29mph

LEFT: **The Diamond T Models 967, 968 chassis was also used for the Model 969 medium wrecker, with Holmes twin-boom recovery gear. The vehicle is being used to recover a captured Panzer III tank.**

Diamond T Models 967, 968

The Diamond T Model 967 was a 4-ton 6x6 cargo truck produced for the US Quartermaster Corps (QMC) in 1940. Approximately 1,000 examples were manufactured. At the same time, the QMC purchased similar 4-ton trucks from Autocar, White and Ward LaFrance, but it was the Diamond T that became standardized in this class in 1941, as the slightly modified Model 968.

For both models, the power unit was an 8,669cc Hercules RXC six-cylinder petrol engine driving through a five-speed gear-box (with overdrive as top gear) connected to all three axles via a two-speed transfer box. Suspension was by semi-elliptical leaf springs, inverted at the rear.

The chassis was built in two wheelbase lengths (4,369mm/172in and 3,835mm/151in), and was generally fitted with a front-mounted 7½-ton capacity winch driven from a power take-off on the transfer box. The short-wheelbase version was bodied as a cargo vehicle. The long-wheelbase variant was fitted with a cargo/pontoon body for use by the US Corps of Engineers. From around 1943, the manufacturer's attractive closed cab was replaced by a standard military open cab with a canvas cover. One vehicle out of four off the production line was fitted with a machine-gun ring mount.

Special versions of what was essentially the same chassis were also produced for the Canadian Army, designated Models 975 and 975A. Chassis and cab units were available for the fitting of special bodies, for example a crane, photographic-processing or workshop van. The Model 968 chassis was also used to provide a 4-ton dump truck (Model 972), and twin-boom wrecker (Model 969). The latter was occasionally fitted with a canvas cover to make it resemble a cargo vehicle from the air. By the time production came to an end in 1945, almost 31,500 examples of the 4-ton chassis had been produced, of which around 9,000 were bodied as cargo vehicles.

ABOVE: **The Diamond T was the standard US Army 4-ton truck from 1941 and was produced in a number of variants. The Model 975 shown is the longer wheelbase version produced for the Royal Canadian Army.**

Diamond T Models 967, 968

Type: Truck, 4-ton, cargo, 6x6

Manufacturer: Diamond T Motor Car Company; Chicago, Illinois

Production: 1940 to 1945

Powerplant: Hercules RXC; six cylinders in-line; petrol; water-cooled; 8,669cc; side valves; power output, 106bhp at 2,300rpm

Transmission: 5F1Rx2; part-time 6x6

Suspension: Live axles on semi-elliptical multi-leaf springs

Brakes: Air-pressure

Electrical system: Hybrid 6V/12V

Dimensions: Length – 6,832mm/269in, 7,544mm/297in
Width – 2,438mm/96in
Height – tilt in place, 2,997mm/118in; minimum, 2,540mm/100in
Wheelbase – 3,835mm/151in, 4,369mm/172in
Bogie centres – 1,321mm/52in

Weight: Unladen – 7,938kg/17,500lb
Payload – 7,711kg/17,000lb

Performance: Maximum speed – 64kph/40mph

LEFT: **The Dodge WC53 carryall is one of the more unusual variants of the ³/₄-ton WC series. One role for which the WC53 may have been used was as a convoy lead vehicle on any of the supply routes. A total of 8,400 were built between 1942 and 1943.**

Dodge T214 WC series

The T214-engined ³/₄-ton Dodge WC series was introduced in 1942 to supersede the earlier ¹/₂-ton models which dated back to 1936, and had proved to be too light for many of the anticipated roles. At the time of its introduction, the US Army had not recognized the ³/₄-ton payload as a standard vehicle class, but the design changes which the Dodge engineers introduced resulted in a vastly improved vehicle. The chassis and bodywork were redesigned to give a 450mm/18in reduction in profile and there was increased power and better tyre flotation on soft ground. This was one tough and enormously capable tactical truck which remained in production until 1945 in a range of variants.

Constructed on a robust steel ladder-type chassis, nothing about the vehicle was innovative or ground-breaking,

which is probably the reason why it was so successful. Power came from a Dodge six-cylinder side-valve engine producing close to 100bhp. This had a special tip-proof carburettor which prevented flooding or fuel starvation when the truck was operated at extreme angles and a high-efficiency oilbath-type air cleaner. A four-speed gearbox and single-speed transfer box were fitted, allowing two- or four-wheel drive. The wide-track axles were suspended on semi-elliptical springs and provided excellent stability off-road, particularly when compared to the ¹/₂-ton model which the T214 was replacing. There was a choice of two wheelbase lengths, the longer version being reserved for a telephone maintenance truck. All of the mechanical components were common across the range. A percentage

RIGHT: **The WC64 was known as the "ambulance collapsible, ³/₄-ton 4x4". It was designed so that the body sides and top could be dropped down into the lower part of the body, together with the cab and windscreen. This made it easily transportable by air. Introduced in January 1945, 3,000 were built.**

LEFT: The T223/WC63 was the 6x6 version of the Dodge 214, and was rated for 1½-ton loads. Without the winch it was the WC62. Mechanical components were basically the same as those in the T214. The T223 was widely used after World War II by the armies of France, Greece, Turkey, Israel and Portugal.

of weapons carriers and command cars were fitted with a front-mounted Braden horizontal winch driven by a power take-off on the transmission.

Manufactured at the Fargo Motor Corporation's Mound Road plant in Detroit, standard variants included the weapons carrier (WC51, WC52), carryall (WC53), ambulance (WC54, WC64), 37mm gun motor carriage (WC55), command car (WC56, WC57), radio command car (WC58), and telephone installation and maintenance truck (WC59, WC61). There was also a rail conversion of the WC51, by Evans Auto-Railer, where the truck was equipped with hydraulically raised and lowered railway wheels. A larger 6x6 variant (WC62, WC63) of the weapons carrier shared many components with the 4x4.

A version of the weapons carrier was also assembled by Dodge in Canada, as "truck, 15cwt, 4x4, GS, APT", with a slightly modified engine.

A total of more than 255,000 of the WC series of all types had been built by the time the model was discontinued in 1945. More than half of the production total was of the weapons carrier variant, which was nicknamed "Beep" – commonly believed to mean "Beefed-up Jeep" or "Big Jeep" which rather superbly describes the machine.

The vehicle saw service with all of the Allies, and thousands remained in service, particularly in Europe, until well into the 1970s and later. In US military service, the truck was replaced by the M37 in 1950. A civilian version was also made available under the name Power Wagon.

ABOVE: The WC56 command car was originally intended for use by officers in the field. However, it was soon discovered that the distinctive outline of the vehicle made it an easy target for enemy artillery and anti-tank gun crews. Similar variants included the winch-equipped WC57 and the WC58 radio command car.

Dodge T214 WC series

Type: Truck, ¾-ton, weapons carrier, 4x4; WC51, WC52

Manufacturer: Chrysler Corporation, Dodge Division, Fargo Motor Corporation; Detroit, Michigan

Production: 1942 to 1945

Powerplant: Dodge T214; six cylinders in-line; petrol; water-cooled; 3,772cc; side valves; power output, 92bhp at 3,200rpm

Transmission: 4F1R; part-time 4x4

Suspension: Live axles on semi-elliptical multi-leaf springs; lever-arm shock absorbers (telescopic shock absorbers on WC64)

Brakes: Hydraulic

Electrical system: 6V, 12V, according to variant

Dimensions: Length – without winch, 4,242mm/167in; with winch, 4,470mm/176in
Width – 2,108mm/83in
Height – tilt in place, 2,159mm/85in; minimum, 1,702mm/67in
Wheelbase – 2,150mm/85in, (WC59, WC61), 307mm/121in

Weight: Unladen – 2,563kg/5,650lb
Payload – 204–226kg/450–500lb

Performance: Maximum speed – 87kph/54mph

LEFT: **Model T cargo trucks were used by both British and US forces during World War I.**

Ford Model T

In 1896, Henry Ford began manufacturing motor cars in Dearborn, Michigan. With backing from Thomas H. Murphy, in 1901, he founded the Detroit Automobile Company, but this was closed three years later. The Henry Ford Company was established in 1901, but Ford resigned within a matter of months and the company was reorganized as the Cadillac Automobile Company the following year. By 1903, Ford had established the Ford Motor Company, his first product being the Model A. The Model C was launched in 1904, and in the same year Ford established a plant in Canada. Other models followed, but

BELOW: **Model T ambulances, with female crews, in service with the Royal Navy at a shore-based hospital.**

real success did not come until the development of the Model T, or "Tin Lizzie" in October 1907. By 1909, the vehicle was in volume production and, although the scuttle and wings were redesigned in 1916, it continued virtually unchanged for the next 20 years.

The Model T was a simple, reliable vehicle, designed for the mass production techniques that Ford pioneered. It was powered by a four-cylinder 2,901cc monobloc engine with a detachable cylinder head. Drive to the rear wheels was by a two-speed epicyclic transmission; some Model T trucks had a two-speed rear axle. Suspension was by transverse semi-elliptical leaf springs. The main brake was described as an

"engine brake", and there was also a separate "emergency brake".

During World War I, the Model T was one of the vehicles standardized by the US Army in the "light" class. The first truck, using a long-wheelbase chassis designated Model TT, was launched in 1917. Although Ford himself was a pacifist, he was also an astute business man and he was happy to supply the US Army with more than 12,000 of these vehicles, some 7,000 of which were shipped overseas. There was no civilian production of the Model Ts between 1917 and 1918.

Total US and Canadian production of the Model T amounted to more than 15 million vehicles by the time production ended in 1928. From 1911, the vehicle was also assembled at Ford's Trafford Park factory near Manchester, where some 250,000 were built.

The Model T was widely used by the US and British armies during World War I as a staff car, ambulance, van and cargo truck, even as an artillery tractor, for which application the truck was fitted with twinned rear tyres. Many remained in service into the 1930s.

Ford Model T

Type: Truck, light, cargo, 4x2
Manufacturer: Ford Motor Company; Dearborn, Michigan
Production: 1907 to 1927
Powerplant: Ford; four cylinders in-line; petrol; water-cooled; 2,901cc; side valves; power output, 20bhp at 1,800rpm
Transmission: 2F1R; 4x2
Suspension: Live axles on transverse semi-elliptical multi-leaf springs
Brakes: Mechanical, separately operated "engine" and "emergency" brakes
Electrical system: 6V
Dimensions: (Model TT van variant)
　　Length – 3,480mm/137in
　　Width – 1,702mm/67in
　　Height – 2,108mm/83in
　　Wheelbase – 2,550mm/100in
Weight: Unladen – 544kg/1,200lb
　　Payload – 410kg/904lb
Performance: Maximum speed – 56kph/35mph

LEFT: **A Ford GPA (General Purpose Amphibian) in service with the US Marine Corps after landing at Anzio, January 22, 1944. Many GPAs were supplied to the Soviet Union, where it was copied and produced as the GAZ-46.**

Ford GPA

Ford GPA	
Type: Truck, amphibian, ¼-ton, 4x4	
Manufacturer: Ford Motor Company; Dearborn, Michigan	
Production: 1942 to 1943	
Powerplant: Ford GPA-6005 (licence-built Willys Go-Devil); four cylinders in-line; petrol; water-cooled; 2,199cc; side valves; power output, 54bhp at 4,000rpm	
Transmission: 3F1Rx2; part-time 4x4	
Suspension: Live axles on semi-elliptical multi-leaf springs; hydraulic double-acting shock absorbers	
Brakes: Hydraulic	
Electrical system: 12V	
Dimensions: Length – 4,875mm/192in	
Width – 1,625mm/64in	
Height – 1,727mm/68in	
Wheelbase – 2,134mm/84in	
Weight: Unladen – 1,660kg/3,660lb	
Payload – 290kg/640lb	
Performance: Maximum speed – 88kph/55mph	

In 1941, marine architects Sparkman & Stevens designed a small amphibious vehicle using components from the Jeep. By December, Marmon-Herrington had built a prototype, with a second from Ford in February 1942. Following trials by the US Quartermaster Corps the Ford prototype was chosen for production. Designated GPA – or "GP Amphibian" – the vehicle had a lightweight steel hull together with the Jeep engine, transmission and axles. Propulsion in the water was by a three-bladed propeller. Steering was by a boat-type rudder.

Although similar to the DUKW, it was not a success. On the road, the increased size of the body made the vehicle unwieldy. In the water there was insufficient freeboard when loaded, which reduced safe usage in choppy water. Production ended in June 1943 after about 12,785 vehicles had been built. Many were supplied to the Soviet Union.

Ford GTB

Dating from 1942, the Ford GTB was a low-profile forward-control truck developed for the US Quartermaster

Ford GTB	
Type: Truck, cargo, 1½-ton, 4x4	
Manufacturer: Ford Motor Company; Dearborn, Michigan	
Production: 1942 to 1944	
Powerplant: Ford G8T; six cylinders in-line; petrol; water-cooled; 3,703cc; side valves; power output, 90bhp at 3,400rpm	
Transmission: 4F1Rx2; part-time 4x4	
Suspension: Live axles on semi-elliptical multi-leaf springs; hydraulic double-acting shock absorbers	
Brakes: Vacuum-assisted hydraulic	
Electrical system: 12V	
Dimensions: Length – 4,597mm/181in	
Width – 2,184mm/86in	
Height – tilt in place, 2,540mm/100in; minimum, 2,083mm/82in	
Wheelbase – 2,921mm/115in	
Weight: Unladen – 3,289kg/7,250lb	
Payload – 1,500kg/3,307lb	
Performance: Maximum speed – 72kph/45mph	

ABOVE: **The Ford GTB was developed to a specification issued by the US Quartermaster Corps in 1942.**

Corps for use in combat zones. During 1942, prototypes had been produced by Dodge, Ford, Chevrolet and others in the ¾ and 1½-ton weight classes. Despite testing continuing into 1944, the Ford GTB was the only vehicle to enter production.

The GTB was based on a commercial truck, and the low silhouette was achieved by placing the driver alongside the engine, which was offset to the right. The engine was a Ford six-cylinder driving live axles through a four-speed gearbox and two-speed transfer box. Both single and twin rear wheel variants were produced. Some were equipped with a front-mounted winch.

Total production was 15,274. The US Army and US Navy took 8,218 cargo vehicles (GTBA), and 7,066 of a Mk II variant were supplied to the US Navy.

FWD Model B

The Four Wheel Drive Auto Company (FWD) started building trucks in 1910 and launched the Model B 3-ton 4x4 truck in 1912. The truck was standardized for its class by the US Quartermaster Corps and remained in production throughout World War I.

A 6,375cc Wisconsin four-cylinder engine was fitted under the cab and was connected to a mid-mounted three-speed gearbox via a belt or silent chain. A locking centre differential with shafts connecting the drive was fitted to the front and rear axles. The axles were located by radius rods, and suspension was by semi-elliptical springs. Although originally using solid tyres on spoked or disc wheels, many were converted to pneumatics in the early 1930s. More than 16,000 were supplied to the US Army, many sent to Europe. The trucks were also built by Kissel, Mitchell-Lewis, Premier, and Peerless, the latter destined for Britain.

RIGHT: **An FWD Model B in World War I US camouflage as part of a display in London to encourage people to buy War Bonds. The vehicle was built at the FWD plant at Clifton, Wisconsin, between 1912 and 1919.**

FWD Model B

Type: Truck, cargo, 3- to 5-ton, 4x4
Manufacturer: Four Wheel Drive Auto Company (FWD); Clintonville, Wisconsin
Production: 1912 to 1919
Powerplant: Wisconsin; four cylinders in-line; petrol; water-cooled; 6,375cc; side valves; power output, 36bhp at 1,800rpm
Transmission: 3F1R; full-time 4x4
Suspension: Live axles on semi-elliptical multi-leaf springs
Brakes: Mechanical
Electrical system: None
Dimensions: Length – 5,640mm/222in
Width – 1,930mm/76in
Height – tilt in place, 3,200mm/126in
Wheelbase – 3,150mm/124in
Weight: Unladen – 5,534kg/12,200lb
Payload – road, 4,990kg/11,000lb; cross-country, 2,994kg/6,600lb
Performance: Maximum speed – 24kph/15mph

International M-5-6, M-5H-6

The International Harvester Company was one of the contenders for the US Army's standardized 2¹/₂-ton 6x6 chassis of World War II. The first prototype was produced in 1940 and the M-5-6 went into production the following year. The company built around 40,000 in both long- and short-wheelbase form. Most were supplied to the US Navy and Marine Corps.

The engine was a 5,912cc International RED-361B six-cylinder driving through a five-speed gearbox and two-speed transfer box. Suspension was by semi-elliptical leaf springs, with a Hendrickson-type rear bogie.

Early production vehicles were fitted with an all-steel cab, but this was eventually replaced by the typical canvas-topped open cab. Standard variants included cargo, workshop, fire-fighter, recovery vehicle, dump and fuel tanker; there was also a tractor for semi-trailers. A 6x4 variant was also produced, designated M-5H-6.

LEFT: **The International M-5-6 was produced in 1941, the majority being supplied to the US Navy.**

International M-5-6, M-5H-6

Type: Truck, cargo, 2¹/₂-ton, 6x6
Manufacturer: International Harvester; Chicago, Illinois
Production: 1941 to 1945
Powerplant: International RED-361B; six cylinders in-line; petrol; water-cooled; 5,912cc; overhead valves; power output, 126bhp at 2,500rpm
Transmission: 5F1Rx2; part-time 6x6
Suspension: Live axles on semi-elliptical multi-leaf springs
Brakes: Vacuum servo-assisted hydraulic
Electrical system: 6V
Dimensions: (cargo vehicles)
Length – 6,452mm/254in
Width – 2,337mm/92in
Height – tilt in place, 2,388mm/94in; minimum 1,930mm/76in
Wheelbase – 3,785mm/149in, 4,293mm/169in
Bogie centres – 1,143mm/45in
Weight: Unladen – 6,078kg/13,400lb
Payload – road, 4,536kg/10,000lb; cross-country, 2,427kg/5,350lb
Performance: Maximum speed – 72kph/45mph

LEFT: **The DUKW was essentially the mechanical components of the GMC CCKW truck. The vehicle was designed by Sparkman & Stephens, a firm of marine architects based in New York, from where they continue to design yachts.**

GMC DUKW-353

Dating from 1942, the GMC DUKW is probably the most successful amphibious military vehicle of all time. It was designed in 1941 by New York-based marine architects Sparkman & Stephens working to a brief drawn up by the National Defense Research Council. It was to be built by GMC's Yellow Truck & Coach Division.

The first prototypes, which were successfully trialled in June 1942, were based on the components of the AFKWX-353 forward-control truck. Following the trials, an initial contract was placed for 2,000 vehicles, now using components of the CCKW-353. By the time production ended in 1945, a total of 21,147 had been built.

Power came from a GMC (Chevrolet) six-cylinder overhead-valve engine driving either all six wheels, or a propeller, through a five-speed gearbox, with an overdrive top gear and two-speed transfer box.

The axles were suspended on semi-elliptical leaf springs, inverted at the rear. A rudder was fitted at the rear to provide directional control in the water. Late production models were fitted with a "Central Tyre Inflation System" (CTIS), which allowed the tyre pressures to be set from the driver's position to suit ground conditions when leaving the water. A mechanical winch was installed at the rear.

The welded-steel hull included seating for a driver and co-driver at the front, combined with a spacious cargo area at the rear, over which a full-length canvas cover could be erected.

The DUKW – the name was simply the manufacturer's chassis code indicating the year of development, the drive-line, wheelbase length, and the type of body – was first used in amphibious landings in the Pacific and on Sicily. Although a scheme to use DUKWs equipped with fire escape ladders to scale the cliffs at

Pointe du Hoc was unsuccessful, the DUKW was used very effectively to ferry supplies ashore in the days following the D-Day landings, before the Mulberry Harbours were operational.

The DUKW was used by all of the Allies during World War II and remained in US Army service into the 1960s. It was also used in the post-war years by France, Britain and others. The British Army still retains a small number of DUKWs at the Amphibious Trials & Development Unit (ATDU), Instow, North Devon.

LEFT: **The hull provided seating for a driver and co-driver and had a large open bay at the rear, which could be used for cargo or personnel. A full-length canvas roof could be erected over the cargo bay. Early DUKWs can be identified by the upright windscreen.**

GMC DUKW-353

Type: Truck, cargo, 2¹/₂-ton, amphibian, 6x6
Manufacturer: GMC Yellow Truck & Coach Division; Pontiac, Michigan. After 1943, GMC Truck & Coach Division; Pontiac, Michigan
Production: 1942 to 1945
Powerplant: GMC (Chevrolet) Model 270; six cylinders in-line; petrol; water-cooled; 4,416cc; overhead valves; power output, 92bhp at 2,750rpm
Transmission: 5F1Rx2; part-time 6x6
Suspension: Live axles on semi-elliptical multi-leaf springs, inverted at rear
Brakes: Vacuum-assisted hydraulic
Electrical system: 6V
Dimensions: Length – 9,450mm/372in
    Width – 2,515mm/99in
    Height – tilt in place, 2,690mm/106in; minimum, 2,286mm/90in
    Wheelbase – 2,921mm/164in
    Bogie centres – 1,118mm/44in
Weight: Unladen – 6,750kg/14,880lb
    Payload – 2,268kg/5,000lb
Performance: Maximum speed – 80kph/50mph

LEFT: The GMC CCKW was one of the vehicles which helped to win the war. The truck was used by the Allies and by all arms of the services and was the backbone of the US Army's supply chain. The vehicle shown is fitted with the civilian-type cab and is being loaded on to an LCT at Weymouth, Dorset, in preparation for the D-Day landings, June 6, 1944.

GMC CCKW-352, 353

Known as the "deuce-and-a-half" or the "Jimmy", the GMC 2¹/₂-ton 6x6 was probably the most significant US truck of World War II. And, with a total of some 562,750 produced, it was also the second most numerous vehicle of the war, beaten from the top spot only by the Jeep. The "Jimmy" served in every theatre of the war and with all of the Allied armies. It was produced in a large number of variants.

From 1939, GMC had started supplying a range of lightly militarized, but essentially civilian, 2¹/₂-ton 4x2 and 6x4 trucks to the US Army from 1939. However, the vehicle for which the company became known worldwide was derived from the 6x6 ACKWX which had originally been intended for the French Army. When France fell to the Nazis in 1940, the trucks were diverted to Britain. In January 1941, the ACKWX was modified to produce the standardized CCKW (initially designated CCKWX). The all-steel Chevrolet civilian-type cab

of the original was retained, but the bonnet and radiator grille were replaced. The enclosed cab, with a V-shaped top-hung screen, survived until 1944, when it was replaced by a standardized open military cab with a canvas top and flat, folding windscreen.

The truck was powered by a GMC (Chevrolet) six-cylinder overhead-valve engine, driving all wheels through a five-speed gearbox, (with overdrive top gear) and two-speed transfer case. The front axle drive could be disengaged when not required. Suspension was by semi-elliptical multi-leaf springs, inverted at the rear. During the production run, two types of axle design were used, described as the Timken "split" axle, or the Chevrolet "banjo". The latter was less susceptible to catastrophic failure through over-loading.

Production took place at GMC's Yellow Truck & Coach Division, although after 1943 the company was renamed

RIGHT: Up until 1944, the truck was fitted with a militarized version of the manufacturer's standard civilian cab fitted with the simple military bonnet and mudguards. Later production vehicles had a canvas-covered open cab designed to save materials and reduce the shipping height.

LEFT: **A quarter of GMC CCKW trucks were fitted with a hip ring in the cab roof which allowed the use of a heavy machine-gun. Many convoys were accompanied by trucks equipped with four 0.50in Browning heavy machine-guns in a Maxson M2 electrically operated mount. Each gun had a maximum rate of fire of 450 rounds per minute.**

as GMC Truck & Coach Division. The model code CCKW indicates that the truck was designed in 1941 (first C), was fitted with a normal-control cab (second C), front-wheel drive (K), and rear-wheel bogie drive (W). The "X" suffix, which indicated a non-standard wheelbase, was dropped soon after manufacture began. The vehicle was produced in two chassis lengths, the "353" having a wheelbase of 4,166mm/164in, and the "352" measuring 3,658mm/144in.

The long-wheelbase (CCKW-353) cargo truck was the most numerous in production and while most cargo bodies were of welded-steel construction, timber bodies were also fitted. Both types had fixed sides and a drop tailgate and had folding troop seats fitted in the rear. Five removable hoops were provided to support a canvas cover. There was a multiplicity of other variants, including fuel tanker, water tanker, stake truck, compressor vehicle, workshop vehicle, bomb-service truck, dump truck (tipper) and van body. The

truck was also supplied as a chassis-cab unit for the fitting of specialized bodies. A number of vehicles were fitted with a Gar Wood or Heil 5-ton capacity winch installed on chassis extension ahead of the radiator. One out of four trucks off the production line was fitted with an anti-aircraft machine-gun mount above the passenger seat.

The truck remained in service with the US Army into the 1950s. After the war, thousands were passed to the armies of the liberated European nations, where many remained in service into the early 1980s.

BELOW: **A GMC CCKW-353 mounted with a Le Roi Model D318 air-compressor for road repairs.**

GMC CCKW-352, 353

Type: Truck, 2¹/₂-ton, cargo, 6x6
Manufacturer: Yellow Truck & Coach Manufacturing; Pontiac, Michigan. After 1943, GMC Truck & Coach Division; Pontiac, Michigan
Production: 1941 to 1945
Powerplant: GMC (Chevrolet) Model 270; six cylinders in-line; petrol; water-cooled; 4,416cc; overhead valves; power output, 92bhp at 2,750rpm
Transmission: 5F1Rx2; part-time 6x6
Suspension: Live axles on semi-elliptical multi-leaf springs, inverted at rear
Brakes: Hydraulic with vacuum servo-assistance
Electrical system: 6V
Dimensions: (cargo vehicles)
    Length – (CCKW-352) 5,842mm/230in; (CCKW-353) 6,477mm/255in
    Width – 2,261mm/89in
    Height – tilt in place, 2,770mm/109in; minimum, 1,880mm/74in
    Wheelbase – (CCKW-352) 3,658mm/144in; (CCKW-353) 4,166mm/164in
    Bogie centres – 1,118mm/44in
Weight: Unladen – 4,370kg/9,635lb
    Payload – road, 4,536kg/10,000lb; cross-country, 2,427kg/5,350lb
Performance: Maximum speed – 72kph/45mph

Jeep CJ10A

The Jeep CJ10 was introduced in 1981, and remained in production until 1986. It was available with a choice of diesel or petrol engines, coupled to a four-speed manual or three-speed automatic transmission and two-speed transfer box.

In the mid-1980s, PSI Mobile Products produced 1,500 examples of a CJ10-based short-wheelbase tractor for the US Air Force. Designated CJ10A, it was intended to be used to tow ammunition trailers or as a tug for towing small aircraft and helicopters. The wheelbase was reduced to 2,032mm/80in and there was a minimal, short, rear body incorporating a large fuel tank, and fitted with a stepped towing bumper with three pintle hooks. The centre pintle was designed to telescope and to swing from left to right.

The CJ10A was powered by a Nissan SD-33 six-cylinder diesel engine driving a four-speed manual transmission, with the transfer box locked in the low ratio.

Jeep CJ10A

Type: Air Force aircraft tug, 4x4
Manufacturer: Jeep Corporation; Southfield, Michigan. Modified by PSI Mobile Products
Production: 1985 to 1986
Powerplant: Nissan SD-33; six cylinders in-line; diesel; water-cooled; 3,246cc; overhead valves; power output, 95bhp at 3,500rpm
Transmission: 4F1R; full-time 4x4
Suspension: Live axles on semi-elliptical multi-leaf springs
Brakes: Hydraulic
Electrical system: 24V
Dimensions: Length – 3,683mm/145in
　　　Width – 1,730mm/68in
　　　Height – 1,780mm/70in
　　　Wheelbase – 2,032mm/80in
Weight: Unladen – 2,722kg/6,000lb
　　　Payload – 436kg/1,000lb
　　　Maximum drawbar pull – 1,814kg/4,000lb
Performance: Maximum speed – 40kph/25mph

LEFT: **The Jeep Corporation's CJ10A was used by the USAF as a light aircraft tug.**

Jeep Wrangler TJ-L

Produced in Egypt by Arab American Vehicles (AAV) for the Egyptian Army, the Wrangler TJ-L was a joint-venture project between Daimler-Chrysler and the Egyptian Government. The vehicle was initially powered by a 3,958cc six-cylinder petrol engine, mated to a five-speed manual transmission. From 2005, a VM Motori four-cylinder 2,800cc diesel

engine was also available. The pick-up bed was suitable for mounting a heavy-calibre machine-gun or could be fitted with two rows of seats to carry troops. Production began in August 2003 at the AAV Cairo plant and is running at approximately 1,500 units a year. The Egyptian armed forces' initial order was for 1,000 Wrangler TJ-Ls.

Jeep Wrangler TJ-L

Type: Truck, utility, 4x4
Manufacturer: Arab American Vehicles; Cairo
Production: 2003 on
Powerplant: Daimler-Chrysler Power-Tech I-6; six cylinders in-line; petrol; water-cooled; 3,958cc; overhead valves; power output, 181bhp at 4,600rpm
VM Motori; four cylinders in-line; turbocharged diesel; water-cooled; 2,800cc; overhead valves; power output, 120bhp at 3,800rpm
Transmission: 5F1Rx2; part-time 4x4
Suspension: Live axles on dual-rate coil springs; locating arms, track and stabilizer bars; telescopic gas-filled shock absorbers
Brakes: Power-assisted hydraulic
Electrical system: Dual 12V/24V
Dimensions: Length – 4,420mm/174in
　　　Width – 1,694mm/67in
　　　Height – tilt in place, 1,763mm/69in
　　　Wheelbase – 2,931mm/115in
Weight: Unladen – 1,520kg/3,350lb
　　　Payload – 907kg/2,000lb
Performance: Maximum speed – 113kph/70mph

LEFT: **The Jeep Wrangler TJ-L is in service with the Egyptian Army which placed an initial order for 1,000 vehicles. Although derived from the civilian Wrangler, the TJ-L has a lengthened wheelbase and is fitted with uprated suspension and a heavy-duty rear axle.**

Jeffery Model 4017 Quad

ABOVE: **A Model 4017 Quad fitted with solid tyres. Note the chains on the front wheels for extra traction.**

Jeffery Model 4017 Quad

Type: Truck, 2-ton, cargo, 4x4
Manufacturer: Thomas B. Jeffery; Kenosha, Wisconsin, later Nash-Quad
Production: 1913 to 1928
Powerplant: Buda; four cylinders in-line; petrol; water-cooled; 3,785cc, 4,719cc; side valves; power output, 32–36bhp at 1,800rpm
Transmission: 4F1R; 4x4
Suspension: Live axles on semi-elliptical multi-leaf springs
Brakes: Mechanical
Electrical system: None
Dimensions: Length – 7,544mm/297in
Width – 1,880mm/74in
Height – 1,956mm/77in
Wheelbase – 3,150mm/124in
Weight: Unladen – 3,590kg/7,900lb
Payload – 2,000kg/4,400lb
Performance: Maximum speed – 20kph/12mph

Thomas B. Jeffery started building the 2-ton Quad truck in 1913, and the US Army and Marine Corps were among the first customers, with many seeing service during the Mexican War. The Quad drove, steered and braked on all four wheels. Despite the use of cast-steel wheels and solid rubber tyres, this represented a considerable improvement in mobility when compared with other manufacturers' 4x2 trucks of the period.

A Buda four-cylinder petrol engine was installed ahead of the driver, and transmission was by a four-speed gearbox driving the wheels through ring and pinion gears. Suspension was by semi-elliptical leaf springs. By 1919, four-wheel steering feature was not installed on the military Quad. More than 11,500 examples eventually entered military service.

The trucks were renamed Nash-Quad in 1917, and were also manufactured by Hudson and National and during the latter years of World War I, by Paige-Detroit.

Mack NO1–NO7

Mack NO1–NO7

Type: Truck, 7½-ton, prime mover, 6x6
Manufacturer: Mack Manufacturing Company; New York
Production: 1940 to 1944
Powerplant: Mack EY; six cylinders in-line; petrol; water-cooled; 11,586cc; overhead valves; power output, 170bhp at 2,100rpm
Transmission: 5F1Rx2; part-time 6x6
Suspension: Live axles on semi-elliptical multi-leaf springs
Brakes: Air-pressure; wired for electric trailer brakes
Electrical system: Hybrid 6V/12V
Dimensions: Length – 7,544mm/297in
Width – 2,591mm/102in
Height – tilt in place, 3,099mm/122in; minimum, 2,388mm/94in
Wheelbase – 3,962mm/156in
Bogie centres – 1,473mm/58in
Weight: Unladen – 13,436kg/29,620lb
Payload – 7,031kg/15,500lb
Performance: Maximum speed – 52kph/32mph

The Mack NO was a heavy 6x6 tractor designed to tow the US Army's 155mm and 240mm howitzers. The first example, NO1, was launched in December 1940. This was followed by the NQ of which there was no series production. Subsequent modifications produced the series NO2, NO3, NO6 and NO7. Models NO4 and NO5 were long-wheelbase heavy wrecker variants, but there was no series production.

All variants were powered by an 11,586cc six-cylinder petrol engine driving through a five-speed gearbox and two-speed transfer box. The triple-reduction elevated front axle used bevel gears and revolving kingpins as the final-drive. Suspension was by semi-elliptical springs.

Models NO2 to NO7 were fitted with an open cab and a fabricated steel body

ABOVE: **The Mack NO series was fitted with a large mechanical winch at the front of the vehicle.**

with seating for 12 personnel plus stowage for spare wheels, parts and ammunition. A chain hoist above the tailgate was used for lifting the gun trail.

Pacific TR1 "Dragon Wagon"

Better known as the "Dragon Wagon", the Pacific Car & Foundry TR1 was one of the largest vehicles of World War II. Unhappy with the Diamond T Models 980, 981, which had been produced for the British, the US Army developed the TR1 as a replacement. The armoured cab made the TR1 suitable for use as a battlefield tank recovery vehicle.

The TR1 was prototyped by the Knuckey Truck Company of San Francisco in 1942 but, lacking manufacturing facilities, it was produced by locomotive builders Pacific Car & Foundry. However, even the production version of the vehicle retained Knuckey's huge chain-drive rear bogie.

Aside from massive size, the most striking feature of the original M26 variant is the angular armoured cab with distinctive armoured shutters for the radiator and windows. Later the M26A1, a soft-skinned variant, was produced in October 1944, retaining the angular shape. Both variants were powered by a 17,861cc Hall Scott six-cylinder petrol engine, with a capacity of almost 18 litres, driving all six wheels through a four-speed gearbox and three-speed transfer box. The front axle was suspended on semi-elliptical springs, while at the rear the walking-beam chain-drive bogie was oversprung. Two huge winches were fitted behind the cab to assist with loading disabled tanks.

A folding A-frame allowed the truck to be used as a recovery vehicle.

The standard trailer was the Fruehauf M15, a 45-ton eight-wheeled rear-loading unit. The tractor and trailer together were designated "M25 40-ton tank transporter truck-trailer". The vehicle was produced between 1943 and 1945, with 1,372 tractors completed. The M26 remained in service with the US Army throughout the 1950s. Many were left in Europe after the war and became a popular conversion for heavy-haulage operators.

Pacific TR1 "Dragon Wagon"

Type: Truck-tractor, 12-ton, 6x6; M26, M26A1

Manufacturer: Pacific Car & Foundry Company; Renton, Seattle

Production: 1943 to 1945

Powerplant: Hall Scott Model 440; six cylinders in-line; petrol; water-cooled; 17,861cc; overhead valves; power output, 240bhp at 2,100rpm

Transmission: 4F1Rx3; part-time 6x6

Suspension: Live front axle on multi-leaf semi-elliptical springs; walking-beam rear bogie without suspension

Brakes: Air pressure, rear wheels only

Electrical system: 12V

Dimensions: Length – 7,721mm/304in
 Width – 3,810mm/150in
 Height – 3,480mm/137in
 Wheelbase – 4,369mm/172in
 Bogie centres – 1,600mm/63in

Weight: Unladen – 19,051kg/42,000lb
 Gross train weight – 60,329-64,865kg/ 133,000-143,000lb

Performance: Maximum speed – 42kph/26mph

LEFT: **The Detroit-Diesel powered Oshkosh M1070 was originally designed as a transporter for the US Army's Abrams main battle tank.** BELOW: **Fitted with the Caterpillar C18 engine, the Oshkosh tractor was selected by the British Ministry of Defence as a replacement for the Scammell Commander.**

Oshkosh M1070

Type: Truck-tractor, heavy equipment, 8x8; M1070

Manufacturer: Oshkosh Truck Corporation; Oshkosh, Wisconsin

Production: 1992 to 2003

Powerplant: (M1070) Detroit-Diesel 8V92TA; eight cylinders in V configuration; turbocharged diesel; water-cooled; 12,061cc; overhead valves; power output, 500bhp at 2,100rpm. (M1070F) Caterpillar C18; six cylinders in-line; turbocharged diesel; water-cooled; 18,100cc; overhead valves; power output, 7,00bhp at 1,300rpm

Transmission: automatic 5F1Rx2 (M1070), 7F1R (M1070F); part-time 8x8 (M1070), full-time 8x8 (M1070F); differential locks on rear axles

Suspension: Live axles on semi-elliptical tapered-leaf springs at front; live axles with Hendrickson air suspension at rear

Brakes: Air-pressure

Electrical system: 24V

Dimensions: Length – 9,195mm/362in
Width – 2,591mm/100in
Height – 3,556mm/140in
Wheelbase – 5,461mm/215in
Bogie centres – 1,524+1,524mm/60+60in

Weight: Unladen – 20,058kg/44,220lb
Gross train weight – 99,792–117,936kg/ 220–260,000lb

Performance: Maximum speed – 80–85kph/50–53mph

Oshkosh M1070

In 1990, the Oshkosh Truck Corporation delivered the first prototype to the US Army of the M1070 "Heavy Equipment Transporter" (HET) which was intended to replace the company's earlier M911 tractor. Production began in the spring of 1992 and a total of 1,600 examples were completed.

The M1070 was a massive tractor, rated for a gross train weight of up to 99,792kg/220,000lb and easily capable of carrying an Abrams main battle tank or two smaller armoured fighting vehicles, such as the Bradley "Infantry Fighting Vehicle" (IFV), on the standard four-axle semi-trailer. Power was by a 12,061cc Detroit-Diesel V8 diesel engine driving through an Allison automatic five-speed

transmission and two-speed transfer box, which incorporated a front-axle disconnect. Live axles, with hub-reduction gears, were used front and rear. The front axle was suspended on parabolic tapered-leaf semi-elliptical springs. Hendrickson air suspension was used at the rear. Inter-axle and intra-axle differential locks were fitted. Axles one (front) and four (rear) are used for steering the vehicle.

Three winches were installed behind the cab, above the first of the three rear axles – two 55-ton two-speed hydraulic winches, together with an auxiliary single-speed 1-ton winch used for paying out the steel hawser from the main winches. A "Central Tyre Inflation System" (CTIS) was fitted, with preset

selections for highway, cross-country, mud/snow and emergency conditions.

In 2001, a Caterpillar-engined variant, designated M1070F, was selected by the British Ministry of Defence to replace the ageing Scammell Commander tank transporters. Designed for use with a seven-axle King semi-trailer, the M1070F is rated at 72-tons. A total of 92 of these tractors were built, with deliveries completed by October 2003.

Stewart & Stevenson FMTV

Prototypes for what the US Army was describing as the "Family of Medium Tactical Vehicles" (FMTV) were produced by three companies towards the end of the 1980s – the Tactical Truck Corporation (a consortium formed by General Motors and Bowen-McLaughlin-York), Teledyne Continental and Stewart & Stevenson. Following extensive trials, the Texas-based Stewart & Stevenson company received a five-year $1.2 billion contract to produce 10,843 trucks. Production started in 1991, and further contracts followed requesting a total of 85,000 vehicles.

The FMTV is a forward-control all-wheel drive truck, designed to replace the ageing 2½-ton and 5-ton "M Series", the origins of which date back to the early 1950s. The truck is being produced in two basic variants with an 80 per cent component commonality. The range now encompasses some 14 chassis versions.

The "Light Medium Tactical Vehicle" (LMTV) is a 4x4 design rated for a payload of 2½ tons, while the "Medium Tactical Vehicle" (MTV) is a 6x6 rated at 5 tons. Both vehicles are powered by a Caterpillar six-cylinder diesel engine, with full-time all-wheel drive through an automatic seven-speed gearbox and single-speed transfer box incorporating a torque-bias lockable inter-axle

differential. Suspension is by live axles on parabolic tapered leaf springs. An upgraded "A1" variant was introduced in September 1999, with increased engine power and anti-lock brakes.

An electronic "Central Tyre Inflation System" (CTIS) is standard, and a number of vehicles are fitted with a 5- or 7-ton winch. The cab roof can support a machine-gun ring mount.

The LMTV has been procured in cargo and van variants. The MTV is available in four wheelbase lengths, and standard variants include cargo, crane-equipped cargo, expansible van, tractor, recovery vehicle, dump, flat rack load-handling system and fuel tanker vehicles. The MTV has also been used as a transporter-launcher for the US "High Mobility Artillery Rocket System" (HIMARS). Purpose-designed 2¼-ton and 5-ton trailers have also been produced.

ABOVE: **Rated for a 5-ton payload, the 6x6 "Medium Tactical Vehicle" (MTV) is produced in four wheelbase lengths. Standard variants include cargo (with optional hydraulic crane), expansible van, tractor, recovery vehicle, dump, flat rack load-handling system and fuel tanker.** LEFT: **The 4x4 "Light Medium Tactical Vehicle" (LMTV) is rated for a payload of 2½ tons. Shown here is the latest upgraded "A2" variant.**

Stewart & Stevenson FMTV

Type: Truck, cargo, 2½-ton, 4x4; M1078A1-M1081. Truck, cargo, 5-ton, 6x6; M1083A1-M1096A1
Manufacturer: Stewart & Stevenson, Tactical Vehicle Systems Division; West Sealy, Texas
Production: 1991 on
Powerplant: (LMTV) Caterpillar 3126 ATAAC, (MTV) Caterpillar 3136 ATAAC; six cylinders in-line; turbocharged diesel; water-cooled; 7,200cc; overhead valves; power output, 275–330bhp at 2,400rpm
Transmission: Automatic 7F1R; full-time 4x4 or 6x6; inter-axle differential lock
Suspension: Live axles on parabolic tapered leaf semi-elliptical springs; hydraulic double-acting shock absorbers
Brakes: Air-pressure
Electrical system: 24V
Dimensions: (typical)
Length – (LMTV) 6,420mm/253in; (MTV) 6,960–9,305mm/274–366in
Width – 2,438mm/96in
Height – tilt in place, 2,845mm/112in; minimum, 2,680mm/105in
Wheelbase – (LMTV) 3,900mm/154in; (MTV standard) 4,100mm/161in, (MTV long) 4,500mm/177in, 5,300mm/209in, 5,500mm/216in
Bogie centres – 1,525mm/60in
Weight: Unladen – 7,978–10,287kg/17,589–22,678lb
Payload – (LMTV) 2,268kg/5,000lb; (MTV) 4,536kg/10,000lb
Performance: Maximum speed – 93kph/58mph

Ward LaFrance Model 1000

The US Army's first heavy wrecker was produced by Marmon-Herrington in 1935, with small numbers supplied by Corbitt from July 1937. The design was standardized as "truck, wrecking, heavy, M1" and Ward LaFrance and Kenworth received contracts for 69 and 300 vehicles respectively. Similar in design and appearance, the vehicles featured a Continental petrol engine, Fuller transmission and Gar Wood hand-operated crane. Some 2,030 examples were built, with most coming from Ward LaFrance, before production was halted in favour of the M1A1.

Introduced in 1943, the standardized M1A1 had improved lifting equipment and featured an open cab. Both companies were now producing what was effectively the same vehicle, with a total of 3,735 M1A1s produced before 1945. Ward LaFrance were again responsible for the majority.

The vehicle was assembled around a Continental-powered 6x6 heavy-duty chassis. Ward LaFrance used the same Model 1000 chassis as had been developed for their M1 wrecker, now designated the Series 5. Kenworth's chassis was the Model 573. Transmission

was by a five-speed Fuller gearbox and remote-mounted Timken two-speed transfer box, driving both front and rear axles. Suspension was by semi-elliptical springs, inverted at the rear and located by means of radius rods. Brakes were air-pressure operated. Brake-line connectors at front and rear, as well as a double check valve in the brake lines, allowed the vehicle to be braked by a towing vehicle.

The Gar Wood US 5A crane of the M1 was replaced by the fully powered US 6A unit. Winches were fitted at the front and rear. A massive V-shaped front bumper, and V-shaped tow bar, was fitted which could be used to tow or push a light or medium armoured vehicle. The crane could be slung through 180 degrees to lift at the rear or side. Maximum lifting capacity was 7,276kg/16,000lb. Jacks and triangulated braces were used to support the vehicle during lifting operations.

Production began in 1943 at Kenworth's Seattle plant – production was moved to Yakima, Washington, in 1944 – and at the Ward LaFrance truck factory at Elmira, New York. In 1945, Kenworth was purchased by Pacific Car & Foundry and production was moved back to Seattle.

ABOVE: **Produced by both Kenworth and Ward LaFrance, the Continental-engined M1A1 was the standard US Army heavy wrecker during the last years of World War II. The recovery equipment was manufactured by Gar Wood and featured a power-operated crane.** LEFT: **The M1A1 remained in service throughout the 1950s. This vehicle is with the US Air Force in West Germany.**

Ward LaFrance Model 1000 (M1A1)

Type: Truck, wrecking, heavy, 6x6; M1A1
Manufacturer: Ward LaFrance Truck Division of Great American Industries; Elmira, New York
Production: 1943 to 1945
Powerplant: Continental 22R; six cylinders in-line; petrol; water-cooled; 8,210cc; overhead valves; power output, 145bhp at 2,400rpm
Transmission: 5F1Rx2; part-time 6x6
Suspension: Live axles on semi-elliptical multi-leaf springs, inverted at rear; hydraulic shock absorbers at front
Brakes: Air-pressure
Electrical system: 12V
Dimensions: Length – 8,840mm/348in
　　Width – 2,540mm/100in
　　Height – 2,970mm/117in
　　Wheelbase – 4,600mm/181in
　　Bogie centres – 1,320mm/52in
Weight: Unladen – 14,152kg/31,200lb
　　Maximum weight on crane – 7,276kg/16,000lb
Performance: Maximum speed – 72kph/45mph

Willys MB

In 1940, Willys-Overland, American Bantam and Ford had all contributed prototypes to the US Quartermaster Corps (US QMC) project to develop a light reconnaissance car. In late 1940, following trials at Camp Holabird and elsewhere, officials at the Army and the US QMC appeared unable to make up their mind as to which of the three vehicles offered the best combination of performance and reliability. Each manufacturer was awarded a contract to produce 500 vehicles based on the respective prototypes. This number was subsequently increased to 1,500.

Unsurprisingly, since all three had been based on the same specification, and Willys and Ford engineers had apparently been able to inspect the Bantam prototype before developing their own, all three of the prototypes shared design features. The simple, open-sided four-seater body was provided with a folding windscreen and a removable canvas top. The body was generally assembled from flat panels which would simplify

repairs in the field. A four-cylinder water-cooled petrol engine drove the rear wheels through a three-speed gearbox. Drive to the front axle could be selected via a two-speed transfer box, which allowed all-wheel drive through a set of low-ratio gears. Live axles were suspended on semi-elliptical multi-leaf springs in combination with hydraulic telescopic shock absorbers. A towing pintle was provided at the rear, and a circular plate designed to support a machine-gun pedestal was welded to one of the chassis cross-members.

Once the contracts were issued, staff at the US QMC started to draw-up a specification for a "standardized" Jeep which would embody elements of all three designs. Trials had shown that the Go-Devil engine of the Willys MA offered the best all-round performance. In July 1941, Willys was asked to produce a further 16,000 MA Jeeps.

With this work underway, representatives of the US QMC and the user arms met at Camp Holabird to discuss further changes and improvements to the design. One important aspect of this work was the standardization of components with other US military vehicles of the period. The standardized Jeep, which employed a version of Ford's front end, was designated MB.

By October 1941, it was obvious that Willys lacked the production capacity to keep up with the enormous demand for the vehicle. It would have been the obvious solution to involve both American Bantam and Ford but, for some reason, there was still a reluctance to order further vehicles from Bantam. The Quartermaster General, E. B. Gregory, arranged a meeting with Edsel Ford at which it was agreed that the company would

LEFT: The US Seventh Army in Alsace fitted a number of Jeeps with 4.5in rocket launchers; the 12 rockets could be fired at two-second intervals. Note the steel roof designed to protect the crew.

ABOVE: **Such was the versatility of the Jeep that the US Army used the vehicle in a variety of roles. Several attempts were made to build an armoured reconnaissance vehicle on the Jeep chassis. All were to fail due to the poor power-to-weight ratio.**

ABOVE: **This Jeep has been heavily modified to serve as a royal review vehicle. Note particularly the whitewall tyres and the addition of stylish front and rear mudguards and extended running boards. The occasion was the inspection of Canadian troops by the, then, Princess Elizabeth in January 1951.**

produce Jeeps according to the specification of the Willys MB, with every part interchangeable. Ford received a contract for a further 15,000 Jeeps which the company designated GPW.

Although the two vehicles were effectively identical, and all parts were indeed interchangeable, the products of the two manufacturers can be identified by the radiator cross-member, which is in the form of an inverted U section on the Ford and is circular on the Willys. The modern-day Jeep cognoscenti claim that the GPW was a better product, but it is doubtful that there is any practical difference. However, Ford did make subtle changes to better suit their mass-production methods, and stamped a script "F" on as many components as possible, including bolt heads, to indicate that this was a Ford product.

The needs of mass production, combined with shortages of components and materials forced myriad small changes during the production run. Early on, the welded slat grille, used only by Willys, was replaced with the familiar pressed-steel

grille. The manufacturer's name, which had been stamped into the rear panel, was omitted, and a jerrycan holder was fitted. In late 1945, the original Willys Type 441 engine was replaced by the improved Type 442, which featured a redesigned oil pump and a gear train in place of the former timing chain set-up.

No further changes were made to the design and by the time production ended in 1945, some 639,245 MB/GPW Jeeps had been completed. Willys built 361,349 and Ford was responsible for 277,896. Jeeps served with all of the Allied armies during World War II and the design went on to be copied by many other manufacturers.

The Ford GPA amphibian was built using the same engine, the same automotive transmission and suspension. There were also experiments with armoured, half-tracked and 6x6 variants.

ABOVE: **Jeeps were successfully equipped with both .30 and .50 calibre Browning heavy machine-guns as an early exponent of the "shoot and scoot" philosophy. This vehicle carries both weapons.**

Willys MB

Type: Truck, 1/4-ton, 4x4

Manufacturer: Willys-Overland Motors; Toledo, Ohio. GPW produced by Ford Motor Company; Dearborn, Michigan

Production: 1941 to 1945

Powerplant: Willys Go-Devil Type 441, 442; four cylinders in-line; petrol; water-cooled; 2,199cc; side valves; power output, 60bhp at 4,000rpm

Transmission: 3F1Rx2; part-time 4x4

Suspension: Live axles on semi-elliptical multi-leaf springs; hydraulic telescopic shock absorbers

Brakes: Hydraulic

Electrical system: 6V

Dimensions: Length – 3,353mm/132in
Width – 1,575mm/62in
Height – tilt in place, 1,772mm/70in; minimum, 1,322mm/52in
Wheelbase – 2,032mm/80in

Weight: Unladen – 1,113kg/2,453lb
Payload – 363kg/800lb

Performance: Maximum speed – 105kph/65mph

Willys, Ford, Kaiser Jeep, AM-General, M151

In March 1951, the Ford Motor Company started design work for a new Jeep-type vehicle, initially known as the XM151. It was intended to offer reduced weight when compared to its predecessors, combined with maximum cross-country capabilities, high flotation, air-drop capability and ease of maintenance. The production vehicle, introduced into service from 1960, was ultimately manufactured by Ford, Willys, Kaiser-Jeep and AM-General, as the M151.

It was designed on a radical low-cost "throw-away" principle using a unitary chassis-less construction. Conventional live axles were replaced by independent suspension using swing axles and coil springs. Power was provided by a 2,319cc Continental overhead-valve engine, giving the vehicle a respectable speed and excellent off-road performance.

However, the combination of swing axles and a relatively high centre of gravity also led to difficult handling

ABOVE: **Designed by the Ford Motor Company in 1951, the M151 was intended to replace all the US Army's existing Jeeps. The suspension of the original M151 was modified in an attempt to improve the handling.**

and a roll-over problem that was never satisfactorily resolved despite two modifications. The M151A1, introduced in 1964–65, had stiffer springs, firmer mountings and an extra rubber bump stop to reduce rebound. This was replaced by the M151A2 in 1969–70, which had a completely redesigned suspension at the rear using semi-trailing arms, which allowed the wheels on each side to assume different angles. Although this improved the handling considerably, it did not entirely eliminate the problem. In 1986, the US Army started installing a "Roll-Over Protection System" (ROPS) to reduce injuries. There was also an M151A2LC variant built in small numbers, which used live axles and semi-elliptical springs.

Despite a lower profile, in appearance the vehicle was not unlike the original Jeep, with an open-sided body and folding windscreen. Alongside the basic cargo variant, it was produced as a front-line ambulance (M718); as a communications vehicle with rear-facing passenger seat (M107, M108); as a platform for the 106mm M20 recoilless rifle (M151A1C and M825); and as a US Marine Corps "fast-attack" vehicle. There were also experiments with extended wheelbase 6x6 and 8x8 variants.

Production continued until 1985 and was resumed briefly in 1988. Around 100,000 M151 and M151A1 vehicles were built, and 332,000 of the M151A2. Some early examples were

ABOVE: **Military vehicle enthusiasts in a restored M151A1 originally produced in 1964.**

assembled by Willys, but Ford was the primary supplier until late 1970, when contracts were awarded to Kaiser-Jeep and AM-General. All of the variants were fitted with bodies built by Fruehauf. The M151 saw service with around 100 countries worldwide.

Willys, Ford, Kaiser Jeep, AM-General, M151

Type: Truck, 1/4-ton, utility, 4x4

Manufacturer: AM-General Corporation; South Bend, Indiana. Ford Motor Company; Dearborn, Michigan. Kaiser Jeep Corporation; Toledo, Ohio. Willys-Overland; Toledo, Ohio

Production: 1960 to 1988

Powerplant: Continental L-142; four cylinders in-line; 2,319cc; petrol; water-cooled; overhead valves; power output, 72bhp at 4,000rpm

Transmission: 4F1Rx1; except model M151A2LC, 3F1Rx1; part-time 4x4

Suspension: Independent suspension using coil springs and swing axles front and rear; except model M151A2LC, semi-elliptical springs

Brakes: Hydraulic

Electrical system: 24V

Dimensions: Length – 3,510mm/133in
Width – 1,650mm/65in
Height – tilt in place, 1,800mm/71in; minimum, 1,321mm/52in
Wheelbase – 2,159mm/85in

Weight: Unladen – 1,066–1,089kg/2,350–2,400lb
Payload – road, 340kg/750lb
cross-country, 250kg/550lb

Performance: Maximum speed – 105kph/65mph

TAM 110T7BV

In 1947, Tovarna Automobilov Maribor (TAM) started manufacturing Praga trucks under licence at Marburg, in the former Yugoslavia. By 1957, TAM had become the largest motor manufacturer in Yugoslavia, and the Praga had been phased out in favour of a range of TAM-designed civilian and military 4x2, 4x4 and 6x4 trucks using licence-built KHD (Deutz) diesel engines.

The high-mobility 1½-ton 110T7BV was launched in 1976 and is effectively a version of the German-built Magirus-Deutz 130T7FAL under licence. Power was by a 5,880cc air-cooled four-cylinder diesel engine driving both axles through a five-speed gearbox, together with a mid-mounted two-speed transfer box which included a front-axle disconnect. Live axles were fitted front and rear, suspended on semi-elliptical leaf springs. Both were fitted with ZF self-locking differentials for improved mobility in difficult conditions.

The steel forward-control cab was open-topped and the windscreen could be folded forward to reduce the profile.

Unusually for a vehicle of this size, the cab was designed to tilt forward to allow improved access to the engine. At the rear, there was a steel drop-side cargo body with a drop-down tailgate. Collapsible bench seating was provided for 12 personnel. A 2½-ton capacity front-mounted under-floor mechanical winch was fitted and driven by a power take-off on the transfer box. There was

also a 6x6 variant (TAM150T11BV), rated at 3 tons and fitted with a V6 diesel engine.

Export sales were handled through SDPR, the Yugoslav Federal Directorate of Supply and Procurement in Belgrade. Following bankruptcy in 1996 the company became MPP Vozila, but the TAM name is still used on vehicles.

ABOVE: **The high-mobility 1½-ton TAM 110T7BV was launched in 1976. It was effectively a version of the Magirus-Deutz 130T7FAL built by Tovarna Automobilov Maribor (TAM) under licence in the former Yugoslavia. There was also a 3-ton 6x6 variant fitted with a more-powerful engine.**

LEFT: **A tilting cab is unusual in a vehicle of this size, but clearly allows improved access to the engine.**

TAM 110T7BV

Type: Truck, 1½-ton, cargo/personnel, 4x4
Manufacturer: Tovarna Automobilov Maribor (TAM); Marburg
Production: 1976 to 1996
Powerplant: Deutz licence TAM F4L-413R; four cylinders in-line; direct-injection diesel; air-cooled; 5,880cc; overhead valves; power output, 115bhp at 2,650rpm
Transmission: 5F1Rx2; part-time 4x4
Suspension: Live axles on semi-elliptical multi-leaf springs; hydraulic double-acting shock absorbers
Brakes: Air-assisted hydraulic
Electrical system: 24V
Dimensions: Length – 4,850mm/191in
Width – 2,270mm/89in
Height – tilt in place, 2,470mm/97in; minimum, 880mm/35in
Wheelbase – 2,850mm/112in
Weight: Unladen – 4,500kg/9,921lb
Payload – road, 2,500kg/5,511lb
cross-country, 1,500kg/3,307lb
Performance: Maximum speed – 90kph/56mph

Index

ABOVE: **The Hallford was typical of early British Army trucks used in World War I. This 1914 model was powered by a 5,300cc four-cylinder petrol engine and had a four-speed gearbox with chain drive to the rear wheels.**

ABOVE: **The funeral procession for victims of the R101 airship crash. The vehicle is a Morris-Commercial in RAF service, bedecked with floral tributes including a representation of the airship, October 11, 1930.**

ABOVE: **New vehicles outside the Marmon-Herrington factory in Indianapolis circa 1933. These 2¹/₂-ton TL29-6 6x6 trucks were designed for use as an artillery prime movers.**

ABOVE: **Auto-Traction 4x2 tractor towing a light single-axle tailer carrying a Renault FT17 tank.**

ABOVE: **Morris-Commercial C8 4x4 with the 62nd Anti-Tank Regiment on exercise near Tilshead, Salisbury Plain, England.**

ABOVE: **The Mack NO series was fitted with a large mechanical recovery winch at the front of the vehicle.**

ABOVE: **A 4¹/₂-ton Mercedes-Benz L4500A 4x4 heavy cargo truck in** *Luftwaffe* **service being unloaded from a transport ship in a North African port, October 1, 1941.**

ABOVE: **Designed by the US company American Bantam and the US Ordnance Department, the Jeep was the first vehicle of the type that effectively replaced the motorcycle in military service.**

ABOVE: **Men of the Swedish Air Force driving a Volvo TL11 P214 aircraft-starter truck tow a Saab J29 *Tunna* (Barrel) jet fighter out of an underground hangar.**

ABOVE: **The BJ212 was fitted with an open-topped four-door body. The vehicle was powered by a 2,445cc four-cylinder water-cooled petrol engine.**

ABOVE: **The Timoney independent suspension system is by double wishbones on each wheel, with twin variable-rate coil springs and concentric dampers.**

ABOVE: **Produced by the Minsk Wheel Tractor Plant, the Volat 74135 is a massive 8x8 tractor and is rated for a gross train weight of more than 200 tons.**

ABOVE: **The armoured DURO 4x4SP intended for the cargo, personnel and ambulance roles undergoing trials at a military test facility.**

Acknowledgements

Picture research for this book was carried out by Pat Ware and Jasper Spencer-Smith, who have selected images from the following sources: JSS Collection, Warehouse Publications, Getty Images, Tank Museum, Imperial War Museum, Archives of Canada and Ullstein Bild.

Much of the colour material has been supplied by the following (l=left, r=right, t=top, b=bottom, m=middle):

Mark Barnes: 172b.

John Blackman: 38t; 42br; 47tr; 47b;

50b; 78m; 93t; 109t; 109b; 150b; 173t; 179t; 180b; 192t; 203t; 207b; 212b; 213t; 213b; 216t; 220t; 221b; 224b; 231b; 235b; 246b.

Paul Costen: 79tr.

Phil Royal: 39m, 39b; 44t; 45bl; 45br; 51b; 72b; 78t; 78b; 79tl; 79b; 85t; 85b; 94–95; 108t; 108b; 152t; 237t.

Simon Thomson: 43t; 45t; 46t; 46bl; 47tl; 50t; 50tl; 70t; 70br; 71t; 72t; 72b; 73t; 73b; 74t; 75t; 82t; 82b; 103b; 107t; 115t; 118t; 119tl; 120b; 126t; 126b; 129b; 140t; 141t; 141b; 144t; 144b; 145t; 146t; 150t; 153t; 154t; 163b; 171t; 175t; 177t; 178t; 187t; 188t; 189t; 191t; 194b; 198t; 202t; 205t; 205b; 206m; 210t; 211t; 225t; 228t; 230t; 232t; 234t; 239t; 240t; 242b; 245t; 248t.

Every effort has been made to acknowledge photographs correctly, however we apologize for any unintentional ommissions. These will be corrected in future editions.

ABOVE: **A Mack tractor unit of the Israeli Army in a convoy moving heavy equipment out during the first withdrawal phase from Southern Lebanon, January 2001.**

Key to flags

For the specification boxes, the national flag that was current at the time of the vehicle's use is shown.

 Australia

 Austria

 Belarus

 Belgium

 Canada

 China

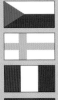 Czechoslovakia

Finland

France

Germany – World War II

West Germany – post-World War II

Hungary

 India

Ireland

Italy

 Japan

Netherlands

Poland

Soviet Union

Spain

Sweden

Switzerland

 United Kingdom

United States of America